Borders in Cyberspace

Borders in Cyberspace

Information Policy and the Global Information
Infrastructure

edited by Brian Kahin and Charles Nesson

A Publication of the Harvard Information Infrastructure Project

The MIT Press, Cambridge, Massachusetts, and London, England

Third printing, 1999

© 1997 The President and Fellows of Harvard College

This book was printed and bound in the United States of America.

Library of Congress Cataloging-in-Publication Data

Borders in cyberspace : information policy and the global information infrastructure /
    edited by Brian Kahin and Charles Nesson.
        p. cm. — (A publication of the Harvard Information Infrastructure Project)
    Includes index.
        ISBN 0-262-11220-5 (hc : alk. paper). — ISBN 0-262-61126-0 (pb : alk. paper)
        1. Transborder data flow—Law and legislation. 2. Online information services—Law
    and legislation. 3. Data protection—Law and legislation. 4. Privacy, Right of. 5. Internet
    (Computer network) I. Kahin, Brian. II. Nesson, Charles R. III. Series.
    K4305.4.B67 1997
    025.04—dc21   96-49898
                                                                                                                        CIP

Contents

Preface

Our experience of geographic space has been transformed by the information revolution, as it was by the railroad and air travel. But the transformation now underway on the Internet is not only greater and qualitatively different. It has collapsed the world, transcending and blurring political boundaries in the process. It gives individuals instant, affordable access to other individuals, wherever they may be, and it enables each to publish to the world.

With this empowerment comes enormous potential for unbalancing, even upending, social, business, political, and legal arrangements. Like advances in transportation and the globalization of international trade, it contains both opportunities and threats. For countries committed to free markets and free trade, the opportunities seem too great to pass up despite threats of criminal activity, cultural invasion, and "information warfare." How substantial are these threats? Can they be addressed effectively? How can national policy and law be designed in this permeable and rapidly changing environment? Can international harmonization proceed, perhaps with diminished expectations? Can technology resurrect the boundaries that it has blurred?

Some of these issues are familiar from the controversies over "transborder data flows" and the "New World Information Order" that enjoyed considerable air time ten to twenty years ago. But that was a different world, sparsely populated by mainframes and private networks connecting small circles of like-minded users and still in awe of the power of broadcasting.

The Internet has since become the data equivalent of the public switched network. But unlike the public switched network, the cost of using the Internet is distance-insensitive and often time-insensitive. It is a publishing as well as a communications medium, and it has muddied the difference between the two.

The development of Internet-related law is in its infancy. Indeed, the Internet has been remarkably unimpeded by regulatory agencies. Because it is built on existing communications facilities (dial-up lines and leased lines), Internet access providers in the United States and other industrialized countries have not needed government licenses. For this reason, the Internet escaped the regulatory and political struggles that characterized the early development of cable television and cellular telephone. Its volatile energy and potential for stimulating economic and social growth make the administrative bureaucracies wary of steering it. Their understanding of its multifaceted technology is too limited, their processes are too slow, and their ability to predict the consequences of their own actions is too uncertain.

The Internet has clearly done well without their help. According to its chairman, the U.S. Federal Communications Commission is unlikely to assert regulatory authority over the development of Internet telephony, despite its potential for fundamentally reworking the architecture of national and international long-distance communications. At least in the United States, the prevailing attitude seems to be, "let's see what develops." However, courts are less able to keep hands off the Internet. Judicial process is easily invoked by individual parties who feel aggrieved, and where there is an injury, courts strive to provide a remedy, sometimes with remarkable absence of caution.

In 1980, *Playboy* magazine obtained from a federal district court in New York an injunction based on trademark law against an Italian publisher. The injunction prevented the publisher from distributing in the United States *Playman* magazine, which the publisher had been producing and distributing in Italy. *Playman* ceased distribution in the United States, but in January 1996, *Playboy* discovered that the same Italian publisher had created an Internet site featuring the name *Playmen*. The site, located on a server in Italy, makes available images of the cover of the Italian magazine, as well as its "Women of the Month" feature and other sexually explicit photographic images.

The federal court in New York, on *Playboy*'s motion, reacted by ordering that *Playmen* "either shut down its Internet site completely" or deny access to anyone from the United States. "The simplest method of prohibiting access by United States users," said the court, "is to . . . require users of the . . . service to acquire free passwords and user IDs in order to access the site. In this way, users residing in the United States can be filtered out and refused access." In a footnote the court added yet a further constraint to cover the possibility that users wanting access from the United States would route their requests through other countries: "If technology cannot identify the country of origin of email addresses, these passwords and user IDs should be sent by [postal] mail."

Here is a U.S. court trying to impose obligations that will affect users of a foreign-based Internet site around the world, either eliminating the site entirely or imposing constraints on access to the site that are costly, unfriendly, and inefficient to all users. The court's justification is straightforward: "Only in this way can the Court be assured that United States users are not accidentally permitted access to [the *Playmen* site]." (The case is *Playboy Enterprises, Inc. v. Chuckleberry Publishing, Inc.*, 1996 WL 396128 [S.D.N.Y. 7/16/96].)

Given a global Internet in which publication anywhere means publication everywhere, the *Playboy* case is representative of the kinds of conflict that will increasingly drive parties to court. Conflicts will not be limited to protection of trademarks but will occur over content that is allegedly obscene, blasphemous, racist, invasive of privacy, libelous, infringing of intellectual property rights, or otherwise actionable.

Internet businesses would undoubtedly like "to structure their primary conduct with some minimum assurance as to where the conduct will and will not render them liable to suit." This quote is from the U.S. Supreme Court's opinion in *World-Wide Volkswagen*, 444 U.S. at 297, holding that Oklahoma could not exercise jurisdiction over the defendant car dealer on the theory that the dealer should have anticipated that a car sold in New York could be involved in an accident anywhere in the United States. Unfortunately, lawyers cannot now give Internet businesses such assurance. In its most recent consideration of the reach of long-arm jurisdiction the Supreme Court split four to four on the question whether merely putting a product into "the stream of commerce" should be sufficient to support jurisdiction wherever the stream runs (*Asahi Metal Industrial Co. v. Superior Court*, 480 U.S. 102 [1987]). The Internet stream runs everywhere, which suggests that publication anywhere on the Internet might mean not only publication everywhere but also jurisdiction everywhere.

The specter of law thus looms over the Internet. Legal issues will proliferate along with its commercial development, and hosts of young lawyers are eager to raise and grapple with them. Responding to the need for new thinking on the legal issues of the Internet, Harvard Law School has established a Center for Law and Information Technology. Internet law is not yet a field, but it promises to become one, characterized by cross-border legal conflicts resulting from the borderless nature of electronic space and by cross-category conflicts resulting from the convergence of what were formerly distinct media. Through this Center, Harvard intends to play a constructive role in articulating this new field of law, drawing its strands together from existing legal domains.

This volume explores much of the territory that the Center will address. The first part tackles the nature of "cyberspace;" the recurrent themes of globalization, democratization, disintermediation, and arbitrage, and the cross-cutting issues of process: jurisdiction, conflict of laws, extraterritorial enforcement and effect, comity, harmonization, and alternative dispute resolution. The second part looks at transborder problems in six substantive areas: intellectual property; censorship; privacy; cryptography; government information; and consumer protection.

This project, which marks the public debut of the Center, was undertaken in collaboration with the Science, Technology and Public Policy Program and the Center for Business and Government at the John F. Kennedy School of Government. We also acknowledge with gratitude the collaboration of the Global Information Infrastructure Commission on this and a companion project on national information infrastructure initiatives: Brian Kahin and

Ernest J. Wilson III, editors, *National Information Infrastructure Initiatives: Vision and Policy Design* (Cambridge: MIT Press 1996). We are grateful for funding provided by Advanced Network and Services, EDS, Motorola, and Nynex as well as the general sponsors of the Harvard Information Infrastructure Project: AT&T, Bellcore, Hughes, and IBM. Finally, we wish to thank the presenters and participants at the conference, as well as the authors represented in this book.

Brian Kahin and Charles Nesson

Life and Law on the Frontier

The Rise of Law on the Global Network

David R. Johnson and David G. Post

Introduction

Global computer-based communications cut across territorial borders, creating a new realm of human activity and undermining the feasibility—and legitimacy—of applying laws based on geographic boundaries. While these electronic communications play havoc with geographic boundaries, a new boundary, made up of the screens and passwords that separate the virtual world from the "real world" of atoms, emerges. This new boundary defines a distinct cyberspace that needs new law and legal institutions of its own. Territorially based law-making and law-enforcing authorities find this new environment deeply threatening, but established territorial authorities may yet learn to defer to the self-regulatory efforts of cyberspace participants who care deeply about this new digital trade in ideas, information, and services. Separated from doctrine tied to territorial jurisdictions, new rules will emerge in a variety of online spaces to govern a wide range of new phenomena that have no clear parallel in the nonvirtual world. These new rules will play the role of law by defining legal personhood and property, providing a mechanism for resolving disputes, and crystallizing a collective conversation about core values.

Territorial Borders in the "Real World"

We take for granted a world in which geographic borders—boundaries separating physical spaces—are of primary importance in determining legal rights and responsibilities: "All law is *prima facie* territorial."[1] Territorial borders, generally speaking, delineate areas within which different sets of legal rules apply. There has until now been a general correspondence between borders drawn in physical space (between nation-states or other political entities) and borders in "law space." For example, if we were to superimpose a "law map" (delineating areas where differing rules apply to particular behaviors) onto a political map of the world, the two maps would overlap to a significant degree, with clusters of homogenous applicable law and legal institutions fitting within existing physical borders, distinct from neighboring homogenous clusters.

Consider a specific example to which we will refer throughout this article: trademark law—schemes to protect the associations between words or images and particular commercial enterprises. Trademark law is distinctly based on geographic separations.[2] Trademark rights typically arise within a given country, usually on the basis of use of a mark on physical goods or in connection with the provision of services in specific locations within that country. Different countries have trademark laws that differ on matters as central as whether the same name can be used in different lines of business. In the United States, the same name can be used even for the same line of business if there is sufficient geographic separation of use to avoid confusion. In fact, there are many local stores, restaurants, and businesses with identical names that do not interfere with each other because their customers do not overlap; Ritz crackers can coexist with the Ritz hotel, or the Lutece restaurant with Lutece cosmetics.[3] In addition, physical cues provided by different lines of business allow most marks to be used in multiple lines of commerce without dilution of the other users' rights. There is no global registration scheme; protection of a particularly famous mark on a global basis requires registration in each country. Trademark owners must be constantly alert to territorially based claims of both abandonment and dilution arising from uses of confusingly similar marks, and they must also master the different procedural and jurisdictional laws of various countries that apply in each such instance.

Physical borders are not, of course, simply arbitrary creations. Although they may be based on historical accident, geographic borders for law make sense in the real world. Their relationship to the development and enforcement of legal rules is logically based on a number of related considerations.

Power. Control over physical space, and the people and things located in that space, is a defining attribute of sovereignty and statehood.[4] Law making requires some mechanism for law enforcement, which in turn depends (to a large extent) on the ability to exercise physical control over, and to impose coercive sanctions on, law violators. The ability of the sovereign to claim personal jurisdiction over a particular party, for instance, turns importantly on the party's relationship to the physical jurisdiction over which the sovereign has control, e.g., the presence of the party or assets belonging to the party within the jurisdiction or the existence of activities of the party that are directed to persons or things within the jurisdiction. Similarly, the law chosen to apply to a contract, tort, or criminal action has historically been influenced primarily by the physical location of the parties or the action in question. The U.S. government does not impose its trademark law on a Brazilian business operating in Brazil, at least in part because imposing sanctions on the Brazilian business would require assertion of physical control over those responsible for the operation of that business. Such an assertion of control would conflict with the Brazilian government's recognized monopoly on the use of force with its citizens.[5]

Effects. The correspondence between physical boundaries and boundaries in "law space" also reflects a deeply rooted relationship between physical proximity and the effects of any particular behavior. That is, Brazilian trademark law governs the use of marks in Brazil because that use has a more direct impact on persons and assets located within that geographic territory than anywhere else. For example, the existence of a large sign over "Jones's Restaurant" in Rio de Janeiro is unlikely to have an impact on the operation of "Jones's Restaurant" in Oslo, Norway, for we may assume that there is no substantial overlap between the customers or the competitors of these two entities. Protection of the former's trademark does not—and probably should not—affect the protection afforded the latter's.

Legitimacy. We generally accept the notion that the persons residing within a geographically defined border are the ultimate source of law-making authority for activities within that border.[6]

The "consent of the governed" implies that those subject to a set of laws must have a role in their formulation. The category of persons subject to a sovereign's laws will consist primarily of individuals who are located in particular physical spaces. Similarly, allocation of responsibility among levels of government proceeds on the assumptions that, for many legal problems, physical proximity between the responsible authority and those most directly affected by the law will improve the quality of decision making and that it is easier to determine the will of those individuals in physical proximity to the decision maker.

Notice. Physical boundaries are also appropriate for the delineation of "law space" in the physical world because they can give "notice" that the rules change when the boundaries are crossed. Proper boundaries have signposts that provide warning that we will be required, after crossing, to abide by different rules; physical boundaries — lines on the geographical map — generally serve this signpost function.[7]

The Absence of Territorial Borders in Cyberspace

Cyberspace radically undermines the relationship between legally significant phenomena and physical location. The rise of the global computer network is destroying the link between geographic location and (1) the *power* of local governments to assert control over behavior; (2) the *effects* of behavior on individuals or things; (3) the *legitimacy* of the efforts of a local sovereign to enforce rules applicable to global phenomena; and (4) the ability of physical location to give *notice* of which sets of rules apply. The Net thus radically subverts a system of rule making based on borders between physical spaces, at least with respect to the claim that cyberspace should naturally be governed by territorially defined rules.

Cyberspace has no territorially based boundaries because the cost and speed of message transmission on the Net is almost entirely independent of physical location: messages can be transmitted from any physical location to any other without degradation, decay, or substantial delay and without any physical cues or barriers that might otherwise keep certain geographically remote places and people separate from one another.[8] The Net enables transactions between people who do not know, and in many cases cannot know, the physical location of the other party. Location remains vitally important, but only location within a *virtual* space consisting of the "addresses" of the machines between which messages and information are routed. The system is indifferent to the *physical* location of those machines, and there is no necessary connection between an Internet address and a physical jurisdiction. Although a domain name, when initially assigned to a given machine, may be associated with a particular Internet Protocol address corresponding to the territory within which the machine is physically located (e.g., a ".uk" domain name extension), the machine may move in physical space without any movement in the logical domain name space of the Net. Alternatively, the owner of the domain name might request that the name become associated with an entirely different machine in a different physical location.[9] Thus, a server with a ".uk" domain name may not necessarily be located in the United Kingdom, a server with a ".com" domain name may be anywhere, and users, generally speaking, are not aware of the location of the server that stores the content that they read. Physical borders no longer can function as signposts informing individuals of the obligations assumed by entering into a new, legally significant place, because individuals are unaware of the existence of those borders as they move through virtual space.

The power to control activity in cyberspace has only the most tenuous connections to physical location. Many governments respond first to electronic communications crossing their territorial borders by trying to stop or regulate the flow of information as it crosses their borders.[10] Rather than deferring to efforts by participants in online transactions to regulate their own affairs, many governments establish trade barriers, seek to tax any border-crossing cargo, and respond especially sympathetically to claims that information coming into the jurisdiction might prove harmful to local residents. Efforts to stem the flow increase as online information becomes more important to local citizens. In particular, resistance to "transborder data flows" (TDFs) reflects the concerns of sovereign nations that the development and use of TDFs will undermine their "informational sovereignty," will negatively impact on the privacy of local citizens, and will upset private property interests in information.[11]

But efforts to control the flow of electronic information across physical borders—to map local regulation and physical boundaries onto cyberspace—are likely to prove futile, at least in countries that hope to participate in global commerce. Individual electrons can easily, and without any realistic prospect of detection, "enter" any sovereign's territory. The volume of electronic communications crossing territorial boundaries is just too great in relation to the resources available to government authorities to permit meaningful control. U.S. Customs officials have generally given up. They assert jurisdiction only over the physical goods that cross the geographic borders they guard and claim no right to force declarations of the value of materials transmitted by modem. Banking and securities regulators seem likely to lose their battle to impose local regulations on a global financial marketplace.[12] And state Attorneys General face serious challenges in seeking to intercept the electrons that transmit the kinds of consumer fraud that, if conducted physically within the local jurisdiction, would be more easily shut down.

Faced with their inability to control the flow of electrons across physical borders, some authorities strive to impose their boundaries onto the new electronic medium through filtering mechanisms and the establishment of electronic barriers. For example, German authorities, seeking to prevent violations of that country's laws against distribution of pornographic material, ordered CompuServe to disable access by German residents to certain global Usenet newsgroups. Anyone inside Germany with an Internet connection could, however, easily find a way to access the prohibited news groups during the ban. Although initially compliant, CompuServe subsequently rescinded the ban on most of the files by mailing users a new program that enabled them to choose for themselves which items to restrict.[13] Similarly, Tennessee has insisted indirectly, through enforcement of a federal law that defers to local community standards that an electronic bulletin board in California install filters that prevent offensive screens from being displayed to users in Tennessee if it is to avoid liability under obscenity standards.[14] Other states have been quick to assert the right to regulate all online trade insofar as it might adversely impact local citizens. The Attorney General of Minnesota, for example, has asserted the right to regulate gambling on a foreign Web page that was accessed and "brought into" the state by a local resident.[15] The New Jersey securities regulatory agency has similarly asserted the right to shut down any offending Web page accessible from within the state.[16]

But such protective schemes are likely to fail. First, the determined seeker of prohibited communications can simply reconfigure her or his connection to appear to reside in a different location, outside the particular locality, state, or country. Because the Net is engineered to work on the basis of "logical" not geographic locations, any attempt to defeat the independence of messages from physical locations would be as futile as an effort to tie an atom and a bit together. Moreover, assertions of law-making authority over Net activities on the ground that those activities constitute "entry into" a physical jurisdiction can just as easily be made by any territorially based authority. If Minnesota law applies to gambling operations conducted on the World Wide Web because such operations foreseeably affect Minnesota residents, so, too, must the law of any physical jurisdiction from which those operations can be accessed. By asserting a right to regulate whatever its citizens may access on the Net, local authorities are laying the groundwork for an argument that Singapore or Iraq or any other sovereign state can regulate the activities of U.S. companies operating in cyberspace from a location physically within the United States. All such Web-based activity, in this view, must be subject simultaneously to the laws of all territorial sovereigns.

Nor are the effects of online activities tied to geographically proximate locations. Information available on the World Wide Web is available simultaneously to anyone with a connection to the global network. The notion that the effects of an activity taking place on a Web site should radiate from a physical location over a geographic map in concentric circles of decreasing intensity, however sensible that may be in the nonvirtual world, is meaningless when applied to cyberspace. A Web site physically located in Brazil, for example, has no more effect on individuals in Brazil than a Web site physically located in Belgium or Belize that is accessible in Brazil. Usenet discussion groups, to consider another example, consist of continuously changing collections of messages that are routed from one network to another with no centralized location at all; they exist, in effect, everywhere, nowhere in particular, and only on the Net.[17]

Nor can the legitimacy of any rules governing online activities be naturally traced to a geographically situated polity. There is no geographically localized set of constituents with a stronger claim to regulate it than any other local group; the strongest claim to control comes from the participants themselves, and they could be anywhere.

The rise of an electronic medium that disregards geographic boundaries also throws the law into disarray by creating entirely new phenomena that require clear legal rules but that cannot be governed satisfactorily by any current territorially based sovereign entity. For example, electronic communications create vast new quantities of transactional records and pose serious questions regarding the nature and adequacy of privacy protections. Yet the communications that create these records may pass through or even simultaneously exist in many different territorial jurisdictions. What substantive law should we apply to protect this new, vulnerable body of transactional data?[18] May a French policeman lawfully access the records of communications traveling across the Net from the United States to Japan? Similarly, whether it is permissible for a commercial entity to publish a record of all of any given individual's postings to Usenet newsgroups or whether it is permissible to implement an interactive Web page application that inspects a user's "bookmarks" to determine which other pages that user has visited, are questions not readily addressed by existing legal regimes—both because the phenomena are new and because any given local territorial government cannot readily control the relevant, globally dispersed actors and actions.[19]

Because events on the Net occur everywhere but nowhere in particular, are engaged in by online personae who are both "real" (possessing reputations and capable of performing services and deploying intellectual assets) and "intangible" (not necessarily or traceably tied to any particular person in the physical sense), and concern "things" (messages, databases, standing relationships) that are not necessarily separated from one another by any physical boundaries, no physical jurisdiction has a more compelling claim than any other to subject these events exclusively to its laws.

The question of who should regulate or control Net domain names presents an illustration of the difficulties faced by territorially based law making. The engineers who created the Net devised a "domain name system" that associates numerical machine addresses with easier-to-remember names. Thus, an Internet Protocol machine address such as "161.164.10.69" can be derived, by means of a lookup table, from "georgetown.edu." Certain letter extensions (".com," ".edu," ".org," and ".net") have evolved to represent global domains with no association to any particular geographic area. Although the Net creators designed this system as a convenience, it rapidly developed commercial value because it allows customers to learn and remember the location of particular Web pages or e-mail addresses. Currently, domain names are registered with specific parties who relay the information to "domain name servers" around the world. Registration generally occurs on a "first come, first served" basis,[20] generating a new type of property akin to trademark rights but without inherent ties to the trademark law of any individual country. Defining rights in this new, valuable property presents many questions, including those relating to transferability, conditions for ownership (such as payment of registration fees), duration of ownership rights, and forfeiture in the event of abandonment, however defined. Who should make these rules?

Consider the placement of a "traditional" trademark on the face of a World Wide Web page. This page can be accessed instantly from any location connected to the Net. It is not clear that any given country's trademark authorities possess, or should possess, jurisdiction over such placements. Otherwise, any use of a trademark on the Net would be subject simultaneously to the jurisdiction of every country. Should a Web page advertising a local business in Illinois be deemed to infringe on a trademark in Brazil just because the page can be accessed freely from Brazil? Large U.S. companies may be upset by the appearance on the Web of names and symbols that overlap with their valid U.S.-registered trademarks. But these same names and symbols could also be validly registered by another party in Mexico whose "infringing" marks would be suddenly accessible from within the United States. Upholding a claim of infringement or dilution made by the holder of a U.S.-registered trademark solely on the basis of a conflicting mark on the Net would expose that same trademark holder to claims from other countries when the use of their U.S.-registered mark on the Web would allegedly infringe a similar mark in those foreign jurisdictions.

Almost everything involving the transfer of information can be done online: education, health care, banking, the provision of intangible services, all forms of publishing, and the practice of law. The laws regulating many of these activities have developed as distinctly local and territorial. Local authorities certify teachers, charter banks with authorized "branches," and license doctors and lawyers. The law has in essence presumed that the activities conducted by these regulated persons cannot be performed without being tied to a physical body or building subject to regulation by the territorial sovereign authority and that the effects of those activities are most distinctly felt in geographically circumscribed areas. These distinctly local regulations cannot be preserved once these activities are conducted through the Net by globally dispersed parties. When many trades can be practiced in a manner that is unrelated to the physical location of the participants, these local regulatory structures will either delay the development of the new medium or, more likely, be superseded by new structures that better fit the online phenomena in question.

Any insistence on "reducing" online transactions to something that is subject to a legal analysis based on geography presents, in effect, a new "mind-body" problem on a global scale. We know that the activities that have traditionally been the subject of regulation are still engaged in by real people who are, after all, at distinct physical locations. But the interactions of these people now somehow transcend those physical locations. Efforts to determine "where" the events in question occur are decidedly misguided, if not altogether futile.

A New Boundary for Cyberspace

Although geographic boundaries may be irrelevant in defining a legal regime for cyberspace, a more legally significant border for the "law space" of the Net consists of the screens and passwords that separate the tangible from the virtual world. Traditional legal doctrine treats the Net as a mere transmission medium that facilitates the exchange of messages sent from one legally significant geographic location to another, each of which has its own applicable laws. Yet, trying to tie the laws of any particular territorial sovereign to transactions on the Net, or even trying to analyze the legal consequences of Net-based commerce as if each transaction occurred geographically in a particular place, is most unsatisfying.

Cyberspace as a Place

Many of the jurisdictional and substantive quandaries raised by border-crossing electronic communications could be resolved by one simple principle: conceiving of cyberspace as a distinct "place" for purposes of legal analysis and recognizing a legally significant border between cyberspace and the "real world." Using this new approach, we would no longer ask the unanswerable question of "where" in the geographical world a Net-based transaction occurred. Instead, the more salient questions become: What rules are best suited to the often unique characteristics of this new place and the expectations of those who are engaged in various activities there? What mechanisms exist or need to be developed to determine the content of those rules and the mechanisms by which they can enforced? Answers to these questions will permit the development of rules better suited to the new phenomena in question, more likely to be made by those who understand and participate in those phenomena, and more likely to be enforced by means that the new global communications media make available and effective.

Treating cyberspace as a separate "space" to which distinct laws apply should come naturally because entry into this world of stored online communications occurs through a screen and (usually) a "password" boundary. There is a "placeness" to cyberspace because the messages accessed there are persistent and accessible to many people. You know when you are "there." No one accidentally strays across the border into cyberspace. To be sure, cyberspace is not a homogenous place; groups and activities found at various online locations possess their own unique characteristics and distinctions, and each area probably will develop its own set of distinct rules.[21]

But the line that separates online transactions from our dealings in the real world is just as distinct as the physical boundaries between our territorial governments—perhaps more so.[22]

Crossing into cyberspace is a meaningful act that would make application of a distinct "law of cyberspace" fair to those who pass over the electronic boundary. As noted, a primary function and characteristic of a border or boundary is its ability to be perceived by the one who crosses it.[23] As regulatory structures evolve to govern cyberspace-based transactions, it will be much easier to be certain which of those rules apply to your online activities than to determine which territorially based authority might apply its laws to your conduct. For example, you would know that you should abide by the "terms of service" established by CompuServe or America Online when you are in their online territory rather than having to guess whether Germany or Tennessee or the SEC will succeed in asserting their right to regulate your activities and those of the "placeless" online personae with whom you communicate.

The ultimate question of who should set the rules for uses of names on the Net presents an apt microcosm for examining the relationship between the Net and territorially based legal systems. There is nothing more fundamental, legally, than a name or identity. The right to legally recognized personhood is a predicate for the amassing of capital including the reputational and financial capital, that arises from sustained interactions. The domain name system and other online uses of names and symbols tied to reputations and virtual locations exist operationally only on the Net. These names can, of course, be printed on paper or embodied in physical form and shipped across geographic borders, but such physical uses should be distinguished from electronic use of such names in cyberspace because publishing a name or symbol on the Net is not the same as intentional distribution to any particular jurisdiction. Instead, use of a name or symbol on the Net represents distribution to all jurisdictions simultaneously. Recall that the non-country-specific domain names such as ".com," and ".edu" led to the establishment of online addresses on a global basis. And through such widespread use, the global domain names gained proprietary value. In this context, assertion by any local jurisdiction of the right to set the rules applicable to the "domain name space" is an illegitimate extraterritorial power grab.

Conceiving of the Net as a separate place for purposes of legal analysis will have great simplifying effects. For example, a global registration system for all domain names and reputationally significant names and symbols used on the Net would become possible. Such a Net-based regime could take into account the special claims of owners of strong global marks (as used on physical goods) and "grandfather" these owners' rights to the online use of their marks. But a Net-based global registration system could also fully account for the true nature of the Net by treating the use of marks on Web pages as a global phenomenon, by assessing the likelihood of confusion and dilution in the online context in which such confusion would actually occur, and by harmonizing any rules with applicable engineering criteria, such as optimizing the overall size of the domain name space.

A distinct set of rules applicable to trademarks in cyberspace would greatly simplify matters by providing a basis for resisting the inconsistent and conflicting assertions of geographically local prerogatives. If one country objects to the use of a mark on the Web that conflicts with a locally registered mark, the rebuttal would be that the mark has not been used inside the country at all, but only on the Web. If a company wants to know where to register its use of a symbol on the Net, or to check for conflicting prior uses of its mark, the answer will be obvious and cost effective: the designated registration authority for the relevant portion of the Net itself. If we need to develop rules governing abandonment, dilution, and conditions on uses of particular types of domain names and addresses, those rules—applicable specifically to cyberspace—will be able to reflect the special characteristics of this new electronic medium.

Once we take cyberspace seriously as a distinct place for purposes of legal analysis, many opportunities to clarify and simplify the rules applicable to online transactions become available.

Defamation Law

Treating messages on the Net as transmissions from one place to another has created a quandary for those concerned about liability for defamation: messages may be transmitted between countries with very different laws, and liability may be imposed on the basis of "publication" in multiple jurisdictions with varying standards.[24] In contrast, the approach that treats the global network as a separate place would consider any allegedly defamatory message to have been published only on the Net, or in some distinct subsidiary area thereof, at least until such time as distribution on paper occurs.[25] A person who uploads a potentially defamatory statement would more readily be able to determine the rules applicable to her or his own actions. Moreover, because the Net has distinct characteristics, including an enhanced ability of the allegedly defamed person to reply, the rules of defamation developed for the Net could take into account these technological capabilities—perhaps by requiring that the opportunity for reply be taken advantage of in lieu of monetary compensation for certain defamatory Net-based messages.[26] The distinct characteristics of the Net could also be taken into account when applying and adapting the "public figure" doctrine in a context that is both global and highly compartmentalized and that blurs the distinction between private and public spaces.

Regulation of Net-Based Professional Activities

The simplifying effect of taking cyberspace seriously likewise arises in the context of regimes for regulating professional activities. As noted, traditional regulation insists that each professional be licensed by every territorial jurisdiction in which she or he provides services.[27] Meeting this requirement is infeasible when professional services are dispensed over the Net and potentially provided in numerous jurisdictions. Establishing certification regimes that apply to such activities on the Net would greatly simplify matters. Such regulations would take into account the special features of Net-based professional activities such as telemedicine or the global practice of law by addressing the need to avoid the special risks associated with giving medical advice online without direct physical contact with a patient or answering a question regarding local law from a remote location. Using this new approach, we could also override the efforts of local school boards to license online educational institutions, treating attendance by students at online institutions as analogous to "leaving home for school" rather than characterizing the offering of education online as prosecutable distribution of disfavored materials into a potentially unwelcoming community that asserts local licensing authority.

Fraud and Antitrust

Even an area that might otherwise be thought to favor the assertion of jurisdiction by a local sovereign—protection of local citizens from fraud and antitrust violations—shows the beneficial effects of a cyberspace legal regime. How should we analyze "markets" for antitrust and consumer protection purposes when the companies at issue do business only through the World Wide Web? cyberspace could be treated as a distinct marketplace for purposes of assessing concentration and market power. Concentration in geographic markets would only be relevant in the rare cases in which such market power could be inappropriately leveraged to obtain power in online markets—for example by conditioning access to the Net by local citizens on their buying services from the same company (such as a phone company) online. Claims regarding a right to access to particular online services, as distinct from claims to access particular physical pipelines, would remain tenuous as long as it is possible to create a new online service instantly in any corner of an expanding online space.

Consumer protection doctrines could also develop differently online—to take into account the fact that anyone reading an online ad is only a mouse click away from consumer protection agencies and discussions with other consumers. Can Minnesota prohibit the establishment of a Ponzi scheme on a Web page physically based in the Cayman Islands but accessed by Minnesota citizens through the Net? Under the proposed new approach to regulation of online activities, the answer is clearly no. Minnesota has no special right to prohibit such activities. The state lacks enforcement power, cannot show specially targeted effects, and does not speak for the community with the most legitimate claim to self-governance. But that does not mean that fraud might not be made "illegal" in at least large areas of cyberspace. Those who establish and use online systems have an interest in preserving the safety of their electronic territory and preventing crime. They are more likely to be able to enforce their own rules. And, as more fully discussed below, insofar as a consensually based "law of the Net" needs to obtain respect and deference from local sovereigns, new Net-based law-making institutions have an incentive to avoid fostering activities that threaten the vital interests of territorial governments.

Copyright Law

We suggest, not without some trepidation, that "taking cyberspace seriously" could clarify the current intense debate about how to apply principles of copyright law in the digital age. In the absence of global agreement on applicable copyright principles, the jurisdictional problems inherent in any attempt to apply territorially based copyright regimes to electronic works simultaneously available everywhere on the globe are profound. As Jane Ginsburg has noted:

A key feature of the GII [global information infrastructure] is its ability to render works of authorship pervasively and simultaneously accessible throughout the world. The principle of territoriality becomes problematic if it means that posting a work on the GII calls into play the laws of every country in which the work may be received when . . . these laws may differ substantively. Should the rights in a work be determined by a multiplicity of inconsistent legal regimes when the work is simultaneously communicated to scores of countries? Simply taking into account one country's laws, the complexity of placing works in a digital network is already daunting; should the task be further burdened by an obligation to assess the impact of the laws of every country where the work might be received? Put more bluntly, for works on the GII, there will be no physical territoriality.... Without physical territoriality, can legal territoriality persist?[28]

But treating cyberspace as a distinct place for purposes of legal analysis does more than resolve the conflicting claims of different jurisdictions; it also allows the development of new doctrines that take into account the special characteristics of the online "place."

The basic justification for copyright protection is that bestowing on authors an exclusive property right to control the reproduction and distribution of works will increase the supply of such works by offering authors a financial incentive to engage in the effort required for their creation.[29] But even in the "real world," much creative expression is entirely independent of this incentive structure because the author's primary reward has more to do with acceptance in a community and the accumulation of reputational capital through wide dissemination than it does with the licensing and sale of individual copies of works; for example, the creative output of lawyers and law professors—law review articles, briefs and other pleadings, and the like—may well be determined largely by factors completely unrelated to the availability or unavailability of copyright protection for those works because that category of authors, generally speaking, obtains reputational benefits from wide dissemination that far outweigh the benefits that could be obtained from licensing individual copies.[30] And that may be generally true of authorship in cyberspace; because authors can now, for the first time in history, deliver copies of their creations instantaneously and at virtually no cost anywhere in the world, one might expect authors to devise new modes of operation that take advantage of, rather than work counter to, this fundamental characteristic of the new environment.[31] One such strategy has already begun to emerge: giving away information at no charge— what might be called the "Netscape strategy"[32]—as a means of building up reputational capital that can subsequently be converted into income (e.g., by means of the sale of services). As Esther Dyson has written:

Controlling copies (once created by the author or by a third party) becomes a complex challenge. You can either control something very tightly, limiting distribution to a small, trusted group, or you can rest assured that eventually your product will find its way to a large nonpaying audience - if anyone cares to have it in the first place. . . .

Much chargeable value will be in certification of authenticity and reliability, not in the content. Brand name, identity, and other marks of value will be important; so will security of supply. Customers will pay for a stream of information and content from a trusted source. For example, the umbrella of the *New York Times* sanctifies the words of its reporters. The content churned out by *Times* reporters is valuable because the reporters undergo quality-control, and because others believe them. . . .

The trick is to control not the copies of your work but instead a relationship with the customers—subscriptions or membership. And that's often what the customers want, because they see it as an assurance of a continuing supply of reliable, timely content.[33]

A profound shift of this kind in regard to authorial incentives fundamentally alters the balance between the costs and benefits of copyright protection in cyberspace, calling for a reappraisal of long standing principles. So, too, do other unique characteristics of cyberspace severely challenge traditional copyright concepts. For example, consider the very ubiquity of file "copying"—the fact that one cannot access any information whatsoever in a computer-mediated environment without making a "copy" of that information.[34] As a consequence, any simple-minded or simplistic attempt to superimpose traditional notions of the author's exclusive rights over the making of "copies" on cyberspace transactions are likely to have perverse results; "[I]f the very act of getting a document to your screen is considered the 'making of a copy' within the meaning of the Copyright Act, then a high proportion of the millions of messages traveling over the Internet each day potentially infringes on the right of some file creator . . . to control the making of copies. And, if the very act of reading such documents on line involves copying, then some form of a license . . . would, in this view, be required for virtually every one of those message transmissions."[35] Similarly, application of the "first sale" doctrine (allowing the purchaser of a copyrighted work to freely resell the copy she or he purchased) is problematic when the transfer of a lawfully owned copy technically involves the making of a new copy before the old one is eliminated.[36] Defining "fair use" is also difficult when a work's size is indeterminate, ranging from (1) an individual paragraph sold separately on demand in response to searches to (2) the entire database from which the paragraph originates, something never sold as a whole unit.

Treating cyberspace as a distinct location allows for the development of new forms of intellectual property law applicable only on the Net that would properly focus attention on these unique characteristics of this new, distinct place while preserving doctrines that apply to works embodied in physical collections (such as books) or displayed in legally significant physical places (for example theaters). Current debates about applying copyright law to the Net often do, implicitly, treat it as a distinct space, at least insofar as commercial copyright owners somewhat inaccurately refer to it as a "lawless" place.[37] The civility of the debate might improve if everyone assumed that the Net should have its own law, including a special law for unauthorized transfers of works from one realm to the other. We could, in other words, regulate the smuggling of works created in the physical world by treating the unauthorized uploading of a copy of such works to the Net as infringement of copyright. This new approach would help promoters of electronic commerce focus on developing incentive-producing rules to encourage authorized transfers into cyberspace of works not available now while also reassuring owners of existing copyrights of valuable works that changes in the copyright law for the Net would not require changing laws applicable to distributing physical works. It would also permit the development of new doctrines of implied license and fair use that, with regard to works first created on the Net or imported with the author's permission, would appropriately allow the transmission and copying necessary to facilitate their use within the electronic realm.[38]

Will Responsible Self-Regulatory Structures Emerge on the Net?

Even if we agree that new rules should apply to online phenomena, questions remain about who sets the rules and how they are enforced. We believe the Net can develop its own effective legal institutions.

In order for the domain name space to be administered by a legal authority that is not territorially based, new law-making institutions will have to develop. Many questions that arise in setting up this system will need answers; decisions will have to be made whether to create a new top-level domain, whether online addresses belong to users or service providers, and whether one name impermissibly interferes with another, thus confusing the public and diluting the value of the preexisting name. The new system must also include procedures to give notice of conflicting claims, to resolve these claims, and to assess appropriate remedies (including, possibly, compensation) in cases of wrongful use. If the cyberspace equivalent of eminent domain develops, questions may arise over how to compensate individuals when certain domain names are destroyed or redeployed for the public good of the Net community. Someone must also decide threshold membership issues for cyberspace citizens, including how much users must disclose (and to whom) about their real-world identities to use e-mail addresses and domain names for commercial purposes. Implied throughout this discussion is the recognition that these rules will be meaningful and enforceable only if cyberspace citizens view those making these decisions as a legitimate governing body.

Experience suggests that the community of online users and service providers is up to the task of developing a self-governance system.[39] Every system operator who dispenses a password imposes at least some requirements as conditions of continuing access, including paying bills on time or remaining a member of a group entitled to access (e.g., students at a university).[40] System operators (sysops) have an extremely powerful tool at their disposal to enforce such rules—banishment.[41] Moreover, communities of users have marshaled plenty of enforcement weapons to induce wrongdoers to comply with local conventions such as rules against flaming, shunning, mailbombs, and the like. And both sysops and users have begun explicitly to recognize that formulating and enforcing such rules should be a matter for principled discussion, not an act of will by whoever has control of the power switch.[42]

While many of these new rules and customs apply only to specific, local areas of the global network, some standards apply through technical protocols on a nearly universal basis. And widespread agreement already exists about core principles of "Netiquette" in mailing lists and discussion groups[43]—although, admittedly, new users have a slow learning curve and the Net offers little formal "public education" regarding applicable norms. Dispute resolution mechanisms suited to this new environment also seem certain to prosper.[44] Cyberspace is anything but anarchic; its rules are becoming more robust every day.

Perhaps the aptest analogy to the rise of a separate law of cyberspace is the origin of the law merchant—a distinct set of rules that developed with the new, rapid boundary crossing trade of the Middle Ages.[45] Merchants could not resolve their disputes by taking them to the local noble, whose established feudal law mainly concerned land claims. Nor could the local lord easily establish meaningful rules for a sphere of activity he barely understood, executed in locations beyond his control. The result of this jurisdictional confusion, arising from a then-novel form of boundary-crossing communications, was the development of a new legal system—*lex mercatoria.*

[D]uring this period, because of the need for uniform laws of commerce to facilitate international trade, . . . the basic concepts and institutions of modern Western mercantile law—lex mercatoria—were formed, and, even more important, it was then that mercantile law in the West first came to be viewed as an integrated, developing system, a body of law. Virtually every aspect of commercial transactions in all of Europe (and in cases even outside Europe) were "governed" by this body of law after the eleventh century. . . . This body of law was voluntarily produced, voluntarily adjudicated and voluntarily enforced. In fact, it had to be. There was no other potential source of such law, including state coercion.[46]

The people who cared most about and best understood their new creation formed and championed this new body of law, which did not destroy or replace existing law regarding more territorially based transactions (e.g., transferring land ownership). Arguably, exactly the same type of phenomenon is developing in cyberspace right now.[47]

Governments cannot stop electronic communications coming across their borders, even if they want to do so. Nor can they credibly claim a right to regulate the Net based on supposed local harms caused by activities that originate outside their borders and that travel electronically to many different nations. One nation's legal institutions should not, therefore, monopolize rule making for the entire Net. Even so, established authorities are likely to continue to claim that they must analyze and regulate the new online phenomena in terms of some physical locations. After all, the people engaged in online communications still inhabit the material world. And, so the argument goes, local legal authorities must have authority to remedy the problems created in the physical world by those acting on the Net. The rise of responsible law-making institutions within cyberspace, however, will weigh heavily against arguments that would claim that the Net is "lawless" and thus tie regulation of online trade to physical jurisdictions. As noted, sysops acting alone or collectively have the power of banishment to control wrongful actions online. This enforcement tool is not perfect—any more than the tool of banishing merchants from the medieval trade fairs was perfect for the development of the law merchant.[48] Individuals intent on wrongdoing may be able to sneak back on the Net or into a particular online area with a new identity. But the enforcement tools used by legal authorities in the real world also have limits. We do not refrain from recognizing the sovereignty of our territorial governments just because they cannot fully control their physical borders or all of the actions of their citizens. Thus, for online activities that minimally impact the vital interests of sovereigns, the self-regulating structures of cyberspace seem better suited than local authorities to deal with the Net-related legal issues.[49]

Local Authorities, Foreign Rules: Reconciling Conflicts

What should happen when conflicts arise between the local territorial law (applicable to persons or entities by virtue of their location in a particular area of physical space) and the law applicable to particular activities on the Net? The doctrine of "comity" along with principles applied when delegating authority to self-regulatory organizations provide us with guidance for reconciling such disputes.

The doctrine of comity, in the Supreme Court's classic formulation, is "the recognition which one nation allows within its territory to the legislative, executive, or judicial acts of another nation, having due regard both to international duty and convenience, and to the rights of its own citizens or of other persons who are under the protections of its law."[50] It is incorporated into the principles set forth in the Restatement (Third) of Foreign Relations Law of the United States, in particular Section 403, which provides that "a state may not exercise jurisdiction to prescribe law with respect to a person or activity having connections with another state when the exercise of such jurisdiction is unreasonable,"[51] and that when a conflict between the laws of two states arises, "each state has an obligation to evaluate its own as well as the other state's interest in exercising jurisdiction [and] should defer to the other state if that state's interest is clearly greater.").[52] It arose as an attempt to mitigate some of the harsher features of a world in which law-making is an attribute of control over physical space but in which persons, things, and actions may move across physical boundaries, and it functions as a constraint on the strict application of territorial principles that attempts to reconcile "the principle of absolute territorial sovereignty [with] the fact that intercourse between nations often demand[s] the recognition of one sovereign's lawmaking acts in the forum of another."[53] In general, comity reflects the view that those who care more deeply about and better understand the disputed activity should determine the outcome. Accordingly, it may be ideally suited to handle, by extension, the new conflicts between the aterritorial nature of cyberspace activities and the legitimate needs of territorial sovereigns and of those whose interests they protect on the other side of the cyberspace border. This doctrine does not disable territorial authorities from protecting the interests of those individuals located within their spheres of control, but it calls upon them to exercise a significant degree of restraint when doing so.

Local officials handling conflicts can also learn from the many examples of delegating authority to self-regulatory organizations. Churches are allowed to make religious law.[54] Clubs and social organizations can, within broad limits, define rules that govern activities within their spheres of interest. Securities exchanges can establish commercial rules, long as they protect the vital interests of the surrounding communities. In these cases, government has seen the wisdom of allocating rule-making functions to those who best understand a complex phenomenon and who have an interest in assuring the growth and health of their shared enterprise.

Cyberspace represents a new permutation of the underlying issue: how much should local authorities defer to a new, self-regulating activity arising independently of local control and reaching beyond the limited physical boundaries of the sovereign? This mixing of tangible and intangible boundaries leads to a convergence of the intellectual categories of comity and local delegation by a sovereign to self-regulatory groups. In applying both the doctrine of "comity" and the idea of "delegation" to cyberspace, a local authority is called upon to defer to the self-regulatory judgments of a population partly, but not wholly, composed of its own subjects.

Despite the seeming contradiction of a sovereign deferring to the authority of those who are not its own subjects, such a policy makes sense, especially in light of the underlying purposes of both doctrines. Comity and delegation represent the wise conservation of governmental resources and allocate decisions to those who most fully understand the special needs and characteristics of a particular "sphere." Although cyberspace represents a new sphere that cuts across national boundaries, the fundamental principle remains. If the sysops and users who collectively inhabit and control a particular area of the Net want to establish special rules to govern conduct there, and if that rule set does not fundamentally impinge upon the vital interests of others who never visit this new space, then the law of sovereigns in the physical world should defer to this new form of self-government.

Consider, once again, the trademark example. A U.S. government representative has stated that since the government paid for the initial development and administration of the domain name system, it "owns" the right to control policy decisions regarding the creation and use of such names.[55] Obviously, government funds helped create this valuable and finite new asset, but the government's claim based on its investment is not particularly convincing. In fact, the United States may be asserting its right to control the policies governing the domain name space primarily because it fears that any other authority over the Net might force it to pay again for the ".gov" and ".mil" domain names used by governmental entities.[56] To assuage these concerns, a Net-based authority should concede to the governments on this point. For example, it should accommodate the military's strong interest in remaining free to regulate and use its ".mil" addresses.[57] A new Net-based standards-setting authority should also accommodate the government's interests in retaining its own untaxed domain names and prohibiting counterfeiting. Given responsible restraint by the Net-based authority and the development of an effective self-regulatory scheme, the government might well then decide that it should not spend its finite resources trying to wrest effective control of nongovernmental domain names away from those who care most about facilitating the growth of online trade.

Because controlling the flow of electrons across physical boundaries is so difficult, a local jurisdiction that seeks to prevent its citizens from accessing specific materials must either outlaw all access to the Net—thereby cutting itself off from the new global trade—or seek to impose its will on the Net as a whole. This would be the modern equivalent of a local lord in medieval times either trying to prevent the silk trade from passing through his boundaries (to the dismay of local customers and merchants) or attempting to assert jurisdiction over the known world. It may be most difficult to envision local territorial authorities deferring to the law of the Net when the perceived threat to local interests arises from the very free flow of information that is the Net's most fundamental characteristic—when, for example, local authorities assert an interest in seeing that their citizens are not adversely affected by information that the local jurisdiction deems harmful but that is freely (and lawfully) available elsewhere. Examples discussed earlier include the German government's attempts to forbid its citizens access to prohibited materials or the prosecution of a California bulletin board operator for making material offensive to local "community standards" available for downloading in Tennessee. Local jursidictions may insist that their interest in protecting their citizens from harm is paramount and easily outweighs any interest in making this kind of material freely available. But the opposing interest is not simply the interest in seeing that individuals have access to ostensibly obscene material; it is the "meta-interest" of Net citizens in preserving the global free flow of information.

If there is one central principle on which all local authorities within the Net should agree, it must be that territorially local claims to restrict online transactions in ways unrelated to vital and localized interests of a territorial government should be resisted. This is the Net equivalent of the First Amendment, a principle already recognized in the form of the international human rights doctrine protecting the right to communicate.[58] Participants in the new online trade must oppose external regulation designed to obstruct this flow. This central principle of online law bears importantly on the "comity" analysis because it makes clear that the need to preserve a free flow of information across the Net is as vital to the interests of the Net as the need to protect local citizens against the impact of unwelcome information may appear to be from the perpective of a local territorial jursidiction. Moreover, the right of individuals to participate in various online realms depends critically on their obtaining information about those realms. Insofar as any territorial government merely asserts the moral superiority of its laws and values, it is not well situated to oppose a free flow of information that might lead its citizens to disagree, because this would be the equivalent of defending ignorance as a necessary ingredient of preservation of the values espoused by the local state. This view is unlikely to persuade external rule-makers who do not share those values. For the Net to realize its full promise, online rule-making authorities must not respect the claims of territorial sovereigns to restrict online communications when they are unrelated to vital governmental interests.

Internal Diversity

One of a border's key characteristics is that it slows the interchange of people, things, and information across its divide. Arguably, distinct sets of legal rules can develop and persist only where effective boundaries exist. Therefore, the development of a true cyberspace law depends upon a dividing line between this new online territory and the nonvirtual world. Our argument so far has been that the new sphere is cut off, at least to some extent, from rulemaking institutions in the material world and requires the creation of distinct law.

But we hasten to add that cyberspace is not, a homogeneous or uniform territory where information flows without further impediment. Although it is meaningless to speak of a French or Armenian portion of cyberspace because the physical borders dividing French or Armenian territory from their neighbors cannot generally be mapped onto the information flow, the Net has other kinds of internal borders delineating many distinct internal locations that slow or block the flow of information. Distinct names and (virtual) addresses, special passwords, entry fees, and visual cues—software boundaries—can distinguish subsidiary areas from one another. The Usenet newsgroup "alt.religion.scientology" is distinct from "alt.misc.legal," each of which is distinct from a chat room on CompuServe or America Online which, in turn are distinct from the cyberspace Law Institute listserver or Counsel Connect. Users can access these different forums only through distinct addresses or phone numbers, often navigating through login screens, the use of passwords, or the payment of fees. Indeed, the ease with which internal borders consisting entirely of software protocols can be constructed is one of cyberspace's most remarkable and salient characteristics. Listservers, for example, can be set up on any network or Internet server by means of simple instructions given to one of several widely available software programs (listproc or majordomo). A Usenet discussion group in the "alt." hierarchy can be established by sending a simple request to the "alt.config" newsgroup.[59]

Cyberspace not only permits the effective delineation of internal boundaries between online spaces but also allows for effective delineation of distinct online roles within different spheres of activity and as to which different rules apply. In the nonvirtual world, we slip in and out of such roles frequently; the rules applicable to the behavior of a single individual in a single territorial jurisdiction may change as he or she moves between different legally significant persona (acting as an employee, a member of a church, a parent, or the officer of a corporation, for example). cyberspace may make the boundaries between these different roles easier to maintain, given that explicit "tags"—distinct "signature files," or screen names—can relatively easily be attached to messages originating from the author's different roles.

The separation of subsidiary "territories" or spheres of activity within cyberspace and the barriers to exchanging information across these internal borders allow for the development of distinct rule sets and for the divergence of those rule sets over time.[60] The processes underlying biological evolution provide a useful analogy.[61] Speciation—the emergence over time of multiple, distinct constellations of genetic information from a single, original group—cannot occur when the original population freely exchanges genetic material among its members. In other words, a single, freely interbreeding population of organisms cannot divide into genetically distinct populations. While the genetic material in the population changes over time, it does so more or less uniformly. For example, a single interbreeding population of the species *Homo erectus* can become a population of *Homo sapiens,* but cannot give rise to more than one contemporaneous, distinct genetic set.

Speciation requires, at a minimum, some barrier to the interchange of genetic material between subsets of the original homogeneous population. Ordinarily, a physical barrier suffices to prevent one subgroup from exchanging genetic data with another. Once this "border" is in place, divergence within the gene pool—the aggregate of the underlying genetic information—in each of the two subpopulations can occur.[62] Over time, this divergence may be substantial enough that even when the physical barrier disappears, the two subgroups can no longer exchange genetic material—that is, they have become separate species.

Rules, like genetic material, are self-replicating information.[63] The internal borders within cyberspace will allow for differentiation among distinct constellations of information—in this case rule sets rather than species. Content or conduct acceptable in one "area" of the Net may be banned in another. Institutions that resolve disputes in one "area" of cyberspace may not have support or legitimacy in others. Local sysops can, by contract, impose different default rules regarding who has the right, under certain conditions, to replicate and redistribute materials that originate with others. And while cyberspace's reliance on bits instead of atoms may make *physical* boundaries more permeable, the boundaries delineating digital online "spheres of being" may become *less* permeable. Cyberspace, as Ethan Katsh has written, is a "software world" where "code is the Law."

To a considerable extent, networks really are what software allows them to be. The Internet is not a network but a set of communications protocols. [T]he Internet is software. Similarly, the World Wide Web is not anything tangible. It is client-server software that permits machines linked on a network to share and work with information on any of the connected machines."[64]

And software specifications can be unforgiving (as anyone who has tried to send an e-mail message to an incorrectly spelled network recipient can attest):

Entry of messages into, and routing of messages across, digitally-based electronic networks . . . are controlled by more effective protocols [than generally govern non-electronic communications networks in the "real world"]: *each network's technical specifications (typically embodied in software or*

switching mechanisms) constitute rules that precisely distinguish between compli-
ant and non-compliant messages. This boundary [is not an] artificial construct
because the rules are effectively self-enforcing. To put the matter simply, you can't
"almost" be on the Georgetown University LAN or America Online—you are either
transmitting LAN- or AOL-compliant messages or you are not. "[65]

Individual network communities can be configured to bar all (or some specified portion of) internetwork traffic with relative ease, and securing online systems against unauthorized intruders may prove an easier task than sealing physical borders from unwanted immigration. Groups can establish online corporate entities or membership clubs that tightly control participation in, or even public knowledge of, their own affairs. Such groups can reach agreement on or modify these rules more rapidly via online communications. Accordingly, the rule sets applicable to the online world may quickly evolve away from those applicable to more traditional spheres and may develop greater variation.

How this process of differentiation and evolution will proceed is one of the more complex and fascinating questions about law in cyberspace—and a subject beyond the scope of this paper. We should point out, however, an important dimension of the proliferation of these internal boundaries between distinct communities and distinct rule sets and the process by which law will evolve in cyberspace. Cyberspace may be an important forum for the development of new connections between individuals and mechanisms of self-governance by which individuals attain an increasingly elusive sense of community. Commenting on the erosion of national sovereignty in the modern world and the failure of the existing system of nation-states to cultivate a "civic voice," a moral connection between the individual and the community (or communities) in which she or he is embedded, Sandel has written:

The hope for self-government today lies not in relocating sovereignty but in dispersing it. The most promising alternative to the sovereign state is not a cosmopolitan community based on the solidarity of humankind but *a multiplicity of communities and political bodies—some more extensive than nations and some less—among which sovereignty is diffused.* Only a politics that disperses sovereignty both upward [to transnational institutions] and downward can combine the power required to rival global market forces with the differentiation required of a public life that hopes to inspire the allegiance of its citizens. . . . If the nation cannot summon more than a minimal commonality, it is unlikely that the global community can do better, at least on its own. A more promising basis for a democratic politics that reaches beyond nations is a revitalized civic life nourished in the more particular communities we inhabit. In the age of NAFTA the politics of neighborhood matters more, not less."[66]

Furthermore, the ease with which individuals can move between different rule sets in cyberspace has important implications for any political philosophy that derives justification for the state's exercise of coercive power over its citizens from their consent to the exercise of that power. In the nonvirtual world, this consent has a strong fictional element: "State reliance on consent inferred from someone merely remaining in the state is particularly unrealistic. An individual's unwillingness to incur the extraordinary costs of leaving his or her birthplace should not be treated as a consensual undertaking to obey state authority."[67]

To be sure, citizens of France, dissatisfied with French law and preferring, say, Armenian rules, can try to persuade their compatriots and local decision makers of the superiority of the Armenian rule set. In Hirschman's terms, they have a "voice" in the development of French law, at least to the extent that French law-making institutions represent and are affected by citizen participation, but their "exit" option is limited by the need to physically relocate to Armenia to take advantage of that rule set.[68] In contrast, in cyberspace, any given user has a more accessible exit option—from one virtual environment's rule set to another's—thus providing a more legitimate "selection mechanism" by which different rule sets will evolve over time.

The ease with which individuals may move between communities or inhabit multiple communities simultaneously also implies that cyberspace may provide the necessary and sufficient conditions for something more closely resembling the optimal collective production of a particular set of goods—namely, "laws"—than can be achieved in the real world. cyberspace may closely approximate Tiebout's idealized model for the allocation of local goods and services, in which optimal allocation of locally produced public goods is provided by small jurisdictions competing for mobile residents.[69] The Tiebout model of intergovernmental competition has four components: (1) a perfectly elastic supply of jurisdictions, (2) costless mobility of individuals among jurisdictions, (3) full information about the attributes of all jurisdictions, and (4) no interjurisdictional externalities.[70] In a Tieboutian world,

> each locality provides a package of local public goods consistent with the preferences of its residents (consumer-voters). Residents whose preferences remain unsatisfied by a particular locality's package of goods and services would (costlessly) move. . . . Escape from undesirable packages of goods and services is feasible as a result of two explicit characteristics of the Tiebout model: absence of externalities and mobility of residents.[71]

We suggest that cyberspace may be a closer approximation to ideal Tieboutian competition between rule-sets than exists in the nonvirtual world, a consequence of (1) the low cost of establishing an online "jurisdiction," (2) the ease of exit from online communities, (3) the relative ease of acquiring information about the practices of online communities, and (4) the greater impermeability of the internal, software-mediated boundaries between online communities in cyberspace, which may mitigate (at least to some extent) the problem of intercommunity externalities.

The ability of inhabitants of cyberspace to cross borders at will between legally significant territories many times in a single day is unsettling. This power seems to undercut the validity of developing distinct laws for online culture and commerce: how can these rules be "law" if participants can literally turn them on and off with a switch? Frequent online travel might subject relatively mobile human beings to a far larger number of rule sets than they would encounter traveling through the physical world over the same period. Established authorities, contemplating the rise of a new law applicable to online activities, might object that we cannot easily live in a world with so many different sources and types of law, particularly those made by private (nongovernmental) parties, without breeding confusion and allowing antisocial actors to escape effective regulation.

But the speed with which we can cross legally meaningful borders or adopt and then shed legally significant roles should not reduce our willingness to recognize multiple rule sets. Rapid travel between spheres of being does not detract from the distinctiveness of the boundaries as long as participants realize the rules are changing. Nor does it detract from the appropriateness of rules applying within any given place any more than changing commercial or organizational roles in the physical world detracts from a person's ability to obey and distinguish rules as a member of many different institutional affiliations and to know which rules are appropriate for which roles. Nor does it diminish the enforceability of any given rule set within its appropriate boundaries as long as groups can control unauthorized boundary crossing of groups or messages. Alternating between different legal identities many times during a day may confuse those for whom cyberspace remains an alien territory, but for those for whom cyberspace is a more natural habitat in which they spend increasing amounts of time it may become second nature. Legal systems must learn to accommodate a more mobile kind of legal person. As Sandel has observed, "Self-government today . . . requires a politics that plays itself out in a multiplicity of settings, from neighborhoods to nations to the world as a whole. Such a politics requires citizens who can abide the ambiguity associated with divided sovereignty, who can think and act as multiply situated selves."[72]

Conclusion

Global electronic communications have created new spaces in which distinct rule sets will evolve. We can reconcile the new law created in this space with current territorially based legal systems by treating it as a distinct doctrine, applicable to a clearly demarcated sphere, created primarily by legitimate, self-regulatory processes, and entitled to appropriate deference—but also subject to limitations when it oversteps its appropriate sphere.

The law of any given place must take into account the special characteristics of the space it regulates and the types of persons, places, and things found there. Just as a country's jurisprudence reflects its unique historical experience and culture, the law of cyberspace will reflect its special character, which differs markedly from anything found in the physical world. For example, the law of the Net must deal with persons who "exist" in cyberspace only in the form of an e-mail address and whose purported identity may or may not accurately correspond to physical characteristics in the real world. In fact, an e-mail address might not even belong to a single person. Accordingly, if cyberspace law is to recognize the nature of its "subjects," it cannot rest on the same doctrines that give geographically based sovereigns jurisdiction over "whole," locatable, physical persons. The law of the Net must be prepared to deal with persons who manifest themselves only by means of a particular ID, user account, or domain name.[73]

Moreover, if rights and duties attach to an account itself rather than an underlying real world person, traditional concepts such as "equality," "discrimination," or even "rights and duties" may not work as we normally understand them. New angles on these ideas may develop. For example, when America Online users joined the Net in large numbers, other cyberspace users often ridiculed them based on the ".aol" tag on their e-mail addresses—a form of "domainism" that might be discouraged by new forms of Netiquette. If a doctrine of cyberspace law accords rights to users, we will need to decide whether those rights adhere only to particular types of online appearances, as distinct from attaching to particular individuals in the real world.

Similarly, the types of "properties" that can become the subject of legal discussion in cyberspace will differ from real world real estate or tangible objects. For example, in the real world the physical covers of a book delineate the boundaries of a "work" for purposes of copyright law; those limits may disappear entirely when the same materials are part of a large electronic database. Thus, we may have to change the "fair use" doctrine in copyright law that previously depended on calculating what portion of the physical work was copied. Similarly, a Web page's "location" in cyberspace may take on a value unrelated to the physical place where the disk holding that Web page resides, and efforts to regulate Web pages by attempting to control physical objects may only cause the relevant bits to move from one place to another. On the other hand, the boundaries set by "URLs" (Uniform Resource Locators, the locations of documents on the World Wide Web) may need special protection against confiscation or confusingly similar addresses. And because offensive material may be located in these "places," we may need rules requiring (or allowing) groups to post certain signs or markings at these places' outer borders.

The boundaries that separate persons and things behave differently in the virtual world but are nonetheless legally significant. Messages posted under one e-mail name will not affect the reputation of another e-mail address even if the same physical person authors both messages. Materials separated by a password will be accessible to different sets of users, even if those materials physically exist on the very same hard drive. A user's claim to a right to a particular online identity or to redress when that identity's reputation suffers harm may be valid even if that identity does not correspond exactly to that of any single person in the real world.

Clear boundaries make law possible, encouraging rapid differentiation between rule sets and defining the subjects of legal discussion. New abilities to travel or exchange information rapidly across old borders may change the legal frame of reference and require fundamental changes in legal institutions. Fundamental activities of law-making—accommodating conflicting claims, defining property rights, establishing rules to guide conduct, enforcing those rules, and resolving disputes—remain very much alive within the newly defined, intangible territory of cyberspace. At the same time, the newly emerging law challenges the core idea of a current lawmaking authority—the territorial nation-state, with substantial but legally restrained powers.

If the rules of cyberspace thus emerge from consensually based rule sets and the subjects of such laws remain free to move among many different online spaces, then considering the actions of cyberspace's system administrators as the exercise of a power akin to "sovereignty" may be inappropriate. Under a legal framework by which the top level imposes physical order on those below it and depends for its continued effectiveness on the inability of its citizens to fight back or leave the territory, the legal and political doctrines we have developed over the centuries are essential to constrain such power. In that situation, where exit is impossible, costly, or painful, then a right to a voice for the people is essential. But when the "persons" in question are not whole people, when their "property" is intangible and portable, and when all concerned may readily escape a jurisdiction they do not find empowering, the relationship between the "citizen" and the "state" changes radically. Law, defined as a thoughtful group conversation about core values, will persist. But it will not, could not, and should not be the same law as that applicable to physical, geographically defined territories.

Notes

1. *American Banana Co. v. United Fruit Co.*, 213 U.S. 347, 357 (1909).

2. See Jerome Gilson, *Trademark Protection and Practice* §9.01 (New York: Bender, 1991); Dan L. Burk, "Trademarks Along the Infobahn: A First Look at the Emerging Law of Cybermarks," 1 *U. Rich. J.L. & Tech.* 1 (1995), available at http://www.urich.edu/~jolt/v1i1/burk.html.

3. See *Restaurant Lutece, Inc., v. Houbigant, Inc.*, 593 F. Supp. 588 (D.N.J. 1984).

4. See "Restatement (Third) of Foreign Relations Law of the United States," §201 (1987) ("Under international law, a state is an entity that has a defined territory and a permanent population, under the control of its own government . . . ."); §402 (a state has "jurisdiction to prescribe law with respect to (1)(a) conduct that, wholly or in substantial part, takes place within its territory; (b) the status of persons, or interests in things, present within its territory; (c) conduct outside its territory that has or is intended to have substantial effect within its territory.").

5. See generally, Henry H. Perritt, Jr., *Law and the Information Superhighway*, ch. 12 (New York: Wiley, 1996).

6. See "Declaration on Principles of International Law Concerning Friendly Relations and Cooperation Among States in Accordance with the Charter of the United Nations," G.A. Res. 2625, 35th Sess. (1970); see also Lea Brilmayer, "Consent, Contract, and Territory," 74 *Minn. L. Rev.* 1, 6, 11–12 (1989) (noting the significance of state authority derived from sovereignty over physical territory in the context of social contract theory and discussing contractarian theories of state sovereignty and legitimacy).

7. Some "signposts" are culturally understood conventions that accompany entry into specialized places, such as courtrooms, office buildings, and churches. But not all signposts and boundaries dividing different rule sets are geographically or physically based. Sets of different rules may apply when the affected parties play particular roles, such as members of self-regulatory organizations, agents of corporate entities, and so forth. But even these roles are usually clearly marked by cues of dress or by formal signatures.

8. As Woody Allen once quipped, "Space is nature's way of keeping everything from happening to you." Although there is distance in online space, it behaves differently than distance in real space. See generally, M. Ethan Katsh, *Law in a Digital World* (New York: Oxford University Press, 1995), 57–59, 218.

9. See Burk, "Trademarks Along the Infobahn," 12–14, for a general description of the Domain Naming System; see also Bush, Carpenter, and Postel, "Delegation of International Top-Level Domains, Internet-Draft ymbk-itld-admin-00,"

http://www.internic.net; "RFC 882, Domain Names—Concepts and Facilities," ftp://ds.internic.net/rfc/rfc882.txt; "RFC 883, Domain Names—Implementation and Specifications," ftp://ds.internic.net/rfc/rfc883.txt.

10. See Jon Auerbach, "Fences in Cyberspace; Governments Move to Limit Free Flow of the Internet," *Boston Globe*, Feb. 1, 1996, at 1 (surveying "digital Balkanization" of the Internet through government censorship and filtration); Seth Faison, "Chinese Cruise Internet, Wary of Watchdogs," *New York Times*, Feb. 5, 1995, at A1; see also note 14 below (describing the German government's attempts to interrupt German citizens' access to certain Usenet discussion groups).

11. See generally Anthony Paul Miller, "Teleinformatics, Transborder Data Flows and the Emerging Struggle for Information: An Introduction to the Arrival of the New Information Age," 20 *Colum. J. L. & Soc. Probs.* 89, 105–118, 127–132 (1986); see also "Book Publishers Worry About Threat of Internet," *New York Times*, Mar. 18, 1996, at A1 (describing appearance of *Le Grand Secret*, a book about former French President Francois Mitterand, on the Internet despite its having been banned in France and the general concern of book publishers about unauthorized Internet distributions).

12. See Walter B. Wriston, *The Twilight of Sovereignty* (New York: Scribner, 1992) at 61–62: "Technology has made us a 'global' community in the literal sense of the word. Whether we are ready or not, mankind now has a completely integrated international financial and information marketplace capable of moving money and ideas to any place on this planet in minutes. Capital will go where it is wanted and stay where it is well treated. It will flee from manipulation or onerous regulation of its value or use, and no government power can restrain it for long."

13. See Karen Kaplan, "Germany Forces Online Service to Censor Internet," *Los Angeles Times*, Dec. 29, 1995, at A1; "Why Free-Wheeling Internet Puts Teutonic Wall over Porn," *Christian Sci. Monitor*, Jan 4, 1996, at 1; "Cyberporn Debate Goes International; Germany Pulls the Shade On CompuServe, Internet," *Washington Post*, Jan. 1, 1996, at F13; Auerbach, "Fences in cyberspace," at 15; see also "CompuServe Ends Access Suspension: It reopens all but five adult-oriented newsgroups. Parents can now block offensive material," *Los Angeles Times*, Feb. 14, 1996, at D1.

14. See *United States v. Thomas*, 74 F.3d 701 (6th Cir. 1996) (affirming the convictions of a California couple for violations of federal obscenity laws stemming from electronic bulletin board postings made by the couple in California but accessible from and offensive to the community standards of Tennessee). See generally Electronic Frontier Foundation, "A Virtual Amicus Brief in the Amateur Action Case," Aug. 11, 1995, http://www.eff.org/pub/Legal/Cases/AABBS_Thomases_Memphis/Old/aa_eff_vbrief.html.

15. The Minnesota Attorney General's Office distributed a "Warning to All Internet Users and Providers," (available at http://www.state.mn.us/cbranch/ag/memo/txt), stating that "persons outside of Minnesota who transmit infor-

mation via the Internet knowing that information will be disseminated in Minnesota are subject to jurisdiction in Minnesota courts for violations of state criminal and civil laws." The conclusion rested on the Minnesota general criminal jurisdiction statute, which provides that "a person may be convicted and sentenced under the law of this State if the person . . . (3) Being without the State, intentionally causes a result within the state prohibited by the criminal laws of this State." *Minn. Stat. Ann.* §609.025 (West 1987). Minnesota also began civil proceedings against Wagernet, a Nevada gambling business which posted an Internet advertisement for online gambling services. See Complaint, Minnesota v. Granite Gate Resorts, Inc. (1995) (No. 9507227), http://www.state.mn.us/ebranch/ag/ggcom.txt. The Florida Attorney General, by contrast, contends that it is illegal to use the Web to gamble from within Florida but concedes that the Attorney General's office should not waste time trying to enforce the unenforceable. 95-70 Op. Fla. Att'y Gen. (1995), http://legal.firn.edu/units/opinions/95-70.html. For a general discussion of these pronouncements, see Mark Eckenwiler, "States Get Entangled in the Web," *Legal Times,* Jan. 22, 1996, at S35.

16. See "State Regulators Crack Down on 'Information Highway' Scams," *Daily Rep. For Exec.* (BNA), July 1, 1994, available in Westlaw, BNA–DER database, 1994 DER 125 at d16.

17. See generally "What Is Usenet?" and "Answers to Frequently Asked Questions about Usenet," available at http://www.smartpages.com/bngfaqs/news/announce/newusers/top.html.

18. See Joel R. Reidenberg, "The Privacy Obstacle Course: Hurdling Barriers to Transnational Financial Services," 60 *Fordham L. Rev.* S137 (1992); David Post, "Hansel & Gretel in Cyberspace," *Am. Law.*, Oct. 1995, at 110.

19. Privacy, at least, is a relatively familiar concept, susceptible to definition on the Net by reference to analogies with mail systems, telephone calls, and print publication of invasive materials. But many new issues posed by phenomena unique to the Net are not so familiar. Because electronic communications are not necessarily tied to real world identities, new questions about the rights to continued existence, or to protection of the reputation, of a pseudonym arise. The potential to launch a computer virus or to "spam the net" by sending multiple offpoint messages to newsgroups, for example, creates a need to define rules governing online behavior. When large numbers of people collaborate across the net to create services or works of value, we will face the question whether they have formed a corporate entity or partnership—with rights and duties that are distinct from those of the individual participants—in a context in which there may have been no "registration" with any particular geographic authority and the rights of any such authority to regulate that new "legal person" remain unsettled.

20. Conflicts between domain names and registered trademarks have caused Network Solutions, Inc. (NSI), the agent for registration of domain names in the United States, to require that registrants "represent and warrant" that they have

the right to a requested domain name and promise to "defend, indemnify and hold harmless" NSI for any claims stemming from use or registration of the requested name. See Network Solutions, Inc., NSI Domain Name Dispute Policy Statement (Revision 01, effective Nov. 23, 1995), ftp://rs.internic.net/policy/internic/internic-domain-4.txt. For a useful overview of the domain name registration system and of the tensions between trademark rights and domain names, see Gary W. Hamilton, "Trademarks on the Internet: Confusion, Collusion or Dilution?," 4 *Tex. Intell. Prop. L.J.* 1 (1995). See also Proceedings of the NSF/DNCEI & Harvard Information Infrastructure Project, Internet Names, Numbers, and Beyond: Issues in the Coordination, Privatization, and Internationalization of the Internet, Nov. 20, 1995, http://ksgwww.harvard.edu/iip/nsfmin1.html (discussing protection of the "trademark community" on the Net).

21. See the section below on Internal Diversity (discussing internal differentiation among rulesets in different online areas).

22. See notes 64–65 below.

23. Having a noticeable border may be a prerequisite to the establishment of any legal regime that can claim to be separate from preexisting regimes. If someone acting in any given space has no warning that the rules have changed, the legitimacy of any attempt to enforce a distinctive system of law is fatally weakened. No geographically based entity could plausibly claim to have jurisdiction over a territory with secret boundaries. And no self-regulatory organization could assert its prerogatives while making it hard for members and nonmembers to tell each other apart or disguising when they are (or are not) playing their membership-related roles.

24. See, e.g., Henry H. Perritt, Jr., "Tort Liability, the First Amendment, and Equal Access to Electronic Networks," 5 *Harv. J. L. & Tech.* 65, 106–108 (1992).

25. Subsequent distribution of printed versions might be characterized as publication without undermining the benefits of applying this new doctrine because it is much easier to determine who has taken such action and where (in physical space) it occurred, and the party who engages in physical distribution of defamatory works has much clearer warning regarding the nature of the act and the applicability of the laws of a particular territorial state.

26. Edward A. Cavazos, "Computer Bulletin Board Systems and the Right of Reply: Redefining Defamation Liability for a New Technology," 12 *Rev. Litig.* 231, 243–247 (1992). This "right of reply" doctrine might apply differently to different areas of the Net, depending on whether these areas do in fact offer a meaningful opportunity to respond to defamatory messages.

27. In the context of "telemedicine," early efforts to avoid this result seem to take the form of allowing doctors to interact with other doctors in consultations, requiring compliance with local regulations only when the doctor deals directly with a patient. See Howard J. Young and Robert J. Waters, "Licensure Barriers to the Interstate Use of Telemedicine" (1995), available at http://www.arentfox.

com/newslett/tele1b.htm. The regulation of lawyers is muddled: regulations are sometimes based on where the lawyer's office is (as in the case of regulation of advertising by the state of Texas), sometimes based on the content of legal advice, and sometimes based on the nature and location of the client. See Katsh, *Law in a Digital World*, at 178–181.

28. Jane C. Ginsburg, "Global Use/Territorial Rights: Private International Law questions on the Global Information Infrastructure," *J. Copy Soc.* 318, 319–320 (1995).

29. See generally Friedman, "Standards as Intellectual Property," 19 *U. Dayton L. Rev.* 1109 (1994); William Landes & Richard Posner, "An Economic Analysis of Copyright Law," 18 *J. Legal Stud.* 325 (1989).

30. See Stephen Breyer, "The Uneasy Case for Copyright: A Study of Copyright in Books, Photocopies, and Computer Programs," 84 *Harv. L. Rev.* 281, 293–309 (1970) for an analysis of the incentive structure in the scholarly publishing market.

31. There is a large and diverse literature on the new kinds of authorship that are likely to emerge in cyberspace as a function of the interactive nature of the medium, the ease with which digital information can be manipulated, and new searching and linking capabilities. Among the more insightful pieces in this vein are Pamela Samuelson, "Digital Media and the Changing Face of Intellectual Property Law," 16 *Rutgers Computer and Tech. L. J.* 323 (1990); Katsh, supra note 8, chaps. 4, 8, and 9; Euguene Volokh, "Cheap Speech," 94 *Yale L. J.* 1805 (1994); and Sherry Turkle, *Life on the Screen: Identity in the Age of the Internet* (New York: Simon & Schuster, 1996).

32. Netscape Corp. gave away, at no charge, over four million copies of their Web browser; it is estimated that they now control over 70 percent of the Web browser market, which they have managed to leverage into dominance in the Web *server* software market, sufficient to enable them to launch one of the most successful initial public offerings in the history of the United States. See "Netscape IPO booted up;: Debut of hot stock stuns Wall Street veterans," *Boston Globe*, Aug. 10, 1995, at 37; "With Internet Cachet, Not Profit, A New Stock Is Wall St.'s Darling," *New York Times*, Aug. 10, 1995, at 1. Other companies are following Netscape's lead; for example, Realaudio, Inc. is distributing software designed to allow Web browsers to play sound files in real time over the Internet, presumably in the hopes of similarly establishing a dominant market position in the server market. See http://www.realaudio.com.

33. Esther Dyson, "Intellectual Value," *Wired* (Aug. 1995).

34. "Browsing on the World Wide Web, for example, necessarily involves the creation of numerous 'copies' of information; first, a message is transmitted from Computer A to (remote) Computer B, requesting that Computer B send a copy of a particular file (e.g., the 'home page' stored on Computer B) back to Computer A. When the request is received by Computer B, a copy of the requested file is made and transmitted back to Computer A (where it is copied

again—'loaded' into memory—and displayed). And the manner in which messages travel across the Internet to reach their intended recipient(s)—via intermediary computers known as 'routers,' at each of which the message is 'read' by means of 'copying' the message into the computer's memory—[involve] innumerable separate acts of . . . 'reproduction.' File copying is not merely inexpensive in cyberspace, it is ubiquitous; and it is not merely ubiquitous, it is indispensable . . . . Were you to equip your computer with a 'copy lock'—an imaginary device that will prevent the reproduction of any and all information now stored in the computer in any form—it will, essentially, stop functioning." David G. Post, "Controlling Cybercopies," *Legal Times* (Apr. 8, 1996) at 44.

35. David G. Post, "New Wine, Old Bottles: The Evanescent Copy," *Am. Law.*, May 1995, at 103; see also Jessica Litman, "The Exclusive Right to Read," 13 *Cardozo Arts & Ent. L. J.* 29, 40–42 (1993); Pamela Samuelson, "The Copyright Grab," *Wired* (Jan. 1996) at 137; Pamela Samuelson, "Legally Speaking: Intellectual Property Rights and the Global Information Economy," 39 *Commun. Assoc. Computing Machinery* 23, 24 (1996).

36. Neel Chatterjee, "Imperishable Intellectual Creations: Use Limits of the First Sale Doctrine," 5 *Fordham Intell. Prop. Media & Ent. L.J.* 383, 384, 415–418 (1995) (discussing Information Infrastructure Task Force proposal to exclude transmissions from the first sale doctrine).

37. Benjamin Wittes, "A (Nearly) Lawless Frontier: The Rapid Pace of Change in 1994 Left the Law Chasing Technology on the Information Superhighway," *Legal Times*, Jan. 3, 1995, at 1.

38. For example, we could adopt rules that make the "caching" of Web pages presumptively permissible, absent an explicit agreement, rather than adopting the standard copyright doctrine to the contrary. (Caching involves copying Web pages to a hard drive so that future trips to the site take less time to complete.) Because making "cached" copies in computer memory is essential to speed up the operation of the Web and because respecting express limits or retractions on any implied license allowing caching would clog up the free flow of information, we should adopt a rule favoring browsing. See Cyberspace Law Institute, "Caching and Copyright Protections" (Sept. 1, 1995), http://www.cli.org/; Samuelson, "Legally Speaking," at 26–27 (discussing copyright issues raised by file caching).

39. See David G. Post, "Anarchy, State, and the Internet: An Essay on Law-Making in Cyberspace," 1995 *J. Online L.* art. 3, para. 10, http://www.law.cornell.edu/jol/jol.table.html.

40. Typical rules also require refraining from actions that threaten the value of the online space or increase the risk that the system operator will face legal trouble in the real world. Many coherent online communities also have rules preserving the special character of their online spaces, rules governing posted messages, discouraging "flaming" (sending an insulting message) or "spamming" (sending the same message to multiple newsgroups), and even rules mandating certain professional qualifications for participants.

41. See Robert L. Dunne, "Deterring Unauthorized Access to Computers: Controlling Behavior in cyberspace Through a Contract Law Paradigm," 35 *Jurimetrics J.* 1, 12 (1994) (suggesting that system operator agreements to banish offenders would deter unauthorized computer access more effectively than current criminal sanctions).

42. Jennifer Mnookin, "Virtual(ly) Law: A Case Study of the Emergence of Law on LambdaMOO" (May 15, 1995) (unpublished manuscript on file with the authors) (describing the emergence of a legal system in the LambdaMOO virtual community).

43. Hambridge, RFC 1855: "Netiquette Guidelines" (Oct. 1995) ftp://ds.internic.net/rfc/rfc1855.txt.

44. See Henry H. Perritt, Jr., "Dispute Resolution in Electronic Network Communities," 38 *Vill. L. Rev.* 349, 398–399 (1993) (proposing an alternative dispute resolution mechanism that could be implemented by a computer network service provider); Henry H. Perritt, Jr., "President Clinton's National Information Infrastructure Initiative: Community Regained?," 69 *Chi.–Kent L. Rev.* 991, 995–1022 (1994) (advocating the use of new information technology to facilitate dispute resolution); I. Trotter Hardy, "The Proper Legal Regime for 'Cyberspace,'" 55 *U. Pitt. L. Rev.* 993, 1051–1053. One such dispute resolution service, the Virtual Magistrate, has already arisen on the Net. See http://vmag.law.vill.edu:8080/.

45. See generally Hardy, "The Proper Legal Regime for 'Cyberspace,'" at 1020; Leon E. Trakman, *The Law Merchant: The Evolution of Commercial Law* 11–12 (Littleton, CO: Rothman, 1983). Benson describes the development of the law merchant as follows:

> With the fall of the Roman Empire, commercial activities in Europe were almost nonexistent relative to what had occurred before and what would come after. Things began to change in the eleventh and twelfth centuries [with the] emergence of a class of professional merchants. There were significant barriers to overcome before substantial interregional and international trade could develop, however. Merchants spoke different languages and had different cultural backgrounds. Beyond that, geographic distances frequently prevented direct communication, let alone the building of strong interpersonal bonds that would facilitate trust. Numerous middlemen were often required to bring about an exchange . . . . All of this, in the face of localized, often contradictory laws and business practices, produced hostility towards foreign commercial customs and led to mercantile confrontations. There was a clear need for Law as a "language of interaction."

Bruce L. Benson, "The Spontaneous Evolution of Commercial Law," 55 *Southern Econ. J.* 644, 646–647 (1989).

46. Benson, "The Spontaneous Evolution of Commercial Law," 647.

47. See Hardy, "The Proper Legal Regime for 'Cyberspace,'" 1019 ("The parallels [between the development of the law merchant and] cyberspace are

strong. Many people interact frequently over networks, but not always with the same people each time so that advance contractual relations are not always practical. Commercial transactions will more and more take place in cyberspace, and more and more those transactions will cross national boundaries and implicate different bodies of law. Speedy resolution of disputes will be as desirable as it was in the Middle Ages! The means of an informal court system are in place in the form of on-line discussion groups and electronic mail. A 'Law cyberspace' co-existing with existing laws would be an eminently practical and efficient way of handling commerce in the networked world."); Post, "Anarchy, State, and the Internet," par. 43 and n. 15.

48. See Paul R. Milgrom, Douglass C. North, and Barry R. Weingast, "The Role of Institutions in the Revival of Trade: The Law Merchant, Private Judges, and the Champagne Fairs," 2 *Econ. & Pol.* 1 (1990) (describing the use of banishment and other enforcement mechanisms during development of law merchant).

49. The social philosopher Michael Sandel has made a similar point in writing of the need for new transnational law-making institutions if the "loss of mastery and the erosion of community that lie at the heart of democracy's discontent" is to be alleviated: "In a world where capital and goods, information and images, pollution and people, flow across national boundaries with unprecedented ease, politics must assume transnational, even global, forms, if only to keep up. Otherwise, *economic power will go unchecked by democratically sanctioned political power*. . . . We cannot hope to govern the global economy without transnational political institutions." Michael Sandel, "America's Search for a New Public Philosophy," *Atlantic Monthly*, Mar. 1996, at 72–73 (emphasis added).

50. *Hilton v. Guyot*, 115 U.S. 113, 163–164 (1995). See also *Lauritzen v. Larsen*, 345 U.S. 571, 582 (1953) ("International or maritime law . . . aims at stability and order through usages which considerations of comity, reciprocity and long-range interest have developed to define the domain which each nation will claim as its own."). Good general treatments of the comity doctrine can be found in Swanson, "Comity, International Dispute Resolution Agreements, and the Supreme Court," 21 *Law & Policy in Int'l Bus.* 333 (1990); Paul, "Comity in International Law," 32 *Harv. Int. L.J.* 1 (1991); Yntema, "The Comity Doctrine," 65 *Mich. L. Rev* 9 (1966); James S. Campbell, "New Law for New International Trade," 5 (Dec. 3, 1993) (on file with the authors); Mark W. Janis, *An Introduction to International Law*, 250ff. (Boston: Little, Brown, 1988); Lea Brilmayer, *Conflict of Laws: Foundations and Future Directions*, 145–190 (Boston: Little, Brown, 1991).

51. "Restatement (Third) of Foreign Relations Law of the United States," §403(1) (1987).

52. Ibid., at §403(3).

53. Maier, "Remarks," 84 *Proc. Am. Soc. Int'l Law* (1990), 339, 339; also 340 (principle of comity informs the "interest-balancing" choice of law principles in the Restatement). Paul, "Comity in International Law," 12 (comity arose out of "the need for a more sophisticated system of conflict resolution . . . in connection with the emergence of the nation state and the rise of commerce that brought

different nationalities into more frequent contact and conflict with one another"); also at 45–48 (noting that although the relationship between the "classical doctrine of comity" and the Restatement's principle of "reasonableness" is uncertain, the former "retains a significant function in the Restatement"); also at 54 (comity principle "mitigates the inherent tension between principles of territorial exclusivity and sovereign equality").

54. Cf. Adam Gopnik, "The Virtual Bishop," *New Yorker,* March 18, 1996, at 63 ("'Of course, the primitive Church was a kind of Internet itself, which was one of the reasons it was so difficult for the Roman Empire to combat it. The early Christians understood that what was most important was not to claim physical power in a physical place but to establish a network of believers—to be on line,'" quoting French Bishop Jacques Gaillot).

55. See David W. Maher, "Trademarks on the Internet: Who's in Charge?" (Feb. 14, 1996), available at http://www.aldea.com/cix/maher.html (noting the "arrogance" of the Federal Networking Council's position on this issue).

56. Ibid.

57. Ibid. (noting "the .mil domain is excluded" from the jurisdiction of the private corporation that assigns addresses).

58. The free flow of information principle has been defined as a necessary part of freedom of opinion and expression. See Article 19 of the Universal Declaration of Human Rights, *G.A. Res.* 217(III)A, 3(1) *U.N. GAOR Resolutions* at 71, 74–75, U.N. Doc. A/810 (1948) (stating that freedom of expression includes "freedom to hold opinions without interference and to seek, receive and impart information and ideas through any media and regardless of frontiers"). See also Jonathan Graubert, "What's News: A Progressive Framework for Evaluating the International Debate Over the News," 77 *Cal. L. Rev.,* 629, 633 (1989) ("The guiding principle in international communications since World War II has been the U.S.-inspired goal of a 'free flow of information.' According to this principle, 'freedom of information implies the right to gather, transmit and publish news anywhere and everywhere without fetters.'") (citing *G.A. Res.* 59 (I), 1(2), *U.N. GAOR Resolutions* at 95, U.N. Doc. A/64/Add. 1 (1947).

59. See sources cited in note 17.

60. Post, "Anarchy, State, and the Internet," art. 3, at par. 7 (asserting that the individual network "organizations" will probably determine the substantive rule-making for cyberspace); David R. Johnson and Kevin A. Marks, "Mapping Electronic Data Communications onto Existing Legal Metaphors: Should We Let Our Conscience (and Our Contracts) Be Our Guide?," 38 *Vill. L. Rev.* 487, 489–489 (1993) (explaining that communication service providers, owners of disks carrying centralized databases, and people presiding over electronic discussion groups have the power to select applicable rules).

61. For illuminating discussions of the many parallels between biological evolution and social evolution in cyberspace, see Kevin Kelly, *Out of Control: The Law of Neo-Biological Civilization* (London: Fourth Estate, 1994); John Lienhard,

"Reflections on Information, Biology, and Community," 32 *Hous. L. Rev.* 303 (1995); Michael Schrage, "Revolutionary Evolutionist," *Wired* (July 1995).

62. This geographic barrier merely permits divergence to occur; it does not guarantee it. Speciation will occur, for example, only if the two divided subpopulations are subject to different selection pressures or at least one of them is small enough to accrue significant random changes in its gene pool ("genetic drift"). For good, nontechnical descriptions of evolutionary theory, see Daniel C. Dennett, *Darwin's Dangerous Idea: Evolution and the Meanings of Life* (New York: Simon & Schuster, 1995); John Maynard-Smith, *Did Darwin Get it Right? Essays on Games, Sex, and Evolution* (New York: Chapman & Hall, 1989); John Maynard-Smith, *On Evolution* (Edinburgh: Edinburgh University Press, 1972); George C. Williams, *Adaptation and Natural Selection: A Critique of Some Current Evolutionary Thought* (Princeton: Princeton University Press, 1966).

63. See Richard Dawkins, *The Selfish Gene* (New York: Oxford University Press, 1989). General parallels between biological evolution and the evolution of legal rules are discussed in Friedrich Hayek, *Law, Legislation, and Liberty*, 44–49 (Chicago: University of Chicago Press, 1973); Friedrich Hayek, *The Constitution of Liberty*, 56–61 (Chicago: University of Chicago Press, 1960); see generally Tom W. Bell, "Polycentric Law," 7 *Humane Studies Rev.* (available at http://osf1.gmu.edu/~ihs/w91issues.html).

64. Ethan Katsh, "Software Worlds and the First Amendment: Virtual Doorkeepers in Cyberspace," *Univ. Of Chic. Legal Forum* (forthcoming), at 7, quoting William Mitchell, *City of Bits* (Cambridge: MIT Press, 1995).

65. Post, "Anarchy, State, and the Internet," at par. 20 (emphasis added).

66. Sandel, "America's Search for a New Public Philosophy," 73–74 (emphasis added).

67. Brilmayer, "Consent, Contract, and Territory," 5.

68. Albert O. Hirschman, *Exit, Voice and Loyalty*, 106–119 (Cambridge: Harvard University Press, 1970). See also David G. Post, "The State of Nature and the First Internet War," *Reason*, Apr. 1996, at 33:

> There has always been a strong fictional element to using this notion of a social contract as a rationale for a sovereign's legitimacy. When exactly did you or I consent to be bound by the US Constitution? At best, that consent can only be inferred indirectly, from our continued presence within the US borders—the love-it-or-leave-it, vote-with-your-feet theory of political legitimacy. But by that token, is Saddam Hussein's rule legitimate, at least as to those Iraqis who have "consented" in this fashion? Have the Zairois consented to Mobutu's rule? In the world of atoms, we simply cannot ignore the fact that real movement of real people is not always so easy, and that most people can hardly be charged with having chosen the jurisdiction in which they live or the laws that they are made to obey. But in cyberspace, there is an infinite amount of space, and movement between online communities is entirely frictionless. Here, there really is the opportunity to obtain consent to a social contract; virtual communities can be

established with their own particular rule-sets, power to maintain a degree of order and to banish wrongdoers can be lodged, or not, in particular individuals or groups, and those who find the rules oppressive or unfair may simply leave and join another community (or start their own).

69. See Charles Tiebout, "A Pure Theory of Local Expenditures," 64 *J. Pol. Econ.* 416 (1956).

70. See Robert P. Inman and Daniel L. Rubinfeld, "The Political Economy of Federalism," Working Paper No. 94-15, Boalt Hall Program in Law and Economics (1994), at 11–16; reprinted in D. Mueller (ed.), *Developments in Public Choice* (Cambridge: Cambridge University Press, 1995).

71. Gillette, "In Partial Praise of Dillon's Rule, or, Can Public Choice Theory Justify Local Government Law," 67 *Chi–Kent L. Rev.* 959, 969 (1991).

72. Sandel, "America's Search for a New Public Philosophy," 74. To be sure, sophisticated analysis of even traditional legal doctrines suggests that we appear before the law only in certain partial, conditional roles. Joseph Vining, *Legal Identity: The Coming of Age of Public Law,* 139–169 (New Haven: Yale University Press, 1978). But this partial and conditional nature of "persons" who hold rights and duties is more pronounced in cyberspace.

73. For example, the expanded uses to which pseudonymity may be put in online communities will affect the extent to which information about the applicant's identity must be disclosed in order to obtain a valid address registration. See David G. Post, "Pooling Intellectual Capital: Thoughts on Anonymity, Pseudonymity, and Limited Liability in Cyberspace," *Univ. Chic. Legal Forum* (forthcoming), http://www-law.lib.uchicago.edu/forum/ (discussing the value of pseudonymous communications); A. Michael Froomkin, "Flood Control on the Information Ocean: Living With Anonymity, Digital Cash, and Distributed Databases" (Dec. 4, 1995) (exploring the use and possible regulation of computer-aided anonymity) http://www.law.miami.edu/~froomkin; A. Michael Froomkin, "Anonymity and Its Enmities," 1995 *J. of Online Law,* art. 4, http://www.law.cornell.edu/jol/jol.table.html (discussing the mechanics of anonymity and how it affects the creation of pseudonymous personalities and communication on the Net). And any registration and conflict-resolution scheme will have to take into account the particular ways in which Internet addresses and names are viewed in the marketplace. If shorter names are valued more highly (jones.com being more valuable than jones@isp.members.directory.com), this new form of "domain envy" will have to be considered in developing applicable policy.

Universalism and Particularism: The Problem of Cultural Sovereignty and Global Information Flow

Ingrid Volkmer

The Internet: A Global Medium?

As the fastest growing communications medium, the Internet can be regarded as an icon of a globalized media world that has shifted global communication to a new level. Whereas television was a harbinger of this new era of global communication by reaching a worldwide audience with worldwide distribution and innovative global programming (such as that of CNN and MTV), the Internet reveals the full vision of a global community. The implications of this new global communication—or interactive society—are quite obvious: national borders are increasingly disappearing within cyberspace; facts, issues and opinions interact anonymously; hypertexts produce new cultural linkages. Thanks to new modes of communication, a free flow of information, interactively raised by new voices, now exists; the World Wide Web in particular serves as a forum for both broad- and narrow-cast crosscultural, crossnational unregulated free discourses. A closer look at the most recent developments of this medium reveals not only that about 20–40 million people worldwide use the Internet but that—especially in 1995—the infrastructure of the Internet has been profoundly renewed.

In 1995, it first became obvious that the World Wide Web is a multifunctional global forum. This observation is based on the fact that the aggregate growth of host computers outside the United States for the first time exceeded domestic growth. Although North

America still has the largest number (4.5 million hosts in July 1995), Western Europe is already ranked second with 1.4 million hosts (compared to 730,000 in July 1994), followed by the Asian Pacific region and Eastern Europe. Africa (specifically Southern Africa), Central and South America and the Middle East also reveal a slow but very steady development (*Internet World*, 1995a, p. 48). This global expansion has been accompanied by an increase in language variety. For example, a recently launched net browser allows the user to state a language preference (*Financial Times*, 1995a); the growing number of non-English-language on-line publications also reflects the increasingly multilingual segmentation of Web content. The disproportional growth of the transnational commercial domain (.com), the increasing commercialization of browsers such as Yahoo!,[1] which is used by more than 800,000 people daily (*Financial Times*, 1995c), as well as a developing market for advertising, confirm that the World Wide Web and other Internet segments such as e-mail (involving new services such as Pobox.com[2]) are undergoing tremendous commercialization.

The World Wide Web has already become a virtual market, not only for products and services but also for conventional international, national and local broadcast and print media. Cyberspace is shaping new types of program organization by creating virtual networks, new syndication models and interaction modes of fragmented audiences on specific issues. Not only have traditional and virtual media outlets dramatically expanded on the World Wide Web, but the transnational domains of networks (.net) and organizations (.org) grew exponentially in 1995. Departments and individuals discovered on-line publishing, which in some cases replaces or challenges official views. These developments indicate that there is not only life after television (Gilder, 1992) but also life after the Information Age of globally distributed news channels. This new era enables the news junkie-cybernauts of New York, Mexico City, Cape Town, Beijing, Moscow and Berlin not only to watch breaking news on CNN International but also to interact with journalists covering these events (via sites such as Microsoft Network's political e-zine "Slate") and exchange views with each other. This new communication level not only redefines Marshall McLuhan's vision of a global village by creating worldwide communities, but also creates new uses for the computer terminal, which has been transformed from a data-processing machine to a multi-functional tool for on-line interactivity.

Of course, it can be argued that these developments must be regarded from a more realistic and less enthusiastic viewpoint. In countries with less developed infrastructure where Internet access is expensive (e.g., in Germany), the "gold rush" attitude toward this medium is skeptically viewed. These developments can also be seen as a traditional element of the internationalization of the mass media, which began in the early 1950s as a one-way flow from modern to traditional societies (Lerner 1958), from central to peripheral countries (Galtung and Ruge 1965), or from the developed Northern to the developing Southern hemisphere (UNESCO 1980). This global media expansion was based on the utilization of media for modernization—that is, democratization processes—and in the satellite television decade of the 1980s, it was primarily a commercial enterprise aimed at gaining lucrative segments of a widening international media market.[3] It can be argued that the new international ownership structures, media conglomerates, new distribution channels and programming that evolved during this period, in conjunction with the current cyberspace market, have simply transformed these structures and completed the global expansion.

From another perspective, the debate on cultural sovereignty could be considered obsolete since Internet access is unregulated and the program flow is potentially open and occasionally self-balancing ("spamming"). The concept of cultural imperialism that arose from the earlier expansion of the international media and demanded "proportionate reciprocation of influence by the country so affected" (Boyd-Barrett 1977:17) seems outdated. However, the increasing internationalization of the media, as well as the growing concern for the protection of cultural autonomy that continues to be represented in both national and international media regulations (such as Television Without Frontiers in Europe[4]), must be seen within the context of an increasingly homogenized world in which modern liberalism, values and ethics are spread globally. The world today can still be described as a global village, but one with a new network of superhighways that connect to a new main street as well as small side streets. These fundamental changes raise new questions of cultural—or cybercultural—sovereignty. New commercialized technologies such as satellite transmission systems, new global media channels such as CNN Internationl and new global programs[5] have shaped a global media market in which traditional views of media imperialism must be replaced if we are to examine global communications from a new angle and find patterns in this newly shaped global infrastructure. In order to understand the new communication architecture, we must replace the conceptual framework of modern international communication with a new globalized perspective that permits interpretation of new communication segments arising within the global context of interrelated communication structures and options.

From this globalized perspective, worldwide cybercasting facilities represent a new public sphere in which the public is no longer a substantial element of the political system of a single society (Habermas 1991), but has been transformed into a somewhat autonomous global public sphere that can be described as a common or collective space not between the public and the state but between the state and an extrasocietal, global community. Within this global public sphere of the World Wide Web events of global concern (predominantly ecological and human rights issues) that have been primarily shaped by television are supplemented by "local" (regional or national) viewpoints and other hyperlink information networks. Furthermore, traditional political reporting has been reconstituted because of a new parallelism (as well connectedness) among the perspectives of conventional coverage ("parachute" journalism[6]), local authenticity, and the interactivity of worldwide discourse.

This sphere is autonomous, sovereign unto itself and widely independent of state and national regulation as well as of the two international regulatory and advising bodies (the International Telecommunications Union [ITU] and UNESCO). This gives the available services the advantage of autonomy in terms of log-in access, content and communication modes. However, the repercussions of such unregulated autonomy include state restrictions on providing technical access (China, for example, has restricted computer access to universities and special privileged groups) and censorship of domestic on-line publications. This global public sphere has neither center nor periphery. Instead, it can be characterized by content relativity. Issues relate or hyperlink to each other without any reference to actual geographical locations: a computer located in New Jersey may provide information on human rights abuse in China, or a computer in England may update on-line news on military activities in Bosnia. Furthermore, hyperlinked information provides a variety of horizontal knowledge by referencing Web sites instead of in-depth contexts. Events raised in this global public sphere are ahistorical, which is creating a new historicity of short time periods. According to McLuhan's (1966) thesis that the medium is the message, the specifity of on-line services is characterized by being fast, up-to-date, brief, and focused. Redundancy and historical links are provided in focused menu archives but not by semantics or topics. Within this global public sphere, parallelism among the media (primarily print, television and electronic media) and a new global vertical integration of television stations, newspapers and software programs (e.g., Pearson in the United Kingdom; Microsoft and Turner Broadcasting System in United States) provide crossmarket program flows and new outlets for selling repackaged programs. This new type of vertical integration has produced its own journalism models by reproducing existing content and program structures (on-line editions), developing new modes of journalistic presentation for the World Wide Web, and, significantly, regarding the Internet facilities of e-mail, newsgroup and Web services as authentic sources for news gathering (sometimes even replacing news agency material). Whereas in the first phase of cybercasting, primarily print media were involved in World Wide Web publication, the second phase has been characterized by the additional involvement of television and, more recently, radio stations. This development will likely entail a megamerger of the telecommunications, broadcasting, electronic and cable industries in the near future. Finally, technological advances and globally homogenized interactive languages (e.g., Java), on the one hand, and the creation of network technologies that make it easier to access specified Web facilities, on the other, make it easier for individuals to create html pages and support Intranet information circuits.

These dimensions of global communication can be refined in view of global cultural sovereignty. From this perspective, culture is defined by the differences from others and cultural sovereignty increasingly becomes a matter of global groups of communities as well as of nations. This is a rather irritating process since it implies a diversity of extrasocietal global cultures, such as the homogenization of pop-culture (which Barber [1994] described as "McWorld") and localism of various types. This new global network comprises a parallelism of homogeneous and heterogeneous components, universal and particular.[7] The tension between cultural homogenization and heterogenization can be regarded as the "central problem of today's global interactions" (Appadurai 1990, p. 5). It has globalized factionalism, which has consequences for the global perspective on media infrastructure and television developments as well as the new interactive medium of the Internet and new journalism structures.

Cybercasting

Such a theoretical framework of global communication allows an analysis of the global expansion of the Internet that focuses on both universal and particular elements of the new global communication architecture. This parallelism of universalism and particularism, the dynamic of oscillating global and factional communication "particles," reveals new global knowledge segments, general and specific viewpoints that contribute substantially to the definition of cultural sovereignty in a global context. Whereas this universalism includes the globalization implied by McLuhan's global village and encompasses the global spread of values and moral standards, pop culture icons (whether Mozart, Madonna, or Adidas) and political issues (Bosnia and the Middle East), new communication channels with interactively transmitted, fragmented content are adding another level of global communication that is transforming the global whole into a broad range of worldwide communities, factions, fractions and worldviews. This new particularism is also represented by the increasing language variety on the World Wide Web. Very specific modes of communication are beginning to create global language communities in the same way that "the Internet provides outlets for users interested in microbreweries or in stamp collecting" (*Financial Times*, 1995a). Accordingly, French, Chinese, Russian, Spanish, Italian and German speakers "all over the globe get in touch with each other on the Internet. For an expatriate living in New York, that can be a great way to socialise with people who speak your native language" (*Financial Times*, 1995a). This multilingual advance encourages non-English speakers—as well as the advertising industry—to use the Internet. Critics claim that this development will cause the Internet to lose its coherence. Other indications of fledgling particularism include the parallelism of international and national as well as regional and local media on the World Wide Web. On-line editions of local newspapers are increasing in remote, loosely populated regions such as Canada's Yukon Territory and in international and national regions experiencing political tensions or cultural identity irritations. Particularism also reveals new forms of global localism that communicate local issues globally. Within the global public sphere of the World Wide Web, economic and pop cultural issues can be regarded as universal fields, whereas social and cultural issues arise in particularized global communications (Mowlana 1993).

Media organizations in "peripheral" countries have also increased their global dissemination.[8] Within a globalized media world, "peripheral" countries include not only developing countries (as assumed in the viewpoint of media imperialism) but countries and regions located on the borderline of major satellite footprints, such as some areas of Scandinavia, Portugal, Malta and Ireland, or characterized by underdeveloped telecommunications infrastructure, as well as remote regions that can gain access to the global public sphere by offering a local viewpoint on issues.

Although originally the Internet itself and the World Wide Web represented a universal communication sphere, recent developments reveal the presence of particular or factional elements. The differing characteristics of cybercasting networks in various world regions, in terms of participation and representation structures as well as agendas and content, have given rise to this particularization. The buzzword "cybercasting" signifies new communication content, specific organizational arrangements and new presentation formats, thus revealing a specific global agenda for journalism on the World Wide Web.

Cybercasting Networks

With the advent of diverse satellite channels, the traditional models of "gatekeeping" have been eroded and new types of global journalism have developed (Volkmer 1995). On-line providers have replaced conventional modes of gatekeeping (such as editorial consent) by providing various carrier segments within program options. These carrier segments, such as headlines, are increasingly supplied by conventional news agencies, predominantly Reuters, which have transformed themselves from news wholesalers to direct sale companies. Other topical segments, such as politics and economics, are provided by on-line versions of broadcasting or print media outlets. Within this context, the selection process of the topical agenda and the presentation of news is replaced by the leasing of journalistic space and program segments (such as by Microsoft Network). This development is refining ethics, social responsibilty and journalistic values. Although gatekeeping can be regarded in practice as the climate of the newsroom, a bureaucratic professional milieu that influences the news selection process (see Donohue, Tichenor and Olien 1972 and Wilke and Rosenberger 1991), the lack of editorial transparency in carrier packages, and the logic and goals of selection require new roles for on-line journalists to moderate issues and lead to related contexts. Gatekeeping transparency creates a news atmosphere that helps people select not only a favorite newspaper but also a preferred on-line network. On-line providers, search engines and Internet software packages represent new types of communication outlets that disseminate information and provide interactive and communication services. Although these cybernetworks are under no legal obligation or restriction, they increasingly monitor internal information flows, select menu topics, present editorials, and permit the participation of organizations, nations and regions in this process. However, as the CompuServe case[9] in Germany revealed, on-line providers can be viewed critically by public authorities and held responsible for the decency of their information flow. The subsequent public discussion in this case also called for moral and legal obligations for providers.

This growing public awareness of Internet content and its increasing commercialization indicate that newsgroups and Web sites are no longer countercultural enterprises but are about to become public networks. Although the Internet is considered a universal, globally accessible but variegated means of communication, there are differences already in types of on-line providers around the world. These variations include different development phases for on-line access packages, differences in types of groups targeted, different regional technical infrastructures and differing communication demands and regional political restrictions. The first generation of on-line providers included the Internet itself, which was established in the United States in 1969,[10] CompuServe, founded in 1979, and America Online, established in 1985. The second generation has brought about a rapid differentiation of on-line provider services in terms of organization and worldwide expansion as well as internal structure. Whereas the Internet was originally designed for an electronic community consisting of computer professionals, recent developments (e.g., the founding of Europe Online) reveal a mass-market focus as well as increasing organizational differentiation. The establishment of conventional on-line providers can be regarded as the founding era of electronic outlet organization, which has been followed by a pragmatic commercial on-line mass market that has brought about new types of syndication and network models. In the second phase, the United States and Europe have developed a mass market and on-line services have caused "homespun initiatives to go commercial" (*Internet World*, 1995a, p. 44). Examples include Lycos from Carnegie Mellon University and Yahoo! at Stanford (*Internet World*, 1995a, p. 44). On-line providers have not only broadened their commercial interests by expanding their services to enable users to send and receive e-mail, read usenet news, browse the World Wide Web, publish information on the Web, and use telnet, FTP and Gopher, but they have also targeted groups, and consequently their selection of cybermedia and optional agendas also varies. The target groups can be divided into professionals and specialized consumers, such as frequent travellers and home office employees, but there are also regional differences in terms of usage and content of the different on-line provider services.

The third phase of development among on-line providers commenced in 1994 in the United States and Europe. Publishing and broadcasting companies started becoming more involved in the on-line provider market in order to gain another sales outlet for their print and broadcast products. For example, Delphi, the on-line provider of Rupert Murdoch's News Corporation, provides agency news (UPI and Reuters) and stock market news and offers an Internet relay for news group access. The German media company Bertelsmann has invested in America Online, while the publishing houses Burda (Germany) and Hachette (France) have set up networks primarily for their national markets. In this third phase, television and radio companies are also involved in program dissemination on the Web via speaker systems, thus bridging the traditional gap between the telecommunications and broadcasting markets with recorded as well as live newscasts (via RealAudio software [see Dejesus 1996, p. 53]). Global subsidiaries of U.S. on-line providers have also established a presence in new international markets with tailored programs, such as CompuServe in Russia and Europe and America Online in Europe.

The provision of on-line services in other regional markets has begun and largely parallels U.S. and European developments. The first phase, which began around four years ago in Eastern Europe, Asia and Africa, was characterized by e-mail links that either distributed information within remote areas (e.g., Russia) or within wartorn states (e.g., Angola, Bosnia). Whereas Western on-line providers still primarily target a global business audience (either financial professionals or consumers), East European and African Internet services (and this characterizes the second phase of on-line provider development in these regions) mainly center around regional communication issues. A good example is Africa Online,[11] which regards itself as the continent's prime gateway to the Internet and chronicles daily news reports from local African news networks and other selected news-gathering organizations. Its proclaimed goal is involvement of the community, and it even offers home pages within its Web Site to anyone who wants to discuss issues related to Africa. The service also requests material related to Africa that can be posted in the sections "Market Place," "Kids Only," "Fax" services, "Classifieds," "Jobs," "Sports," "Organizations" or "Women" (a usenet group on women's issues). Africa Online is operated by Karisi Communications in Kenya,[12] where it has 750 subscribers (mostly private companies) (*Internet World,* 1995d, p. 105), and it is currently expanding to Côte d'Ivoire. The service not only addresses regional issues but also involves regional newspapers (*Kenya News, Uganda News, Tanzania News, The Zambia Post* and the *South African Electronic Guardian and Mail*).

In the second phase, U.S. on-line providers in Africa (as in Eastern Europe) have developed a strong regional focus and clearly defined target audiences. Because of the low density of telecommunications in most African countries (primarily connecting business centers) and an illiteracy rate of around 70 percent, the target audience can be clearly identified. (In Eastern Europe as well, telecommunications infrastructure is still developing.) One enterprise is AngoNet in Angola, which began as an e-mail link in 1991 and currently connects 66 organizations, academic institutions and government agencies, which together account for 35 percent of its content. Women's groups, regional organizations, businesses and personal users comprise the other 65 percent (*Internet World,* 1995d, p. 102). Zamnet, a Zambian Internet service, was established in March 1994 to sell Internet access. As of November 1995 it had 240 subscribers and was growing by 30 new accounts per month (*Internet World,* 1995d, p. 102). Zamnet also offers an on-line edition of the *Zambia Post,* and thematic options include "Government in Zambia," "University of Zambia," "Health" and "Zambian Business," as well as background information on Zambia provided by a Canadian and an U.S. Web site. All options are strictly national. Zimbabwe is served by one of South Africa's 20 Internet service providers, Internet Africa, and has 1,000 users.[13]

South Africa is the only African country with a sophisticated telecommunication infrastructure and booming Internet connections. "A rough estimate of 150,000 to 200,000 of South Africa's 25 million residents are connected to the Internet, either via the academic network Uninet, which connects 27 universities, or by one of the 20 local Internet service providers" that create new home pages for 15 to 30 new clients a month (*Internet World,* 1995d, p. 104). CompuServe and America Online also have several regional outlets in South Africa. "There is still a major economic gap in

South Africa between the black and white populations. One is hard-pressed to find indigenous Xhosa- or Zulu-speaking Internet users. SangoNet, a privately funded noncommercial Internet access provider, has helped remedy this situation by supplying affordable electronic communication and networking services to the more deprived areas of the country" (*Internet World,* 1995d, p. 104). The regional focus in Southern Africa is reinforced by on-line school networks with their own servers, such as Western Cape Schools Network and MISANET, established by the Media Institute for Southern Africa, which allows newspapers in the region to share information.

In Eastern Europe, CompuServe and America Online are expensive. Services such as Russia Online and Relcom have became Russia's largest commercial provider. The on-line market is comprised of small enterprises that "need the communication but don't have the money to pay for terribly expensive service" (*Central European Economic Review,* 1995, p. 21). Because of this economic necessity to communicate, on-line providers in Russia currently serve two major communities: business and education. In the first phase, on-line service was provided by a computer-linked network ("The Net"), and in the second phase it was offered by commercial enterprises such as engineering, computer and financial companies and by universities and other educational organizations. On-line providers are primarily located in Moscow and St. Petersburg. In the third phase, pan-European services such as EUnet/Novell[14] are establishing regional outlets in Eastern Europe that primarily provide information services for travelling business professionals. Print media have already begun on-line editions (e.g., *Izvestia, Moscow News, St. Petersburg Press* and *European Business Contact*). On-line editions of print media are also available in the Slovak Republic, Poland and Slovenia. In Poland, there is a link between the provider Internet Technologies Polska and a Polish financial services supplier, and this service "offers up-to-date on-line information about the economies and financial sectors of Central and Eastern Europe. The company gets its raw data from news sources and government agencies, and offers analysis, including strategic reports from CS First Boston on investment opportunities throughout the region" (*Central European Economic Review,* 1995, p. 21).

Syndication Models

Whereas in the television market the term "syndication" applies to programs "sold, licenced, distributed or offered to television stations licensees in more than one market" (Bittner 1984, p. 276), in reference to the World Wide Web it signifies on-line editions of various media available in these markets and beyond. On-line syndication is primarily related to print media. Print media on-line editions are easily produced, inexpensive, prestigious, and, since the majority of on-line publications are simply transferred into the electronic medium, require little editorial work. Television and radio journalism are also slowly entering the on-line market. CNN's interactive on-line service—a quite advanced example of cybercasting—transforms television journalism through interactivity and the presentation of images and text. Other broadcasters available on-line include the British Broadcasting Corporation (BBC) and the Canadian Broadcasting Corporation (CBC)). Despite the paucity of on-line broadcast services, syndication models are established by presenting a specific type of print media, targeted to "branded," specified on-line communities. The following can be regarded as models of on-line syndication.

Electronic Newsstand

The Electronic Newsstand (www.enews.com) describes itself as the "single Internet source for the widest selection of articles from the world's leading magazines, newsletters, newspapers and more." The Newsstand provides 351 on-line editions of newspapers and magazines as well as virtual editions under the headings "Business," "Computers and Technology," "Entertainment," "Automotive/ Health," "Politics," "Travel," "Sports and Recreation," "Renaissance Room," "Books," "News Services," "Catalogs" and "Newspapers." Its home page also offers a selection of editorials, headlines (provided by Reuters, hyperlinked to Yahoo!) and daily news reports on developments in business, technology, politics, sports and entertainment. The Electronic Newsstand's "Politics" category includes a broad section on U.S. politics and government and a smaller one on international organizations. The subsection "Politics, News and Media Publications" includeds 37 publications, of which two (which are related to the Internet) can be described as virtual publications.[15] Half of these on-line editions simply offer a standard home page that contains a statement of purpose (without any hyperlinks) and a general hyperlink menu that offers subscription information, an archive, the current issue and an invitation to contact the editor with comments and requests. Of these sites, 33 are U.S.-based publications, two are Irish and two are Canadian. There are seven thematic categories for these cyberpublications:

• "Politics/Government" includes 14 publications, of which 13 are related to U.S. magazines and one to a Canadian political journal (Maclean's). Of these 14 magazines, nine represent a U.S. perspective on international and domestic politics, three monitor international democratic movements and two espouse particular factional views on specific political issues (special political interests and women's issues).[16]

• "Business/Economy" lists three publications, two of which are virtual editions. Two target Internet businesses and the third is a general U.S. business magazine.[17]

• "International Affairs/Foreign Policy" includes five publications on U.S. foreign policy and diplomatic issues.[18]

• "Culture/Human Interest" encompasses nine publications. Two of these focus on historical issues, two are satirical/countercultural publications, and four address cultural topics in general. Eight are U.S. magazines and one is Canadian. Two are local publications from New York and one focuses on Irish culture for the American Irish community. One publication represents a universal viewpoint.[19]

• "Newspapers" includes only the *Irish Times*, which presents a particular political viewpoint.

• "Social Affairs" lists one publication which focuses on social movements and communitarianism.[20] "Academic Journals" includes four U.S. publications, of which two focus on media/politics, one on international politics and one on international economics.[21]

The "Politics" category is divided into various universal and specialized segments. There is a variety of thematic differentiation, as well as special segmented viewpoints that address, for example, local concerns, a cultural community,or women's issues. Other sections of the Electronic Newsstand focus on special interests such as particular businesses, hobbies and travel. Universal issues include health, food, world history, nature and technology/electronics. Nine different countries are represented on the Electronic Newsstand: South Africa (one title), Australia (two titles), Canada (one title), Hungary (one title), United Kingdom (one title), Ireland (three titles), Israel (two titles), Poland (one title), and Singapore (one title). Whereas the South African and Canadian publications target politics in general, the Australian edition covers computer issues, the on-line editions from Hungary, Poland and Singapore focus on business topics, the UK title addresses financial issues, and the Irish and Israeli publications cover culture and politics.

Universal issues represented include human rights (provided by Amnesty International), astronomy, computer/Internet (around 40 publications are specifically dedicated to computer issues) and the environment.

The New York Times Syndication

The new role of print media syndication is exemplified by the *New York Times*. The New York Times Syndication includes the New York Times News Service, which has 2,000 media clients worldwide and reaches around 85 million readers, issues-related Web pages (developed by the *Times* itself) and a small variety of on-line editions of international print media. This syndication model thus comprises a new combination of in-house news service (which will be expanded over time) and conventional on-line syndication. The virtual on-line services go beyond conventional journalism and specifically target business professionals. Besides providing a news service syndication, this model also offers specific Web sites, updated daily, on computer news and health news and the Times Fax, which is a daily fax digest of the *New York Times* with about 150,000 subscribers. Whereas the Electronic Newsstand model is not related to any company that provides the service, the *New York Times* is responsible for the content and syndicated editions of its syndicates. Its own editorial sites include an archive, which contains the paper's database, and "New Media/New Products," which develops new on-line products. The syndicated on-line editions involve 15 Web sites, of which six are international print editions from Brazil, Italy, Israel, Japan and Norway and nine originate in the United States.

Microsoft Network

Microsoft Network (MSN) represents the third model of cybercasting syndication. By including a syndicated World Wide Web package with its software services, Microsoft has widened its on-line target group. MSN combines a search engine (Infoseek) and news sources. Infoseek has customized its service to give MSN users the look and feel of the Windows interface (*Internet World,* 1995c, p. 45). The American broadcaster NBC provides news and entertainment software and is participating in the launch of a cable-television news service called MSNBC Cable News. Within the next five years, a cable and on-line service will be provided. On-line news and backup data will be provided by NBC's existing sources (*Financial Times,* 1995b).

Besides these syndication models, cybercasting also encompasses new types of journalism involving the arrangement of Web sites and the gathering of various points of interest. These thematic sections, when combined, represent a new type of media product: a network. One of the most successful of these new cybercasting networks is Yahoo!, which was founded in April 1994 by David Filo and Jerry Yang, students at Stanford University who wanted to find a way to share their favorite Web sites with other students. Yahoo! began selling advertising space in April 1995. Today the site draws 800,000 people daily, and it has recorded as many as ten million clicks in a 24-hour period (*Financial Times,* 1995c). Yahoo! offers 26 topical options, including a headline news service provided by Reuters, business and commercial news services, and focused usenet newsgroups on health, the Internet, legal matters and World Wide Web issues as well as on-line editions of U.S. and international high school and college newspapers. In total, Yahoo! offers 161 print media editions, of which about one-third are international papers.

Five are virtual on-line editions: India World (which is an on-line news service); *Kamloops Daily News Online*, Canada; *Star Online*, Malaysia; *Austria Online*; and *Independent Online*, South Africa. "Yahoo!" also offers a gateway to Canadian newspapers via Vannet, based in Vancouver.

The range of on-line editions of papers available on Yahoo! covers transnational, national, regional and local issues. Regional papers are available from the United Kingdom (Middlesex and Somerset counties), France (Alsace), Canada, Portugal and Sweden as well as *People's Day* from China and several from "peripheral" countries such as Iceland and Ireland. Most on-line editions originate in Germany or United Kingdom, while other European countries such as France, the Netherlands, Norway, Sweden, Italy and Portugal are represented by one edition. The only Middle Eastern country that offers an on-line edition is Israel; Canada and the United States provide one each; Latin America contributes two (Brazil and Mexico); and South Africa and Australia each provide one on-line edition.

These syndication models are becoming information networks and are developing specific communities. Web users can join a community that is defined by thematic issues (Electronic Newsstand), special on-line services for clearly defined target groups (New York Times Syndication) and software systems (Microsoft) and obtain almost anything without leaving their computer terminals.

Cyberjournalism

Newswire services are becoming increasingly involved in cybercasting and have discovered that the new syndication networks reach an additional market. Yahoo! offers a hyperlink to 17 wire services. Reuters is not only the most innovative wire service but also the most active on-line news agency. In addition to traditional wire services, small target group agencies have also entered the on-line market. For example, services such as the Global Student Newswire Project and NewsWire (from nine University of California campuses) provide an information hotline for U.S. student newspapers and offer information on U.S. student issues for the world community. Other new wire services include the Global Internet News Agency and a virtual outlet of the Voice of America, which, in accordance with U.S. law, exclusively targets audiences outside the United States.

U.S. and West Europe broadcasters began to enter the on-line market in 1995 by developing print editions of various news segments. Unlike ABC, NBC and CBS, which all use on-line editions as marketing tools for program promotion, the BBC has developed an approach that encourages the use of on-line communication. Because of this educational purpose, the BBC established a networking Club to "catalyse the public's knowledge and usage of the Internet" (BBC promotional web page at www.bbcnc.org). This project concluded on December, 31, 1995, and was succeeded by a multimedia centre that aims to enhance activities involving new media, including on-line and CD-rom productions.

Besides these national programs, globally distributed specialized programs such as CNN and MTV also use the on-line market as a secondary channel for programming. For CNN, the Web site is just another channel for disseminating news that has already been produced, supplementing its established market niches such as out-of-home markets and five different CNN cable channels. Since news has become an attractive on-line segment, CNN might well expand within the Web market by providing specific services (such as special topical services or an expansion of breaking news stories for worldwide media organizations). The optional menu of a graphical tree already gives an impression of the variety of news available on the CNN Web site. CNN's cyberjournalism includes the presentation of facts, images (both still and moving) and audio clips and also provides links for the user to expand a story. Whereas in other models the links are incidentally installed to provide a gateway to other sites, CNN provides links to other contexts. According to the editor in chief of CNN Interactive, "If the link is on a CNN page, it's a link to a source you can trust" (www.cnn.com). CNN's Web service links to the Lexis-Nexis Information Service, which offers the largest international archive of newspapers, magazines and broadcast editions.

CNN's cyberjournalism provides access to a large variety of topical fields,[22] involves other CNN networks (CNN, CNNI, CNNfn,

Headline News, CNN Radio, etc.), links topical issues to other reliable sources and encourages individual researchers to use the Lexis-Nexis data bank. This model reveals the different levels of cyberjournalism, which includes much more than editing and presenting news stories that have been repackaged from other news channels. Cyberjournalism requires the arrangement of topics in new formats and various selection options for the user. Therefore the stories must be presented at a variety of levels of detail because the user selects the research proceeding from one story (from CNN's Headline to the Lexis-Nexis archive). Cyberjournalism must fulfill different requirements for each news-gathering sequence on the Web site. CNN's Web site covers universal as well as particular elements of news. The first level of presentation includes universal news issues, such as the option "World News." More specialized news issues go into greater detail.

Whereas CNN's cyberjournalism provides a variety of universal and particular issues and encourages the user to engage in personal news research, *The Financial Times* has developed a very successful model of cyberjournalism that is based on conventional print journalism. The menu of its Web site includes eight clearly defined options besides the home page: "News in Brief," "Top Story," "Europe," "Americas," "Asia/Pacific," "Technology" and "Letters to the Editor." The top story is chosen from *The Financial Times* international edition (circulated in 150 countries and printed in France, Germany, Sweden, the United States and Japan), which covers more international issues than the British edition does. The top story is precisely defined and focuses either on politics, economy, business or finance. An archive of stories from the last five days is also provided for all topical options. This archive does not include all *Financial Times* stories within this time period, only the on-line stories. *The Financial Times* Web site contains hyperlink advertisement (though no hyperlinks other than to its own sites) and requires registration. This model represents a typical on-line newspaper with a clear editorial statement and a selection of on-line articles. Unlike CNN Interactive, this on-line model neither supplements nor replaces the original media outlet, but instead gives a brief overview of *The Financial Times'* view of the world for the day.

These examples show that cyberjournalism has already developed specific modes of communication or interaction that transcend conventional journalism in terms of presentation and news-gathering. Whereas conventional journalism is targeted to a news consumer who does not have access to either raw or edited news material, the on-line user can browse or hyperlink Web sites or context material, including archives, databases and news agencies. This different attitude toward news and information consumption not only encompasses editorial requests (within a general option menu) and e-mail comments and ideas, but also involves an interactive user with a variety of possible responses. This can include a focused discussion among worldwide users on a particular news item. This affects the role of the journalist, who now serves as a moderator as well as a presenter of information. The on-line moderator provides additional material and responds to comments and arguments.

Interactivity also implies that the user will be guided through raw information and across various levels of cyberjournalism. One on-line magazine, *Body Politic*, available on the Electronic Newsstand, requests not only comments but also issue-related clippings and other material that will subsequently be published on-line. Although archive material is provided by almost all cybercasting Web sites, the quality of cyberjournalism depends not only on archival material from different time periods but also on other clearly defined sources. In order to provide a potentially global on-line community with global information and knowledge, it is essential to link universal as well as particular source material. For example, a CNNs headline on an earthquake in Japan should be linked with seismographic research organizations as well as Japanese Web sites. Ideally these hyperlinks should not only be presented by keywords but also be introduced and defined by a brief description of the hyperlink option's content. Transparency about the organizational background and information presentation and gathering goals of the on-line cybercasting outlet helps the user to interpret the issues presented. In addition, optional news sources and hyperlinks need to be defined, and the selection process for Headlines and other highlighted material must be identified. Background information should also include the update intervals of the material presented. Although on-line editions are derived from other daily media (newspaper, broadcast), the news material sometimes dates back weeks or even months. Universal as well as particular elements involve not only the topic itself if it is one of universal or particular relevance but also its presentation as well as its topic field (e.g., environment is a universal field while stories on the American football league are particular). In order to provide a worldwide audience with global information, cyberjournalism may develop different ways of presenting universal and particular issues. Issues that concern a worldwide audience might be presented in a particular light for different audiences. One example is CNN's story "Ecstasy is Buzzword in Jakarta's Night Life" (CNN Interactive, January 14, 1996) on the worldwide Techno music scene from one particular slant. An example of a particular story with a universal context was the 1995–1996 U.S. budget crisis ("Budget Impasse Continues," Reuters New Media/Yahoo!, December 28, 1995). Cyberjournalism thus allows both multilateral and bilateral viewpoints. Originally, cyberjournalism involved both journalism on-line, which implies that the Web is an additional or secondary publishing site and simply transforms conventional journalism, and on-line journalism, which implies virtual "e-zines" and papers. Whereas journalism on-line is exercised by traditional media outlets (primarily newspapers), on-line journalism was established with a focus on global issues (such as women, electronics or human rights).

The second phase of on-line journalism was marked by the creation of bulletin boards by governments and organizations such as the United Nations. In the third phase, on-line outlets of commercial enterprises such as news agencies were established. Today, the two forms of journalism are about to be combined through the creation of on-line departments within large media organizations (such as CNN) that develop their own specific combinations, relationships and interactivity (e.g., for news-gathering purposes). Cyberjournalism relates to contexts that arise not only from hyperlink connections but also from the specific relationship between the original medium and its on-line counterpart. Whereas currently almost no such relations can be identified in the original media, in the near future the Web site will also influence off-line journalism.

Global Internet Environments

Which of these models of cyberjournalism will dominate in the various regions of the world? The answer to this question will depend on the surrounding media environment. For this reason, cybercasting developments must be interpreted within the context of diverse global media environments. With this in mind, five different worldwide information environments can be identified that reveal specific cybercasting profiles (i.e., regulation of access, technology infrastructure, web site content). Even though the computer has developed from a PC into a gateway to a multifunctional worldwide network (see, for example, *Financial Times* 1996b), it is nevertheless essential to know where any specific computer is located and to recognize the specific information needs of the user of each environment. The determination of such a specific profile also helps to clarify different attitudes and the various communication "ideologies" of the global sphere as well as information topic preferences that arise in the context of the surrounding communication environment (i.e., which media are available). Profiles vary from envrionment to environment. I propose to characterize these environments in light of overall media structures in order to determine specific Internet profiles within the overall media setting. This will help to clarify the role of media interaction within an environment that is widely developed in a pluralist society but restricted by strong governmental influence in a state-regulated media environment. These specifications also allow styles of journalism to be identified both within and among environemnts.

Spillover Environment

Spillover environments can be characterized by a low level of technical infrastructure. They are geographically located either within or on the border of relay-satellite footprints of major media environments. Although some international television channels can be received within spillover regions, the program content does not target their audiences but is geared toward the large media markets for which it is produced. The received satellite footprints of this environment connect the gap between other large and major media settings. The term "spillover" relates to this relay function of major satellite footprints (for example, Central Africa is a relay or borderline environment of Arabsat 10, which connects Northern Africa and the Middle East). Spillover thus applies to an incidental international program flow.

This spillover environment is also characterized by a relatively low degree of regulation of international program flow and a low level of regional representation within the international media. The term "spillover" implies not active state intervention to restrict broadcasting but that from a global broadcasting perspective the region is not a particularly attractive market. Remote areas such as the Yukon as well as various Asian countries can be considered spillover environments. The profile of Internet use in spillover environments affects both community communication and the professional infrastructure.

The Internet can be used in remote regions to facilitate community-wide communication that would be impossible otherwise. Of the 46 African countries, only 30 have access to the Internet, and of these, only Ghana, Kenya, Tunisia, Zambia, Zimbabwe and South Africa have full Internet connectivity. The African spillover environment is also characterized by low telecommunications density, which of course affects the Internet infrastructure and has led to a special regional development. Whereas satellite television is easily accessed, access to the older medium of the telephone is still uneven in Africa. The problem stems from the fact that Africa has "12% of the world's people, but just 2% of the world's main telephone lines. Put another way, Africa has the lowest growth in teledensity (main telephone lines per 100 inhabitants) of any developing region over the last 10 years" (*Internet World*, 1995d, p. 103). Moreover, around half of these telephones are located in the major cities and business capitals. Thus, it is much easier to place satellite speed-dial calls to Europe via INTELSAT (the only organization that provides comprehensive global satellite coverage and offers telephone, television and data distribution services to billions of people on every continent) than to call other African countries or even other regions within a country. Whereas television connects African countries to the world via the same global programming and program access (for example, CNN International broadcast by satellite and hotel distribution), the Internet has the potential to bridge gaps within these communication systems by establishing a network for community-wide communication. This application of Internet and World Wide Web is very different from their use in pluralist environments like the United States where the Internet is regarded as a tool for global communication.

There are various levels of community-wide communication via the Internet in Africa. For example, Africa Online has a strong regional emphasis that is evident in topics such as "Government" and "Health," regional headlines (such as the role of journalists as watchdogs, provided by the *Zambia Post*), and an on-line tourist guide, as well as clearly defined links to information related to Africa provided by hosts located in other parts of the world (such as the African Studies Web site of the University of Pennsylvania) and on-line newspapers. Although computer access is limited in Africa, the first cybercafes have been set up in Ghana; they sell food and drinks as well as offering Internet usage and free Internet classes (*Internet World*, 1995d, p. 102). Community-wide communication improves contacts not only with neighboring countries but also between cities and remote areas.

A number of communication projects have been established to provide technical support, such as Capacity Building for Electronic Communications in Africa (CABECA), which was established by the United Nations and Canada. Universities serve as hubs in various African regions. Another project was established in May 1994 by the South African Development Community (SADC). The participating countries agreed on principal communications policies and standards for a system that would help link the SADC countries (Angola, Kenya, Malawi, Mozambique, Namibia, South Africa, Swaziland, Tanzania, Zambia, Zaire and Zimbabwe). This network links SADC governments and provides databases about countries in the region to enable African businesses, universities and individuals to learn about Africa (*Internet World*, 1995d, p. 104). This kind of communication provides regional information not only to residents but also to Africans living abroad and to a broader international audience.

Improving the journalistic infrastructure is also necessary in spillover regions. In order to support journalism within Southern

Africa, for example, the Media Institute for Southern Africa (MISA) established the MISANET project to improve the flow of information among newspapers in the region (*Internet World*, 1995d, p. 105). "Until recently, international news came almost exclusively from Reuters, the South African Press Agency, and Associated Press. What Africans knew about their neighboring countries was determined by editors in London. To improve the situation, the journalists developed MISANET, an e-mail system located in Windhoek, Namibia. It is a simple text-only bulletin board where editors can send local stories and where MISA members from the region and around the world can reach each other" (*Internet World*, 1995d, p. 105). This project has helped to improve the situation tremendously: "It now takes just five minutes to upload a story to the Internet, plus another six hours for the message to work its way through the store-and-forward system used to get the message out of Namibia. Six hours my seem an eternity" (*Internet World*, 1995d, p. 105). In addition to speeding up the communication flow, this network is cost effective. Africa Online has 750 subscribers (as of November 1995) who send and receive e-mail and news from Reuters and reports from East Africa to compile daily news stories "which a Nairobi features-syndicate group then sends to the American office to put up on the Web site" (*Internet World*, 1995d, p. 106). This Web site is accessible from Kenya but will soon be available in Uganda as well. Such projects improve cross-border communication in Africa. The Hornet project based in Addis Ababa, Ethiopia, is a free computer networking service established in early 1994 to exchange information in the Horn of Africa via electronic communication. Users of this service include academics, governments, nongovernmental organizations, UN agencies, businesses and diplomats.

State-Regulated, Limited International Commercialization Environment

This second environment model is defined by the fact that although governments can own, manage and regulate domestic media, they have only minimal control over international commercial broadcasting. For example, although the Internet was introduced in China in the late 1980s, it was specifically used as an information tool during the student revolution in 1989. Whereas in those days e-mail was primarily used to connect protesting students and distribute information nationally and internationally, the development of other Internet segments such as the World Wide Web has been slow in China. There are several rasons for this slow development. Computer access in China is restricted to privileged groups within universities and scientific organizations. Recently China established officially controlled information ports to monitor the flow of electronic information on the Internet. This new regulation requires that "any network offering Internet service be subject to close supervision by the Ministry of Post and Telecommunications or one of the other designated Government agencies" (*The New York Times*, February, 6, 1996). Another reason for the slow expansion is the language problem: "The vast majority of communications on the Internet are in English, and the English-speaking ability of Chinese university professors and researchers—who comprise the largest number of Internet users—is spotty" (*Internet World*, 1995e, p. 110). The on-line edition of *People's Daily*, the official newspaper of the Communist Party of China (which is published in English and Chinese), targets a global audience. It is published by the Information Center of People's Daily.

Within this environment, an important issue is reciprocal communication. In such a restricted context where access to communication infrastructure is extremely limited and closely monitored, Web sites that allow true interactivity and information exchange have to be set up outside the region. Because the Internet's program flow is global, Web sites dealing with domestic Chinese issues may be located anywhere. One of these sites, the Digital Freedom Network, publishes the writings of Chinese political prisoners and monitors human right abuse not only in China but also in Burma and Bangladesh. This kind of reciprocal communication and interaction is another example of the new opportunities of cybercasting. Reciprocal Web sites target problems of a particular society but are geographically located outside of that society.

Another type of reciprocal communication is the use of the Internet by political minorities or opposition groups within a restricted media environment. This type of reciprocal communication was recently employed by opposition parties in Singapore, where the official media are constrained by the government's unwillingness to permit full freedom of political expression (*Financial Times*, 1996a).

Post-communist Transition Environment

Mass media (including electronic media) in societies undergoing the transition from communism toward democracy are characterized by an ill-defined legal situation (or none at all), a still vivid history of socialist media policy and a commercial market in which international and domestic broadcasters exist alongside various unlicensed local and regional stations. In terms of the Internet, "the original users, in Central Europe and elsewhere, tended to be the academic and scientific communities. But new entrepreneurial energy, combined with an urgent need to establish basic computer-based business systems, has led to a stampede of businesses crowding on-line" (*Central European Economic Review*, 1995, p. 19).

The critical need for effective business communication in Russia led to the establishment of an e-mail network among new small businesses in Russia as well as internationally. Communicating by e-mail is cheaper than by telephone in Russia. This new network also involves bulletin board messages that include advertisements as well as business information. Internet use has helped people overcome the telecommunications problems of Eastern Europe and the former Soviet Union. The region's growth rate is one of the fastest in the world. Internet use has increased by more than 30 percent in Eastern Europe, compared with levels of only 3–4% in Western Europe (*Central European Economic Review*, 1995, p. 19). On-line editions of East European newspapers include several that are relevant to national and international businesses; such as *European Business Contact* and *Analytica Moscow* (both published in Moscow), *Gazeta Biuro i Komputer* (Warsaw) and *Pravda* (Bratislava).

Other businesses have also entered the virtual market in Eastern Europe and the former Soviet Union, such as the "flirt-line" in Russia and a virtual pub in the Czech Republic that provides recipes for brewing beer (*Central European Economic Review*, 1995, p. 20). Occasionally, pop-culturel issues also target the worldwide audience via bulletin boards from the region: "One Romanian ... claims that Elvis Presley roams the cellars of Bucharest's Curtea Veche (Old Princely Court) every Tuesday evening singing 'In the Ghetto'" (*Central European Economic Review* 1995, p. 20).

Pluralist Environment

This fourth type of media environment is characterized by basic media regulations and a broad market of both media types and content. In pluralist environments, the media are primarily regarded as commercial enterprises. Accordingly, Internet growth is profound. In the United States in particular, there was a tremendous increase in the number of commercial Web sites in 1995. "From July 1994 to July 1995, the number of hosts counted rose from 3.2 million to 6.6 million" (*Internet World*, 1995a, p. 47), with an estimated 120 million machines expected to be connected to the Internet in the year 2000. Currently, more than half of all computers connected to the Internet are located in the United States. Within this pluralist environment, the capacities of the Internet and especially the World Wide Web have been fully unfolded. The development of the World Wide Web involves new cybercasting models for its organization, presentation and commercialization. The United States also contributes the largest variety of on-line publications, and many U.S.-based Web sites are also involved in reciprocal communication processes (e.g., the Digital Freedom Network at the University of Pennsylvania has a Web site on Africa). Around 335 U.S.-based newspapers provide on-line editions on the World Wide Web. These include six national papers and 329 local and regional papers. The greatest number of these (54) originates in Illinois. This tremendeous variety of regional media underscores the enormous technical and financial capacity of the United States as well as the advanced level of journalistic professionalism needed to produce such a broad range of on-line editions.

Because of the growth of the new Internet market, the media industries are merging in order to gain lucrative program or technical market segments. Although this trend primarily affects the television and entertainment markets, it also influences Internet content (e.g., the Time Warner/CNN Pathfinder Web site) and syndication. The downloading industries also exploit this market. U.S. cable and telecommunications companies are expanding their original services into the new electronic markets of data transmission services. The three largest U.S. cable operators— Tele-Communications Inc. (TCI), Time Warner and Comcast—are already offering commercial data transmission services in selected markets and are competing with telephone companies by offering downloading services via coaxial cable as opposed to conventional (copper) phone lines; this advance is speeding up the downloading process tremendously. On-line provider services such as CompuServe, the second largest U.S. on-line provider with about 4.3 million subscribers (America Online is ranked first with about 7 million subscribers and Prodigy third), are tailoring markets to new segments of Internet services (e.g., Sprynet) and to small, clearly defined Internet audiences such as novice computer users (*New York Times,* 1996b). The same applies to America Online and its new GNN, and AT&T now offers Internet access to its telephone customers via its Worldnet Services. Modem markets are also expanding in the United States and internationally. Companies like Intel Corporation, U.S. Robotics and Sun Microsystems have designed cable modems and computer hardware specifically for Internet use. Besides domestic differentiation strategies, international expansion has already begun to commercialize Internet services in other environments.

Dualist Environment

Finally, the dualist environment is characterized by a parallelism of public service programs and internationally operating commercial channels. It applies especially to Western Europe, and involves various models of state-regulated public service broadcasting and distinct restrictions on commercial television in both the national and international context. Whereas Western Europe's television industries are legally regulated, the Internet remains unencumbered by legal restrictions and has become both an additional market for broadcasters and print media and a countercultural virtual territory. In 1995, Internet growth in Western Europe was quite remarkable.

West European print and—more recently—broadcast media are increasingly entering the on-line market. Meanwhile, public service broadcasters are also on-line. The BBC, in accordance with its public service programming goals, provides an educational and informational Web site, as does Deutsche Welle in conjunction with the Canadian Broadcasting Corporation and Voice of America. Commercial broadcasters (such as Germany's RTL and SAT 1) focus primarily on entertainment content. West European media have also established Web sites. These are primarily the large national papers such as *Frankfurter Allgemeine* and news magazines like *Der Spiegel.* The German market is a good example of a dualist environment with about one million subscribers to on-line services. The United Kingdom has a similar on-line subscription rate, whereas France has one of the highest in Europe (although its provider is Minitel-Service, which has to be reorganized to make it compatible with current software standards) (Zimmer 1995).

In the dualist environment of Western Europe, the media are regarded as an integral element of a national culture that includes societal and public responsibilities as well as (limited) commercial enterprises. Because of this structure, media commercialization is limited and a public concern regulated by law.

These five environments demonstrate that the particularism of the Internet comprises not only different approaches to cybercasting but different ideologies associated with Internet technology. The Internet also has different significance and functions in the various media regions that are also associated with various access modes, such as from a workplace or university, local or national dial-up access provider, regional, national or international telephone company, mass-market information utility (e.g., America Online, CompuServe or MSN) or cable television company (which will soon be possible in the United States).

The Internet and the World Wide Web are closely related to other media channels and regional communication demands that are the background to its specific significance and cultural context. Thus, cyberjournalism as a new type of journalism within a global community is confronted with particular problems in each of the media environments described above. In each environment, the World Wide Web is associated with specific demands and opportunities, such as increasing regional communication, linking otherwise unbridgeable technological gaps and providing reciprocal Web sites. The increasing multilingualism of the World Wide Web and the language problem in general highlight another aspect that is relevant to different environments. Because of the increase in regional as well as extrasocietal reciprocal Web sites, language variety is essential (Web sites should be at least bilingual with English as a general option) to establishing regional communication and disseminating information worldwide. In addition to these particular aspects, cyberjournalism (as opposed to conventional journalism) communicates both within one media environment and across worldwide environments. This duality requires specific modes of comprehension, presentation and topic selection.

Cultural Sovereignty

Within the last 15 years, global communication has achieved a complexity that is increasingly difficult to comprehend. Global communication now enables us to "eyewitness" news events taking place in remote locations as well as world capitals of policy and commerce and to become informed about issues of global, regional or local relevance. These global processes, in which information and knowledge, values and ethics, aesthetics and lifestyles are exchanged, are becoming increasingly autonomous and are actually creating a "third culture" (Featherstone 1990, p. 1). This entails a "generative frame of unity within which diversity can take place" (Featherstone 1990, p. 2). Global communication thus represents far more than the expansion of modernization. As Niklas Luhmann has argued, the universalism of worldwide communication dynamically develops autonomously operating "systems" (Luhmann 1982). These temporary and permanent global communication networks, however, increasingly have an impact on the national and social realities. Within this worldwide framework, the information society not only affects the information flow by providing a global free flow but also encourages a "commoditization" of information that seems to grow in direct proportion to the decline of cultural values. Thus the information society does not produce more knowledge. Rather, it alters knowledge so that it becomes increasingly ahistorical (Marvin 1987, p. 59).

The new theory of global communication could, however, help to redefine or even substitute for conventional concepts of international communication. The growing complexity, or even anarchy, of conventional global political communication unfolds in "fact" narratives of worldwide "news." Different definitions of the meaning and importance of specific political events, news hierarchies and political issues are remixed in a global context. The autonomy of global communication, however, implies new definitions of "free speech" and "cultural sovereignty." These terms must be redefined in light of universal and particular global communication, of on-line organizational issues (representation, participation, access) and new communication challenges (moderation, interactivity). Broad regulatory models must be developed to support and protect a differentiated global culture, with a particular focus on communication content and global network organization. In order to ensure a variety of universal and particular elements, transparency of editorial content is also essential. This transparency must also be applied to available services and access modes. Information about the new communication infrastructure includes not only information about the World Wide Web but also a clear definition of moderation and of the goals of cyberjournalism and its information structure. Cultural sovereignty can be defined not only in light of the Internet but also against the background of other media and the special interrelation of media and communication cultures in various regions of the world. Today television covers global topics and the Internet covers smaller segments that can be transmitted around the world. Both media are important because the new media age of the next century will require a new concept of the world as a whole that also takes into account its cultural variety.

Notes:

1. This is the acronym for Yet Another Hierarchical Officious Oracle (*Financial Times*, 1995c).

2. Pobox.com is a recently launched e-mail service that forwards a message to a local Internet provider while the user is traveling. This allows the user to have an e-mail address outside of the office or private home.

3. This expanding global market implies a fundamental change in broadcasting from international to global programming.

4. *Television Without Frontiers* (Luxembourg: European Community, 1989) regulates the inflow of global television programs into Europe and serves as the basis for many national media policies in Europe.

5., One example of new global programming are 'tailored' programs, developed by global broadcasters in order to target different geographical world regions from a global perspective, such as CNN Asia, MTV Europe.

6. This term refers to a specific type of international journalism in which a journalist "parachutes" into an international event and reports from a domestic viewpoint.

7. The debate on universalism and particularism has its roots in ancient philosophy. The terms are used here, without strong reference to the philosphical debates and their specific relationship and concepts, to indicate simply that worldwide 'common' as well as factional issues characterize global communication.

8. This involves the irony that somebody in New Zealand can access the local paper of a small Yukon community on the World Wide Web before a local resident walk across the street to get it, as one resident reports (*Internet World*, 1995b, p. 120).

9. CompuServe, a U.S.-based on-line service was forced by the German authorities to suspend access to more than 200 newsgroups because pornographic material was made available by these discussion group. This is the first case in which an Internet provider restricted access to newsgroups in response to the threat of legal action (see also *Financial Times*, 1995d).

10. The first international connections were established to Norway and England four years later.

11. Africa Online represents a specific type of on-line provider that is a hybrid of a traditional on-line provider and a Web site.

12. http://www.afrique.com.

13. In many African countries the telecommunications infrastructure is concentrated in cities and regional business centers. The postal system is also regionally undeveloped: a letter may take only one week to reach England, but may take one month to reach an African state and may never reach a neighboring country.

14. The service is available in 27 countries, including six East European states (Bulgaria, the Czech Republic, Poland, Romania, Slovenia, and Slovakia) as well as Russia and the Commonwealth of Independent States.

15. Virtual Publications are defined as regularly published Web pages that are freely accessible and can be subscribed to.Examples include: dot.Com and The Internet Letter.

16. These on-line publications are: *Body Politic, Dissent, Federal Employees' News Digest, Journal of Democracy, Maclean's, National Review, The National Times, New*

Perspectives Quarterly, The New Republic, On the Issues, Policy Review, Political Science Quarterly, Reason Magazine, and *The Washington Monthly.*

17. This group includes *Business Week, dot.Com, Internet Letter.*

18. These are: *Foreign Affairs, Foreign Policy, The Washington Quarterly, World Affairs, World Politics.*

19. This category includes: *Civilization* (Library of Congress), *Current History, Irish Voice, Mother Jones, The New Yorker, Saturday Night Magazine, Slick Times, The Village Voice, The Whole Earth Review.*

20. The only edition listed in this category is *The Responsive Community.*

21. These are: *American Journalism Review, Harvard International Journal of Press/ Politics, International Security, International Organization.*

22. Recently the University of Indiana counted 12,850 "e-zines," the most popular of which reach 100,000 subscribers. They cover a great variety of topics, ranging from computer topics to sex, leisure activities and sports, cyberpunks, etc. (*Die Zeit* 1.12.95, p. 92). About 90 percent are in English; just recently the share of titles originating in Europe increased while none come from Latin America, Asia or Africa.

References

Appadurai, Arjun (1990). "Disjuncture and Difference in the Global Cultural Economy," in Mike Featherstone, ed., *Global Culture. Nationalism, Globalization and Modernity* (London: Sage).

Barber, Benjamin (1994). "Zwischen Dschihad und McWorld," *Die Zeit* (October 14, 1994), p. 64.

Boyd-Barrett, Oliver (1977). "Media Imperialism: Towards an International Framework for the Analysis of Media Systems," in James Curran, Michael Gurevitch, and Janet Woollacott, eds., *Mass Communication and Society* (London: Edward Arnold).

Bittner, John R. (1984). *Law and Regulation of Electronic Media.* Englewood Cliffs, NJ: Prentice-Hall.

Central European Economic Review (1995). "Internet. The East Is Wired" (June 1995), pp. 18–22.

Dejesus, Edmund X. (1996). "How the Internet will Replace Broadcasting," *Byte* (February 1996), pp. 51–64.

Donohue, George A., Philip J. Tichenor, and Clarice N. Olien (1972). "Gatekeeping: Mass Media Systems and Information Control," in Gerald Kline and Philip J. Tichenor, eds., *Current Perspectives in Mass Communication Research* (London: Sage).

Die Zeit (1995). "Selbst ist der Verlag" (December 1, 1995), p. 92.

Featherstone, Mike, ed. (1990). *Global Culture. Nationalism, Globalization and Modernity*. London: Sage.

Financial Times (1995a). "Travellers on the Infobahn Start to Speak in Tongues" (October 23, 1995), www.ft.com.

Financial Times (1995b). "NBC and Microsoft to Launch All-News TV Service" (December 15, 1995), www.ft.com.

Financial Times (1995c). "Yahoo! Swiftly Turns Commercial" (December 18, 1995), www.ft.com.

Financial Times (1995d). "Online Provider" (December 29, 1995), www.ft.com.

Financial Times (1996a). "Singapore Election Fever Draws Net Fans" (January 23, 1996), www.ft.com.

Financial Times (1996b). "Heretic's Vision" (March 1, 1996), www.ft.com.

Galtung, Johan and Mari Holmboe Ruge (1965). "The Structure of Foreign News," *Journal of Peace Research*, No. 2, pp. 64–91.

Gilder, George (1992). *Life after Television*. New York: Norton.

Habermas, Jürgen (1991). *The Structural Transformation of the Public Sphere*. Cambridge, MA: MIT Press. (Original: *Strukturwandel der Öffentlichkeit*. Frankfurt/Main: Luchterhand, 1962.)

Internet World (1995a). "Internet '95" (November 1995), pp. 47–52.

Internet World (1995b). "Northern Exposure" (November 1995), pp. 119–120.

Internet World (1995c). "The Unfolding Net" (November 1995), pp. 42–45.

Internet World (1995d). "New Lifelines" (November 1995), pp. 102–106.

Internet World (1995e). "Dragons at the Gates" (November 1995), pp. 109–111.

Lerner, Daniel (1958). *The Passing of Traditional Society: Modernizing the Middle East*. Glencoe, IL: The Free Press.

Luhmann, Niklas (1982). "The World Society as a Social System," *Journal of General Systems*, No. 8, pp. 131–138.

Marvin, Carolyn (1987). "Information and History," in Jennifer Daryl Slack and Fred Fejes, eds., *The Ideology of the Information Age* (Norwood, NJ: Ablex), pp. 49–62.

Mowlana, Hamid (1993). "The New Global Order and Cultural Ecology," *Media Culture and Society*, No. 15, pp. 9–27.

The New York Times (1996a). "China Issues Rules To Monitor Internet" (February 6, 1996).

The New York Times (1996b). "CompuServe Is Joining Push To Broaden Internet Access" (February 7, 1996).

McLuhan, Marshall (1966) *Understanding Media*. New York: McGraw-Hill.

UNESCO (1980). *Many Voices, One World*. Paris: Unesco Press.

Volkmer, Ingrid (1995). *Between Universalism and Particularism—Global Spheres of*

Mediation: A Study of CNN and Its Impact on Global Communication. Bielefeld: University of Bielefeld.

Wilke, Jürgen, and Bernhard Rosenberger (1991). *Die Nachrichten-Macher. Zu Strukturen und Arbeitsweisen von Nachrichtenagenturen am Beispiel von AP und dpa.* Cologne: Böhlau.

Zimmer, Jochen (1995). "Online-Dienste für ein Massenpublikum?," *Media Perspektiven*, No. 10, pp. 476–488.

Governing Networks and Rule-Making in Cyberspace

Joel R. Reidenberg

Introduction

The information infrastructure has significant implications for the governance of an Information Society. Despite the popular perception, the global information infrastructure (GII) is not a "lawless place." Rather, the GII poses a fundamental challenge for effective leadership and governance. Laws, regulations, and standards can, do, and will affect infrastructure development and the behavior of GII participants. Rules and rule-making do exist. However, the identities of the rule makers and the instruments used to establish rules will not conform to classic patterns of regulation.

The global network environment defies traditional regulatory theories and policy-making practices. At present, policymakers and private sector organizations are searching for appropriate regulatory strategies to encourage and channel the GII.[1] Most attempts to define new rules for the development of the GII rely on disintegrating concepts of territory and sector while ignoring the new network and technological borders that transcend national boundaries.[2] The GII creates new models and sources for rules. Policy leadership requires a fresh approach to the governance of global networks. Instead of foundering on old concepts, the GII requires a new paradigm for governance that recognizes the complexity of networks, builds constructive relationships among the various participants (including governments, systems operators, information providers, and citizens), and promotes incentives for the attainment of various public policy objectives in the private sector.

The Disintegration of Traditional Sovereignty Paradigms

Global communications networks challenge the way economic and social interactions are regulated. In the past, legal rules usually governed behavior in distinct subject areas for defined territories. These national and substantive borders formed the sovereignty paradigms for regulatory authority and decision-making. For example, intellectual property rights and privacy rights—each critical for the ordering of an Information Society—are designed as distinct bodies of law. Copyright, patent, trademark, and trade secret law protect specific attributes of information and its economic value, while privacy law guards specific information about individuals from particular harms. Customarily, such distinct rules applied only in the rule maker's geographically defined territory.[3] Few transnational rights in the economic and social sphere truly exist; international treaties and regional obligations typically establish some degree of harmonized, national standards instead of a single, unique "global" right.[4] With the GII, however, territorial borders and substantive borders disintegrate as key paradigms for regulatory governance.

Permeable National Borders

For centuries, regulatory authority derived from the physical proximity of political, social, and economic communities. International law grants legitimacy to a governing authority if it exercises sovereignty over a physical territory and its people.[5] Constitutional governance predicates sovereignty on the existence of geographically distinct political and social units.[6]

Regulatory power has always been defined in terms of national borders. Key rights establishing the structure of an Information Society, such as intellectual property protections, fair information practice standards, and competition rules, are all territorially based.[7] The adjudication of disputes also typically depends on territorially empowered courts. Similarly, police powers to enforce regulatory policies and decisions through property seizures or incarceration are territorially restricted.

Transnational information flows on the GII undermine these foundational borders and erode state sovereignty over regulatory policy and enforcement. Geographic limits have diminishing value. Physical borders become transparent and foreign legal systems have local relevance. Network activities may make participants subject to legal rules of distant jurisdictions. Political and economic communities based predominantly on geographic proximity and physical contact have less relevance in cyberspace because network communities can replace physically proximate communities. Political discourse can ignore national borders while affinities and affiliations transcend distances and human contact. Internet listservs[8] and Usenet groups[9] involve participants from around the world communicating directly with each other on topics of mutual interest. Economic relationships need no physical situs. With electronic cash and new means of electronic stored value such as Cybercash and Mondex, Internet transactions may take place entirely on the network without the physical delivery of goods or services and without the resort to any national payment system. Even social relationships now evolve in the absence of physical contact. Online chat rooms provide live, but remote contact, and cybersex offers very intimate, albeit electronic, relationships.[10]

The permeability of national borders destabilizes territorial rights. Inevitably, differences will exist among various key national rights in an Information Society. The scope, for instance, of intellectual property rights is not uniform across state lines.[11] Even the mechanisms by which countries may assure rights such as privacy may vary significantly.[12] Yet, the GII creates simultaneous global rightholders. A given activity may be subject to differing rights at the same time such as trademark and anti-trust protection because the activity transcends the borders of any single nation. This by itself imposes conflict. In addition, the temptations to apply national laws and standards extraterritorially further compound legal uncertainty. The patent law of the United States, for example, has extended to restrict foreign activities that were legal where conducted,[13] while the new data protection directive of the European Union requires the evaluation of foreign data processing standards.[14] Nevertheless, the erosion of national borders places an important degree of network activity beyond the physical grasp of state authorities. While states may still force corporations or people within their borders to behave in particular ways, the enforcement problem challenges the uniformity of any right.

Ambiguous Substantive Borders

Beyond the disintegration of territorial borders, the GII also undermines substantive legal sovereignty. Governance has relied historically on clear distinctions and borders in substantive law. For example, telecommunications law has been distinct from financial services law and intellectual property law has been distinct from privacy law. Similarly, the borders of protection within any particular field were usually well-defined. A "common carrier" had a set of regulations quite apart from those of a "cable" provider[15] or a broadcaster.

The GII obscures these substantive boundaries. The new technological abilities of a telephone company to offer video dial tone and a cable company to propose voice communications undercut the well-defined borders of communications law. The digital environment challenges the applicability of basic Information Society rights such as copyright as well as the boundaries among other intellectual property rights. Designers of information products can, to a certain extent, package their works to pick and chose legal protection. Processing instructions can, for example, be embedded in a semi-conductor chip to benefit from sui generis legal protection[16] or can be stored on a floppy disk to be covered under copyright[17] or incorporated in a device to obtain patent protection.[18] This substantive blurring of rights creates significant uncertainty; the degree and scope of protection becomes variable.

In addition, network interactions defy clear disciplinary categorization. The regulation of an information transfer or transaction can easily cross sectoral lines. For example, a packet of information may contain electronic cash or payment instructions along with digitally reconstructed images of an individual. In such a case, the legal interests cross many sectoral lines, including telecommunications, financial services, intellectual property, and privacy. Even pure information processing activity may cross sectoral lines. For example, a third-party may process transaction information for a retail chain and may perform payment netting. In one sense, this activity is unregulated information processing, yet in another sense it is a banking activity and might be subject to bank safety and soundness requirements.

More significantly, digitalization and the information infrastructure enable the objectives of one distinct body of law such as privacy law to be achieved by application of the rules of another field such as intellectual property law. Secondary use of personal data, for example, is a core issue for information privacy law, but in the multimedia context, copyright law can also regulate the manipulation of data relating to individuals.[19] In essence, functional activity is more relevant than sectoral legal boundaries.

The Emergence of Network Sovereignty

Just as traditional foundations for governance are breaking down, new boundaries are emerging on the GII. The infrastructure itself contains visible borders. Network borders replace national borders. Both network service providers and the infrastructure architecture each establish rules of participation for defined network areas. These rules form visible borders on the GII. In addition to these visible borders, network communities also develop distinct sovereign powers. Infrastructure organizations acquire attributes of traditional territorial sovereigns.

Visible Network Borders

The demarcation lines among network service providers such as America Online, CompuServe, EUNet, or Prodigy create important boundaries. Private contractual arrangements determine the availability and the conditions of access for network connections. These contractual arrangements define distinct borders between service providers. Participants on the GII will be subject to different contractual rules, benefit from different resources, and adhere to different pricing plans according to network service agreements.[20] In essence, the reach of a service provider's network establishes an important boundary line in an Information Society.

Network architecture also creates a significant type of border. System design imposes rules of order on an Information Society. Technical choices are policy decisions that have inherent consequences for network participants. For example, ISDN technology and the World Wide Web transmission protocol offer better interactive capabilities and choice than analog technology and simple file transfer protocols. Gateways between different systems or between a proprietary network like America Online and the Internet establish fundamental rules of conduct; without a gateway, interactions are effectively prohibited. In effect, technical standards exert substantial control over information flows.[21] The degree of system interoperability thus determines the openness of the Information Society and determines whether network architectural "borders" can be crossed.

Technical standards set default boundary rules in the network that tend to empower selected participants. For example, transmission protocols can embed rules of control on the use of personal information collected by the network. World Wide Web browsers such as Netscape record transaction data on the hard drives of Internet users and make the information available to host sites.[22] The JavaScript in Netscape similarly allows Web sites to collect real-time data on visitors' activities and to examine the directory of a visitor's hard drive.[23] These designs set as a default rule the empowerment of Web sites. Yet, at least in the case of Netscape, the software allows savvy users to override the recording feature.[24] Other protocols tend to enable producer choice in the use of intellectual property.[25] For example, copy protection techniques for digital audio tapes assist producers in controlling the reproduction of perfect digital copies.[26] Electronic rights management protocols are emerging to enable online protection of intellectual property.[27]

These visible network borders arise from complex rule-making processes. Technical standardization may be the result of a purely market-driven process or alternatively may be adopted through a standards body. The classic example of a market promulgated standard is the QWERTY keyboard. Once the now famous keyboard configuration became popular, public acceptance of other more user-friendly configurations was unlikely. In contrast, standards bodies seek to identify and recommend technical specifications for particular network needs such as security. Standards bodies range from industry groups to combined industry/government organizations. These organizations, such as the American National Standards Institute (ANSI) and the International Organization for Standards (ISO), play a critical role in the development and promotion of technical standards. In essence, these organizations assure and reinforce the contours of network borders.

Powerful Network Communities

In addition to the new "geography" of borders, networks may now supplant even substantive, national regulation with their own rules of citizenship and participation.[28] Networks themselves take on political characteristics as self-governing entities; networks determine the rules and conditions of membership. Private contracts mediate the rights and responsibilities of participants.[29] Different service providers offer different terms of adherence. America Online and Prodigy, for example, have different policies on user privacy,[30] while Counsel Connect has different message posting rules for lawyers than for law students. Discussion groups on the Internet have their own rules of access and participation. "Usenet" groups are open to all, while "listserv" groups are available only to subscribers authorized by the list owner according to criteria such as knowledge of a particular field, though a list owner may open the list to anyone without restriction.

Networks also determine the rules of participant behavior. This characteristic can result in rules that reverse established territorial laws. For example, by private contract with network participants, Counsel Connect, in effect, reversed the traditional copyright allocation of rights of authorship for bulletin board message postings.[31] Alternatively, network conduct rules may be sui generis. Microsoft, for example, is endorsing a ratings system for information distributed on the World Wide Web to allow voluntary screening of material inappropriate for children.[32] In contrast, CompuServe and Netcom each initially chose to exclude all participants world-wide from various Internet discussion groups because of a provincial state German prosecutor's inquiry into the availability of pornographic content and the fear of potential criminal liability. These online services could have more narrowly tailored the restrictions, if in fact, they would have incurred German liability for use of their networks within Germany. For the non-proprietary Internet, an entire body of customary rules of behavior has even been formulated as "netiquette."[33]

Like nation states, network communities have significant powers to enforce rules of participant conduct. In the case of proprietary networks, such as America Online or CompuServe, service providers may terminate access for offending participants. "Netiquette" rules for the Internet may even be enforced by individual members of the network community through technical means. For example, the Internet has the equivalent of self-appointed policemen and policymakers. "Spamming," the sending of unsolicited messages, results in "cancelbots," programs that delete messages circulating on the Internet originating from offending senders. Even the Guardian Angels have begun to patrol the net with their "CyberAngels" to look for crime and safety problem areas.[34] Similarly, "technologies of justice" will regulate and enforce behavioral standards or expectations.[35] For example, software developers have created filters for the World Wide Web protocol that allow network participants to mask commercial advertisements while viewing Web sites. Even collective efforts to adjudicate disputes are likewise emerging in the network community. There is at least one mechanism, the Virtual Magistrate, for online dispute settlement with network-based tribunals of experts.[36]

The Incongruity of Traditional Regulatory Policy-Making

When faced with these new dimensions of network governance, existing regulatory approaches are incongruous and ill-situated to resolve the challenges of the network environment. Despite the fundamental impact of the GII on governance, U.S. regulation, for example, and the American policy decision-making process remain wedded to the traditional paradigms of distinct legal fields and territorial borders. The U.S. approach to regulation and its philosophical preference for narrowly targeted law obscures the dramatic evolution of the Information Society. At the same time, European regulation similarly anchors rules in territorial and substantive jurisdictional areas, though it also tends to favor proactive government intervention. These differing approaches offer a contrasting set of difficulties arising from the problems governments have in coping with the speed and magnitude of change in this area.

Obscured Vision

The U.S. approach to regulatory policy obscures decision-makers' vision of the new structural boundaries on the GII. The American legal tradition eschews a powerful state role in society and draws on a deep-seated philosophical belief in limited government.[37] The constitutional structure itself, by emphasizing a citizen's rights against the state expresses, a commitment to limits on state power. Even in the wake of increases in government regulation following the New Deal and the Progressive Era, U.S. law-making rhetoric remained hostile toward the regulation of industry.[38] Legal standards evolve primarily in response to discrete identified problems or crises and jurisdictional lines are vitally important, whether the boundary is between the federal and state governments or between legal disciplines.

In the area of information policy, the U.S. approach has a distinct preference for self-regulation in the private sector. For example, important fair information practice standards are typically not found in legislation, but rather determined by company activities.[39] Legal rules tend to be narrowly drawn, such as the strong protections for video rental records[40] and scant protections for health care records,[41] or purport to seek only minor adjustments to existing regimes such as the National Information Infrastructure Task Force white paper on intellectual property rights.[42] Over the last decade, intellectual property laws and information privacy rules have evolved only modestly in contrast to the dramatic evolution of information technology. Perhaps the most significant legal response to the GII thus far has been the arduous process of telecommunications reform.[43] This two-year effort resulted in the Telecommunications Act of 1996. Despite the de facto restructuring of communications industries, fragmented policymaking in Congress had extraordinary difficulty dealing with the complexity of the change in information technology and the complexity of special interests. The resulting law is a striking display of the power of well-funded special interest lobbying.[44] Congress did not even try to deal with many of the intertwined issues of privacy and intellectual property.

The consequence of the U.S. approach is that policymaking for global information flows is widely dispersed and ill equipped to face the governance challenges.[45] Under the U.S. system, no single government organization is in a position to assess the restructuring of traditional regulatory borders. Multiple federal agencies including the State Department, the United States Trade Representative, the Federal Communications Commission, and the Commerce Department's National Telecommunications and Information Administration and the National Institute for Standards and Technology each have narrow and overlapping claims to various discrete aspects of information policy. Regulators then compete with one another for jurisdictional power. The National Telecommunications and Information Administration, the Federal Trade Commission, and the Federal Communications Commission have each, for example, tried to stake out claims to privacy issues.[46] The significance of the paradigmatic shift in borders becomes lost in the bureaucratic maze. For example, government agencies do not generally have the combination of technical skills and public policy mandates to examine the impact of choices in technological standards on regulatory policy or objectives. No agency has a complete perspective on the structural changes taking place in society as a result of the GII. Even the Clinton Administration's present effort to develop a vision for the information infrastructure and its governance through the work of the Information Infrastructure Task Force remained captive to sectoral thinking and reactive tendencies. The task force established study groups divided along sectoral lines and some of the most time consuming group projects like privacy and intellectual property remain focused on territorial borders and the transposition of status quo interests to cyberspace. In addition, the study groups compete with each other for recognition. For privacy alone, the U.S. Advisory Council (expert advisors to the IITF), the Working Group on Privacy, the Government Services Group, and the Security Issues Forum have each issued separate privacy policy statements.

Although the GII has its origins in the United States, the U.S. regulatory policy process seems to be a serious impediment for effective leadership. The incongruity of American regulatory practices with the GII's multidisciplinary character and rapid technological pace seems to enshrine significant inefficiency and narrowness in the development of GII policies. The United States can no longer assume that its legal and policy standards will dominate the GII merely by the strength of the American market. In the case of information privacy, the European Union has already set the global agenda with its 1995 data protection directive. The United States, like other countries, must develop new governance paradigms that encompass the shifting borders of the GII.

Overloaded Vision

In contrast to the American experience, other regulators outside the United States confront the GII from comprehensive vantage points. In Europe as compared to the United States, comprehensive government regulation is not anathema to society.[47] For example, European policy making often comes from centralized institutions such as independent "data protection agencies" who play an important role in the formulation of information policy with mandates that attach to information flows rather than narrow sectoral regulations.[48] Omnibus rules such as data protection legislation[49] and sui generis laws such as the relatively new rules on intellectual property rights[50] present far-reaching views on information policy rather than ad hoc solutions to narrow problems. Central government agencies with comprehensive powers institutionalize broad policy planning and wide-ranging debates on issues. The European Union, for example, has established an Information Society Project Office to coordinate a number of wide-ranging European Commission activities. Yet, at the same time, even an omnibus view cannot simultaneously address the full scope of issues confronting the GII. Centralized agencies will not have sufficient staff or technical expertise. An illustration of this crucial problem is the fact that the European Commission had to narrow the range of issues addressed in its recent Green Paper on copyright.[51]

While the omnibus approach to regulation may offer a broader vision for public policy in a global network environment than the U.S. approach, the vision inherent in European efforts still tends to preserve important, yet evaporating, foundations based on territorial principles and sectoral distinctions. National application remains preeminent. The principle of "subsidiarity" in European Community law reflects this continued commitment to territorial and sectoral boundaries.[52] Under "subsidiarity," the European

Community may act only on matters that are not more properly within the boundaries of member-state competence. When actions are taken at the European level through "Directives," each European member state must enact conforming national rights that implement the legal standards defined in the relevant Directive; Directives do not in themselves create supranational rights that can be invoked directly by citizens.

The broad approach also illustrates the problems of omnibus control. No matter how an omnibus regulatory policy is decided, the extraterritorial impact foreshadows difficulties. Under European data protection rules, for example, personal information may not be transferred outside the European Union unless adequate privacy protections exist at the destination.[53] The very omnibus character of European rules makes appropriate comparisons to other legal systems like the United States complex.[54] Similarly, reciprocity provisions in intellectual property rules offer disparate treatment depending on the type of available foreign protections.

In the rapidly developing GII, the institutionalized vigilance for information flows that follows from an omnibus approach risks becoming rigid. The very process of adopting and implementing a European Directive is slow. For example, the first draft of the data privacy directive was released in 1990, the final text adopted in 1995, and member states are not required to implement the Directive before the end of 1998. By the time standards are implemented in national legislation, some rules may be obsolete due to the rapid pace of technological development. Similarly, bureaucratic processes do not lend themselves well to rapidly changing technologies. The information system registration schemes common in some European countries over the last 20 years frequently relied on concepts such as "data files." While this made sense initially, techniques for the storage of personal information in an age of distributed data bases no longer associate data with particular identifiable locations.

Because the omnibus approach encourages extensive, and customarily slow, deliberation, regulatory policies risk being circumvented on the network. If participants structure their network activities to avoid a jurisdiction, the omnibus approach makes a government response difficult and enforcement uncertain.

A Network Governance Paradigm

The development of a new model for governing networks is crucial for effective policy leadership on the GII. The new paradigm must recognize all dimensions of network regulatory power. As a complex mix of rulemakers emerges to replace the simple, state sovereign model, new policy instruments must appear that are capable of establishing important norms of conduct for networks. Policy makers must begin to recognize network sovereignty and begin to shift the regulatory role of states toward indirect means that develop network rules.

Complex Mix of Rule Makers

On the GII, governance can no longer be viewed as an exercise in state edict. The relationships among the different participants in the information infrastructure become interactive. States have direct interests in the development of an Information Society. The private sector has a crucial role in the creation of the GII. Technologists have a pivotal position in the choices of policy, and the GII empowers citizens to establish rules of their own. Policy-making among these different interest centers is intertwined. For example, technological choices may frustrate or support state interests or citizen goals. Overlapping jurisdiction and the rapid evolution of information technology defy the traditional forms of state control.

For global networks, governance should be seen as a complex mix of state, business, technical, and citizen forces. Rules for network behavior will come from each of these interest centers. Within this framework, the private sector must be a driving force in the development of the Information Society and governments must be involved to protect public interests. At the same time, policy-making cannot ignore technological concerns and technologically driven decision-making.

New Policy Instruments

The recognition of new network borders opens new instruments for the achievement of regulatory objectives. Executive and legislative fora lose a degree of relevance to technical standards organizations. Standards decisions affect fundamental public concerns and are no longer technical rules of purely commercial interest. Standards now contain significant policy rules. The availability of "clickstream" data such as those contained in the Netscape file <cookies.txt> is, for example, a default policy rule.[55] The debate over encryption standards and key escrow mechanisms similarly reflects the critical new instrumentality of standards setting.[56]

In the network governance paradigm, standards bodies will not be able to avoid robust public policy debates. Already, the Canadian Standards Association has tried to incorporate policy debate through the promulgation of a privacy standard[57] and other national government agencies are encouraging technical decision-makers to implement policy objectives.[58] This recognition will change the decision-making process at standards organizations. At present, citizen interests are either weakly or indirectly represented in standards decision-making. For example, the American National Standards Institute (ANSI) is an umbrella organization in the United States that has prepared a framework for identifying the requirements for national information infrastructure standards.[59] The Information Infrastructure Standards Panel only indirectly considers user needs through standards developers and technology vendors.[60] Governments can and should seek standards that facilitate or incorporate broader policy objectives. Without a widening of the policy concerns inherent in technical standards, the results may be distorted. For instance, standards of electronic rights management for intellectual property may transgress policy goals for fair information practices if the technical decisions do not consider the privacy implications. The Canadian experience and growing government interest in technologies of privacy including encryption are beginning to force this broader consideration at standards bodies.

Nevertheless, the practicality and consequence of embedding regulatory policy in technical standards poses a number of important dilemmas. If technical systems implement policy decisions through particular standards, desirable policy changes might necessitate rebuilding the infrastructure. Various policy objectives might also be more readily incorporated in standards than others.

For example, the basic data protection principle that personal information not be retained any longer than necessary to accomplish the purpose for which it was collected may easily translate into a standard for data purging, but the principle that data may only be used for the purpose for which it was collected is far more difficult to build into the system since data may be re-used and recycled.

Network Federalism

Governance in the network environment suggests a need to recognize network systems as semi-sovereign entities.[61] Networks have key attributes of sovereignty: participant/citizens via service provider membership agreements, "constitutional" rights through contractual terms of service, and police powers through taxation (fees) and system operator sanctions. In effect, network users become stakeholders in transnational political and economic communities. As CompuServe's elimination of certain Internet usenet groups illustrates, network management affects participant discourse.[62] These characteristics warrant a degree of network independence from state intervention.

Nevertheless, where networks develop in parallel to physical society, traditional governments retain crucial public responsibilities and retain significant interests. For example, distance learning through video conferencing may substitute for local schools but it does not diminish or replace the public interest in an educated citizenry. Similarly, physical points of contact between networks and states as a result of the location of users and network infrastructure such as cables and nodes give states a direct interest in network activities.

The overlap of interests between the physical world and the virtual world suggests a governance model that contains distinct rules for the separation of powers. Territorial borders will retain an important role in structuring overlaps between network boundaries and state jurisdictions. Principles of federalism offer a valuable lesson for the relationship between territorial governments and cyberspace. Just as *lex mercatoria* did not displace the law of the situs of trade fairs,[63] a new *lex informatica* suggests that sovereign state should act only within particular spheres or zones of influence.[64] State governments can and should be involved in the establishment of norms for network activities, yet state governments cannot and should not attempt to expropriate all regulatory power from network communities. In some ways, the European principle of subsidiarity[65] fits the network model. States can act to govern behavior on networks only when state competence and direct state interests are established or when states are more capable of doing so than networks.

Role of the State

Even though national borders have less meaning in an Information Society, states retain a critical ability to influence rule making by networks themselves. States can provoke the creation of network standards, as in the development of content filters on the CompuServe network.[66] With power over physical situs points (users and infrastructure), states have the capability to set conditions of network operations, such as free expression or minimal service obligations, in exchange for legally permissible access to users or infrastructure situs points. States have a potent tool in the ability to impose and enforce a certain degree of liability on networks and their participants. This power, thus, gives states the capacity to influence network behavior as well as the capacity to create legal conflicts.

As the GII moves forward, the state's role in the governance of networks suggests a movement toward a system of state-provided incentives through encouragement as well as allocations of liability that will induce networks themselves to adopt desirable public policies.[67] For example, as stakeholders in a network system, users may pressure networks to adopt principles of democracy in network decisions as seen in the vigorous online debates regarding CompuServe's action suppressing Usenet access in response to a German prosecutor's inquiry. However, under different circumstances, public interests may dictate that governments actively seek elements of network democracy as a condition of network operation. With physical power over persons and infrastructure, states can exercise control over key network situs points. The allocation of liability might evolve as a policy instrument to promote network self-regulation. Yet, this policy instrument requires cautious use. State intervention that imposes excessive burdens of liability may impede the advantages of a robust network and result in censorship of valuable information flows.

Conclusions

The GII poses a fundamental challenge to the conventional foundations of governance. Global networks structurally alter regulatory decision making. National borders and sectoral boundaries lose an important degree of relevance while network borders and network communities gain prominence. Basic regulatory policy making, whether under the anti-statist American approach or under the comprehensive European approach, are ill suited to the GII. Instead, a new network governance paradigm must emerge to recognize the complexity of regulatory power centers, utilize new policy instruments such as technical standardization to achieve regulatory objectives, accord status to networks as semi-sovereign entities, and shift the role of the state toward the creation of an incentive structure for network self-regulation.

Notes

Adapted from Joel R. Reidenberg, "Governing Networks and Rule-Making in Cyberspace," 45 *Emory L. Rev.* — (1996).

1. See, e.g., Chair's Conclusions, G-7 Ministerial Conference on the Information Society, Brussels (Feb. 25–26, 1995), available on World Wide Web at <http://www.ispo.cec.be/g7/keydocs/G7en.html>.

2. See, e.g., National Information Infrastructure Task Force, "Report of the Working Group on Intellectual Property and the National Information Infrastructure" (Sept. 1995), available on World Wide Web at <http://www.uspto.gov/niiip.html> [hereinafter NII White Paper]. Various equivalent foreign reports from Canada, the European Union, and Japan tend to focus similarly on changes to national laws and the applicability in specified territories of "Information Society" rights.

3. See, e.g., Paris Convention for the Protection of Industrial Property, Mar. 20, 1883, as last revised, Stockholm, July 14, 1967, 21 U.S.T. 1583, 423 U.N.T.S. 305; Berne Convention for the Protection of Literary and Artistic Works, Sept. 9, 1886, as last revised, Paris, July 24, 1971, 828 U.N.T.S. 221; Robert A. Gorman and

Jane C. Ginsburg, *Copyright for the Nineties*, 4th ed., 873–901 (Charlottesville, VA: Michie, 1993).

4. See, e.g., The Final Act Establishing the World Trade Organization, General Agreement on Tariffs and Trade, Uruguay Round, Marakesh, Apr. 15, 1994, Annex 1C, available on World Wide Web at <http:://itl.irv.uit.no/trade_law/ documents/freetrade/wta-94/art/ii.html>. Recommendation of the Council Concerning Guidelines Governing the Protection of Privacy and Transborder Flows of Personal Data, O.E.C.D. Doc. C58 final (Oct. 1, 1980), reprinted in 20 I.L.M. 422 (1981); Council of Europe, Convention for the Protection of Individuals with Regard to Automatic Processing of Personal Data, Eur. T.S. No. 108 (Jan. 28, 1981), reprinted in 20 I.L.M. 317 (1981), also available on World Wide Web at <http:://www2.echo.lu/legal/en/dataprot/ counceur/conv.html>.

5. See Restatement (Third) of Foreign Relations Law, §201 (1987).

6. See, e.g., U.S. Constitution, amendment IX. Even in non-democratic states, sovereignty was internally equated with distinct territorial borders. See John N. Hazard, William E. Butler, and Peter B. Maggs, *The Soviet Legal System: The Law in the 1980s*, 14–17, 25–29 (New York: Oceana Publications, 1984)

7. See, e.g., Paul B. Stephan III, Donald Wallace, Jr., and Julie A. Roin, *International Business and Economics: Law and Policy*, 397–405, 420–421 (Charlottesville, VA: Michie, 1993).

8. A listserv is a feature of electronic mail software that automatically distributes messages to subscribers of a specified list. To participate, a computer user sends a subscription message to the host computer. Once the host computer accepts the subscriber, the person may post messages to all participants on the list by sending a single e-mail to the host. Depending on the type of list, each single, incoming message may automatically be copied to all members of the list whether the list has 10 or 10,000 members or may only be copied to all members of the list after screening by a list moderator.

9. Usenet groups allow computer users to post messages on a bulletin board at a host site. Access to the bulletin board is unrestricted.

10. For an illustrative experience, adult-oriented chat rooms may be found on the World Wide Web at <http:://chat.bianca.com/cgi-bin/displaychat/shack/ quickref.html>. See also Anastasia Toufexis, "Romancing the Computer," *Time*, Feb. 19, 1996, at 53 (reporting on cyber-romances and the filing of a divorce petition in New Jersey because of a spouse's alleged "online affair").

11. See, e.g. Symposium: Fordham Conference on International Intellectual Property Law and Policy, 4 *Fordham Intell. Prop. L. J.* 1–500 (1993).

12. See Joel R. Reidenberg, "The Privacy Obstacle Course: Hurdling Barriers to Transnational Financial Services," 60 *Fordham L. Rev.* S137 (1992); Paul M. Schwartz, "European Data Protection Law and Restrictions on International Data Flows," 80 *Iowa L. Rev.* 17 (1995).

13. See 35 U.S.C. §271(g) (extending the scope of U.S. process patent protection to prevent the importation of legally manufactured foreign products.)

14. See Directive 95/46/EC of the European Parliament and of the Council, O.J. L281, 31 (Nov. 23, 1995), Art. 25–26 [hereinafter Privacy Directive].

15. See Robert R. Bruce, Jeffrey P. Cunard, and Mark D. Director, *From Telecommunications to Electronic Services*, 153–168 (Boston: Butterworths, 1986).

16. See 17 U.S.C. §§901–914.

17. See 17 U.S.C. §§101–102, 106, 117.

18. 35 U.S.C. §§1–376.

19. See Joel R. Reidenberg, "Multimedia as a Challenge and Opportunity in Privacy: The Examples of Sound and Image Processing," in *Berliner Datenschutzbeauftragter*, 22, Materialien zum Datenschutz: Symposium Multimedia und Datenschutz (1995).

20. See Robert L. Dunne, "Deterring Unauthorized Access to Computers: Controlling Behavior in Cyberspace through a Contract Law Paradigm," 35 *Jurimetrics* 1 (1994) (arguing for model contracts).

21. See Mark A. Lemley, "Shrinkwraps in Cyberspace," 35 *Jurimetrics* 311, 322 (1995) (arguing for technical self-help as an alternative to model contracts).

22. Netscape creates a log file (usually named <cookies.txt>) in the program directory that allows web sites to record the pages viewed by the user. The web site may access this data from the user's personal computer when the user revisits the site. See Cookies Technical Specifications, available on World Wide Web at <http::/ /home.netscape.com/std/ newsref/cookie_spec.html>.

23. See John Robert LoVerso, "Netscape Navigator 2.0 Exposes User's Browsing History," *Risks Digest*, Feb. 23, 1996, available on World Wide Web at <http::// catless.ncl.ac.uk/Risks/17.79html> (describing bug that allows collection of real-time data); John Robert LoVerso, "Report of Netscape 2.01 JavaScript Problems," available on World Wide Web at <http::/ /www.osf.org/~loverso / javascript/www-sec-Mar22.html> (describing ability to browse a user's directory).

24. Users concerned about their privacy may disable the feature by changing the attributes of the <cookies.txt> file to a read-only file.

25. See, e.g., Peter H. Lewis, "Microsoft Backs Ratings System for the Internet," *New York Times*, March 1, 1996, at D1–2.

26. See Julie E. Cohen, "Reverse Engineering and the Rise of Electronic Vigilantism: Intellectual Property Implications of Lock-Out Programs," 68 *Calif. L. Rev.* 1091 (1995); Pamela Samuelson, "Technological Protection for Copyrighted Works," 45 *Emory L. J.* (1996).

27. See U.S. Congress Office of Technology Assessment, *Information Security and Privacy in Network Environments*, 110 (1994) [hereinafter Information Security]; Interactive Media Assoc., "IP Requirements Forum: Electronic Commerce for Content," available on World Wide Web at <http::/ /www.ima.org/forums/ip/ ip_meet.html>.

28. See David Johnson and David Post, "Law and Borders: The Rise of Law in Cyberspace," 49 *Stanford L. Rev.* (1996).

29. Networks have the rule making capability of private associations. See I. Trotter Hardy, "The Law of Cyberspace," 55 *U. Pitt. L. Rev.* 993, 1028–32 (1994).

30. Compare Prodigy, "User Service Agreement," §§6–7 (Dec. 11, 1995) with America Online, "Terms of Service Agreement: Rules of the Road," §7c (both available on World Wide Web at <http:://www.cdt.org/privacy/online_services/chart.html>.

31. See Hardy, "The Law of Cyberspace," at 1031.

32. See Lewis, "Microsoft Backs Ratings System for the Internet," at D1.

33. An Internet guide to netiquette is available on the World Wide Web at <ftp://ds.internic.net/rfc/rfc1855.txt>.

34. See Guardian Angels Internet World Wide Web page, <http:://proxis.com/~safetyed/cyberangels/cyberangels05.html>.

35. See Lawrence Lessig, "The Constitution in Cyberspace," 45 *Emory L. J.* (1996).

36. The Virtual Magistrate Project was launched in March 1996 to "assist in the rapid, initial resolution of computer network disputes" by a pool of on-line neutral arbitrators. The project is based on the World Wide Web at <http:://vmag.law.vill.edu:8080/>. The National Center for Automated Information Research, a prominent non-profit foundation, is similarly supporting work exploring online dispute mediation and held an invitational meeting, "The On-Line Dispute Resolution Conference," in May 1996.

37. See Joel R. Reidenberg, "Setting Standards for Fair Information Practice in the U.S. Private Sector," 80 *Iowa L. Rev.* 437 (1995).

38. See Morton J. Horwitz, "The History of the Public/Private Distinction," 130 *U. Pa. L. Rev.* 1423, 1426 (1982).

39. See Reidenberg, "Setting Standards for Fair Information Practice," at 508–511.

40. 18 U.S.C. §2710 (1988).

41. See Paul M. Schwartz, "The Protection of Privacy in Health Care Reform," 48 *Vand. L. Rev.* 295 (1995).

42. See NII White Paper (note 2 above). But, these adjustments are not truly minor.

43. Telecommunications Act of 1996, Pub. L. No. 104–104, 110 Stat. 56 (1996).

44. Ibid.; "Telecomm Bill Rates One of Top Sweetheart Deals in 1995," *Wash. Telecomm. News,* Jan. 8, 1996, available on LEXIS, Nexis library, Curnws file.

45. See, e.g., William Drake, ed., *The New Information Infrastructure: Strategies for U.S. Policy* (New York: Twentieth Century Fund, 1995).

46. See, e.g., U.S. Dept. of Commerce, National Telecomm. and Info. Adm., "Privacy and the NII: Safeguarding Telecommunications-Related Personal In-

formation" (Oct. 1995); Fed. Communication Commission, "Calling Number Identification Service," 60 *Fed.Reg.* 29489 (June 5, 1995); Fed. Trade Commission Workshop, "Consumer Protection and the Global Information Infrastructure" (April 10–11, 1995), available at <http::/ /www.ftc.gov/opp/gii.htm>. The Federal Trade Commission also runs a privacy discussion listserv on the World Wide Web at <http::/ /www.ftc.gov/ftc/privacy.htm>.

47. See Mary Ann Glendon, *Rights Talk: The Impoverishment of Political Discourse*, 1–17 (New York: Free Press, 1991) (observing differences in the political culture of "rights" between the United States and European societies).

48. See Privacy Directive (note 14 above).

49. See Spiros Simitis, "From the Market to the Polis: The EU Directive on the Protection of Personal Data," 80 *Iowa L. Rev.* 445 (1995).

50. See "Council Directive on the Legal Protection of Computer Programs," O.J. 91/250/EEC (requiring European Community member states to adopt a special set of rules for the copyright protection of computer software). Previously, France, when faced with the problem of software protection, added an essentially sui generis protection into the French copyright law. See Loi No. 85-660 du 3 juillet, 1985.

51. See European Commission, "Green Paper on Copyright and Related Rights in the Information Society," reprinted in 43 *J. Copyright Society* 50, 55 (1995) (noting that the Green Paper addresses only a subset of intellectual property issues for the information society).

52. The Maastricht Treaty on European Union, done at Maastricht, Feb. 7, 1992, Eur. O.J. C 224/1 (Aug. 31, 1992). See also George Bermann, Roger Goebel, William Davey, and Eleanor Fox, *Cases and Materials on European Community Law*, 1995 Supp., 11–14 (St. Paul, MN: West, 1995); George Bermann, "Taking Subsidiarity Seriously: Federalism in the European Community and the United States," 94 *Columbia L. Rev.* 331 (1994).

53. See Privacy Directive (note 14 above), art. 25.

54. See Paul M. Schwartz and Joel R. Reidenberg, *Data Privacy Law: A Study of United States Data Protection* (Michie, 1996).

55. See note 22 above.

56. See Information Security (note 27 above), 111–34; U.S. Congress, Office of Technology Assessment, "Issues Update on Information Security and Privacy in Network Environments," 1–34 (June 1995); Joel R. Reidenberg and Françoise Gamet-Pol, "The Fundamental Role of Privacy and Confidence in the Network," 30 *Wake Forest L. Rev.* 105, 109 (1995).

57. See Canadian Standards Assoc., "Model Code for the Protection of Personal Information" (1996).

58. See "Joint Report of the Netherlands and Ontario Privacy Commissions on Privacy Enhancing Technologies: The Path to Anonymity" (Aug. 1995).

59. See ANSI, "Framework for Identifying Requirements for Standards for the National Information Infrastructure," April 11, available on World Wide Web at <http:://www.ansi.org/iisp/fram4nii.html>.

60. Ibid., at para. 1.

61. See, e.g., Johnson and Post, "Law and Borders" (arguing that cyberspace should be recognized as its own jurisdiction).

62. See text accompanying notes 33–34.

63. See Hardy, "The Law of Cyberspace," at 1020.

64. Ibid., at 1025.

65. See note 52 above.

66. See Michael Meyer, "A Bad Dream Come True in Cyberspace," *Newsweek*, Jan. 8, 1996, 65.

67. I. Trotter Hardy makes a similar point in arguing for strict liability of network operators as the best means of achieving a desired regulatory policy outcome. See Hardy, Hardy, "The Law of Cyberspace," at 1041–48. This runs the risk, however, that network operators will adopt a policy of "when in doubt, take it out" and consequently engage in broad censorship.

The Third Waves

Christopher R. Kedzie

During the last quarter of the twentieth century, two books with nearly identical titles but ostensibly different subject matter described current revolutions likely to have profound long-term consequences. In his 1984 book *The Third Wave*, social critic Alvin Toffler outlined the emerging worldwide impacts of improved information and communication technologies. Those effects were still so new and unfamiliar, he observed, that "We grope for the words to describe the power and reach of this extraordinary change. Some speak of a looming Space Age, Information Age, Electronic Era, or Global Village" (1980: 9). Samuel P. Huntington, a professor of government at Harvard University, in his 1991 book entitled *The Third Wave: Democratization of the Late Twentieth Century*, analyzed "an important—perhaps the most important—global political development of the late twentieth century: the transition of some thirty countries from nondemocratic to democratic political systems" (1991b: xiii).

The coincidence of the two titles is merely that, for Toffler's and Huntington's concepts of the first and second waves bear no relationship to each other. The coincidence of the revolutions to which they refer, however—outbreaks of democracy around the globe and breakthroughs in communication and information technologies—has inspired the notion that these two distinct third-wave phenomena may be positively correlated.

Coincidence of the Third Waves

A diverse and growing array of professionals are commenting on these third-wave phenomena and suggesting a relationship between them. Eugene Skolnikoff, a professor at the Massachusetts Institute of Technology, has surmised that "It is therefore a reasonable, though qualitative, conclusion that the introduction of information technologies (and other technologies that play a synergistic role) tends, on balance, to have consequences that are biased in the direction of increased limitations on the centralization of political power and toward greater openness within a society" (1993: 101). The context of this statement augments its significance; it is a book in which Skolnikoff argues that the effects of science and technology on international affairs have by and large posed "only limited challenges to traditional assumptions and concepts."

Bureaucrats have more boldly extolled the revolutionary potential of new technologies to promote democratic freedoms. Sam Pitroda, Chairman of the India Telecom Commission and an original member of the World Telecommunications Advisory Council of the International Telecommunications Union, enthused that "as a great social leveler, information technology ranks second only to death. It can raze cultural barriers, overwhelm economic inequalities, even compensate for intellectual disparities. In short, high technology can put unequal human beings on equal footing, and that makes it the most potent democratizing tool ever devised" (1993: 66).

Journalists have observed and reported a causal connection. Scott Shane, Moscow bureau chief for the *Baltimore Sun* and witness to the disintegration of the Soviet Union, wrote:

It was a revolution driven by information that the coup was designed to halt; information that had undermined ideology, exposed the bureaucracy, and shattered the Soviet family of nations. But it was also the liberating power of information that doomed the coup to failure—both the information that over five years had changed people's views of the world, and the information that now fueled the resistance with minute-to-minute reports. People were better informed than ever before about the past consequences of totalitarianism, helping them better understand now what was at stake. (1994: 261)

Statesmen, likewise, have claimed a causal relationship - sometimes to advance a political agenda. During a visit to Moscow, Bill Clinton proclaimed in a 1994 address carried on Russian television that "Revolutions [in] information and communication and technology and production, all these things make democracy more likely."

Not surprisingly, both Huntington and Toffler were also keenly aware of a connection between the central topics of their books. Huntington's analysis affirmed the importance of the new information and communication technologies in democratization. "Thanks in large part to the impact of global communications, by the mid-1980a the impact of a 'worldwide democratic revolution' undoubtedly had become a reality in the minds of political and intellectual leaders in most countries of the world" (1991b: 102). Toffler's work concluded with a chapter about the effect of these technologies on democracy around the globe.

Until recently the evidence of an association between democracy and communication has been almost exclusively anecdotal. Phillips Cutright was among the first researchers to use country data and statistical tests to demonstrate a correlation. With respect to technologies that were conventional in the 1960s—newspapers, telephones, and postal mail—Cutright found the communication index to be "a better predictor of political development than is economic development" (1963: 257). This is a powerful statement, given the venerated linkage between democracy and wealth. Huntington himself has remarked that "Few relationships between social, economic and political phenomena are stronger than that between the level of economic development and the existence of democratic politics" (1991a: 30). It is worth noting, however, that in Seymour Martin Lipset's seminal study employing statistical analyses to show a significant correlation between democracy and economic development—a study which concluded that the latter was "related causally" to the former—his metric for economic wealth consisted of communication measures such as numbers of radios, telephones, and newspapers per thousand persons (1959). In other words, the association of democracy with economic development may be at least partially attributable to the effects of communication.

There are good theoretical reasons to expect that the new technologies may be conducive to democratic processes. The late communications scholar Ithiel de Sola Pool, who called himself a "soft technological determinist," characterized as follows the effects of changing communication technologies on political freedom through the centuries: "Freedom is fostered when the means of communication are dispersed, decentralized, and easily available, as are printing presses or microcomputers. Central control is more likely when the means of communication are concentrated, monopolized, and scarce, as are great networks" (1983: 5).[1]

The new technologies for communication are not only dispersed, decentralized, and easily accessible, but they also offer a historically unprecedented multidirectional mode of communication that appears to be democracy enabling. The essence of multidirectional communication, as distinct from unidirectional broadcast and bidirectional interactive communication, is that many individuals can receive information on the same network and can also participate equally within the context of a single discussion. Indeed, the expressed goal for the Internet's predecessor, the ARPANET, was that "It should effectively allow the illusion that those in communication with one another are all within the same soundproofed room" (Baran 1964: 1). The multidirectional communication mode (often, though somewhat inaccurately, referred to as "many-to-many") may inherently be conducive to more democratic institutions and interactions (Ronfeldt 1993).[2] Electronic computer networks are also prodemocracy standouts when compared with conventional communication media along several other key dimensions such as low cost, high speed, independence of national and natural boundaries, and capability to transmit both politically arousing images and easily manipulable data (Kedzie 1996b).

More recent empirical studies and statistical evidence that measure the independent communication variable in terms of electronic communication networks are consistent with both Cutright's findings and notions that the new communication technologies have a special relationship with democracy. Visual evidence of a correlation between levels of democracy and communication is rather provocative. Freedom House, a leading publisher of democracy data, annually reports democracy ratings for all of the countries of the world. If we compare their map for a given year to a comparable world projection showing the major worldwide computer networks involved in the exchange of electronic mail (e-mail)—assigning shadings in such a way that darker shading indicates higher levels of democracy on the political map and greater levels of connectivity on the network map—we find a striking congruence of the patterns on every continent. While overlaying maps is certainly not a form of rigorous analysis, the correspondence revealed is sufficiently intriguing to motivate such analysis.

Is There a Correlation between the Third Waves?

The first task that must be undertaken to ascertain a statistical relationship is to define and quantify the principal variables. Democracy is an abstract concept difficult to measure. Assigning each country a single number to represent a relative level of democracy is a method subject to many risks. First, democracy is a subjective quality and therefore subject to interpretive biases. Second, countries are complex systems. A nominally democratic country may have decidedly nondemocratic organizations and practices, and vice versa. Third, democracy is multidimensional. Flattening and compressing democracy into a single number oversimplifies and truncates important descriptive information. The inherent problems associated with developing a useful and robust measure for democracy now command substantial attention in academic circles.[3]

Measurement difficulties notwithstanding, relative democracy rankings by independent authorities using different criteria agree quite broadly. This concurrence suggests that although the concept of democracy may be difficult to describe explicitly, it is nonetheless well understood intuitively (at least by Western analysts):

[D]emocracy is a distinctive and highly coherent syndrome of characteristics such that anyone measuring only a few of the salient characteristics will classify nations in much the same way as will another analyst who also measured only a few qualities but uses a different set of characteristics, so long as both have selected their indicators from the same larger pool of valid measures. Far from being like the elephant confronting the blind sages, democracy is more like a ball of wax. (Inkeles 1990: 5)

Freedom House obtains the measurements for the *Comparative Survey of Freedom* from a pair of annual world-wide surveys on political rights and civil liberties. Each year, Freedom House reports a rating from 1 to 7 for every country, from the greatest freedom to the least, respectively. Since both political rights and civil liberties are recognized as fundamental elements of democracy, and since these are highly correlated, the democracy variable used in this study is the simple average of these two. This scale is then inverted and normalized to 100 for intuitive convenience. The result of these cosmetic conversions is a metric with 13 discrete values; the maximum democracy rating is 100 (instead of 1), and the minimum is 0 (instead of 7).[4]

Quantifying the principal independent variable is also problematic, both definitionally and functionally. As communication technologies increasingly overlap, a phenomenon Ithiel de Sola Pool termed "convergence of modes" (1983: 23), what to include becomes less clear. Computers can send faxes; audio and video can be combined; radio waves and television cables can transmit e-mail messages. This study focuses on electronic mail because e-mail is the technology that enables people to engage in multidirectional, potentially democratizing discourse across borders in ways that have never before been possible.

The term for this metric is "interconnectivity."[5] Four e-mail networks are globally dominant: Internet, BITNET, UUCP, and FidoNet. Record keeping has not been consistent, regular, or accurate across the networks. The most comprehensive and best available data consist of node counts, although nodes themselves are not equal, even within the same network. A node may consist of a single computer and user or an entire organization with many of both. Matrix Information Directory Service (MIDS) tracks and maintains these data, aggregated by country. The first year for which comprehensive data are available is 1993. Thus, the basic unit of measure for interconnectivity in this report is the number of nodes in the four primary networks, as compiled by MIDS in October 1993.

The numerical value of a country's interconnectivity variable derived from these aggregated data is transformed in one of three different ways throughout this study:

- *The Linear Transformation.* Countries are first ranked by network according to number of nodes and scored with a number from 0 to 4 according to the relative extent of their per capita interconnectivity in each. A 0 is assigned to all countries with no nodes in a particular network. Numbers from 1 to 4 are assigned to countries by increasing quartile for each network. The highest quartile countries receive a score of 4. The sum of the four scores determines the level of interconnectivity on a scale from 0 to 16. This scale is a useful metric for evaluating the relative levels of democracy and interconnectivity.

- *The Logarithmic Transformation.* The algebraic sum of the nodes on all four networks is divided by the population and then transformed using the natural logarithm. However, the total node count in 1993 was 0 for approximately one-third of the countries, and 0 does not transform logarithmically. Therefore, an additional binary variable is paired with the log transformation to indicate the existence, or not, of an electronic mail network in each country. This is the preferred transformation for comparison between and among communication media since televisions, telephones, and computer network nodes all have similarly skewed distributions with long tails on the right.

- *The Square-Root Transformation.* The algebraic sum of the nodes on all four networks is divided by the population and then transformed by taking the square root. This transformation preserves some of the magnitude effects of the logarithmic transformation without requiring another variable for countries with zero interconnectivity. This transformation is useful to describe the change in connectivity over time.

All three formulations are per capita measures that give equivalent weight to each of the four networks. Assumed equivalence does introduce a theoretical potential for inconsistencies. Although the ability to exchange e-mail is a relatively generic capability, the networks are not necessarily comparable in other respects. For instance, the Internet, with specialized services such as the World Wide Web and remote logon, has more functional capacity than the others, creating a possibility of perverse results. For example, a country with fewer nodes and thus a lower interconnectivity score could have more communications capability than a country with

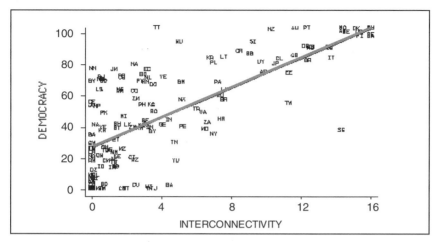

Figure 1 Democracy and Interconnectivity.

more nodes if a the former's nodes were Internet nodes. In practice this is not likely to occur because interconnectivity evolves progressively. The analyses exhibit none of the potential degradation of this variable.

The scatterplot and accompanying regression line in Figure 1 confirms the correlation between democracy and electronic network interconnectivity suggested by the map correlations (which were based on linear scales). This correlation is not only substantial but also more substantial than that between democracy and any of its other traditional correlates. The correlation matrix in Table 1 provides this comparison. The coefficient for per capita GDP, for example, which has often been considered the most important of democracy's correlates, is more than 15 percentage points smaller.

The strength of this correlation is impressive, but, of course, correlation does not prove causality. While Figure 1 shows an undeniable trend in which greater interconnectivity pairs with greater democracy, there are several alternative explanations that would belie a conclusion that the former causes the latter. Probing causality is implicitly central to this investigative endeavor; explicitly proving causality is not, for causality can never be determined conclusively without well-controlled experimentation, which is rarely, if ever, possible in international affairs. The lack of conclusive causal proof notwithstanding, if alternative plausible causal

Table 1   First Order Correlations between Democracy and Selected Variables

	Dem	Int	Sch	Per	Lif	Eth	Log
Democracy	1.00						
Interconnectivity	0.73	1.00					
Schooling	0.67	0.82	1.00				
Per Capita GDP	0.57	0.84	0.79	1.00			
Life Expectancy	0.53	0.71	0.87	0.71	1.00		
Ethnicity	0.27	0.26	0.35	0.23	0.42	1.00	
Log (population)	−0.09	0.07	0.10	0.05	0.07	0.11	1.00

explanations fail to conform to available data, the powerful correlation between democracy and communication highlights this nexus as an area ripe for future research and possibly fruitful policy.

When considering causal connections, one would want to know about the interactions between and among the other key variables. What is the relationship between interconnectivity and democracy when economic well-being and schooling and the other important correlates of democracy are held constant? This question can be explored by correlating democracy with various combinations of the other potentially influential variables.

Second, one would want to consider whether economic development might be a confounding factor that similarly and simultaneously influences both democracy and interconnectivity such that they rise together. One way to test this hypothesis would be to compare the relative correlation between democracy and electronic networks with the correlation between democracy and various other communication media. If different technologies that nominally have comparable associations with wealth differ in their relationship to democracy, then it is unlikely economic development is the fundamental cause of both.

Third, it is conceivable that Figure 1 is merely a picture of different country groups with common characteristics inhabiting their own respective areas of the graph. If, for example, all the points in the top right-hand corner represented the rich Western democracies and all the points in the bottom left were poor, undemocratic, and unconnected Sub-Saharan African countries, with the in-between countries lying somewhere in the middle, Figure 1 might be a reasonable description of the world, but in this case the correlation between interconnectivity and democracy might be meaningless. Do the data exhibit such regional clustering? This possibility can be tested by regressing democracy with its correlates in various regions separately.

Fourth, Figure 1 is a single snapshot in time. Is it possible that either the already established democracies chose higher levels of interconnectivity or that the correlation is simply a circumstantial coincidence of two phenomena with ascending but independent prevalence? In either case, one would want to know not only whether the introduction of the network communication technologies correlated with levels of democracy, but also whether it correlated with changes in the levels of democracy.

Some of these alternative causal explanations have been addressed in considerable detail elsewhere, as indicated below. The following paragraphs summarize, synthesize, and supplement those findings.

Are the Other Variables Responsible for the Correlation?

When interconnectivity and democracy are the only two variables being considered, a visibly strong correlation is undeniable. However, in regression analysis, the exclusion of other important variables can often lead to spurious correlations. If someone were to discover, for instance, a correlation between democracy and the number of restaurants in a country or between democracy and the number of poets, any causal argument that did not include wealth or education would clearly be indefensible. The same is true for interconnectivity. Multiple linear regressions have been conducted that include traditional correlates for democracy, in various combinations, to explore the correlation between democracy and interconnectivity. These regressions consistently reveal interconnectivity as the single predictor that is dominant over economic development, schooling, ethnic homogeneity, life expectancy, and population size. Representative results of these statistical tests regularly indicate that with a greater than 99.9 percent certainty, higher than that for any other correlate, one can reject a hypothesis that there is no relationship between democracy and interconnectivity (Kedzie 1995: 161).

The effects of the likely multicollinearity between the included independent variables would tend to reduce the efficiency of the intertwined predictors. Reduced efficiency means that the reported statistical significance may be less than the actual because the standard errors will be excessively large. In practical terms, however, inferences regarding the relationship between interconnectivity and democracy would not change, because the reported statistical significance is already great and if multicollinearity were influencing these results, the "true" correlation would be even greater.

Furthermore, the coefficient on interconnectivity in these regression models is typically quite large. A single point increase on the interconnectivity scale corresponds to an increase of 5 points in democracy rating. It appears, therefore, that excluded variables and multivariate interactions are not solely responsible for the strong correlation between democracy and interconnectivity.

Does Economic Wealth Account for the Correlation?

The results of multiple regressions are informative but not definitive. The interactions between the independent variables are too numerous and too complex. Isolating any specific relationship between variables through regression techniques can be hazardous when nearly everything is connected to everything else. An alternate exploratory tack would be to determine the relative effects of various communication technologies on democratization. If unidirectional broadcast, bidirectional telephony, and multidirectional network technologies differ in their relative effects on democracy, the difference may then be more attributable to the characteristics of the technology itself, since each communication technology is similarly, although not necessarily identically, dependent on wealth.

As before, this analytic approach employs regression modeling to predict democracy as a function of economic development, education, and population. Per capita numbers of television sets proxy for unidirectional communication, telephone instruments for bidirectional, and e-mail nodes for multidirectional.

In accordance with the theory of the "Dictator's Dilemma," one could reasonably expect the investigation to produce the following results.[6] Unidirectional communication technologies, the preferred communication instrument for exerting the influence of an autocratic dictator, are likely to be the least correlated or perhaps even negatively correlated with democracy. Bidirectional communication, as essential for autonomous market activity, will probably have an indeterminate or nonstatistically significant correlation. Multidirectional communication technologies, as simultaneous enhancers of influence and autonomy, will presumably correlate most highly with democracy.

The statistical results conform precisely to the logic above (Kedzie 1996a). Both variables related to electronic mail networks—the binary variable indicating presence and the continuous variable indicating prevalence—predict democracy with the highest level of statistical significance. The confidence level is again greater than 99.9 percent. In both cases the substantive values are also large. A 1 percent increase in networks associates with a 4 point increase on the democracy scale. The mere existence of networks in a country predicts a democracy level above half the entire democracy scale.

The regression coefficient on the television variable is also statistically significant, but the sign is negative. Increasing the number of televisions by a certain percentage corresponds with a decrease in democracy on the same order that increasing networks corresponds with an increase in democracy. The coefficient on telephones is positive but not statistically significant. No meaningful conclusions can be based on its magnitude or sign.

Not only do networked communications appear to be the most statistically significant predictor, they also predict the greatest percentage of the variance in democracy relative to the other communication technologies—almost 60 percent. Televisions predict just over half of the variance in democracy, and telephones predict even less.

Two conclusions emerge from these results. First, economic wealth cannot account for the correlation between democracy and interconnectivity, because it does not explain the markedly different relationships between the various media and democracy. Second, relative to conventional media, multidirectional communication does exhibit an especially close relationship with democracy.

Can Cultural and Historical Factors Explain the Correlation?

Debates continue as to whether certain cultures or civilizations are favorably disposed or fundamentally disinclined to embrace democratic principles.[7] It is not difficult to believe that historical factors influence the characterization of the political regimes and the appreciation of personal liberties. Similarly, culture and history can be expected to shape the ways in which various people utilize communication technologies. To control for these effects, six regional categories were defined that incorporated elements of culture, history, geography, and religion: Africa, Asia, Eurasia, Latin America, the Middle East, and Western Europe. Demarcation between cultures can never be exact. Identifying certain countries with any regional category could be subject to contention, but the regression results are robust, independent of individual country classifications.

Regional regressions are shown in Figure 2. Outputs vary little with the inclusion or exclusion of other important correlates such as economic development and schooling. In all the regions the correlation is positive. In half of the regions, the correlation coefficient is both substantial and statistically significant. Moreover, correlation is strongest precisely in those regions undergoing dramatic political and economic transformation, namely Eurasia and Africa (Kedzie 1995: 164).

If the correlation were positive only where the establishment of democracy has long preceded the information revolution—for example, in the stable Western democracies—one might argue that the latter could have strengthened the former, but certainly one would not be able to contend that the latter caused the former. The evidence shows otherwise, however: the relationship is weakest in regions characterized by mature democracies and strongest in regions that are cultivating nascent democracies. Cultural or regional effects are inadequate to explain the apparent association of interconnectivity with democracy. While the nominal purpose of these regional tests is to account for cultural influences, they have

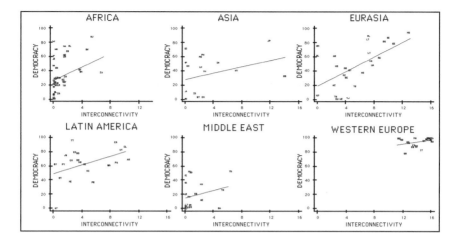

Figure 2   Regional Regressions and Scatterplots.

the additional benefit of emphasizing the time dimension, albeit
indirectly through the regional categorization. Instead of correlating democracy and interconnectivity levels, a more direct approach would be to examine the correlation between these two
variables with respect to changes over time.

Is the Correlation a Circumstantial Artifact?

A salient question that these one-time cross-sectional regressions
fail to answer is, Did the level of democracy change in countries that
increased interconnectivity? Addressing this question requires
temporal comparisons, the data for which, unfortunately, are
scant. International interconnectivity data were not recorded until
electronic networks were already a global phenomenon. It was also
not until 1991 that the Internet started sampling and recording
country data. Nevertheless, an earlier period when interconnectivity
levels are known almost exactly is the early 1980s, when electronic
networking was still an experiment conducted almost exclusively
within the research community of the United States. At the end of
1983, for instance, the level of interconnectivity for almost every
country other than the U.S. was identically zero.[8] In that year
FidoNet was invented and BITNET was still in the early development stages. In the following year, the British and Japanese imple-

mented their own national versions of the Internet, JANET (Joint Academic Research Network) and JUNET (Japanese Unix Network). In the United States, the total number of Internet hosts was still less than 1,000, compared to more than 1,000,000 ten years latter (Hobbes). The decade from 1983 to 1993, although somewhat arbitrarily defined, also brackets the major surge in the number of democratic states at the end of the 1980s.

The change in interconnectivity from 1983 to 1993 is everywhere nonnegative but spans several orders of magnitude. The clearest way to show the relative relationships between changes in interconnectivity and changes in the level of democracy is to transform the interconnectivity variable as the square root of the number of networks per million population.

The dependent variable here is the change in democracy over the period from 1983 to 1993 in the republics of the former Soviet Union and the splinter states of Yugoslavia.[9] The difference across the decade is extracted as before from the Freedom House surveys for 1983/84 and 1993/94. Countries that appeared after 1983 assume the value of their predecessor state. States that merged take the value of the dominant partner (West Germany and North Yemen).

Possible values for the change in democracy over the decade are structurally truncated at both ends of the scale because the democracy scale itself is finite. In other words, if a country with the lowest democracy rating were to become even less free, the value for the change would nevertheless be zero. Therefore, comparisons of democratic change are meaningful only for countries that had similar democracy ratings in 1983/84. Freedom House groups countries into three categories: "Not Free" (defined by a democracy rating below 33), "Partially Free" (from 33 through 67), and "Free" (above 67). The country group that inspires the greatest interest, from both an analytic perspective and from a policy perspective is the "Not Free," which are the countries that have the most room for democratic improvement. "Not Free" countries are also those for which policy initiatives to support democracy can have the most dramatic impacts. While the need for programs to encourage democratic development is most pressing in these countries, the success of such programs historically has been

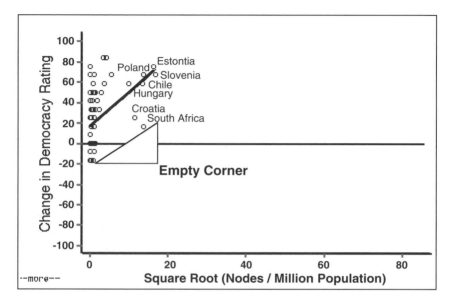

Figure 3 Interconnectivity and Democratic Change in "Not Free" Countries, 1983–93.

elusive. This group is also particularly interesting because it contains a majority of countries in the world, more than double the number of either "Partially Free" or "Free" countries.

A finding of no correlation between changes in democracy and changes in interconnectivity in these least democratic countries could cast serious doubt on the underlying basis of the correlations noted earlier. This is not the case, however: a strong correlation, consistent with all previous results, is apparent from the scatterplot and corresponding regression line in Figure 3. Interconnectivity proves to be a statistically significant predictor of the change in democracy for the "Not Free" group. Again the confidence level is more than 99.9 percent.

The empty corner at the bottom right of the data is perhaps more intriguing than the regression line. There is not a single case of even a moderate increase in the level of interconnectivity that is not also accompanied by at least a moderate increase in the level of democracy. Conversely, in the opposite corner, there are numerous cases of minimally or nonconnected countries becoming more democratic. The latter occurrence is expected; many countries became stable democracies decades or even centuries before the information revolution. This is not to say, however, that connectivity may not have had an important impact even in these states that remained relatively less connected. The demonstration and neighborhood effects emanating from more connected states may have powerfully affected political reforms throughout their sphere of influence. Conjecture aside, the dispersion of data in the top right corner does prove that electronic interconnectivity is not a necessary condition for democratization.

Sufficiency, on the other hand, is not so easily discounted in the absence of data to the contrary. The two countries closest to the edge of the empty corner are extreme cases; Croatia was at war in 1993, and South Africa had a bifurcated society consisting of a connected minority and a large unconnected majority. Even under these circumstances, both of these countries reported respectable democratic gains, and since that time South Africa has democratized further. Perhaps as these countries become more "normal," the empty corner will expand.

The empty corner corroborates the notion of the "Dictator's Dilemma"—that greater connectivity can come only at the expense of political control. President Gorbachev provided the most dramatic example of an authoritarian leader who sought the economic benefits of information and communication while trying to maintain political control. The record shown in Figure 3 indicates that neither he nor anyone else has yet been successful in exploiting networked communication technologies while simultaneously avoiding political liberalization.

The shattering of the Soviet Union resembles, in some aspects, a controlled experiment. The initial state was arguably monolithic. The constituent elements, subject to different levels of intervention (interconnectivity and otherwise), diverged toward disparate outcomes. The results of this "quasi-experiment" are depicted in Figure 4. The correlation, characterized by a line rising to the right, is consistent with the notion that among similar countries, those which were the most interconnected were also those that experienced the greatest democratic gains.

Figure 3 can be combined with similar plots for the "Partially Free" and "Not Free" states. The composite picture in Figure 5

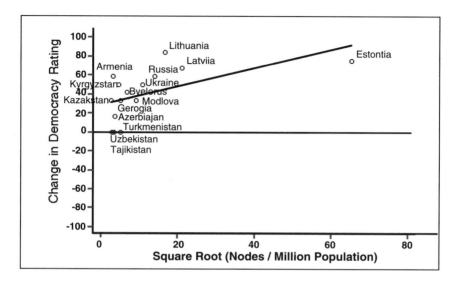

Figure 4   Interconnectivity and Democratic Change in the USSR, 1983–1993.

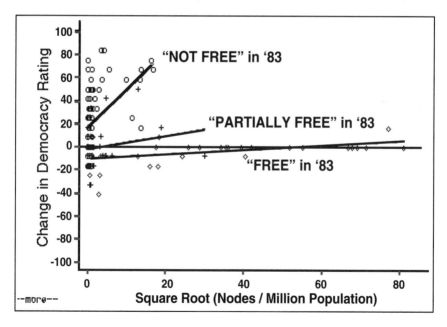

Figure 5   Interconnectivity and Democratic Change Worldwide.

produces interesting and potentially instructive comparisons. As we go from "Not Free" to "Free," the slopes of the lines decrease and the locations of the regression lines descend. The former attests to the decreasing political volatility as democracies take root. The latter results from the truncation at both ends of the democracy scale. "Not Free" states have a lot of room for improvement, but there is nowhere for "Free" states to move except down, although few do because they are more stable.

The triangular area that was identified as the empty corner in the "Not Free" segment and that represented the difficult choices facing current dictators is no longer empty. It is now populated with several observations. The level of connectivity that associates with substantial democracy gains among "Not Free" states, such as 100 nets per million population, corresponds with a minimal gain in "Partially Free" states and even democracy losses in "Free" states. The general inference is that increasing levels of democracy have correspondingly greater communication requirements. The communication and information needs within stable, functioning democracies are quite profound. Meeting these needs would seem to be helpful in securing democracy. Conversely, failing to meet these needs leaves open the possibility of a democratic slide, perhaps a corollary to the "Dictator's Dilemma." The countries that made a great leap into democracy recently might be expected to slip back somewhat unless or until their communication capabilities come on par with the communication needs that are associated with their new levels of democracy.

Ultimately, the most significant inference is that not only does interconnectivity correlate well with the level of democracy, but it also correlates well with the change in democracy over a 10-year period.

Conclusions

Empirical evidence confirms a postulated correlation between Huntington's and Toffler's "Third Wave" phenomena. Despite the inherent limitations of statistical analyses, every analytic perspective, every model, and every set of statistical tests in this study consistently verify that interconnectivity is a powerful predictor of democracy, more so than any of democracy's traditional correlates. As a single independent variable, interconnectivity more strongly correlates with democracy than any other variable. In multiple linear regression, interconnectivity is exclusively the dominant predictor. Among communication media, the strong positive correlation between democracy and electronic networks is unique, diminishing the importance of potentially confounding economic factors. Within regional tests, the correlation of interconnectivity with democracy is everywhere positive, and it has both the largest substantive value and greatest statistical significance in regions characterized by dynamic political transformations. Interconnectivity correlates strongly not only with the level of democracy but also with the change in democracy over ten years. While many of the least democratic states became more democratic without becoming interconnected, not a single one of them became even moderately interconnected without also becoming more free. Tests of alternative causal explanations invariably fail.

While provocative, even compelling, these results still cannot conclusively determine causality in the correlation between democracy and electronic computer networks. Despite the persistence of the unanswerable causal question, the consistent test results should nevertheless influence the relevant policy debates for several reasons. First, to the extent that the United States and other Western democracies aim to encourage the development of democracy worldwide, they do so primarily through programs to improve such indicators as economic development, educational levels, and health. Yet the causal connection supporting those programs is no stronger, and in many instances quite a bit weaker, than can be inferred in the case of networked communication technology.

Second, the backdrop behind the empirical results presented here is a crescendo of anecdotal and theoretical arguments that cast electronic communications networks to the front among factors that may contribute to the development of democracy. These statistical results reinforce the validity and credibility of the more subjective analyses.

Third, causal relationships in international affairs are rarely either simple or in one direction only. The most plausible relationship between democracy and networked communication (and perhaps economic development) is probably a virtuous circle with substantial positive feedback in several directions. Even if a causal argument positing an alternate explanation of the correlation, such as "greater democracy causes greater interconnectivity," could be established with complete irrefutability, the existence of such an argument would not negate or diminish the importance of a likely stream of causality in the opposite direction. Furthermore, the total weight of evidence makes denying the likelihood of the latter causal flow nearly untenable.

If the United States and other democratic countries seek to influence international democratic development effectively and efficiently, then, they ought to be thinking about how to enhance the resonance of the coinciding "Third Waves."

Notes

1. It is important to recognize that the word "network" as Pool used it in this citation refers to large physical networks, such as those used in broadcasting, and not to virtual electronic networks as the term is used throughout this chapter.

2. "Many-to-many" is the term often used to distinguish electronic networks from broadcast ("one-to-many") and from telephony many "one-to-ones". The problem with this distinction is that the number-to-number terminology risks misinterpretation. The connotation of "many" in one-to-many can be the billion or so people around the globe who watch soccer's World Cup. Although some electronic newsletter such as China News Digest may boast of 35,000 subscribers or more, the many-to-many on the scale of the World Cup would be impossibly unwieldy. More importantly, quantifying the number of participants misses the fundamental quality of the innovation in the new technology. Independent of how many people are involved—even if there are only three—electronic networking technology creates a different communication dynamic and thus can be expected to foster different political outcomes.

3. Many of the measurement and statistical difficulties are addressed in considerable depth by Inkeles et al. (1990) and Dahl (1971).

4. For similar precedents, see Rowen (1995) or Muller and Seligson (1994)

5. "Interconnectivity" is a term popularized by Larry Landweber for his measures of the proliferation of global e-mail networks.

6. The "Dictator's Dilemma" is essentially the choice either to allow multidirectional electronic communication networks and risk losing social control or to outlawing the networks and relinquish opportunities for economic growth. A

thorough explanation of the dilemma and its theoretical basis can be found in Kedzie (1996b).

7. For characteristic arguments from both sides of the debate, see Huntington (1984) and Schifter (1994).

8. The first international connections to the ARPANET were England and Norway in 1973, but even in these countries, interconnectivity was very close to nil until after 1983 (Hobbes).

9. Missing or inconsistent data entries precluded the inclusion of the Czech and Slovak Republics and Bosnia-Herzogovina in these analyses. Namibia, which did not exist in 1983, is also excluded from these statistical tests.

References

Baran, Paul. 1964. *On Distributed Communications: XI. Summary Overview*, RM-3767-PR, Santa Monica, CA: RAND.

Central Intelligence Agency, *World Fact Book 1994*, Washington DC.

Clinton, Bill. 1994. Remarks by the President in live telecast to Russian people, Ostankino TV Station, Moscow, Russia, January 14. Available via ftp from info.tamu.edu in the directory /.data/politics/1994/tele.0114.

Cutright, Phillips. 1963. "National Political Development: Measurement and Analysis," *American Sociological Review* 28 April, 253–264.

Dahl, Robert A. 1971. *Polyarchy: Participation and Opposition*, New Haven, CT: Yale University Press, 1971.

Hobbes, Robert, n.d. *Hobbes 1960. Internet Timeline* v2.3 Available Online via WWW at http://info.isoc.org/guest/zakon/Internet/History/HIT.htmL.

Huntington, Samuel P. 1984. "Will More Countries Become Democratic?" *Political Science Quarterly*, 99, no. 2 (Summer): 193–218.

Huntington, Samuel P. 1991a. "Democracy's Third Wave," *Journal of Democracy* 2, no. 2 (Spring): 12–34.

Huntington, Samuel P. 1991b. *The Third Wave: Democratization in the Late Twentieth Century*. Norman, OK: University of Oklahoma Press.

Inkeles, Alex. 1990. "Introduction: On Measuring Democracy," *Studies in Comparative International Development*, 25, no. 1 (Spring): 3–6.

Kaplan, Roger, ed. 1994. *Freedom Review*, 25, no. 1 (January).

Kedzie, Christopher R. 1996a. "A Brave New World or a New World Order?" in Sara Kiesler, ed., *Social Psychology of the Internet*, Mahwah, NJ: Lawrence Erlbaum.

Kedzie, Christopher R. 1996b. "International Implications for Global Democratization," in *Universal Access to E-Mail: Feasibility and Societal Implications*, MR-650-MF, Santa Monica, CA: RAND.

Kedzie, Christopher R. 1995. *The Dictator's Dilemma*. MR-678.0-RC, Santa Monica, CA: RAND.

Landweber, Larry. 1994. *International Connectivity*, Versions 2 through 10 15 February, available online at ftp.cs.wisc.edu in the connectivity_table directory.

Lipset, Seymour Martin. 1959. "Some Social Requisites of Democracy: Economic Development and Political Legitimacy," *American Political Science Review* no. 53: 69–105.

Matrix Information and Directory Services, Inc. (MIDS). 1993. Unpublished data, Austin, TX, October.

Merit, Inc. Internet statistics, available online via ftp nic.merit.edu in the directory nsfnet/statistics Ann Arbor MI.

Muller, Edward N., and Mitchell A. Seligson. 1994. "Civic Culture and Democracy: The Question of Causal Relationships," *American Political Science Review*, 88, no. 3 (September).

Office of Technology Assessment. 1995. *Global Communications: Opportunities for Trade and Aid*. OTA-ITC-642, Washington, DC: U.S. Government Printing Office.

Pitroda, Sam. 1993. "Development, Democracy, and the Village Telephone," *Harvard Business Review* (November–December): 66–79.

Pool, Ithiel de Sola. 1983. *Technologies of Freedom*, Cambridge, MA: Harvard University Press.

Ronfeldt, David. 1993. *Institutions, Markets and Networks: A Framework about the Evolution of Societies*. DRU-590-FF Santa Monica, CA: RAND.

Rowen, Henry S. 1995. "The Tide Underneath the 'Third Wave,'" *Journal of Democracy*, 6, no. 1 (January): 52–64.

Schifter, Richard. 1994. "Is there a Democracy Gene?" *The Washington Quarterly* (Summer): 121–127.

Shane, Scott. 1994. *Dismantling Utopia: How Information Ended the Soviet Union*. Chicago, IL: Ivan R. Dee.

Skolnikoff, Eugene B. 1993. *The Elusive Transformation: Science, Technology and the Evolution of International Politics*. Princeton, NJ: Princeton University Press.

Toffler, Alvin. 1980. *The Third Wave*. New York: Bantam Books.

United Nations Development Programme. 1993. *Human Development Report*. New York: Oxford University Press.

World Bank 1991. *World Bank Development Report*.

The Internet as a Source of Regulatory Arbitrage

A. Michael Froomkin

The Modern Hydra?

Hydra was a mythical beast with many heads, one of which was immortal.[1] Every time one of its heads was cut off it grew two more. To regulators, the Internet may seem like a modern Hydra. Almost every attempt to block access to material on the Internet, indeed anything short of an extraordinarily restrictive access policy, can be circumvented easily. Hydras can be killed by heroic measures: according to Greek mythology, Hercules ultimately destroyed Hydra by cauterizing its stumps and severing the immortal head from its body. The Internet, too, could be killed, or a nation could choose to allow access on a restricted basis. Yet, the more a nation pursues a restrictive Internet policy, the less value it will derive from the network and the more it risks being left out of the information revolution.

Three technologies underlie the Internet's resistance to control. First, the Internet is a *packet switching network*, which makes it difficult for anyone, even a government, to block or monitor information flows originating from large numbers of users. Second, users have access to powerful military-grade cryptography that can, if used properly, make messages unreadable to anyone but the intended recipient. Third, and resulting from the first two, users of the Internet have access to powerful anonymizing tools. Together, these three technologies mean that anonymous communication is within reach of anyone with access to a personal computer and a link to the Internet unless a government practices very strict access control, devotes vast resources to monitoring, or can persuade its population (whether by liability rules or criminal law) to avoid using these tools.

The vision of the Internet as a threat may in any case be flawed. Hydra was a dangerous monster; the Internet, despite the real difficulties it will pose for certain types of regulation, may be predominantly benign.

Packet Switching

The Internet is not a thing; it is the interconnection of many things—the (potential) interconnection between any of millions of computers located around the world. Each of these computers is independently managed by persons who have chosen to adhere to common communications standards, particularly a fundamental standard known as TCP/IP,[2] which makes it practical for computers adhering to the standard to share data even if they are far apart and have no direct line of communication. TCP/IP is the fundamental communication standard on which the Internet has relied: "TCP" stands for Transmission Control Protocol, while "IP" stands for Internet Protocol. There is no single program one uses to gain access to the Internet; instead there are a plethora of programs that adhere to these Internet Protocols. A computer connected to the Internet may have any number of users, all or none of whom may have any of widely varying levels of access to other computers in the network.[3]

The TCP/IP standard makes the Internet possible. Its most important feature is that it defines a packet switching network, a method by which data can be broken up into standardized packets which are then routed to their destinations via an indeterminate number of intermediaries.[4] Under TCP/IP, as each intermediary receives data intended for a party further away, the data are forwarded along whatever route is most convenient at the nanosecond the data arrives. It is as if rather than telephoning a friend one were to tape record a message, cut it up into equal pieces, and hand the pieces to people heading in the general direction of the intended recipient. Each time a person carrying tape would meet anyone going in the right direction, he or she would hand over as many pieces of tape as the recipient could comfortably carry. Eventually the message would get where it needed to go.

Neither sender nor receiver need know or care about the route that their data take and there is no particular reason to expect that data will follow the same route twice. (More importantly from a technical standpoint, the computers in the network can all communicate without knowing anything about the network technology carrying their messages.) Indeed, it is likely that multiple packets originating from a single long data stream will use more than one route to reach the far destination where they will be reassembled. This decentralized, anarchic method of sending information appealed to the Internet's early sponsor, the Defense Department, which was intrigued by a communications network that could continue to function even if a major catastrophe (such as a nuclear war) destroyed a large fraction of the system.[5] The Internet can use dedicated lines or messages can travel over ordinary telephone connections. This built-in resilience is the primary reason that any effort to censor the Internet is likely to fail.

The widespread use of TCP/IP enables the functions that have come to be identified with the Internet, notably: electronic mail (e-mail), Usenet, the World Wide Web, file transfer protocol (FTP), Gopher, Wide Area Information Server (WAIS), Internet Relay Chat (IRC), Multiple User Dungeons/Domains (MUDs), and MUD Object Oriented (MOOs), to name only the most commonly used functions. A user who has access to one of these functions does not necessarily have access to others because the user's level of access is determined by the type of computer used, the capacity of the Internet connection, the cost of access, the software used, and the policy of the person or organization operating that computer. Some national governments impose additional constraints on Internet connectivity. Today it is still possible for a government to restrict access to the Internet; once a person is connected, however, it is currently beyond the power of any government to limit what is accessible via the Internet.

Decentralized Standard Setting

The Internet standard-setting process is also decentralized. Standards are set by an international unincorporated nongovernmental organization known as the Internet Engineering Task Force (IETF). The IETF allows unlimited grassroots participation and operates under a relatively large, open agenda. The IETF has no general membership; instead, it is made up primarily of volunteers, many of whom attend the organization's triennial meetings. Meetings are open to all; similarly, anyone can join the e-mail mailing list in which potential standards are discussed.[6] Although the IETF plays a role in the selection of other groups that help define the basic Internet protocols, the IETF is not part of or subject to those groups. Indeed, it is not entirely clear to the membership who if anyone "owns" the IETF or for that matter who is liable if it is sued.[7] An amorphous body of this sort may be difficult to sue; it is even harder to control.

The IETF has a complex relationship with three more traditionally bureaucratic structures that ensure its continued existence and cohesion: the Internet Society (ISOC), the Internet Architecture Board (IAB), and the IETF Secretariat. The ISOC was founded in January 1992 as an independent, international "professional society that is concerned with the growth and evolution of the worldwide Internet, with the way in which the Internet is and can be used, and with the social, political, and technical issues which arise as a result."[8] The ISOC Board of Trustees must approve all nominations to the IAB. The IAB, formerly the Internet Activities Board, is a technical advisory sub-group of the ISOC responsible for providing oversight of the architecture of the Internet and its protocols. The IAB enjoys a veto over standards proposed by the IETF. Randomly selected members of the IETF control the nominations for the IAB, but the IETF is not formally part of or subject to the IAB. The IAB also retains considerable control over the assignments given to the almost ad hoc task forces that do most of the IETF's work. The IETF Secretariat organizes the triennial meetings and provides institutional continuity between meetings, e.g., by maintaining a World Wide Web site. The Secretariat is administered by the Corporation for National Research Initiatives, with funding from U.S. government agencies and the ISOC. The Secretariat also maintains the on-line Internet Repository, a set of IETF documents.[9]

Growing Uses and User Base

In 1983 there were perhaps 200 computers on the ARPANET, the precursor of the Internet. As of January 1993, there were more than 1.3

million computers with a regular connection to the system. In January 1996 there were about 9.4 million Internet *hosts*, computers regularly connected to the Internet,[10] with a substantial fraction, but probably less than half, located outside the United States. Each of these computers is likely to have at least one user, and some have many more. In 1983 only a handful of networks existed;[11] a 1993 estimate suggested that the Internet connected to approximately 50,000 networks and 30 million users, although that estimate seems high. Access has been doubling annually.[12] Current estimates of connectivity vary; one study suggests 40 million users worldwide.[13] The most careful recent study of U.S. usage found 28.8 million adults with potential or actual access but only 16.4 million people 16 years and over who actually used the Internet in the previous three months.[14] Whatever the actual numbers, there seems to be a consensus that usage is growing exponentially and that non-U.S. users will soon reach 50% of the total. At this rate of growth, the Internet cannot help but penetrate deeply into the general population of industrialized countries.

The two most successful Internet applications have been electronic mail—an estimated 25 billion e-mail messages were exchanged in 1995[15]—and the World Wide Web. The Web is an Internet client-server hypertext-distributed information retrieval system.[16] Within two years of its introduction to the public in 1991, the amount of Web traffic traversing the NSFNET Internet backbone reached 75 gigabytes per month, or one percent of the total. By July 1994 Web traffic was one terrabyte (one million megabytes) per month,[17] and a recent estimate puts it at 17.6% of the total Internet traffic.[18] Web browsing programs such as Netscape or Explorer allow the user to navigate the Web in hypertext. Hypertext links inserted by document authors refer the reader to other documents using Uniform Resource Locators (URLs). A mouse click on a link refers the user to remote documents, images, sounds, or even movies that have been made Internet-accessible. A Web browser can retrieve data via FTP, Gopher, Telnet or news, as well as via the http protocol used to transfer hypertext documents.[19]

How the Internet Enables Anonymous Communication

Communicative anonymity allows users to engage in political speech without fear of retribution, to engage in whistle blowing while greatly reducing the risk of detection, and to seek advice about embarrassing personal problems without fear of discovery. It also has costs, since it vastly reduces the chances of identifying the authors of libel, hate speech, and other undesirable communications.

Thanks in large part to the easy availability of powerful cryptographic tools, the Internet provides the ability to send anonymous electronic messages at will. Cryptography alone, however, is not enough. Full communicative privacy and anonymity requires the services of third parties such as *remailer operators*, who volunteer to operate anonymous *remailer* programs. As described in more detail below, the anonymously mailed e-mail cannot, when properly formatted by the sender for transmittal via these intermediaries, be traced back to its originator. In addition, by using remailers two or more persons can communicate without knowing each other's identity while preserving the untraceable nature of their communications.

It is useful to distinguish between four types of communication in which the sender's physical (or "real") identity is at least partly hidden: *traceable anonymity, untraceable anonymity, untraceable pseudonymity,* and *traceable pseudonymity.* These categories allow one to disentangle concepts that are otherwise conflated: whether and how an author identifies herself as opposed to whether and how the real identity of the author can be determined by others.[20] By untraceable anonymity and pseudonymity I mean a communication transmitted in a manner that provides no information that would aid in identifying the author. For example, if Alice drops an unsigned leaflet that is free of fingerprints on Bob's doorstep in the dead of night when no one is looking, her leaflet might be "untraceably anonymous" if the paper and typeface were sufficiently generic.

The traditional anonymous leaflet required a printing and distribution strategy that avoided linking the leaflet with the author. If the leaflet risked attracting the attention of someone armed with modern forensic techniques, great pains were required to avoid identifying marks such as distinctive paper or fingerprints. In contrast, on the Internet communications are all digital; the only identifying marks they carry are information inserted by the sender, the sender's software, or by any intermediaries who may have relayed the message while it was in transit. For example, an e-mail message ordinarily arrives with the sender's return address and routing information describing the path it took to get from sender to receiver; were it not for that information, or perhaps for internal clues in the message itself ("Hi Mom!"), there would be nothing about the message to disclose the sender's identity.

Enter the anonymous remailer. A remailer receives and automatically forwards communications in a manner that disguises the identity of the original sender. If Alice, the original sender, uses a little care and sends a message via a series of remailers that take advantage of cryptographic tools, the remailer operators need not be known to be trustworthy. Instead, as shown below, Alice's anonymity is protected against anything but the most determined eavesdropping and message-tracing effort so long as any one operator in the chain of intermediaries does not conspire with all the other intermediaries to learn the sender's identity. The more remailers in the chain, however, the longer it may take the message to get to its destination and the greater the chance that an operator in the chain will fail to pass the message on down the line.[21]

Remailers vary, but all serious remailing programs share the common feature that they delete all identifying information about incoming e-mails, substituting a predefined header identifying the remailer as the sender or using a cute tag such as nobody@nowhere.[22] By employing easily automated cryptographic precautions widely available on the Internet and routing a message through a series of remailers, Alice can ensure three outcomes conducive to high security anonymity: (1) None of the remailer operators (except possibly the last in the chain) will be able to read the text of the message because it has been multiply encrypted in a fashion that requires the participation of each operator in turn before the message can be read. (2) Neither Bob, the recipient, nor any remailer operator in the chain (other than the first in the chain) can identify Alice without the cooperation of every prior remailer's operator. (3) It is therefore impossible for the Bob to connect Alice to the text unless every single remailer in the chain both keeps a log of its message traffic and is willing to share this information with the recipient (or is compelled to do so by a court or other authority). Since some remailer operators refuse to keep logs as a matter of principle, there is a good chance that the necessary information does not exist. Even if logs exist, it could be prohibitively expensive for a private litigant to compel all of the operators to divulge their logs because the user can select remailers located in different countries, exposing the would-be plaintiff to the expense of hiring foreign legal counsel and possibly to language difficulties. Similarly, criminal prosecutions may run into difficulties because many legal systems require that an act be an offense in both jurisdictions before allowing a prosecution, or in some cases even discovery, to proceed.

Any electronic communication, even live two-way "chat" communication, can theoretically be made anonymous.[23] In current practice, anonymous remailer technology applies only to e-mail and hence is used for communication between individuals, for mailing lists, and for newsgroup discussions. Although e-mail remailer technology may not yet be as user-friendly as it could be, it is available to anyone who knows where to look—and can even be found on an easy to use World Wide Web page.[24] Anonymous World Wide Web proxies are currently being tested.

At the simplest level, encryption ensures that the first remailer operator cannot read the message and effortlessly connect Alice to Bob and/or the contents. But encryption also has a far more important and subtle role to play. Suppose that Alice decides to route her anonymous message via Ted, Ursula, and Victor, each of whom operates a remailer program and each of whom has published a public key in a public-key encryption system such as PGP.[25] Alice wants to ensure that no member of the chain knows the full path of the message; anyone who knew the full path would be able to identify Alice from the message Bob will receive. On the other hand, each member of the chain will necessarily know the identity of the immediately previous remailer from which the message came and of course the identity of the next remailer to which the message will be sent.

Alice thus wants Ted, the first member of the chain, to program his remailer to remove all information linking her to the message; she is particularly anxious that Ted not be able to read her message since he is the one party in the chain who will know that Alice sent it. Alice also wants Ted to know only that the message should go to Ursula and to remain ignorant of the message's route thereafter. Alice wants Ursula, the second member of the chain, to know only that the message came from Ted and should go to Victor (and to remove the information linking Ted to the message as extra insurance); Victor should know only that it came from Ursula and should go to Bob, although by the time the message reaches Victor, Alice may not care as much whether Victor can read the message since her identity has been well camouflaged.

Alice achieves these objectives by multiply encrypting her message, in layers, using Ted's, Ursula's, and Victor's public keys. As each remailer program receives the message, it discards the headers identifying the e-mail's origins and then decrypts the message with a unique private key, revealing the next address but no more. If one thinks of each layer of encryption as an envelope with an unencrypted address on it, one can visualize the process as the successive opening of envelopes. Thus Alice sends a message to Ted which reads:

To: Ted
Message encrypted with Ted's private key

> Please forward to: Ursula
> Message encrypted with Ursula's public key
>
>> Please forward to: Victor
>> Message encrypted with Victor's public key
>>
>>> Please forward to: Bob
>>>
>>> Text of anonymous message.
>>>
>>> Ideally, this is encrypted with Bob's public key,
>>> but even if it is plaintext, Victor should be unable
>>> to connect it to Alice as long as Alice remembers
>>> not to sign her name.

Chaining the message through Ted, Ursula, and Victor means that no remailer operator alone can connect Alice either to the text of the message or to Bob. Of course, if Ted, Ursula and Victor are in a cabal, or all in the same jurisdiction and keep logs that could be the subject of a subpoena, Alice may find that Bob is able to learn her identity. All it takes to preserve Alice's anonymity, however, is a single remailer in the chain that is not a member of the cabal and either erases her logs or is outside the jurisdiction. In theory, there is no limit to the number of remailers in the chain; Alice can, if she wishes, loop the message through some remailers more than once to throw off anyone attempting *traffic analysis,* which is the study of the sources and recipients of messages, including messages that the eavesdropper cannot understand.[26]

Nothing is foolproof, however. If Alice has the bad luck to use only compromised remailers whose operators are willing to club together to reveal her identity, she is out of luck. However, if Alice uses both encryption and chaining and one member of the chain refuses to cooperate in the effort to unmask her, Bob should not be able to trace the message's path from himself back to Alice. An extraordinarily determined eavesdropper, able to track messages going in and out of multiple remailers over a period of time (perhaps using wiretaps on telephone lines), might be able to conduct traffic analysis and correlate messages leaving one remailer with those arriving at another. To foil this level of surveillance, which has nothing to do with the bad faith of the remailer operators, requires even more exotic techniques including introducing random delays into the remailing process, having the remailers alter the size of messages, and ensuring that they are not remailed in the order they are received.[27]

The supply of remailer operators is the major potential constraint on Internet anonymity. Remailer programs are currently operated by a relatively small number of volunteers located in a few countries; at present they receive no compensation for this service, and in the absence of anonymous electronic cash or the equivalent it is difficult to see how an electronic payment system could be constructed that would not risk undermining the very anonymity the remailers are designed to protect.

The remailer operator's problem is a simple one. No operator can control the content of the messages that flow through the remailer. Furthermore, the last remailer operator in a chain has no reliable way of concealing the identity of the sender's machine from the message's ultimate recipient. Suppose, to return to the example above, Alice wants to send an anonymous death threat to Bob via remailers operated by Ted, Ursula, and Victor. If Victor does nothing to mask his e-mail address, Bob will know he was the last to remail the message. Victor can make any attempt to identify him more difficult by forging his e-mail address in the message to Bob, but Victor cannot be certain that this will work. Indeed, he can be almost certain that over time it will fail.

To understand why this is so requires some background in how an ordinary e-mail message is transmitted from Alice's machine to Bob's via the Internet. As we have seen, ordinarily the two computers do not communicate directly. Instead Alice's machine sends the message to a machine that it hopes is in Bob's general direction, and the message passes from machine to machine until it finds one that is in regular communication with Bob's. Each machine that handles the message appends "path" information to the e-mail that identifies it as having taken part in the communication. The final recipient receives the entire set of path data along with the text of the message, but most commercial e-mail packages are designed to avoid displaying this path information to the reader unless she asks for it.

Victor can instruct his computer to lie about its identity, and indeed can forge information suggesting that the message originated elsewhere far away, but he has no way to persuade the machine to which he sends the message to cooperate. As a result, it is possible for a sufficiently motivated Internet detective to identify the first machine to which Victor sent the message, especially if she has several messages to work with.[28] If the machine that communicated with Victor keeps records of its e-mail handling, or if its operator can be persuaded to do start doing so, the Internet detective can identify Victor's machine, and perhaps even Victor, as the source of the remailed message.

Ordinarily, however, no detective work is required to identify the last remailer in a chain because remailer operators do not attempt to hide their identity. The last remailer is thus exposed to the wrath of an unhappy recipient. Additionally, an identifiable person is a potential target for regulation. If, for example, the remailer operators were made strictly liable for the content of messages that passed through their hands, even though they were unable to learn the content of those encrypted messages, most reasonable people probably would find running a remailer to be an unacceptable risk if they resided in a jurisdiction capable of enforcing such a rule.

Some jurisdictions may choose to make life difficult for remailers. Indeed, in the eyes of some, remailers are a public health hazard on the order of AIDS and other virulent diseases. These writers suggest that remailers enable "information terrorism," although they do not define this term with any precision.[29] Already, they suggest, remailers are "frequently used by the Russian (ex-KGB) criminal element" and favored by unspecified parties for engaging the services of unspecified "cybercriminals."[30] However wild, untestable, and indeed irrefutable, these accusations may be, they contain one grain of truth: remailers do allow users to avoid being held responsible for the contents of the messages they send. In theory at least— I am unaware of any documented examples in practice—a third party could set up shop as an honest broker between an anonymous client and an anonymous criminal and plausibly plead ignorance as to the nature of the transaction.

Remailer operators already have come under various forms of attack, most recently the legal proceedings instigated by officials of the Church of Scientology who sought to identify the person they allege used remailers to disseminate copyrighted and secret Church teachings. At some point, if the number of remailers is small, it becomes technically (if not necessarily politically or legally) feasible for the authorities to conduct traffic analysis on all the remaining remailers and make deductions about who sent what to whom. In the absence of a compensation mechanism or a jurisdiction capable of offering a safe haven for remailers, the cornerstone of Internet anonymity currently relies entirely on the charity of strangers.

Why Censorship Is Difficult

In most countries, all that is required for access to the Internet is either a home computer with access to an Internet service provider (ISP) or an account on a computer network that has Internet access, such as those found in most universities. Short of cutting off international telephone service or concluding an international agreement with all industrialized countries to discontinue telephone service with foreign countries that harbor remailers, there is little that governments can do keep out messages from any other country, or indeed to keep citizens from sending messages wherever they like.

Content control today is frequently primitive or nonexistent. For example, *Penthouse* magazine's World Wide Web site announces that the Web site is "not available" in Ecuador, Egypt, Fiji, Formosa, India, Japan, Kenya, Korea, Malaysia, Malta, Mexico, Nigeria, Okinawa, Pakistan, the Philippines, Saudia Arabia, Singapore, South Africa, Spain, St. Lucia, Thailand, Trinidad, Turkey, the United Kingdom, and Venezuela because these nations "prohibit adult material."[31] Nevertheless, I am reliably informed that the materials on this Web site are accessible from a domain in the United Kingdom with an address ending in ".uk."

If the government of Ruritania is intent on preventing communication with Great Britain, Ruritania might attempt to require that Ruritanian ISPs refuse to accept messages from computers whose domain name identifies them as British. British domain names frequently end with ".uk," and Ruritanian routers might be required to return all messages from those domains. Even if technically feasible, such a strategy is unlikely to succeed. First, there are generic domain names such as ".com," ".org," and ".net" that do not identify the country of origin. Second, unless Ruritania has currency and other controls, there is nothing to stop a Ruritanian user from establishing an account in the U.S. and telnetting to it to access British data. (Even currency controls may not prevent users from establishing foreign Internet accounts since some accounts, on so-called "freenets," are free to the public.) Third, short of a robust international convention, there is no way that Ruritania can prevent people outside Britain from running remailers that "launder" messages from Britain and present Ruritanian computers with acceptable domain names. In short, any effort to censor the Internet organized at the national level (or below) is likely to fail.[32] As John Gilmore put it, "the Net interprets censorship as damage and routes around it."[33] Of course, nothing prevents individual users or system operators from blocking the direct receipt of messages from unwanted sources. Users, however, will not find it difficult to circumvent these restrictions for e-mail, although it might be technically feasible to eliminate anonymous postings from Usenet, a distributed bulletin board system, as long as the number of remailers remains small.[34]

Regulatory Arbitrage . . . and Its Limits

The Internet is a multinational phenomenon. Indeed, as long as they share a common language and a reasonably rapid connection, users of the Internet will frequently be indifferent to the physical location of those with whom they communicate. Location matters little for speech; it may matter more for commerce when parties to a transaction are concerned about redress for a transaction that goes badly. To the extent that transactions are immediate (e.g., exchanges of information) or that suitable reputations, performance bonds, or other third-party guarantees enable longer-term relationships,[35] the multinational nature of the Internet makes it possible for users to engage in *regulatory arbitrage*—to choose to evade disliked domestic regulations by communicating/transacting under regulatory regimes with different rules. Sometimes this will mean gravitating to jurisdictions with more lenient rules, or perhaps no rules at all; sometimes it will mean choosing more stringent foreign regimes (e.g., those with strong consumer protection laws) when stricter rules are more congenial.

Censorship Suffers

Simple communication—free speech—is the strongest example of regulatory arbitrage. Other countries that lack a First Amendment may choose solutions to the perceived dangers of anonymous communication that are more or less restrictive than those suggested by U.S. law, which itself remains unclear in important respects. Remarkably, however, the technology for sending e-mail messages anonymously is already in use both here and abroad; the whole world can now enjoy (or suffer) the fruits of anonymous remailers located anywhere. The constitutional status of anonymous electronic speech remains important: if the U.S. will not or constitutionally cannot ban anonymous remailers, then the U.S.'s Internet connectivity ensures that they will be available for the entire Internet to use. Even if the U.S. attempts to ban anonymous remailers, and even if the Constitution is interpreted as allowing this, U.S. law may not be determinative because, as it now stands, the Internet as a whole is not easily amenable to any nation's control. While it is probably within the physical power of the U.S. government to prosecute Internet remailers based in U.S. territory, it is difficult to see how in practice the government could prevent U.S. residents from using remailers located abroad, although it could certainly raise the costs of getting caught.[36]

U.S. law currently imposes few if any legal restrictions on anonymous remailing. U.S. rules can thus be viewed as a baseline; any country with a more restrictive approach to anonymity can expect to see it undermined by U.S. rules unless it is willing and able to cut itself off from the Internet entirely. Similarly, should the U.S.'s rules change to restrict anonymity, as they might some day, these new rules will themselves be undermined by persons in any another country with more than minimal Internet connectivity and a legal regime more congenial to anonymous communication. (For example, the Canadian Copyright Act guarantees the right of an author to write under a pseudonym.[37]) The proponents of measures to regulate Internet speech and eliminate Internet anonymity are thus likely to find themselves in the position of the counselors to King Canute. Indeed, to the extent that countries with good Internet connectivity such as the Netherlands and Finland already have more permissive rules, those rules effectively undercut the U.S.'s ability to enforce what rules it has.

Once it allows its citizens to connect freely to the Internet, the ability of a government to control the flow of information in a meaningful way is greatly reduced. Anyone with access to e-mail, USENET, or the World Wide Web can receive electronic samizdats at will; anyone with access to e-mail or an anonymous Web page can send out information in a manner that is almost impossible to track. Nevertheless, as long as the Internet remains an elite medium rather than a mass medium, government controls on mass communication will retain some effectiveness.

Asian Examples of the Practical Limits to Censorship

The difficulty that governments have in reigning in free speech on the Internet or in living with its consequences is particularly visible in the uneasy relationship that several Asian governments have with the Internet. Only North Korea and Myanmar have chosen to remain completely aloof from it.[38] The Vietnamese government overcame its concerns about free movement of information and allowed a small academic and scientific network, NetNam, to operate because the government saw the Internet as the "fastest, cheapest way" to improve communications with the rest of the world.[39] The Vietnamese government then apparently had second thoughts about unregulated communications and decided to set up its own system using hardware purchased from a U.S. telecommunications company, Sprint. The new system, which is likely to displace NetNam, will have a greater capacity, but Nghiem Xuan Tinh, deputy director of Vietnam Data Communications Company, itself a subsidiary of Vietnam Post and Telecommunication, has stated that the government hopes that it will be controlled more tightly than "for technical and security reasons [and] from the cultural aspect."[40] The government intends to keep out foreign pornography and other harmful information sent by "foreign organizations."[41] Indeed, anti-communist emigrés based in California have already tried to overwhelm the Vietnamese Prime Minister's e-mail inbox.[42] A government spokesman admitted, however, that the government was uncertain as to how it would achieve its goals, but he promised that the government intended to "think about it."[43]

In Singapore, the government has promised penalties for anyone caught transmitting pornographic or seditious matter.[44] It has also ensured that its point of view will be represented in a Usenet discussion group, soc.culture.singapore, frequented by its critics. Government spokespersons routinely post messages giving the official view of issues.[45] Overall, however, the government has chosen to control Internet access since, despite its best efforts, it cannot figure out how to control content:

The Singapore government knows that it cannot do much to censor the Internet. But it refuses to give up without a fight.

The main control is to limit access—the rationale being that only the determined would get at the materials and not the casual users. ...

Singapore's case is instructive in that it is trying to both control information and yet benefit from the Information Age. Current thinking suggests that it is difficult, if not impossible, to achieve both aims. Nevertheless, Singapore is trying.[46]

As part of its campaign against Internet pornography, the Singaporean government searched the files of users of Technet, one of Singapore's major Internet providers. A scan of 80,000 graphics files identified by the extension ".gif" in the file name found five pornographic files, resulting in warnings to their owners.[47] Foreign companies with offices in Singapore became concerned that the Singaporean government would feel free to search their data in the hopes of finding confidential corporate e-mails, and the government had to promise them that it would not conduct such a wide-ranging search again.[48] Meanwhile, one Internet provider in Singapore has promised to block access to "illegal" Web sites.[49]

Other Asian nations have expressed similar concerns about the Internet. The Malaysian government, for example, is studying regulations to penalize those making disparaging remarks about the country on Web pages or in USENET discussion groups.[50]

The People's Republic of China is a special case because although it is industrializing rapidly and its government appears to be committed to increasing Internet access, the government also appears to be intent on retaining the highest possible degree of state control.[51] Although Internet usage is growing quickly on both campus and commercial servers, albeit from a low base, the Chinese government is seeking to limit Internet access by keeping the costs of local service artificially high while it formulates a long-term policy.[52] China's post and telecommunications minister, Wu Juchuan, recently announced that "as a sovereign state China will exercise control" over information. "By linking with the internet, we do not mean the absolute freedom of information."[53]

A sufficiently determined totalitarian government might be able to achieve considerable control over its citizens' use of the Internet by some combination of strict access control, a ban on unlicensed cryptography, random monitoring of stored data and communications, and draconian punishment for sending or receiving unapproved materials. In time, it might also be possible to create tiered access to foreign materials. Behind this hypothetical Great Firewall of China, most users would be allowed to exchange information with foreign sites if they were on the approved list; controls on domestic information exchange might also be possible, although they might be prohibitively expensive unless the default rule were to be no communication at all. Even a firewall aimed only at controlling the content of international communications would require a very significant investment in filtering software and in manpower to keep the approved site list up-to-date, although it might be able to use simple content analysis to filter out some probably troublesome data (e.g., specific banned words or phrases). A content firewall would reduce the economic value of the Internet considerably. Furthermore, since it is impossible to filter only objectionable material, the system will either filter too little or too much. The tighter the filter, the greater the opportunity cost in lost ability to access the rest off the world's data. Nevertheless, a very aggressive firewall combined with the *in terrorem* effects of some well-publicized punishment of violators might at least allow the government to discourage a large fraction of unsanctioned international information exchanges.

In order for such a strategy to have any hope of success, however, the government must be prepared to resist domestic pressure, pressure from abroad, and especially pressure from foreign firms with local offices that, like those established in Singapore, are likely to protest loudly at having their data and communications monitored. The Chinese government's reassertion early in 1996 of the state news agency's monopoly over the transmission into China of all news and business information[54] is only the latest incident suggesting that the Chinese government may be uniquely willing to stand up to such pressure.

A Canadian Example: the Karla Homolka Case

A lurid example of the difficulty of censorship comes from the failure of the Canadian government to control coverage of the criminal trials of Karla Homolka and Paul Bernado. Canadian law imposes a strict blackout on news coverage of criminal trials so that news coverage will not influence criminal juries, which are not sequestered.[55] On July 5, 1993, a Canadian judge entered an order banning publication of anything relating to the sensational sex-murder trial of Karla Homolka in order to avoid prejudice to the forthcoming trial of her accused former husband and accomplice, Paul Bernado.[56]

Within days, Canadians had formed a Usenet group, alt.fan.karla-homolka, which began to carry foreign press accounts of the trial and the cases. Some Canadian universities sought to comply with the court order by deleting the newsgroup from their servers. This may have protected the universities from charges that they were complicit in evading the ban, but it was a futile gesture from the point of view of blocking access to alt.fan.karla-homolka since Canadians, including those connected to Internet-enabled computers at those same universities, could read the same Usenet group by connecting to foreign computers. The Usenet group was soon supplemented by a mailing list, Teale Tales, that e-mailed the details of the trials to Canadians chafing under a blackout that successfully covered newspapers, broadcast media, and cable television.[57] The list, which apparently was run by one or more Canadians, originally used the pseudonymous remailer at anon.penet.fi; at its peak Teale Tales accounted for 90% of the traffic passing through that remailer.[58] When the volume threatened to overwhelm the Finnish remailer, the list moved to a computer in the United States. Although the Canadian government prosecuted persons who broke the publication ban by photocopying and distributing paper copies of foreign articles and videotapes of U.S. news programs,[59] it does not appear to have prosecuted anyone involved in electronic distribution.

Costs and Limits of Uncontrolled Speech

The inability to enforce a ban on anonymous Internet communication will impose real costs in untraceable libel, hate speech, and (perhaps) theft of intellectual property.[60] Despite these considerable costs, at a global level the net effect of untamable anonymous speech is likely to be positive: as we have seen, anonymous communication spells the end of restrictive national policies regarding information. Any government that allows its citizens to become a part of the global electronic network will be forced to live with a freedom of speech even greater than that contemplated by the authors of the First Amendment. The Singaporean example suggests that the ability of any but the most authoritarian government to restrict access to the global information network is limited because businesses value unrestricted access. No democracies, and indeed few other nations, are likely to be as determined and technically adept as Singapore.

Even so, governments are not yet powerless. Governments have it within their power to impose some costs, at least in ease of use, on those who wish to communicate anonymously. However, a country that wishes to ban electronic mail to or from foreign anonymous remailers will find violations hard to detect unless it expends great resources on monitoring all national traffic. Even if monitoring is tried, the monitors will find it difficult to distinguish between ordinary mail and mail to anonymous remailers unless the government either bans encryption or maintains a very up-to-date list of foreign remailers. Indeed, many nations are trying to control the use of cryptography. Such efforts, if successful, make it much more difficult for citizens to communicate anonymously. For example, both France[61] and Russia[62] have relatively comprehensive controls on the use of cryptography—at least on paper. There is as yet little evidence that these laws have had much impact on behavior. A ban on cryptography can in any event be circumvented—at some cost to ease of use—by employing steganography, which is "the art and science of communicating in a way which hides the existence of the communication." Using steganography Alice might hide her messages to Bob inside a an innocuous photograph, encoded in a way that an observer could not even detect that there was a secret message present.[63]

Once a nation's citizenry generates too much traffic to monitor in any systematic way, the prime effect of a single government's attempt to ban anonymous messages will be to make anonymous communication much less easy to use for those concerned about getting caught. Loss of ease of use is a significant factor because the harder a computer technique is to use, the fewer people will use it.

Furthermore, the more difficult a computer technique, the more frequently users will make sloppy mistakes that could lead to their being detected. The leading study of "how cryptographic systems fail in practice" concluded that "many products are so complex and tricky to use that they are rarely used properly. As a result, most security failures are due to implementation and management errors."[64] Criminalization drives use at least partly underground, much like the attempt to control drugs has no doubt reduced but in no way eliminated the use of marijuana and narcotics in the U.S. and other countries.[65] Users of illicit cryptography may be unable to find quality technical support that would help them avoid sloppy mistakes, further increasing the chance of detection.

Despite these real constraints, widespread access to anonymous communication, even if the communication carries some risk, means that citizens armed with computers will be able to criticize their government—and denounce their neighbors—with less fear of retribution than ever before and will have increased access to messages from around the world giving alternative points of view. Meanwhile, at this writing there is little or no risk involved in using a chain of anonymous remailers, and only a little technical skill is required.

As a result, rules seeking to control the export of information such as the International Traffic in Arms Regulations (ITAR) will become ever more difficult to enforce.[66] Again, the Karla Homolka case is instructive. The remailers running the Teale Tales mailing lists were located outside Canada; the case thus demonstrates the difficulty the Internet presents for those charged with keeping information from pouring into a country. But the Homolka saga also demonstrates how hard it is to keep information from escaping across borders: the stories carried on the Teale Tales list and on alt.fan.karla-homolka originated inside Canada. Some were exported by foreign journalists who published in their home newspapers; some were exported directly by Canadians themselves taking advantage of pseudonymous or anonymous remailers.

In the absence of strong international cooperation, the existence of anonymous remailers means that rules seeking to limit the importation of "subversive" or "obscene" speech become impossible to enforce consistently while the recipient country remains connected to the Internet. Like it or not, we live in an age of completely free speech—of one limited and anonymous type—for everyone with access to a computer connected to the Internet.

Increased Transactional Freedom

A border that is porous to "subversive" speech is also open to transactions in which no physical goods are exchanged. Widespread connection to the Internet is thus likely to increase the citizen's ability to opt out of regulatory regimes in certain limited types of commerce. Already, we see transborder gambling and the sale of digital pornography; in time one can reasonably expect to see some transborder trade in other types of information and value-added information services, such as software, editing, and perhaps even securities and other financial transactions. These transactions may be structured to evade taxes or regulations imposed by the jurisdiction in which the customer resides; without cooperation between the two governments involved, however, there may be relatively little that the government whose rules are being flouted can do about what will, in most cases, be victimless crimes without a complaining witness.

Many states have laws against gambling generally or against private gambling; gambling debts are often not enforceable in court. A number of offshore services now advertise their willingness to take bets via the Internet with payment by credit card or electronic cash.[67] Whether the bettor commits an offense by placing a bet abroad is a question of the law of her home state. As a practical matter, it seems unlikely that the government of the bettor's jurisdiction will be able to learn of the offense without either intercepting the communication, unraveling the payment mechanism, or securing the cooperation of the authorities in the bookie's jurisdiction. If the bookie is established in a jurisdiction where private betting is legal and that jurisdiction requires dual criminality, this cooperation is unlikely to be forthcoming.[68] Indeed, if the bookie fails to pay, the debt is likely to be enforceable in his jurisdiction. Similarly, images deemed obscene in one jurisdiction may be legal elsewhere. Since the information can be encrypted, there is little to prevent international traffic in Internet pornography, which in fact already exists.

Although the traditionally illicit businesses have been the pioneers, it seems likely that in the not too distant future other kinds of transborder information transactions will be conducted electronically. Once an electronic cash infrastructure is in place, there will be few practical obstacles to e-cash being used to trade securities, although consumers might have legitimate fears about their ability to secure redress cost-effectively against a foreign-based broker. Where, however, a jurisdiction has regulations that significantly impede the transactional freedom of its citizens or that impose sufficiently large costs on those transactions as to make offshore brokerages appear worth the added risk, one can expect to see significant regulatory arbitrage between securities markets. Alternately, some customers may choose to trade in jurisdictions that offer them more protection against their brokers than is available at home. Whether this form of regulatory arbitrage will result in a "race to the bottom" toward unregulated markets or a "struggle to the top" to more regulated and perhaps more secure markets is impossible to say;[69] the key points are that there will be greater competition between markets and that this competition will impose constraints on the regulations that governments can introduce without securities trading flowing overseas.

Mobility of Personal Data

The international nature of data flows limits the ability of any single nation to enforce its data protection laws.[70] (Whether data protection laws are effective in providing long-term protection of the privacy of personal information is in any case uncertain.[71]) As a result, the European Commission now allows transborder data flows only if the recipient country offers "an adequate level of data protection."[72] However, even a highly organized international effort to control data flows could be undermined by a *data haven*—the information equivalent to a tax haven—a single nation that offers to warehouse data.

The existence of a data haven would undermine data protection laws in several ways. It could be used to store information about individuals that was illegal to store elsewhere. The owners, or the clients, could engage in massive "data mining" to cross-index that information.[73] It could either market the data to companies unable to compile the data themselves, or firms located in the data haven could provide services—for example, direct marketing, detailed asset information, or consumer profiles—that companies located elsewhere are forbidden to acquire or provide. The new European directive on transborder data flows recognizes the international nature of the data protection issue,[74] but even Europewide regulation is insufficient. European law forbids the export of personal data to states that do not provide adequate privacy protection. Personal data, however, are notoriously leaky. Furthermore, once information leaks or is quietly sold to a firm located in a data haven, it may be difficult to trace the leak to its source, and it is likely to be impossible to take action against firms located in the haven. Europe, at least, is making an effort to confront the international aspects of the issue; U.S. law remains mired in the single state paradigm.

It is difficult to see, however, how even a multilateral convention would solve the problem of data leakage unless the convention required participants to subject non-complying states—states that would presumably refuse to join the convention—to very strict penalties. Arguably, nothing less than a world willing to impose severe sanctions on nonparticipants, such as cutting off all telecommunications to them, might suffice, and it is difficult to imagine that a strong enough consensus will emerge to impose such sanctions.

No End to Taxes

Although the implications of anonymous transactions for taxes, product liability, and copyright remain to be worked out, it seems likely that the effects of anonymity will be unevenly distributed. Despite dire warnings to the contrary from some tax authorities, I do not believe that the tax system will be deeply affected by anonymous communication or even anonymous electronic cash since most production and even more consumption involves transactions that are easily monitored for tax compliance. Few of the electronic cash systems offered today include sufficient anonymity to allow tax evasion. Current digital cash systems that rely entirely on software are either not anonymous at all or anonymous only for the payor because the issuing bank always knows the identity of the recipient of the currency. Some electronic cash systems currently being tested use hardware tokens (e.g., smart cards) and are theoretically capable of anonymous peer-to-peer fund transfers. There is, however, no evidence that the owners of these systems intend to enable that capability.[75]

For salaried workers, income tax noncompliance requires payors as well as payees to participate in circumventing reporting requirements. Widespread deduction and reporting of tax at source makes this unlikely. My salary, for example, is paid by an institution that has no incentive to make it easy for me to engage in tax avoidance. True, the prevalence of salaried workers may be lessening; the U.S. economy is said to be shifting toward smaller-sized businesses. But as the numbers of owner-operated businesses and independent contractors increase, the potential for tax fraud grows whether payments are electronic or not. Although some knowledge workers may be able to demand that payment be routed to accounts held at untaxed offshore addresses, thus causing an effect at the margin, I predict such schemes will remain marginal for the foreseeable future.

Furthermore, any transaction that encounters the banking system—for example, short-term deposits—will be easily traceable for tax purposes as long as the bank is located in a jurisdiction that enlists banks as enforcers of its (and perhaps its treaty partners') tax rules. Few nations offer strong banking secrecy today, and the international effort to curb money laundering has reduced their number;[76] some nations that continue to offer strong banking secrecy may lack the political stability necessary to lure risk-averse investors. Conceivably, the tax system might begin to feel the effects if a reputable bank in a country with a stable currency and a trustworthy regulatory system were to offer anonymous electronic cash accounts on terms attractive to ordinary consumers. In that event, other countries would still be able to mitigate the effects by switching to a Value Added Tax (VAT) system since tax cheating under a VAT system would require the participation of more people in the chain of production. Furthermore, the same technology that would enable tax cheating would vastly enhance the capability of tax collectors to amass transactional data about citizens; if the state is willing to collect this data aggressively, tax cheating may actually become more difficult, not more common.[77]

Little Effect on the "Police Power" over Tangible Goods

Finally, it almost goes without saying that most regulation of tangible goods (known in the U.S. as "police power") will remain unaffected by the Internet. Food and drug regulation does not change because research chemists have new ways of communicating. Traffic laws, pension laws, tort law, indeed vast tracts of the legal and social landscape, will no doubt change in the future—but not because of the Internet.

Only if the Internet were to change migration patterns would the Internet significantly alter traditional regulations. Workplace safety rules need not change to lose their effectiveness if the workplace moves. It may be that certain types of knowledge workers based in low-wage areas will be able to increase the market for their services. Mathematicians and programmers have already begun to exploit this opportunity;[78] perhaps editors and artists will be next. As the Internet becomes the leading means to rapidly disseminate scientific, technical, and even social information, people in less developed countries who find themselves isolated in provincial areas or are concerned about keeping abreast of developments in their field may conclude that they no longer have to move to more developed countries and regions to do cutting-edge work or to participate in scholarly exchanges. Consider, for example, the sense of isolation reported by theoretical physicist Abdus Salam upon his return to Pakistan after years in Cambridge and Princeton's Institute for Advanced Studies.[79] An Internet connection does not provide the ambiance of Cambridge or Princeton, but it would lessen the isolation. The increased ability of some persons in traditionally low-wage areas to sell their services on the world market and participate in global dialogues may help stem the so-called "brain drain." Indeed, it may increase the phenomenon of "reverse brain drain" as some expatriates return to their country of origin, perhaps even joined by a new wave of expatriate knowledge workers seeking a lower cost of living.

The Internet as a Promoter of Liberal Democratic Values

For the foreseeable future, the net effect of the continuing internationalization of the Internet will probably be to promote liberal democratic values of openness and freedom and not to detract from modern states' legitimate regulatory powers. Indeed, there is empirical evidence that information interconnectivity is a "powerful predictor of democracy."[80]

The Internet thus continues, even accelerates, a trend that started with CNN. The world's eyes—those of its people as well as its governments—are increasingly acute, omnipresent, and rapidly focused. Globalized communications have already transformed the politics of several countries. For example, electronic mail is credited with contributing to the failure of the 1991 coup attempt in Moscow.[81] Fax communication and the presence of CNN's cameras limited the Chinese government's ability to suppress the Tiananmen Square protests of 1989.[82] The U.S. government's awareness of the presence of TV cameras has greatly shaped the tactics of every foreign military operation since Vietnam.[83]

In the medium term, the existence of anonymous remailers and jurisdictions willing to host them means that communicative anonymity is an inevitable consequence of allowing citizens access to the Internet. The Internet's ability to make everyone with access a secret publisher as well as a secret reader spells the end of censorship for any government that permits widespread access to the Net. As the recent posting of a banned issue of the Zambian *Post* in early 1996 suggests,[84] this phenomenon is already spreading to nations with limited Internet connections. And as the Singaporean example suggests, the costs of denying access will be intolerable to most governments. Access is not costless: regulatory arbitrage will make some regulation, such as the control of digital gambling and pornography, next to impossible and will likely complicate the regulation of information commerce generally. Nevertheless, the state's power to tax and the vast majority of its police power will remain largely unaffected.

Totalitarians will fare worst in this new world, as they will be forced to choose between, on the one hand, limiting access and paying a substantial price in economic growth[85] or, on the other hand, letting go of their control of information, a traditional tool of social control. Libertarians will not, however, find that their promised land naturally materializes, since the effects of regulatory arbitrage are concentrated and leave most of the traditional regulatory functions of the state untouched. Liberal democrats, however, should be pleased since the increase in international communication will promote the emergence of a global civil society[86] and enhance democratic values of openness and citizen participation while making censorship ever more costly to the national well-being of censors.

Not that all is necessary rosy: to know your neighbors is not necessarily to love them.

Notes

1. Thomas Bullfinch, *Bullfinch's Mythology*, ed. Richard Martin (New York: Harper Collins, 1991), p. 130; Edith Hamilton, *Mythology* (New York: New American Library, 1942), p. 231.

2. Information Sciences Institute, University of Southern California, "Internet Protocol" (Network Working Group, Request for Comments No. 791, September 1981), http://ds.internic.net/rfc/ rfc791.txt; Information Sciences Institute, University of Southern California, "Internet Protocol" (Network Working Group, Request for Comments No. 793, September 1981), http://ds.internic.net /rfc/rfc793.txt; Gary C. Kessler and Steven D. Shepard, A Primer On Internet and TCP/IP Tools (Network Working Group, Request for Comments No. 1739, December 1994), http://ds.internic.net/rfc/rfc1739.txt (describing major TCP/ IP-based applications); Vincent Cerf and R. Kahn, "A Protocol for Packet Network Interconnection," in *IEEE Trans Communications*, vCOM-22n5 (May 1974), p. 637.

3. David H. Crocker, "To Be 'On' the Internet" (Network Working Group, Request for Comments No. 1775, March 1995), http://ds.internic.net/rfc /rfc1775.txt.

4. Bruce Sterling, "Short History of the Internet" (February 1993), gopher: //gopher.isoc.org:70/00/Internet/history/short.history.of.internet.

5. Ibid.

6. IETF Secretariat et al., "The Tao of IETF 3" (Network Working Group, Request for Comments No. 1718, November 1994), http://ds.internic.net/rfc/rfc1718.txt [hereinafter IETF Tao].

7. Paul Mockapetris, POISED '95 BOF gopher://ds.internic.net/00/ietf/95apr /poised95-minutes-95apr.txt.

8. Internet Activities Board & Internet Engineering Steering Group, "Internet Standards Process," Revision 2 at 7 (Network Working Group, Request for Comments No. 1602, March 1994), http://ds.internic.net/rfc/rfc1602.txt [hereinafter RFC 1602].

9. David H. Crocker, "Making Standards the IETF Way," 1 *StandardView* 46, 51 (September 1993), http://info.isoc.org/papers/standards/crocker-on-standards.html.

10. Gary H. Anthes, "Summit Addresses Growth Security Issues for Internet," *Computerworld*, April 24, 1995, p. 67.

11. Bernard Aboba, "How the Internet Came to Be," in *The Online User's Encyclopedia*, gopher://gopher.isoc.org:70/00/internet/history/how.internet.came. to.be.

12. Network Wizards, "Internet Domain Survey," (January 1996), http://www.nw. com/zone/WWW/report.html.

13. Louise Kehoe, "Surge of Business Interest," *The Financial Times*, March 1, 1995, p. XVIII.

14. Donna L. Hoffman, William D. Kalsbeek and Thomas P. Novak, "Internet Use in the United States: 1995 Baseline Estimates and Preliminary Market Segments," http://www2000.ogsm.vanderbilt.edu/baseline/1995.Internet. estimates.html.

15. Nina Burns, "E-mail beyond the LAN," *PC Magazine* April 25, 1995, p. 102.

16. "World-Wide Web," in *The Free On-Line Dictionary of Computing*, http: //wombat.doc.ic.ac.uk/?World-Wide + Web.

17. Ibid.

18. Anthony-Michael Rutkowski, Executive Director Internet Society, "Bottom-Up Information Infrastructure and the Internet" (February 27, 1995), http: //www.isoc.org/speeches/upitt-foundersday.html.

19. "World-Wide Web," in *The Free On-Line Dictionary of Computing*.

20. I draw out the distinctions between these four types in my "Information Ocean" article. A. Michael Froomkin, "Flood Control on the Information Ocean: Living With Anonymity, Digital Cash, and Distributed Databases," *University of Pittsburgh Journal of Law and Commerce* 15, (forthcoming 1996).

21. This risk is reduced by the provision of a "remailer pinging service" that regularly checks to see if remailers are forwarding their mail. A list of remailers and their features as well as current information about their recent performance statistics is maintained by a volunteer and published at http://www.cs. berkeley.edu/~raph/remailer-list.html.

22. Anon.penet.fi, probably the best-known "anonymous" remailer, is not in fact an anonymous remailer. It is merely a very user-friendly traceable *pseudonymous* remailer because the anon.penet.fi system keeps a record of each user's e-mail address. The security of the approximately 8,000 messages that pass through

anon.penet.fi daily (see Douglas Lavin, "Finnish Internet Fan Runs Service Allowing Anonymous Transmissions," *Wall Street Journal*, July 17, 1995, p. A7) thus depends critically on the willingness of the operator, Johan Helsingius, a Finnish computer scientist, to refuse to disclose the contents of his index, which maps each anonymous ID to an e-mail address.

In February 1995, the Church of Scientology successfully enlisted the aid of the Finnish police, via Interpol, to demand the identity of a person who, the Church of Scientology claimed, had used anon.penet.fi to post the contents of a file allegedly stolen from a Scientology computer to a USENET group called alt.religion.scientology. Unprepared for the request, Helsingius surrendered the information, believing that the only alternative would have been to have the entire database seized by the police. See http://www.cybercom.net/~rnewman /scientology/home.html#PENET. Differing descriptions of the Scientologists' legal efforts can be found at The Church of Scientology vs. the Net, http://www. cybercom.net/~rnewman/scientology/home.html (critical view); UK Scientology Critics, http://mail.bris.ac.uk/~plmlp/scum.html (even more hostile); Church of Scientology International, http://www.theta.com/goodman/csi.htm (Scientologists' view).

23. Anonymizer FAQ, http://anonymizer.cs.cmu.edu:8080/faq.html.

24. Community Connextion, http://www.c2.org.

25. In a public-key system, each user creates a public key, which is published, and a private key, which is secret. Messages encrypted with one key can be decrypted only with the other key, and vice versa. Whitfield Diffie and Martin E. Hellman, "New Directions in Cryptography," IT-22 *IEEE Transactions Information Theory* (1976), p. 644, and Ralph C. Merkle, "Secure Communication over Insecure Channels," *Communications of the ACM,* April 1978, p. 294; Bruce Schneider, *Applied Cryptography* (New York: John Wiliey & Sons, 1994), p. 29; Whitfield Diffie, "The First Ten Years of Public-Key Cryptography," Proceedings of the IEEE 76 (1988), p. 560.

A strong public-key system is one in which possession of both the algorithm and one key gives no useful information about the other key. Anyone in the world can use the public key to send messages that only the private key owner can read; the private key can be used to send messages that could only have been sent by the key owner.

Thus, if Alice wants to send a secure e-mail message to Bob and they both use compatible public-key cryptographic software, Alice and Bob can exchange public keys on an insecure line. If Alice has Bob's public key and *knows that it is really Bob's* then Alice can use it to ensure that only Bob, and no one pretending to be Bob, can decode the message. A strong public-key system makes it possible to establish a secure line of communication with anyone who is capable of implementing the algorithm. (In practice, this is anyone with a compatible decryption program or other device.) Sender and receiver no longer need a secure way to agree on a shared key. If Alice wishes to communicate with Bob, a stranger with whom she has never communicated before, Alice and Bob can exchange the plaintext of their public keys. Then Alice and Bob can each encrypt their outgoing messages with the other's public key and decrypt their received messages with their own secret, private key. The security of the system evaporates if either party's private key is compromised, that is, transmitted to anyone else.

PGP stands for "pretty good privacy," a type of robust encryption, which when used with a long key is unbreakable in any reasonable period of time by currently known techniques. PGP is available online by FTP from many sites, including ftp://net-dist.mit.edu/pub/, ftp://ftp.ox.ac.uk/pub/crypto/pgp, or a German server: ftp://ftp.informatik.uni-hamburg.de:/pub/virus/crypt/pgp. For a good description of the technical and political workings of PGP, see Simson Garfinkel, *PGP: Pretty Good Privacy* (Sebastopol, CA: O'Reilly & Associates, 1995).

26. A. Michael Froomkin, "The Metaphor Is the Key: Cryptography, the Clipper Chip, and the Constitution," 143 *University of Pennsylvania Law Review* (1995), pp. 709, 747, http://www-swiss.ai.mit.edu/6095/articles/froomkin-metaphor/text.html.

27. Lance Cottrell's home page on Mixmaster: http://obscura.com/~loki/; Remailer-Essay, http://nately.ucsd.edu/~loki/remailer/remailer-essay.html.

28. Spam FAQ, or "Figuring out Fake E-Mail and Posts," http://digital.net/~gandalf/spamfaq.html.

29. Contrary to what some believe, ordinarily there is very little that an e-mail message can do to harm the recipient other than communicate information that the recipient might not desire to know. In any reasonably well-designed software, users do not become susceptible to computer viruses or "trojan horses" merely by reading an e-mail message. Some further action on the recipient's part is required, e.g., attempting to run a program that may have been attached to the e-mail message.

30. Paul A. Strassman and William Marlow, "Risk-Free Access into the Global Information Infrastructure via Anonymous Re-Mailers," http://www.strassman.com/pub/anon-remail.html.

31. Penthouse Magazine, "Not Available in These Countries," http://www.penthousemag.com/resource/nothere.html.

32. Thus Eugene Volokh's radical predictions about the demise of private speech regulation in the United States actually may be too timid because they do not take account of the international nature of the Internet. Eugene Volokh, "Cheap Speech and What It Will Do," *Yale Law Journal* (1995), pp. 1805, 1836.

33. "Redefining Community," *Information Week,* November 29, 1993, p. 28 (quoting Gilmore).

34. Ethan Katsh, "Rights, Camera, Action: Cyberspatial Settings and the First Amendment," *Yale Law Journal* 104 (1995), pp. 1681, 1695 n. 43; George P. Long, III, Comment, "Who Are You?: Identity and Anonymity in Cyberspace," *University of Pittsburgh Law Review* 55 (1994), pp. 1117, 1186–1187 (describing operation of "Automatic Retroactive Minimal Moderation").

35. A. Michael Froomkin, "The Importance of Trusted Third Parties in Electronic Commerce," 75 *Oregon Law Journal* 75 (forthcoming, 1996).

36. Katsch, "Rights, Camera, Action," p. 1695, n. 43.

37. Canadian Copyright Act §14.1.

38. Philip Shenon, "2-Edged Sword: Asian Regimes on the Internet," *New York Times*, May 29, 1995.

39. Ibid.

40. Jeremy Grant, "Vietnamese Move to Bring the Internet Under Control May Backfire," *Financial Times*, September 19, 1995.

41. Ibid.

42. Shenon, "2-Edged Sword."

43. Grant, "Vietnames Move to Bring the Internet Under Control May Backfire."

44. Shenon, "2-Edged Sword."

45. Philip Taubman, "Cyberspace in Singapore," *New York Times,* November 8, 1995.

46. Peng Hwa Ang and Berlinda Nadarajan, "Censorship and the Internet: A Singapore Perspective," http://info.isoc.org/HMP/PAPER/132/txt/paper.txt (the lead author is a professor at the School of Communication Studies, Nanyang Technological University) [hereinafter "Singapore Perspective"].

47. Ibid.

48. Shenon, "2-Edged Sword."

49. "Asianisation of the Internet Predicted," http://www.jaring.my/star/friday /22nett.html (article from Malaysia Star Online).

50. Posting from Dave Farber to "interesting-people mailing list" March 12, 1996.

51. Joseph Kahn et al., "Beijing Seeks to Build Version of the Internet that Can Be Censored," *Wall Street Journal,* January 31, 1996; Tony Walker, "Beijing Tightens Rules on Access to Internet," *Financial Times*, February 5, 1996.

52. Shenon, "2-Edged Sword."

53. Tony Walker and Shi Junbao, "China's Wave of Internet Surfers Sets Censors a Poser," *Financial Times,* June 24, 1995.

54. Tony Walker, "China Threatens Flow of Business Information," *Financial Times,* January 18, 1996.

55. Criminal Code of Canada §486(1)

56. [1993] O.J. NO. 2047, Action No. 125/93, [R. v. Bernardo].

57. Paul Bernardo Teale/Karla Homolka Frequently Asked Questions List (FAQ) Version 4.0, January 12, 1995, Part One, http://www2.magmacom.com /~djakob/censor/karlafaq.txt.

58. Ibid., p. 5.

59. Ibid., §2b.

60. Technical countermeasures, akin to salting each copy of the telephone book with unique false entries to pinpoint the source of any copies, may reduce attractiveness of unsanctioned copying of digitized information. In addition, customers may prefer to buy products from vendors they know and trust. For example, someone posted code on the Internet that produces output identical to RC4, a propriety encryption algorithm of RSA Data Security, Inc. A spokesman for the company stated that sales of RSA licensed products were not affected by this apparent leakage of intellectual property because customers wanted the confidence of dealing with a reputable supplier. Telephone interview with Kurt Stammberger, Director of Technologies Marketing, RSA Data Security, Inc., November 22, 1995.

61. The French rules derive from Law No. 90-1170 (*Journal Officiel*, December 20, 1990). "Crypto Law Survey," http://cwis.kub.nl/~frw/people/koops/lawsurvy. htm#fr; Ross Anderson, "Crypto Policy by Country," Appendix to *Crypto in Europe—Markets, Law and Policy*, ftp://ftp.cl.cam.ac.uk/users/ria14/queensland. ps.Z.

62. Stepoe and Hohnson, "Edict" (unofficial translation), http://www.us.net /~steptoe/edict.htm; Steptoe and Johnson, "Russian Statutes Restricting Use of Encryption Technologies," http://www.us.net/~steptoe/cyber.htm.

63. Markus Kuhn, "Steganography Mailing List," http://www.thur.de/ulf/stegano /announce.html.

64. Ross Anderson, "Why Cryptosystems Fail," *Communications of the ACM* 37 November 11, 1994, pp. 32–41, ftp://ftp.cl.cam.ac.uk/users/ria14/wcf.ps.Z.

65. Steven B. Duke and Albert C. Gross, *America's Longest War: Rethinking Our Tragic Crusade Against Drugs* (New York: Putnam, 1993).

66. The true purpose of the ITAR as applied to cryptographic devices and algorithms may be to restrict the emergence of a standard mass-market encryption product. In that case, anonymous communication will not greatly reduce the ITAR's effectiveness. Until anonymous digital cash is widespread, no commercial software publisher in the United States will risk violating the ITAR since there is no effective means for them to charge for their products and yet maintain the anonymity they would require to avoid any risk of prosecution. ITAR page, ftp://ftp.cygnus.com/pub/export/export.html.

67. http://www.box.eu.org/~dl/inc/play.shtml. A list of Internet-based gambling operations appears at http://businesstech.com/guest/howertable.html.

68. For a survey of judicial assistance treaties that waive the dual criminality requirement see James I. K. Knapp, "Mutual Legal Assistance Treaties as a Way to Pierce Bank Secrecy," *Case Western Reserve Journal of International Law* 20 (1988), p. 405.

69. Caroline Bradley, "The Market for Markets: Competition between Investment Exchanges," in John Fingleton ed. (assisted by Dirk Schoenmaker), *The Internationalisation of Capital Markets and the Regulatory Response* (London: Graham & Trotman, 1992), pp. 183–196.

70. Paul M. Schwartz, "European Data Protection Law and the Restrictions on International Data Flows," *Iowa Law Review* 80 (1995), pp. 471, 472 [hereinafter "European Data Protection Law"]; Paul M. Schwartz, "Privacy and Participation: Personal Information and Public Sector Regulation in the United States," *Iowa Law Review* 80 (1995), pp. 553, 612.

71. David H. Flaherty, *Protecting Privacy in Surveillance Societies: The Federal Republic of Germany, Sweden, France, Canada, and the United States* (Chapel Hill: University of North Carolina Press, 1989), pp. 406–407.

72. Common Position (EC) No/95 With a View to Adopting Directive 94//EC of the European Parliament and of the Council on the Protection of Individuals with regard to the Processing of Personal Data and on the Free Movement of Such Data, 1994, O.J. (C 93, April 13 1995), reprinted in Appendix, *Iowa Law Review* (1995), p. 697; "European Data Protection Law," pp. 480–488.

73. Froomkin, "Flood Control on the Information Ocean."

74. Directive 95/46/EC of the European Parlilament and of the Council of 24 October 1995 on the Protection of Individuals With Regard to the Processing of Personal Data and on the Free Movement of Such Data, 1995 O.J. (L281, November 23, 1995).

75. Froomkin, "Flood Control on the Information Ocean," p. 86.

76. Caroline A.A. Greene, Note, "International Securities Law Enforcement: Recent Advances in Assistance and Cooperation," *Vanderbilt Journal of Transnational Law* 27 (1994), p. 635; Dennis Campbell, *International Bank Secrecy* (London: Sweet & Maxwell, 1992).

77. Froomkin, "Flood Control on the Information Ocean," p. 86.

78. See, e.g., Don Clark, "China Challenges U.S. Export Law With Alliance in Code Technology," Wall Street Journal, February 8, 1996 (describing sale of programming and cryptological services by China).

79. Abdus Salam, "Cooperation for Development," in *UNESCO World Science Report* (1993), p. 167, quoted in Markus Schlegel, "Brain Drain With Regard to Africa," http://www.sas.upenn.edu/African_Studies/Articles_Gen/Brain_Drain.html.

80. Christopher Kedzie, "International Implications for Global Democratization," in Robert H. Anderson et al., *Universal Access to E-Mail: Feasibility and Societal Implications* (Santa Monica, CA: The RAND Corporation, 1995), http://www.rand.org/publications/MR/MR650/mr650.ch6/ch6.html.

81. David Lyon, *The Electronic Eye: The Rise of Surveillance Society* (Minneapolis: University of Minnesota Press, 1994), p. 87.

82. See Steven V. Roberts et al., "New Diplomacy by Fax Americana," *U.S. News & World Reports*, June 19, 1989, p. 32.

83. See, e.g., Matthew J. Jacobs, "Assessing the Constitutionality of Press Restrictions in the Persian Gulf War," *Stanford Law Review* 44 (1992), p. 675.

84. See "Zambia's Newspaper Censorship," http://www.cs.cmu.edu/~declan /zambia/news.html.

85. Kedzie, "International Implications for Global Democratization."

86. For some suggestions about this phenomenon see World Alliance for Citizen Participation, *Citizens: Strengthening Global Civil Society* (Washington, DC: CIVICUS, 1994).

© A. Michael Froomkin, 1996. All rights reserved. Portions of this paper are revised versions of A. Michael Froomkin, "Anonymity and Its Enmities," 1 *J. Online L.*, Article 4 (1995), http://www.law. cornell.edu/jol/froomkin.html, and of A. Michael Froomkin, "Flood Control on the Information Ocean: Living with Anonymity, Digital Cash, and Distributed Databases," 15 *University of Pittsburgh Journal of Law and Commerce* (forthcoming 1996). I am grateful to Caroline Bradley and Bernard Oxman for helpful comments.

Jurisdiction in Cyberspace:
The Role of Intermediaries

Henry H. Perritt, Jr.

Introduction

The Internet has firmly established itself as the model for the global information infrastructure (GII). Its open standards for exchanging information and its common address space are rapidly being accepted even by the most proprietary of electronic publishers, and by software and hardware designers.

Realization of the full potential of this model depends on law to protect against piracy and vandalism. Absent legal protections, safety from pirates and vandals depends on hiding behind technological fortresses. Ultimately, the existence of the rule of law instead of anarchy in cyberspace depends on the availability of conventional civil and criminal courts to resolve the most serious disputes. Promising possibilities exist for nonjudicial dispute resolution, including a new initiative for a Virtual Magistrate organized by the Cyberspace Law Institute, the National Center for Automated Information Research (NCAIR), the American Arbitration Association, the Villanova Center for Information Law and Policy and a number of online service providers. Nevertheless, some disputes can be resolved voluntarily only because of the possibility of judicial remedies, and some wrongdoers can be prevented from engaging in criminal activities only by the potential for successful criminal prosecution. So even as private dispute resolution systems emerge, their effectiveness may depend largely on the practical availability of more conventional courts as a last resort.

Civil and criminal courts derive their power from the willingness of the state to use its power to enforce judicial judgments. Sheriffs, marshals and, in rare cases, military forces execute civil judgments and decrees from courts but not orders unsupported by judicial authority. Law enforcement personnel collect fines and incarcerate convicted criminal defendants only when they are authorized to do so by judicial warrants and judgments of conviction from courts. Legal systems are circular in this respect. Judicial power is derived from the availability of governmental coercion, and governmental coercion is exercised only when backed up by the authority of the courts.

The close relationship between state power and judicial authority historically led to a localization of judicial authority. Judicial jurisdiction (the power of a court over persons, things and disputes) is geographically based. Courts in Maryland have power only over persons and things having some relationship with Maryland. Courts in Israel have jurisdiction only over persons and things having some relationship with Israel.

Cyberspace, of course, is not localized; it is international. The lack of congruence between cyberspace's global, transnational character and the national geographic limitations on the courts leads to some important challenges in civilizing cyberspace through law. For example, a Finn announced his intentions in 1995 to expand anonymous remailer services to enable persons to evade national laws restricting Internet content.[1] This is just the first of many efforts to create international havens for material considered indecent by some countries, for tax avoidance, for gambling that is illegal in some countries, for consumer-fraud scams and eventually, no doubt, for terrorist activities. The same techniques for creating havens in cyberspace can be used to avoid legal responsibility for intellectual property infringement, for defamation or for invasion of privacy.

Whose substantive legal rules apply to a defamatory message that is written by someone in Mexico, read by someone in Israel by means of an Internet server located in the United States, injuring the reputation of a Norwegian?

Whose courts have jurisdiction to adjudicate claims of injury or violation of national standards? Must the Norwegian go to Mexico or the United States to find a legal institution with power over one of the two potential sources of compensation? If not, if jurisdiction exists in Norway, the most convenient forum for the victim, how is a favorable decision by a Norwegian tribunal ordering the Mexican originator or the American intermediary to pay damages to be enforced?

Suppose the message is criminal instead of defamatory, involving child pornography or indecency, or representing some sort of financial fraud or forgery or terroristic threat. Can the wrongdoer be tried only where he is physically found? If the answer is yes, how should extradition or extralegal means of physically moving the alleged wrongdoer to the place of trial be utilized? Whose substantive criminal law should apply?

An inability to answer these questions satisfactorily increases the pressure to hold intermediaries liable, because unsatisfactory answers to the jurisdictional questions make legal recovery from content originators less likely. The Internet tradition of allowing anonymity makes the position of intermediaries even worse. If the victim cannot identify the originator because she is anonymous, immunizing an intermediary leaves a faultless victim bearing the loss.

This chapter[2] explores the jurisdiction of conventional courts, considering the degree to which they may have jurisdiction to adjudicate civil disputes and prosecute crimes arising in cyberspace. After developing an analytical framework for considering civil and criminal jurisdiction, the chapter proceeds to evaluate the position of two types of intermediaries: those facilitating access to potentially illegal materials, such as World Wide Web servers; and those that can perform dispute resolution functions. The second type of intermediary can be public in character, such as an international criminal court, or it can be private, such as an international arbitration panel. The second type of intermediary also can function largely through the Internet itself.

The argument developed here is not so much that private dispute resolution should be substituted for decisionmaking by public institutions such as courts and legislatures, but that decisionmaking by private tribunals organized to decide interests and rights disputes is better than ad hoc censorship by private institutions organized to deliver information and communications services.[3]

Jurisdiction

This part reviews the traditional sources of power for legal institutions and evaluates their suitability for new network environments. It emphasizes that it is not enough to identify a theoretical source of jurisdiction; a legal decision is meaningful only if it can be enforced against property or the person of the defendant.

The Four Overlapping Doctrines of Judicial Power

Four procedural doctrines interact in circumscribing the power of any court to decide a controversy according to particular substantive rules: personal jurisdiction; notice by arrest, service of process or otherwise; choice of law; and venue. A fifth doctrine, limiting enforcement of judgments, encompasses all of the other four.

Historically, venue rules not only determined where suit could be brought, subsuming personal jurisdiction analysis,[4] but also determined what law would be applied. Venue, in turn, depended on whether the cause of action was "local" or "transitory." Local causes of action had only one acceptable venue, while transitory causes of action might have had several. All crimes except piracy were local. Choice of law meanwhile was hardly an issue. It was assumed that any court would apply its own substantive law; choice of venue thus determined choice of law.[5] There was, under these early formulations, little difference between criminal and civil jurisdiction, or between either jurisdiction and venue. For both civil and criminal cases, courts exercised jurisdiction only over those physically before the court. Once a court had jurisdiction over the defendant, it applied its own substantive law.

One of the best examples of the original relationship among venue, personal jurisdiction and enforcement is found in *Livingston v. Jefferson,*[6] a trespass action against Thomas Jefferson. The alleged trespass occurred in New Orleans, and Jefferson was found in Virginia. The circuit court dismissed the action, finding that it was local and therefore could be brought only where the trespass occurred. Jefferson was not found in the judicial district encompassing New Orleans and therefore could not be sued there. In trespass actions, the title and bounds of land might come into question, and only a jury from the vicinage of the land could appropriately determine such facts.[7] Moreover, a judgment for the plaintiff would potentially necessitate execution by the sheriff and his posse to remove the trespasser if necessary. If execution could be had only in one place, then only the court of that place had the power to try the case.[8]

Transitory actions were different: venue existed wherever the defendant could be found. Contract was the archetypal transitory action, based on the legal and moral obligation of the person to perform his promises. Such actions thus were not tied to any particular place.[9] When enforcement required doing something with respect to a piece of property, only the local sheriff could do it. Conversely, when enforcement involved a person who might move around, enforcement could occur wherever the person was found, through imprisonment for debt, or simply through a *capias ad satisfaciendum*[10] or *capias ad respondendum.*[11]

Now, even though interests analysis is the centerpiece of personal-jurisdiction and choice-of-law analysis, the power dimension that dominated the reasoning in the *Jefferson* case, along with an assessment of efficiency and convenience, still is important in deciding where a lawsuit over electronic conduct should be litigated and where judgments resulting from such a lawsuit can be enforced practicably. As in *Livingston v. Jefferson,* the practice limits of judicial power are determined at least to some degree on the location of a human defendant or of identifiable (though not necessarily tangible) assets.

The GII may span geographic boundaries, but its human actors are present in some traditional jurisdiction, and the hardware, software and financial assets used to operate each part of the GII are located in some traditional jurisdiction. Lawsuits and criminal prosecution will be most efficacious in those jurisdictions. In some cases, they will be entirely ineffective anywhere else.

Jurisdiction over Persons and Organizations

Personal jurisdiction refers to the power of a court over the defendant, originally based on physical control or custody over the defendant. It has been relaxed in the civil contexts to allow power to be asserted over persons with certain connections with the forum state who are given formal notice through service of process, even if they are not physically present. In the criminal context, however, personal jurisdiction still signifies physical custody in virtually every case. Personal jurisdiction in cyberspace requires application of the minimum-contacts and fair-play-and-substantial-justice concepts of civil personal jurisdiction, initially articulated in the United States Supreme Court's *International Shoe* case.[12] Those concepts are proving themselves flexible enough to handle typical kinds of electronic relationships crossing political boundaries.

For example, in *Pres-Kap, Inc. v. System One, Direct Access, Inc.*[13] a split panel of the intermediate Florida court held that Florida courts lacked personal jurisdiction over a New York travel agent who contracted to use an airline reservations system with its main database located in Miami. The majority opinion expressed rhetorical concern over allowing the location of computer databases to support suit against those who use them from afar, but offered little real legal analysis. The dissent is more persuasive.[14]

Plus System, Inc. v. New England Network, Inc.,[15] is better reasoned. In that case, a Colorado-based ATM network sued its New England affiliate (in the Colorado courts) for refusing to implement a new royalty charge. In rejecting the challenge to personal jurisdiction, the district court found among other things that the defendant's regular use of the plaintiff's computer system located in Colorado was an availment of Colorado and its law. The defendant benefited from the services provided by the plaintiff's computer system, and it made no difference that the defendant's connection occurred indirectly through a service organization in Wisconsin.[16] There were, to be sure, other contacts, including a visit and tour of the Colorado computer facility by the defendant's personnel, a contractual choice of law clause that pointed to Colorado, and signature by the plaintiff, at least, of the contract in Colorado.[17]

The basic principles of personal jurisdiction applied in these two cases are extended to cases arising throughout the world. The large number of cases involving personal jurisdiction over print publications offer a reasonable conceptual guide to future cases presenting jurisdictional questions related to the World Wide Web and other electronic-publishing activities.

Under this case law, an electronic publisher should be subject to personal jurisdiction in any location to which the electronic publisher intentionally sends its publication. Thus, subscription-based commercial systems like CompuServe or America Online should be subject to personal jurisdiction in places where significant numbers of their subscribers reside. The residence of subscribers is known to these services,[18] they derive revenue from those subscriptions, and there is little reason to distinguish between the electronic subscriber and the print subscriber.

If an electronic publisher (including an individual posting a message to a public electronic space) publishes a statement intended to injure someone, the publisher should be subject to personal jurisdiction in the place where the injured party is located.[19] The rationale, in colloquial terms, is that the actor intended to "reach out and touch" not just "someone," but the specific victim. That constitutes purposeful legal contact with the place where the victim is.

There are many conceivable GII cases in which publication does not support the exercise of personal jurisdiction so strongly. For example, one might post a message to a list, which then disseminates it to all of its subscribers. But the poster usually has no knowledge of the extent of the list and thus the dissemination of his posting to a particular person is usually neither purposeful nor foreseeable, unless other facts indicate specific knowledge of a particular recipient of messages posted to that list. Absent such special facts, the exercise of personal jurisdiction over the sender of the message is not appropriate merely based on the dissemination of messages through the list.

An even weaker case for the assertion of personal jurisdiction arises from placement of material on servers connected to the Internet or Internet-like open architectures. In this instance, the act resulting in the receipt of the message in a particular place is the act not of the publisher, but of the retriever. Publication in these circumstances should not subject the publisher to personal jurisdiction in places where the information is retrieved, under the rationale of *Hansen v. Denckla*.[20] There is a counterargument, not yet accepted by a majority of the Supreme Court,[21] that placing something in the "stream of commerce" constitutes purposeful contact with all the jurisdictions through which that stream flows. According to this argument, the flow of inquiries to a Web server would be a stream of commerce. The sponsor of a Web server would be subject to personal jurisdiction in all those places from which he knows that requests come.

Personal jurisdiction in criminal cases

Jurisdiction over the person in criminal cases also involves "personal jurisdiction."[22] Personal jurisdiction in criminal cases universally is based on physical presence, usually obtained through arrest. Rule 43 of the *Federal Rules of Criminal Procedure* requires the defendant's presence at the trial.[23] Many countries, like the United States, guarantee defendants the right to be tried in their presence.[24] In addition, the International Covenant on Civil and Political Rights specifically prohibits trials in absentia.[25] Once the trial commences, however, the continued presence of the defendant is not always required.[26]

Accordingly, exercising jurisdiction over international computer crimes requires obtaining custody of the individual defendant. Custody can be obtained through the formal process of extradition, or by extra-legal means.[27]

Jurisdiction over things

Minimum contacts and fair play and substantial justice are not the only means of establishing jurisdiction in civil cases. Jurisdiction can be established not only over people and artificial legal persons such as corporations; it also may be established over things. In other words, the Constitution also permits *in rem* jurisdiction when a civil defendant has property located in the forum state and the dispute relates to the property.[28]

This is how Justice Kennedy began a dissent in a 1996 Supreme Court case:

The forfeiture of vessels pursuant to the admiralty and maritime law is a long, well-recognized tradition, evolving as it did from the necessity of finding some source of compensation for injuries done by a vessel whose responsible owners were often half a world away and beyond the practical reach of the law and its processes.[29]

This section considers whether there is a theory of jurisdiction for cyberspace that would replicate the same tradeoff as that represented by admiralty's *in rem* jurisdiction. The first question is to identify something analogous to the vessel; the second is to find a way of limiting liability while still affording meaningful compensation to the injured party—and a meaningful deterrent to the actor. In cyberspace, a digital packet is analogous to the pirate ship. The packet, like the ship, transports the harm to where the victim or her property is located. But if this is the right analogy, *in rem* forfeiture is less satisfactory for the victim in cyberspace than in maritime law. A pirate's or privateer's vessel was valuable in its own right. It could be converted from harmful uses to profitable ones. That is not the case with the packets sent by a wrongdoer in cyberspace. A particular packet has no intrinsic value.

It may be that the analogy between the packet and the ship is the wrong one, however. Maybe the most appropriate analogy is between the pirate and the packet, and between the ship and the instrumentalities that make it possible for the packet to reach its destination. The analogy may be attacked with the objection that the pirate controlled the ship subject to forfeiture, but the wrongdoer and originator of the packet does not control the instrumentalities used for its delivery.

But the very case in which Justice Kennedy dissented was one in which an innocent owner of the instrumentality of a crime (a dilapidated automobile) had her property interest in the automobile extinguished by its forfeiture. Indeed, Justice Kennedy, although disagreeing with the result, also observed about the admiralty practice:

The prospect of deriving prompt compensation from in rem forfeiture, and the impracticality of adjudicating the innocence of the owners or their good faith efforts in finding a diligent and trustworthy master, combined to eliminate the owner's lack of culpability as a defense.[30]

Thus maybe the difficulties of exercising jurisdiction over remote and perhaps unknown wrongdoers in cyberspace might be ameliorated by subjecting to forfeiture the technical instrumentalities that bring the wrongdoer's packets into the place where harm occurs. Under the admiralty principles, the innocence of the owner of the instrumentality would be no defense. The router, the communications line, the modem, the World Wide Web server and client participating in the digital transactions that connect the pirate with the victim all would be subject to *in rem* accountability.

There are at least two problems, however, with this approach. One is that the instrumentalities of wrongdoing in cyberspace, unlike the instrumentalities of piracy 300 years ago, usually perform other, legitimate functions as well, and at the same time that they facilitate the wrongdoing. Rare was the pirate ship or privateer that also engaged in legitimate commerce. Conversely, rare is the Internet router that does not handle many more legitimate and inoffensive packets than harmful packets. Forfeiting the pirate's or privateer's vessel stopped only the piracy or privateering; forfeiting the Internet router or communications channels stops all commerce through that mechanism.

Second, commerce in cyberspace involves mostly information; maritime commerce involved mostly goods. If innocent owners of instrumentalities in cyberspace are induced by the possibility of forfeiture to avoid risky undertakings, with risk being defined by the controversial character of the content, the harm to public discourse is potentially great. Moreover, in advance it is easier to know the difference between maritime piracy and trading than it is to know the difference between robust discussion and defamation or between entrepreneurial adaptation of old ideas and intellectual property infringement.

Accordingly, *in rem* jurisdiction directed against the physical instrumentalities of cyberspace will tend to chill controversial and unpopular communication, and in the process set up communications intermediaries as censors and adjudicators of decency and legitimacy in information.

Privatizing some governmental functions may be desirable, but privatizing adjudication and censorship is not desirable. The guarantees of procedural due process do not operate against private decisionmakers. If the vice admiralty judge condemns my vessel, the law assures adherence to fair procedure. If the owner of the router or the communications channels denies me access, I may be without remedy except that provided by competitive alternatives in the marketplace. This is not quite the right apposition, however. The same procedural due process protections against an *in rem* proceeding against the vessel are available in an *in rem* proceeding against the router. The same absence of due process protections against the owner of the router are absent if the owner of the vessel denies employment to a master or crew who appear interested in cruising the vessel for piracy.

Internet technologies decrease, rather than increase, the likelihood of traditional assets being located in the jurisdiction of the plaintiff. Even if an argument could be sustained that an Internet server used to disseminate the harmful information is vicariously "present" in the forum state, turning the property into money of value to a victorious plaintiff requires the practical exercise of dominion and control over something that cannot be sold, and vicarious presence is not sufficient. If the server is a Sparcstation located in Luxembourg, the plaintiff and judgment creditor will get money only if the Sparcstation can be sold, and that requires obtaining control over it in Luxembourg. Vicarious presence of that computer in Virginia because it is easily accessible from Virginia is not enough to permit it to be sold in Virginia, even though it might support personal jurisdiction of a Virginia court in a theoretical sense.

Nevertheless, at least one aspect of the *in rem* jurisdictional concept is relevant to cyberspace. Under the *quasi in rem* concept[31] a defendant whose contact with the jurisdiction takes the form of property present in the jurisdiction could be subjected to a judicial judgment only to the extent of the property. For example, someone having an automobile in the jurisdiction could be subjected to civil liability even as to matters not related to the automobile, but the legal effect of the judgment extended only to the property interest in the automobile and not more generally against the defendant personally. One could build on this conceptual foundation a jurisdictional theory for cyberspace that would subject cyberspace actors to civil jurisdiction wherever they have a virtual presence, but then limit the effect of any civil judgment to the extent of that virtual presence. One possible application of this concept would allow jurisdiction based on the presence within the jurisdiction of packets originating with a defendant, but would enforce any judgment only against those packets. That might mean executing against a collection of packets representing an economically valuable piece of intellectual property. Or, it might simply mean condemning the packets and disallowing any further packets originating with that defendant—a kind of virtual banishment or outlawry.[32]

It may be that the *in rem* jurisdiction model can be adapted differently, focusing not on the physical instrumentalities of cyberspace, but on new types of quasi property possessed by the wrongdoer himself. Maybe the wrongdoer has intangible interests in reputation, or executory interests in having his traffic handled that might be the subject of attachment in jurisdictions where he does harm. Regardless of how one reconciles *Shaffer v. Heitner* and *Burnham v. Superior Court*, such interests might be reachable by those legal institutions, either on an *in rem* theory directly (the problem would be that the harm may not arise directly out of those things) or on the grounds that they represent a purposeful availment of the benefits of the jurisdiction sufficient to support jurisdiction over the person of the wrongdoer. But jurisdiction is not enough. One also must be able to execute a judgment against something of value, or else the whole process is worthless.

The exercise of judicial power represented by forfeiture, however, was not unlimited.

The tradeoff, of course, was that the owner's absolute liability was limited to the amount of the vessel and/or its cargo.[33]

How does the wrongdoer's reputational interest represent value to the victim and judgment creditor unless it can be sold? How can the executory interest in having traffic handled be turned to the advantage of the victim? Unless satisfactory answers to these questions can be suggested, cyberspace faces an uncomfortable choice between denying relief to victims because meaningful jurisdiction cannot be exercised over wrongdoers, and proceeding against the property of innocent intermediaries, resulting in a kind of timidity on the part of intermediaries that will undermine some of cyberspace's vitality in free communication.

Jurisdiction to Prescribe: Choice of Law

A forum may have personal jurisdiction and venue and nevertheless be obligated by its choice of law rules—perhaps reinforced by the Constitution—to apply the substantive law of another jurisdiction. Choice of law, application of foreign criminal law and extra-territorial application of criminal law all are aspects of jurisdiction to prescribe.[34] Application of a nation's law to a dispute presupposes that the nation has jurisdiction to prescribe rules applicable to that dispute.

Choice of law rules have been worked out in private international law over several centuries. They are complex, but their essence can be summarized fairly simply.

The analysis for tort claims—such as a GII defamation claim—requires determining the state with the most significant relationship to the occurrence and the parties, including consideration of the place where the injury occurred, the place of the conduct causing the injury, the domicile, residence, nationality, place of incorporation and place of business of the parties, and the place where any relationship between the parties is centered.[35] Contracts cases are adjudicated according to the law chosen by the parties or, in the absence of any such chosen law, by the law of the state which has the most significant relationship to the transactions and the parties with respect to a particular issue.[36] The most significant relationship in contract cases is determined based on the place of contracting, the place of negotiation of the contract, the place of performance, the location of the subject matter of the contract, and the domicile, residence, nationality, place of incorporation and place of business of the parties.[37] "If the place of negotiating the contract and the place of performance are in the same state, the local law of this state will usually by applied."[38]

Constitutional due process requirements constrain choice of law to some extent, but Supreme Court jurisprudence on the relationship between due process and choice of law is in an uncertain state and thus not very influential.[39]

Consider a hypothetical situation in which an Internet server in California makes available material that users in Tennessee find offensive. In a lawsuit filed by the Tennessee users against the California server operator, say for intentional infliction of emotional distress, the choice of law question would be whether Tennessee or California law should apply. Assuming there is a difference between the substantive law of the intentional-infliction tort in the two states, Tennessee may have the most significant interests: it seeks to protect its residents against extreme emotional distress intentionally inflicted by others. California, of course, also has interests: ensuring that its citizens are free to publish material that would not under California standards be tortuous. But under the Supreme Court's tests, there would be sufficient Tennessee interest to allow the application of Tennessee law and the refusal of a Tennessee court to apply California law.[40]

In choice of law cases involving defamation, the law of the place where the injured plaintiff is domiciled probably will govern defamation actions arising in the GII. Invasion of privacy claims, like defamation claims, are centered where the plaintiff lives and conducts her affairs because that is where the privacy interest exists. The same is true of emotional distress claims. The same result is also appropriate for intellectual property infringement actions[41] unless the party arguing for the choice of different law can show that adversely affected markets are located somewhere else.[42] Intellectual property claims primarily involve injuries to markets, and where the markets are located should drive the interest analysis.

Choice of law does not function in the criminal arena the way it does in the civil arena. Strict localization of criminal law[43] leads to the usual conclusion that the courts of one jurisdiction may not apply the criminal laws of another. "A court in the United States may try a person only for violation of United States law, not for violation of the penal law of a foreign state."[44] Actually, however, criminal jurisdiction to prescribe is not strictly local.[45] The commentary to §422 of the Restatement (Third) of Foreign Relations notes that some civil law countries try persons whom they cannot extradite for crimes committed in other countries.[46] This constitutes a kind of "transitory" criminal action.

The concept of international crimes has been recognized for over 150 years.[47] Notwithstanding the dominant principle that criminal law is strictly national, there long have existed a few crimes that are characterized as international and thus punishable in any jurisdiction obtaining custody of the actor. Piracy was one such crime.[48] In this century, air piracy and certain other acts of terrorism have been added to the list, albeit by treaty as much as by the extension of customary international law. The move toward an international criminal court has focused attention on enumerating additional international crimes.

Enforcement of Judgments

The winner of a lawsuit enforces her civil judgment by executing against property owned by the judgment debtor. Enforcement of criminal judgments ordinarily requires obtaining custody of the defendant so he may be incarcerated, thus implicating the basic extradition concepts. In addition, some criminal judgments can be enforced by the forfeiture of property.

Turning a judgment into liquid assets becomes more difficult when the judgment comes from another state or another country. The analysis of jurisdictional doctrines in the preceding sections repeatedly emphasized that jurisdiction does little good if the decision cannot be enforced. A plaintiff may have obtained a judgment against an Internet service provider in an Alabama circuit court but may find assets worthy of executing against only in Virginia. Execution thus must be sought in a Virginia court based on the "foreign judgment" from Alabama. Or, an author in Sweden may obtain a judgment in a Swedish court for copyright infringement resulting from an act by the operator of an Internet server in Massachusetts. In order to obtain monetary relief, the victim must enforce the Swedish judgment against assets held by the server operator in Massachusetts.[49]

In both of these cases, the first step conceptually is to obtain recognition of the judgment. When the foreign judgment is from another American state, the full faith and credit clause of the United States Constitution obligates the enforcing state to recognize it. When the foreign judgment is from another country, either state statutory law, the Uniform Recognition of Foreign Judgments Act in about half the states,[50] or comity[51] prescribe the criteria for recognition. Both the uniform statute and comity require recognition unless the party opposing recognition can show violations of procedural due process, or lack of personal jurisdiction by the rendering court,[52] or in rare instances, the judgment violates public policy in the recognition state.[53]

The United States has found it difficult to negotiate judgment recognition treaties with other countries.[54]

Recognition of a foreign judgment does not end the matter. The "owner" of the judgment, usually referred to as the judgment creditor, must find assets subject to execution. Clearly hardware and computer programs are subject to execution. Obligations owing to the judgment debtor also are subject to execution through a process called "garnishment."

Writs of garnishment against local debtors of the judgment debtor, would be attractive and entirely practicable. It was explained above how action might be commenced against a foreign defendant by attaching property owned by the defendant within the forum state. Property subject to attachment includes debts.[55] Once a judgment has been obtained, the plaintiff can enforce the judgment against such property held by third parties as well. In the usual circumstance in which the only property within the jurisdiction is a series of obligations under a service contract, the value of executing against such property may still be worth something to the plaintiff. For example, if the plaintiff can establish the proposition that the obligation by an Internet service provider or router to handle messages or packets sent by the defendant and judgment debtor constitutes property subject to garnishment, the plaintiff effectively can shut off the defendant's access to the domestic market by executing against that obligation.

Intermediaries

The preceding part concerned itself with the scope of traditional legal institutions such as courts and legislatures to decide cyberspace disputes. This part shifts perspective and considers the role of two different types of cyberspace institutions: those intended to facilitate interaction in cyberspace, and newer adaptations of old ideas intended to resolve disputes in cyberspace.

Intermediary Roles in Different Architectures

The national information infrastructure (NII) of the future will be more diverse, more decentralized, more distributed, and less proprietary in important respects than today's converging but still separate telephone, broadcast, cable and computer database markets. In that infrastructure, intermediaries will play an even more important role than do interexchange networks in today's tele-

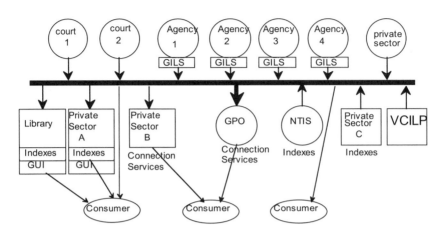

Figure 1 The Internet as a Market for Disaggregating Value Production.

phone system, local broadcast stations in today's network television, local cable franchises in today's cable television system, or
libraries, newsstands and bookstores in today's print distribution
chain.

Figure 1 shows how the Internet and similar architectures permit
value-added products to be unbundled when different elements of
the bundle are supplied by different entities, and the bundling
occurs according to the desires of a particular user at the time the
user wants the complete value-added information product. In this
architecture, suppliers of information content, shown in the figure
by the circles above the solid line,[56] supply their content to anyone
who wants it simply by putting files on computers connected to the
Internet called servers or content servers.

Value-added features are supplied by intermediaries, represented
in the figure by rectangles below the solid line. It is entirely possible
with Internet applications like the World Wide Web for an entity to
supply only index or table-of-contents-type value in the form of
pointers to content. The pointers are implemented through World
Wide Web pages on an Internet server that offers no other kinds of
value. Someone else can provide user-friendly interface software
through another server. Still someone else can provide connection
services that permit connections through dial-up telephone lines
or through higher-speed dedicated links.

When a user wishes to identify and obtain a particular type of content, the user interacts with several Internet servers operated by different entities. The user first establishes a connection to the Internet through a connection services provider, and then to an index provider. From the lists, tables and menus provided by that server, the user identifies one or more items of interest. The index server uploads the pointers (but not the content itself because the index server does not have the content) through the Internet to the user's client computer. Then the user's client computer executes the pointers which automatically causes the indicated content to be downloaded directly from the content server into the client computer.

This is a kind of assembly line for pieces of information value that allows the user to design the product on an ad hoc basis. It produces product just in time rather than producing it in bulk according to someone else's design on the chance that someone might want that particular bundle.

Such an infrastructure is not only two layered; in many cases a pointer points not directly to the full information resource, but to another collection of pointers, which may point to still other collections of pointers and so on, collectively marking a trail to the complete resource. The computer programs involved assemble a trail from the three pointers and then retrieve the desired content from wherever it resides and downloads it directly into the computer of the requester, without the content having to traverse all the intermediary computers. Whether an intermediary points directly or indirectly to the desired resource is inherently an engineering decision driven by performance considerations. In many cases, the decision to maintain copies of a particular information resource is made entirely automatically without any human intervention. A clear example of this is in the caching of recently retrieved resources within a World Wide Web browser such as Netscape.

The typical bulletin board/electronic publisher concept is illustrated in Figure 2. The server not only provides pointers and other finding and retrieval value, represented by the rectangles; it also publishes content, represented by the circle. The client has dealings only with the server, which looks like a conventional publisher.

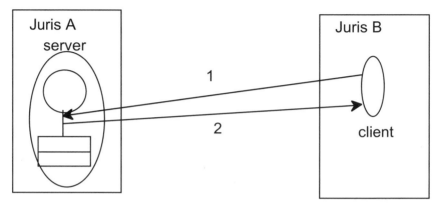

Figure 2

The typical Web server is in a different situation, as shown in Figure 3. Web server X never has possession of the content. It points to server Y, which in turn points to the content on the server of the content originator. Transactions 1 through 4 with servers X and Y are requests for and transmissions of pointers only. The eventual request for and retrieval of the content transpire entirely between the client and the content originator, in 5 and 6. Both types of intermediary—the older type of bulletin board in which the owner of the intermediary facility also controls the content, and the newer type of intermediary, exemplified by a World Wide Web server—potentially get drawn into controversies over harmful content. This may occur because the intermediary facilitates access to a file that infringes on someone else's copyright. It may happen because the intermediary facilitates access to a message posted on a newsgroup that defames someone else, or it may occur because the intermediary facilitates access to pornography.

The Web server that simply points to other content servers is rather like a person who gives directions to the dirty movie studio or the drug dealer. While the supplier of the pointers can be said to be involved in the distribution chain, the operator never comes in contact with the accused material. Certainly, in the copyright setting, this eliminates *prima facie* liability because the server has not engaged in any of the acts reserved exclusively to the copyright owner. However, there is the possibility of vicarious liability under other theories. One of the byproducts of jurisdictional uncertainty

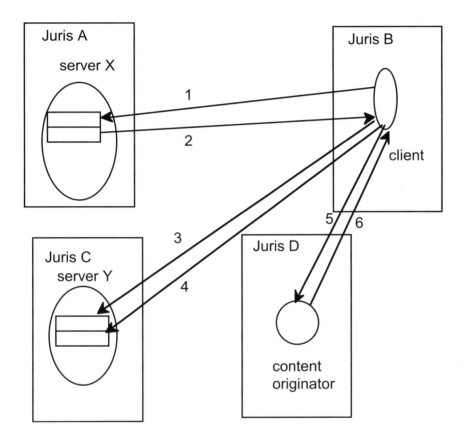

Figure 3

is that intermediaries become even more attractive targets than in the past for criminal prosecution and civil lawsuits. Intermediaries may be easier to identify than originators of harmful content. They may be perceived as having greater financial resources, making it easier to execute judgments against them or to use forfeiture as a criminal penalty. They may be more easily subjected to judicial jurisdiction because they have physical or virtual presence in many more places than content originators.

When intermediaries are subjected to liability they are put in the position of deciding the underlying dispute. An intermediary who responds to a threat of civil liability by refusing to handle controversial material is in effect engaging in a rulemaking function. An intermediary who responds to a particular claim that a particular file infringes a copyright by removing the file is engaging in an adjudicatory function and blocking dissemination of that file based on an accusation and whatever amount of investigation the intermediary thinks appropriate in the particular circumstances.

One could say, therefore, that the threat of liability pushes intermediaries who originally wanted to be only in the information and communications business into the dispute resolution business.

That may be a problem, because people who make good communications and information entrepreneurs may make poor dispute resolvers.

Private Rulemaking and Adjudication

The potential of cyberspace may be better realized if intermediaries and others move more systematically to arrange for dispute resolution in light of the limitations on the jurisdiction of traditional legal institutions and the unwillingness or unsuitability of information intermediaries as dispute resolvers. For example, communities of suppliers and consumers of information technology services can adopt their own rules for defamation, intellectual property infringement, misrepresentation and indecency, and apply these rules through arbitration machinery agreed to through the community.

Conduct would be judged according to norms developed by the users of the network. For example, it would not violate network community norms to post a sexually explicit message to a newsgroup or list which is defined by its participants as exchange for such messages. On the other hand, it would violate community norms to post such a message to another group defined as hosting communications among young children. It would not violate community norms to advertise in electronic spaces devoted to advertising, but it would violate norms to post advertisements to all newsgroups regardless of their nature.

Alleged violations of community norms would be adjudicated through a system of arbitration, probably implemented through spaces on the network itself. Complaints could be made, arbitrators selected, hearings held and arbitral decisions announced through electronic messages and file exchange. Sanctions could include monetary penalties or exclusion from network participation. Arbitration awards could be enforced worldwide under the *New York Convention* on the enforcement of international arbitration awards, or simply by excluding wrongdoers from the benefits of services available through the community.

Private institutional development, particularly arbitration, is appropriate for civil disputes. Public institutional development may be necessary for criminal matters. The following sections develop the arbitration and criminal institutional possibilities more fully.

Arbitration

The best means of reducing uncertainty with respect to personal jurisdiction, choice of law and venue in civil cases is international arbitration. Arbitration is a dispute resolution process in which a binding decision is made by one or more private individuals under an agreement entered into by the disputants.

The legal position of arbitration is enhanced by the willingness of regular courts to channel disputes to the arbitration forum when one of the parties tries to present them to another forum, and to enforce arbitration awards.[57] The first type of relationship between arbitration and the regular courts is frequently referred to as enforcement of the arbitration agreement or "compelling arbitration."[58] The criteria for compelling arbitration and for enforcing arbitration awards are similar because award enforcement is a subset of arbitration agreement enforcement; when one enters into an arbitration agreement, one agrees either expressly or implicitly to comply with the award.

Because the power of an arbitrator is contractual, parties are obligated to arbitrate, and to obey arbitration awards, only when the dispute is within the scope of a valid agreement.[59] Deciding whether a dispute is within a valid arbitration agreement presents the question of substantive arbitrability.[60] Ultimately regular courts decide questions of substantive arbitrability[61] although courts must defer to arbitral decisions on questions of substantive arbitrability when the agreement contemplates arbitrator decisions on those questions.[62]

If a dispute is substantively arbitrable, the parties to the arbitration agreement are obligated to use the arbitration process. Through their agreement they implicitly waive any legal power to present the dispute to a regular court instead of arbitration.[63] Once disputes have been arbitrated and the arbitrator has issued an award, that award is enforceable, either in a breach of contract action seeking specific performance of the arbitration agreement, or in a summary proceeding under an arbitration award enforcement statute.[64] As the footnotes to this section indicate, the basic legal framework for arbitration is the same regardless of whether the arbitration is purely domestic or whether it is international.[65]

Until recently, certain statutory claims were not arbitrable as a matter of public policy in the United States, but the Supreme Court has significantly relaxed this doctrine. Now it is reasonable to presume that almost any subject matter can be arbitrable, at least if the arbitration agreement clearly manifests an intent to make it arbitrable.[66]

Arbitration offers important advantages for cyberspace. Through private dispute resolution arrangements such as contractual arbitration, disputants can provide in advance a channel for submission and resolution of a defined class of disputes. One advantage is that arbitrators can be selected, and arbitration procedures and choice of law can be specified in the arbitration agreement to suit the nature of claims arising in the GII better than regular judicial procedure and generalist judges. A second advantage, given the transnational character of many GII transactions, is that the New York Arbitration Convention provides greater certainty as to the enforceability of international arbitration awards than is available with respect to the enforceability of the judgments of regular courts under the present treaty framework. Personal jurisdiction exists because signing a forum selection clause leading to arbitration waives objections both to personal jurisdiction and venue.[67]

Arbitration procedure is entirely a creature of the arbitration agreement. Thus, whether discovery is permitted, whether fact or notice pleading is to be utilized, and the applicability of different rules of evidence are all matters to be defined by the parties in their arbitration agreement. The parties can allocate costs, providing for prepayment of all or some of the cost by one or both parties. They can, to some degree, allocate decisionmaking responsibility between the private decisionmaker and an enforcing or reviewing court as to the scope (subject matter jurisdiction) of the private forum. They may incorporate by reference rules of procedure issued by various bodies sponsoring arbitration such as the American Arbitration Association, the International Chamber of Commerce, or the UN Commission on International Trade Law (UNCITRAL).[68] Choice of substantive law historically has been a bit trickier, although there is early authority for party autonomy in this regard: the notion that the party should be entirely free to choose the substantive law to be applied.[69] Indeed, there is a growing trend to allow arbitrators to refer to a general commercial law without the necessity of finding any roots in the issuances of national legal institutions. This is an endorsement of *lex mercatoria* in the arbitration context.[70] Arbitrators usually can be given authority to award a variety of remedies, including punitive damages.[71]

Private institutional arrangement can employ whatever modes of communication and recordkeeping the parties wish. For example, there is no legal impediment to writing an arbitration agreement providing that everything, including the hearing itself, be conducted remotely through computer networks.

Because private dispute resolution, as described in this chapter, is a contractual matter, a third party cannot be obligated to arbitrate under an agreement between two others. Nevertheless, this limitation may be more apparent than real in cyberspace. For one thing, the purported third party actually may be a party to contract terms specified in advance by service providers, much as the America Online terms of service constitute the contents of the contract between America Online and a subscriber. There is no reason that the same idea cannot work in a less commercial context, as when a World Wide Web server specifies "terms of service" on a Web page and makes it clear that a user of that page agrees to be bound by those terms of service. Such terms of service can provide for arbitration. While a consumer might seek to avoid the conclusion that she is a party to the contract on the grounds that she had no bargaining power or did not have actual knowledge of the announced terms, existing case law—both substantive contract law and forum selection law—disfavors such arguments. Moreover, even if a third party were not bound to submit a dispute to arbitration, the arbitration arrangement could include a mechanism for making the arbitration forum available on a voluntary basis to the third party. If the arbitration alternative were perceived as fair, cheap and quick, many third parties would resort to it instead of going to court.

A number of those interested in the healthy development of cyberspace have begun putting some of these ideas into practice. They have begun defining a class of intellectual property, personal privacy, consumer protection, defamation, intentional-infliction-of-emotional-distress and intentional-interference-with-contract disputes that would be within the scope of a "Virtual Magistrate" arbitration mechanism.[72] They have drafted a master, or model, arbitration agreement, defining how the procedure works, including all of those procedural elements identified above. Most of the procedural elements are accommodated through electronic networking.

The Villanova Center for Information Law and Policy is the electronic home for the Virtual Magistrate project, and the American Arbitration Association (AAA) is adapting its experience in administering specialized dispute resolution procedures for the project. The AAA has appointed an administrator who will use her offices to persuade uncertain disputants to participate in the mechanism. The results of the initial phase of the Virtual Magistrate project will be evaluated in the summer of 1996. Information about the project is available from http://www.law.vill.edu/vmag.

International Courts

In assessing the jurisdictional limitations of dispute resolution in international cyberspace, it is natural to wonder whether some kind of international court already exists or might be established to address such disputes. The possibility of a private judicial machinery through arbitration already has been considered. This section evaluates another alternative: public international courts.

The International Court of Justice is actually an arbitration body whose jurisdiction is limited to disputes between nations.[73] Some scholars have suggested initiatives to improve its institutional framework for dealing with a broader range of international legal disputes,[74] and at least one has suggested giving the International Court of Justice jurisdiction over international crimes and over state crimes where fugitives have crossed state borders.[75] Nevertheless, there is much more momentum behind a proposal for an international criminal court under United Nations auspices, and it is likely that the International Court of Justice will retain its present jurisdiction and procedure for the foreseeable future.

An International Criminal Court is being discussed under UN auspices.[76] The world could deal with criminal conduct in the GII by bringing certain types of electronic piracy and computer crimes within the jurisdiction of emerging international criminal law institutions such as this proposed court. In addition, problems of international search and seizure such as when the evidence pertinent to a crime in one country is contained on a network server located in another country, can be addressed by broader adoption of legal assistance treaties on the model suggested by the UN draft treaty.[77] Extradition treaties also need to be modernized to include computer crimes within enumerated extradictable offenses.[78]

For this to be a practicable solution, however, computer crimes must be perceived as sufficiently serious to warrant their inclusion in international documents and institutional jurisdictions heretofore focused primarily on war crimes and terrorism.[79] Certain computer crimes, such as terrorism by means of computer,[80] or crimes involving computerized financial transactions, might be an appropriate starting point.[81] Moreover, there is a need for further harmonization of substantive criminal law concepts pertaining to computer crimes, both to make transnational jurisdiction over computer crimes acceptable for new international bodies, and to satisfy the dual criminality requirements of both extradition and legal assistance treaties.

Since politics is important in determining which alternative will be selected, it is useful to assess the likely positions of different groups interested in the development of the global information infrastructure. Intermediaries, frequently known as system operators or "sysops," in the United States almost always prefer to minimize the legal control of their activities. It is likely that they would oppose any new initiative to develop new international or other machinery to enforce legal obligations against participants in cyberspace. While their real interests might be served by harmonizing and internationalizing the legal machinery, especially if it were done through private mechanisms, it may be difficult to get them to understand their own interests in this regard.

The proponents of new laws to restrict indecent material, such as Senator Exon, are likely to oppose the loss of sovereignty they perceive to be associated with international machinery and to focus their efforts on enacting new legislation and enlisting the national prosecutors at the local, state or—at most—national levels.

Indeed, the only group with significant political power likely to favor the establishment of new machinery is that of content originators interested in reducing the incidence of intellectual property infringement, who insisted on inclusion of the Trade Related Intellectual Property appendix in the Uruguay Round of GATT, and have already proposed stronger international machinery to enforce intellectual property rights. While they might support the idea of international institutions with broad jurisdiction, they are more likely to concentrate their efforts on specialized copyright enforcement machinery. Involving them in discussions over the proposed international criminal court would be a useful step.

Also, broader support for internationalization of computer crimes might be enlisted for initiatives involving financial computer crimes.

A Restatement for Cyberspace

Self-government in cyberspace depends on the existence of two primary legal functions of governments in cyberspace: adjudication and rule-making. The Virtual Magistrate project is a significant step toward establishing the adjudicatory mechanism in cyberspace, but for this system to realize its full potential, virtual magistrates must have an appropriate source of law to apply to the disputes before them. To some extent, of course, virtual magistrates can figure it out as they go and develop a kind of common law of cyberspace. But common law evolution is uncertain and from time to time common law decisionmakers come up with a solution that erodes support for their decisionmaking authority.

Legislative bodies help fill the gap; cyberspace needs a legislature. Because cyberspace is not a traditional sovereign, and because it lacks constitutional mechanisms for electing representatives, a real legislature is impracticable for the foreseeable future. But there are other kinds of bodies that develop statements of rules that can be applied by adjudicatory decisionmakers. Perhaps the clearest example in traditional law is the American Law Institute and its development of restatements of law. To some extent, these restatements are syntheses of common law decisions, but to a considerable extent they also break new ground and perform a kind of quasi legislative function (although not one backed by the authority of a traditional legislature).

While cyberspace lacks a legislative hall, it certainly does not lack a hall in which a more informal legislative assembly can be brought together.

Adjudicatory institutions such as a Virtual Magistrate or a new international criminal court may apply conventional legal rules, or they may develop their own common law over time. It also may be useful to codify "netiquette." Such trade custom enjoys considerable respect as a source of law for resolving many types of disputes in conventional legal systems. For example, negligence claims often are decided by reference to industry practice as a reference point for what a reasonable person in the defendant's position would have done. Invasion of privacy cases are decided in large part based on the reasonableness of plaintiff expectations of privacy, influenced by industry practice, and by whether the conduct of the defendant was offensive, often in light of what other similarly situated actors would do. Privileges in defamation cases are determined in part based on projections about the interests of other persons in the community of which the defendant is a part.

In cooperation with Counsel Connect, the author of this chapter has undertaken to develop an initial draft of a Restatement of Cyberspace. Beginning with certain areas in which new technologies present special problems in applying traditional doctrine, he is working with practicing lawyers and law professors to develop succinct statements of norms that can be published on the Internet more generally to provide an opportunity for public comment. While Restatements developed by the American Law Institute have, at least nominally, aimed at synthesizing actual court decisions, the new Restatement effort aims at synthesizing principles actually followed by those active in cyberspace.

Conclusion

Realizing the potential of the global information infrastructure requires new approaches to allocate responsibility for tortious or criminal conduct so that intermediaries do not face sanctions for activities they cannot prevent. At the same time, private and public international institutions must evolve so that the rules for allocating responsibility can be enforced effectively, even against harmful conduct that cannot be localized to any particular state.

The Virtual Magistrate project now in the early stages of implementation is a promising beginning to alleviate jurisdictional problems without thrusting unwilling intermediaries into the position of being judge, jury, prosecutor and potential future defendant. As the Virtual Magistrate project and similar private cooperative undertakings gain in credibility, they can become the principal channels for resolving disputes that otherwise might escape resolution.

Even some matters potentially considered criminal can be addressed within this arrangement. The Virtual Magistrate project has a "public prosecutor" who, in cooperation with the attorneys general of many states, is undertaking investigation and adjudication of conduct in cyberspace that harms the public.

More serious forms of crime and obdurate refusals to participate or cooperate with the Virtual Magistrate's remedial mechanisms may warrant some kind of residual jurisdiction by international criminal institutions. That possibility deserves attention as the plans for an international criminal court mature.

In the meantime, efforts to frame a Restatement for cyberspace can provide a stable, though evolving, set of norms to be applied not only by virtual magistrates but by conventional arbitrators and judges when confronted with disputes involving new technologies where traditional doctrines do not seem to fit.

Notes

1. "Finland Resists Control Efforts: As Regulators Seek to Police Internet, an Offbeat Finnish Service Fights Back," *Wall Street Journal,* July 17, 1995, 1995 WL-WSJ 8733699 (reports on claims by Johan Helsingius to run anonymous remailer service to help frustrate impeding U.S. regulation of indecent material; also reports Finnish police intention to enforce only Finnish law, not U. S. law).

2. The jurisdictional issues addressed in this chapter are explored more fully in Henry H. Perritt, Jr., *Law and the Information Superhighway,* ch. 12 and 13 (New York: John Wiley & Sons, 1996).

3. Both the Virtual Magistrate and Restatement for Cyberspace projects owe their existence in large part to the intellectual vitality and persistence of the author's friend, David R. Johnson.

4. Sir John Fortescue describes the English jury process as involving a kind of reference from the common law courts to the sheriff of a particular county who assembles a jury from "where the fact is suppose to be." Sir John Fortescue, De Laudibus Legum Angliae at 85 (originally written 1471, republished Cincinatti: Robert Clarke & Co., 1874).

5. See A.E. Anton and P.R. Beaumont, *Private International Law* 18, 2nd ed., (Edinburgh: W. Green, 1990) (assumption that choice of judge determined law had to be relaxed as trade spanned boundaries of traditional sovereigns, but intellectual justifications had to be developed for applying foreign law).

6. F. Cas. 660 (C.Ct. D.Va. 1811).

7. Early juries used their own knowledge of the facts as well as testimony adduced from witnesses.

8. *Livingston v. Jefferson,* 15 F. Cas. at 662 (describing two factors).

9. *Livingston v. Jefferson,* 15 F. Cas. at 662. Accord 15 F. Cas. at 664 (Marshall, J.).

10. A writ of execution calling for the arrest of a judgment debtor in order to compel him to satisfy the judgment.

11. A judicial writ directing the sheriff to arrest the defendant and bring him into court to answer a complaint filed against him. See *Vermont National Bank v. Taylor,* 445 A.2d 1122, 1124 (N.H. 1982) (quashing *ex parte capias* procedure used to initiate civil contempt proceeding).

12. *International Shoe Co. v. State of Washington, Office of Unemployment Compensation and Placement,* 326 U.S. 310, 316 (1945) (assertion of jurisdiction by state courts over corporation doing business in the state was constitutional).

13. So.2d 1351 (Fla. Ct. App. 1994),

14. Compare id. at 1353 (expressions of concern about WESTLAW, LEXIS and other databases) with id. at 1354 (Barkdull, J., dissenting).

15. 804 F. Supp. 111 (D. Colo. 1992),

16. 804 F. Supp. at 119.

17. 804 F. Supp. at 118.

18. Personal jurisdiction may be less appropriate if the service can demonstrate that it never knew the address of the plaintiff, as it might for a plaintiff who subscribes on-line and makes payment by a credit card.

19. Compare *Calder v. Jones* with *Madara v. Hall.*

20. U.S. 235 (1958) (unilateral acts of others cannot subject a defendant to personal jurisdiction based on minimum contacts).

21. Four Justices rejected the stream of commerce theory in *Asahi v. Superior Court*, 480 U.S. 162 (1987): "The placement of a product into the stream of commerce, without more, is not an act of the defendant purposefully directed toward the forum State. Additional conduct of the defendant may indicate an intent or purpose to serve the market in the forum State, for example, designing the product for the market in the forum State, advertising in the forum State, establishing channels for providing regular advice to customers in the forum State, or marketing the product through a distributor who has agreed to serve as the sales agent in the forum State. But a defendant's awareness that the stream of commerce may or will sweep the product into the forum State does not convert the mere act of placing the product into the stream into an act purposefully directed toward the forum State." 480 U.S. at 112. In the next paragraph, however, the same four suggested that advertising or otherwise soliciting business in a jurisdiction, and designing products in anticipation of sales in the jurisdiction (along with other factors) could support an inference of purposefulness. 480 U.S. at 112 (O'Connor, J., writing for herself and Powell, C.J. and Scalia, J.J.).

Justices Brennan, White, Marshall and Blackmun disagreed: "The stream of commerce refers not to unpredictable currents or eddies, but to the regular and anticipated flow of products from manufacture to distribution to retail sale. As long as a participant in this process is aware that the final product is being marketed in the forum State, the possibility of a lawsuit there cannot come as a surprise. Nor will the litigation present a burden for which there is no corresponding benefit." 480 U.S. at 1034–1035.

The door thus remains open, at least a crack, for stream of commerce arguments for personal jurisdiction.

22. Jacques Semmelman, "The Doctrine of Specialty in the Federal Courts: Making Sense of United States v. Rauscher," 34 *Virginia Journal of International Law* 71, 71 & n. 3 (1993). Doctrine of Specialty "limits personal jurisdiction in the federal and state courts" to prosecute for a crime other than that for which criminal defendant was extradited).

23. Federal Rules of Criminal Procedure, 43(a) states: "The defendant shall be present at the arraignment, at the time of the plea, at every stage of the trial including the impaneling of the jury and the return of the verdict, and at the imposition of sentence except as otherwise provided by this rule."

24. Cherif Bassiouni, "Human Rights in the Context of Criminal Justice: Identifying International Procedural Protections and Equivalent Protections in Na-

tional Constitutions," 3 *Duke Journal of Comparative and International Law* (1993) 235, 279 n.215.

25. Bassiouni, at 280 nn. 218 (citing *International Covenant on Civil and Political Rights*, G.A. Res. 2200 (XXI), U.N. GAOR, 21st Sess. Supp. No. 16, pt. III, art. 14(d), at 54); Richard J. Terrill, *World Criminal Justice Systems* (1984). Specifically, Professor Terrill describes England, France, Sweden and Japan. Id. at 51–52, 150–151, 209–211, 278. But see *Gallina v. Fraser*, 177 F. Supp. 856, 865–866 (D. Conn. 1959) (ordering extradition to Italy of fugitive despite his argument that he was convicted in absentia).

26. *Federal Rules of Criminal Procedure* 43(b) states that a defendant's continued presence is not required:

> The further progress of the trial to and including the return of the verdict shall not be prevented and the defendant shall be considered to have waived the right to be present whenever a defendant, initially present, (1) is voluntarily absent after the trial has commenced (whether or not the defendant has been informed by the court of the obligation to remain during the trial), or (2) after being warned by the court that disruptive conduct will cause the removal to the defendant from the courtroom persists in conduct which is such as to justify exclusion from the courtroom.

This would apply when the defendant flees during the trial [Bassiouni, "Human Rights in the Context of Criminal Justice," at 280 nn. 216–17; Federal Rules of Criminal Procedure 43(b)(1)] or is removed from the courtroom due to "disruptive conduct"[Id. 43(b)(2)]. Furthermore, under American law, the defendant's presence is not required in four other situations: (1) if the defendant is a corporation it may be represented solely by counsel [Id. 43(c)(1)]; (2) if the offenses are punishable by a fine or imprisonment of not more than one year; (3) the defendant must give the court written consent and the court may then proceed without the defendant's presence "at a conference or argument upon a question of law"; and (4) for a reduction of sentence [*Federal Rules of Criminal Procedure* 43(c)].

27. Ethan A. Nadelmann, "The Evolution of United States Involvement in the International Rendition of Fugitive Criminals," 25 *New York University Journal of International Law and Policy* 813 (1993) (options for U.S. law enforcement officials include requesting extradition, requesting informal methods such as deportation or forcing fugitive out of requested country, requesting that foreign government prosecute fugitive in its own courts, or obtaining custody by abduction or trickery).

28. When a claim to the property is the source of the controversy, "it would be unusual for the State where the property is located not to have jurisdiction." *Shaffer v. Heitner*, 433 U.S. 186, 207 (1977) (invalidating *quasi in rem* jurisdiction unless backed up by minimum contacts).

29. *Bennis v.. Michigan*, 116 S.Ct. 994, 1010 (Mar. 4, 1996) (Kennedy, J., dissenting).

30. Ibid.

31. "A judgment in rem affects the interests of all persons in designated property. A judgment quasi in rem affects the interests of particular persons in designated property. The latter is of two types. In one the plaintiff is seeking to secure a pre-existing claim in the subject property and to extinguish or establish the nonexistence of similar interests of particular persons. In the other the plaintiff seeks to apply what he concedes to be the property of the defendant to the satisfaction of a claim against him." Shaffer, 433 U.S. at 198 n.17 (quoting *Hanson v. Denckla*, 357 U.S. 235, 246 n.12 (1958)).

32. "[A]t early English law, courts dealt with absconding defendants not by way of contempt, but under the ancient doctrine of outlawry, a practice whereby the defendant was summoned by proclamation to five successive country courts and for failure to appear was declared forfeited of all his goods and chattels." *Green v. United States*, 356 U.S. 165, 170 (1958) (citing 4 *Blackstone Commentaries* 283, 319; outlawry never used by federal courts). The use of outlawry as an example mixes criminal and civil concepts, but nevertheless seems a useful illustration of how virtual presence might be applied.

33. Ibid.

34. See Adam W. Wegner, "Extraterritorial Jurisdiction Under International Law: The Yunis Decision is a Model for the Prosecution of Terrorists in U.S. Court," 22 *Law and Policy in International Business* 409, nn. 42–45 (1991) (reviewing preconditions for jurisdiction to prescribe with respect to crimes: (1) territorial jurisdiction based on the location of the crime, (2) national jurisdiction based on the nationality of the offender; (3) protective jurisdiction based on whether the 'national interest in injured; (4) universal jurisdiction based on the theory that some crimes are so universally condemned that any forum that obtains physical custody of the perpetrator may prosecute on behalf of all humanity; and (5) passive personal jurisdiction based on the nationality of the victim) (citing Restatement (Third) of the Foreign Relations Law of the United States §§ 402–404, 421, 431 (1987); "Harvard Research and International Law, Jurisdiction with Respect to Crime," 29 *American Journal of Internatational Law* 435 (Supp. 1935)).

35. Restatement (Second) of Conflict of Laws § 145 (1971).

36. Restatement (Second) of Conflict of Laws § 186 (1971) (general rule); Restatement (Second) of Conflicts of Laws § 187 (1988) (law of the state chosen by the parties); Restatement (Second) of Conflicts of Laws § 188 (1971) (law governing in absence of effective choice by the parties).

37. Restatement (Second) of Conflict of Laws § 188 (1971).

38. Restatement (Second) of Conflict of Laws § 188(3) (1971).

39. Compare *Sun Oil Co. v. Wortman*, 486 U.S. 717, 722 (1988) (allowing application of forum-state statute of limitations to class covered by substantive law of another jurisdiction) with *Phillips Petroleum Co. v. Shutts*, 472 U.S. 797, 815–

816 (1985) (holding unconstitutional application of Kansas law to class action when 97 percent of plaintiffs had no prior connection with state).

40. Cases involving defamation claims against interstate publishers offer some analogies to GII activities. *Vineland v. Hurst Corp.*, 862 F. Supp. 622, 627 (Mass. 1994) (Massachusetts had most significant relationship to defamation claim based on broadcast that originated in Massachusetts and was shown in Massachusetts and surrounding states; plaintiff apparently lived in Texas); *Jean v. Dugan*, 20 F.3d 255, 261 (7th Cir. 1994) (affirming district court choice of Indiana law; Indiana had the most significant contacts to defamation; reputational injury occurred in Indiana although publication occurred both in Indiana and Illinois; defamatory article originated in Illinois); but see *Chevalier v. Animal Rehabilitation Center., Inc.*, 839 F. Supp. 1224, 1229 (N.D. Tex. 1993) (place of injury de-emphasized in multistate defamation cases under Restatement (Second) of Conflicts of Laws § 145 cmt. e (1971); party relationship centered in Texas, Texas was place of injury, many defendants resided in Texas and others injected themselves into Texas activities and most conduct occurred in Texas, thus Texas had most significant relationships). *Zerman v. Sullivan & Cromwell*, 677 F. Supp. 1316, 1318–1319 (S.D.N.Y. 1988) (enumerating nine factors and determining that none of them usually overruled contacts in state of plaintiff's domicile).

41. Of course, choice of law is less important in patent and copyright claims because federal law applies. It may be important, however, in trademark, unfair competition and trade secrets claims.

42. While copyright law is federal, trade secrets and some trademark law is state law, and copyright law varies from country to country.

43. See generally *In re LoDolce*, 16 F. Supp. 455 (W.D.N.Y. 1952) (refusing extradition to Italy of person accused of murder because alleged murder was committed outside territory effectively controlled by Italy during World War II.

44. Restatement (Third) of Foreign Relations § 422(1)(1986). See generally, *United States v. Hudson and Goodwin*, 11 U.S. (7 Cranch) 32 (1812). In *United States v. Hudson and Goodwin*, the Supreme Court held that federal courts may not convict for common law crimes, but only for crimes for which jurisdiction is vested by statute. The rationale was that federal government institutions are institutions of limited jurisdiction. The rationale precludes federal court jurisdiction over crimes defined by foreign states because that jurisdiction has not been given to the courts by Congress. Of course, the rationale permits Congress to define a foreign crime as a U.S. crime within the jurisdiction of a United States federal court.

45. See M. Cherif Bassiouni, *International Extradition and World Public Order,* 203–205 (1974) (identifying five theories of jurisdiction recognized by international law as giving rise to rule-making and rule-enforcing power: (1) territorial; (2) active personality or nationality, based on nationality of the accused; (3) passive personality, based on the nationality of the victim; (4) protective, based on the national interest affected; and (5) universality, based on the international character of the offense).

46. Some commentators suggest that civil law countries are more or less willing to prosecute their own nationals for violation of foreign criminal law as long as a sort of dual criminality principle is satisfied. Nadelmann, 25 *New York University Journal of International Law and Policy* nn. 204–206 (identifying secondary source citing German prosecution of Hungarian national for crimes committed in Hungary, but contrasting U.S. law; characterizing principle as *aut dedere aut iudicare*).

47. Research and drafting for this section was done by Sean P. Lugg, law clerk to the author. See generally, Andre M. Surena, Christopher L. Blakesly, Andreas F. Lowenfeld, Lisa Cacheris, Serge April, and Michael P. Scharf, "Extraterritorial Application of Criminal Law," 85 *American Society of International Law Proceedings* 383, April 20, 1991. See *Tel-Oren v. Libyan Arab Republic*, 726 F.2d 774 (D.C. Cir. 1984) (piracy is a so-called international crime; the pirate is considered the enemy of every state, and can be brought to justice anywhere; every state can punish crimes like piracy or slave trade on capture of the criminal, whatever his nationality).

48. The wording of the U.S. piracy statute makes it clear that international law is being applied: "whoever, on the high seas, commits the crime of piracy as defined by the law of nations, it is afterwards brought into or found in the United States, shall be imprisoned for life." 18 U.S.C. § 1651 (1988).

49. A new concept, worth developing in greater depth, would proceed from the model of *in rem* jurisdiction, and conclude that a judgment supported by personal jurisdiction in the form of electronic presence could be enforced only against the electronic persona, either against assets in the jurisdiction or by excluding that person from electronic contact with that jurisdiction. The author appreciates this suggestion from his friend David R. Johnson.

50. *Uniform Foreign Money Judgments Recognition Act* 13 U.L.A. 261.

51. See *DeLa Mata v. American Life Insurance Co.*, 771 F. Supp. 1375 (D. Del. 1991).

52. Joseph Story, *Commentaries on the Conflict of Laws* XV § 586 at 978 (4th Ed. 1852) (universally accepted that foreign judgment not supported by jurisdiction is treated as a mere nullity, entitled to no respect). The personal jurisdiction and procedural due process standards are essentially American in character.

53. *Matusevitch v. Telnikoff*, 877 F. Supp. 1 (D.D.C. Jan. 27, 1995) (declining to recognize and enforce British libel judgment under Maryland's *Uniform Foreign-Money Judgments Recognition Act* because British libel law lacked constitutional protections applied in the United States).

54. Juenger, 65 *University of Colorado Law Review* at 21–22 & nn. 152–159 (describing difficulties and citing Peter Hay & Roberts J. Walker, "The Proposed Recognition-of-Judgments Convention Between the United States and the United Kingdom," 11 *Texas International Law Journal* 421, 452–459 (1976) (providing text of proposed draft)). Juenger, 65 *University of Colorado Law Review* at 23 n. 159 (citing Fourth Inter American Specialized Conference on Private International Law in Montevideo on July 15, 1989. 29 I.L.M. 73 (1990); Carol S. Bruch, "The

1989 Inter American Convention on Support Obligations," 40 *American Journal of Comparative Law* 817 (1993)). Juenger, 65 *University of Colorado Law Review* at 21 & nn. 152–153 (citing 57 Fed. Reg. 54, 439 (1992) & ABA endorsed 50-hour pro bono minimum, opposes statutory removal of U.S. judges, 61 U.S.L.W. 2482 (Feb. 16, 1993)).

55. Attaching property of the defendant held by a third person usually is called "garnishment."

56. As the figure indicates, content suppliers may be governmental entities, as for statutes and judicial opinions, or private sector entities.

57. An arbitration award is the decision of an arbitrator.

58. See generally *Merrill Lynch, Pierce, Fenner & Smith, Inc. v. Lauer,* 49 F.3d 323 (7th Cir. 1995) (cannot seek to narrow arbitration by suing in district other than district where arbitration is occurring; applying § 4 of the *Federal Arbitration Act* and generally reviewing law under which one sues to compel arbitration).

59. See generally Henry H. Perritt, Jr., "Dispute Resolution in Electronic Network Communities," 38 *Villanova Law Review,* 349 (1993) (exploring difficulty of designing private governance mechanisms that encompass disputes involving third parties not signatory to contracts defining the mechanism).

60. Procedural arbitrability addresses the question of whether appropriate procedures have been followed in presenting the dispute to the arbitrator.

61. *AT&T Technologies, Inc. v. Communications Workers,* 475 U.S. 643 (1986) (courts have the ultimate say on whether a dispute is substantively arbitrable).

62. *First Options v. Kaplan,* 115 S.Ct. 1920, 1923 (May 22, 1995).

63. U.S.C. § 4 (1988) (federal court has power to compel arbitration); UAA § 2 (same power in state court under *Uniform State Act*); *United Nations Convention on the Recognition and Enforcement of Foreign Arbitrable Awards* [hereinafter "New York Arbitration Convention"] art. II § 3 (1958) (requiring courts of contracting states to refer arbitrable agreement to arbitration as long as they find arbitration agreements to be valid). *Howard Fields & Associates v. Grand Wailea Co.,* 848 F. Supp. 890 (D. Hawaii 1993) (staying federal court litigation pending arbitration; explaining relationship between *Federal Arbitration Act* and state arbitration law, acknowledging that *Volt Information Sciences, Inc. v. Board of Trustees of Leland Stanford Junior University,* 489 U.S. 468 (1989), allows choice of law provision in arbitration agreement to apply state arbitration law rather than federal arbitration agreement law).

64. See 9 U.S.C. § 9 (1988) (authorizing federal court enforcement of award if the parties have so provided in their agreement and requiring enforcement unless it can be shown that the award was procured by corruption, fraud or undue means; there was evident partiality or corruption in the arbitrators; where the arbitrators were guilty of misconduct in refusing to postpone the hearing or in refusing to hear pertinent evidence; where the arbitrators exceeded their power); UAA §§ 8, 12 (similar power and criteria for state courts); New York Arbitration Convention Art. III (1958) (providing for enforcement of arbitra-

tion awards); New York Arbitration Convention Art. V § 1 (allowing for refusal of enforcement of arbitration award only if agreement was invalid; party seeking to avoid enforcement was not given appropriate notice; award is outside the scope of arbitration agreement; composition of the arbitral body was in violation of the agreement or the law of the country where the arbitration took place; award has not yet become binding or has been set aside by competent authority where the award was made); New York Arbitration Convention § 2 (allowing for refusal of enforcement if law of country where enforcement is sought does not allow that type of dispute to be arbitrated; enforcement would be contrary to public policy of that country).

65. Accord 9 U.S.C. §§ 201–208 (providing for enforcement of arbitration agreements and awards under New York Convention in accordance with criteria and procedures generally applicable to domestic arbitration). See generally *Jain v. Demere*, 51 F.3d 686 (7th Cir. 1995) (ordering arbitration between non-citizens under agreement providing for application of French law).

66. *Scherk v. Alberto-Culver Co.*, 417 U.S. 506 (1974) (genuinely international arbitration agreement may provide for binding arbitration of statutory securities law claim); *Gilmer v. Interstate/Johnson Lane Corp.*, 111 S.Ct. 1647, 1652 (1991) (allowing arbitration of age discrimination claims under individual employment agreement); *Mitsubishi Motors Corp. v. Soler Chrysler-Plymouth, Inc.*, 473 U.S. 614, 625 (1985) (rejecting presumption against arbitration of statutory claims; contrary presumption applies in international arbitration; finding antitrust disputes to be arbitrable).

67. *National Hydes Systems v. Summit Construction, Inc.*, 731 F. Supp. 264, 266 (N.D. Ill. 1989) (finding waiver).

68. American Arbitration Association Arbitration Rules Art. 20 (1995) (evidence); American Arbitration Association Arbritration Rules Art. 24 (1995) (default provision); UNCITRAL Arbitration Rules Art 24–25 (1976) (evidence and hearings); UNCITRAL Arbitration Rules Art 28 (1976) (default); International Chamber of Commerce Art 24 (1975) (finality and enforceability of award).

69. See generally Okezie Chukwumerije, *Choice of Law in International Commercial Arbitration* (1994) 107–108; but see *Vita Food Products v. Unus Shipping Co.* (1939) A.C. 277 at 290 (choice of law may be disregarded if choice is not bona fide where there is public policy ground for avoiding it).

70. See Chukwumerije at 110–117 (discussing sources of law within *lex mercatoria*, including those of UNCITRAL and International Institute for the Unification of International Private Law (UNIDROIT); *Hutton v. Warren* (1836) 1M & W 466 (endorsing use of extrinsic evidence of custom and usage in disputes over commercial transactions).

71. See *Mastrobuono v. Shearson Lehman Hutton, Inc.*, 115 S.Ct. 1212, 1217–1219 (1995) (contract allowed arbitrator of dispute between securities brokerage and customers to award punitive damages; choice of law provision pointing to New

York law did not require application of New York doctrine against punitive damages by arbitrator because that was procedural and conflicted with the *Federal Arbitration Act*).

72. See http://www.law.vill.edu/vmag/.

73. See generally Shabtai Rosenne, *The World Court: What It Is and How It Works*, 5th ed. (Dordrecht: Martinus, Nijhoff, 1995) 342–343 (reporting on a total of 94 cases filed with the court in its 50-year history).

74. See John H. Barton & Barry E. Carter, "International Law and Institutions for a New Age," 81 *Georgetown Law Journal* 535 (1993) (suggesting consideration of GATT Antitrust Code, at 550; binding arbitration in NAFTA, at 560; making the judgments of the International Court of Justice enforceable in domestic courts as are arbitration awards under New York Convention, at 560; more flexible procedures for the International Court of Justice, at 560; further elaboration of an international common law, at 561; acceptance by the United States that rights recognized by the U.S. Constitution or the International Human Rights Convention govern the U.S. government when it acts abroad, at 561; acceptance by the United States that international treaties and executive agreements can be enforced by the U.S. domestic courts, at 561).

75. See Barbara M. Yarnold, *International Fugitives: A New Role for the International Court of Justice* (1991) 105.

76. See Virginia Morris & M-Christaine Bourloyannis-Vrailas, "The Work of the Sixth Committee at the Forty-Ninth Session of the UN General Assembly," 89 *American Journal of International Law* 607, 613 (1995) (reporting on discussions of a recommendation for an international criminal court, and suggesting that concept might be ripe now for negotiation of a treaty establishing such a court); Madeline K. Albright, "International Law Approaches the Twenty-First Century: A U.S. Perspective on Enforcement," 18 *Fordham International Law Journal* 1595 (1995) (reporting Clinton administration interest in International Criminal Court proposal); Jelena Pejic, "The International Criminal Court: Issues of Law and Political Will," 18 *Fordham International Law Journal* 1762 (1995) (suggesting that international conference of plenipotentiaries may be convened to draft convention on establishing an international criminal court in late 1995); James Crawford, "The ILC Adopts a Statute for an International Criminal Court," 89 *American Journal of International Law* 404 (1995) (reporting on basic parameters for a draft statute developed by International Law Commission); Paul D. Marquardt, "Law Without Borders: The Constitutionality of an International Criminal Court," 33 *Columbia Journal of International Law* 73 (1995); American Bar Association, "American Bar Association Task Force on an International Criminal Court Final Report," 28 *International Law* 475 (1994).

77. See United Nations, *International Review of Criminal Policy* Nos. 43 and 44 paras. 261–273 (1994) [hereinafter "International Review"] (proposing new frameworks for transborder searches of computer databases and mutual assistance in computer crime cases); David McClean, *International Judicial Assistance* (1992).

78. See *International Review* at paras. 274–278 (proposing new frameworks for extradition of those accused of computer crimes). But see 1992 Senate Hearings at 4 (prepared statement of Allen J. Kreczko) (noting advantages of dual criminality instead of enumerated-crimes approach; specifically mentioning that dual criminality approach obviates need to renegotiate treaties to include new offenses such as computer-related crimes).

79. See also United Nations, *Report of the International Law Commission on the Work of its Forty-Seventh Session* (2 May–21 July 1995) (General Assembly Official Records, 50th Sess. Supp. No. 10 (A/50/10) (presenting draft Code of Crimes Against the Peace and Security of Mankind, including international terrorism and drug trafficking, as well as human rights violations and war crimes).

80. Information technology might be the instrument of a terrorist threat aimed at conventional property or person, or a computer system might be the target (e.g., if a terrorist threatened to disable or corrupt a system for managing financial transactions).

81. See *International Review* at paras 245–260 (suggesting ways of harmonizing computer crimes internationally although not emphasizing definitions of new international crimes).

Issues across Borders

The Market for Digital Piracy

Dan L. Burk

Unlike old-fashioned smugglers, the haven pirates never had to physically touch their booty. Data had no substance.[1]

Introduction

In less than a decade since its publication, Bruce Sterling's vision of a computer-linked world in which data havens traffic in purloined knowledge no longer seems the stuff of science fiction. The advent and growth of the global Internet has certainly produced a computer-linked world, and the data pirates may not be far behind. In the United States and elsewhere around the world, politicians are already scrambling to protect precious national information policies from electronic depredation. Such policymakers foresee on the horizon the Jolly Roger of digital buccaneers, striking from within the jurisdictional shelter of information-poor haven nations to plunder the bounty of data-rich information producers.

The reality of such fears remains to be seen. Even data pirates may have their good side; some may rob from the rich and give to the poor, which may not seem so undesirable from the perspective of the poor. Others may rob from monopolists and give to consumers, which may seem desirable from the perspective of consumers. At the very least, the threat of data pirates may force policymakers to batten down the hatches and run a tighter ship, which might be desirable to anyone on board. And in some cases, data pirates may even force some politicians to walk the plank, which might be desirable to nearly everybody.

In this chapter, I shall argue that by promoting international competition in two distinct but interrelated markets, the Internet will profoundly affect national and international information policy. Competition may exist at different levels: at the level of nations, firms, or individuals. I shall principally argue that the Internet will facilitate competition among firms for information products, and among nations for intellectual property regulation. At the same time, the Internet will facilitate externalization of costs in both these markets, undermining efficiency gains from increased competition. In order to understand how these interrelated effects can arise simultaneously, we must begin by briefly considering the nature of the network itself.

The Nature of the Network

The profound effect that the Internet promises to have on competition for information and its related regulation arises from certain technical features of networked communications. First, the Internet is a packet-switching network.[2] Information to be transmitted along the network is broken into discrete packets of bits that are labeled with the address of their final destination. Packets are sent on their way as transmission capacity becomes available, and are reassembled at the point of receipt. Thus, communication channels are not dedicated in real time to a single transmission as with conventional telephony, broadcast, and the like. Instead, packets from a variety of sources may share the same channel as bandwidth allows, promoting more efficient use of available carrying capacity.

Second, the Internet is designed around "smart communications." Because the Internet is a network of computers, mechanical intelligence is available at every node of the network, and the design of the Internet takes full advantage of this characteristic. Computers at each node monitor traffic on the network, and route packets along the least congested path to the next node, from which the process is repeated. Thus, packets comprising a single message may take different paths to their final destination. Although there is no central coordination of traffic, the sum of independent local routing moves packets along the most efficient route as if by an "invisible hand."

Finally, as might be expected from the nature of packet switching, the Internet is relatively transparent to physical distance. Originally designed to promote sharing of scientific equipment and information resources, the network hosts a variety of features that permit remote access to such facilities. Internet users can access computers and information across a continent or around the world as easily as they can access resources in the next room—indeed, depending upon local network traffic, accessing the distant facility may prove to be faster and more responsive. So insensitive is the network to geography that it is frequently impossible to determine the physical location of a resource or user. Such information is unimportant to the network's function or to the purposes of its creators, and the network's design thus makes little provision for geographic discernment.

This network structure already supports access to a wide variety of information utilities, including databases and computational facilities, as well as archives of text, music, graphics, and software. Information and information-based services on the network have traditionally been offered for free, but will increasingly be offered on a commercial basis. At present, commercial traffic on the network usually culminates in an exchange of physical goods, but transfer of digitized information products such as music, photographs, novels, motion pictures, multimedia works, and software can be accomplished entirely within the network itself. Such information products already comprise a sizable portion of the gross national product of developed nations, and that portion is likely to increase worldwide. It is the network's capacity to exchange such products on-line that may challenge certain established notions of market structure.

Location and Migration

The features of the network described above suggest that Internet commerce may not follow conventional models of regional economic organization that were developed to describe and predict the exchange of tangible goods in real space. Such analyses of regional structure draw heavily on the distributional model pioneered by August Lösch, which predicts a spatial distribution of production centers—cities—based on a combination of proximity to production input factors and proximity to points of product sale to consumers.[3] The question of transportation costs is key to such an analysis. At a boundary point some certain distance from the central production facility, transportation of raw materials into the production facility becomes prohibitive. Similarly, at a boundary point some certain distance from the production center, transportation costs limit the edge of the spatial market that can be served by that center. Where these boundaries intersect, a new production facility can be expected to arise, becoming the focal point of a new "cell" of production and market activity.[4]

Commercial exchange over the Internet can be expected to violate the Löschian model, since the characteristics of the Internet obviate certain assumptions inherent in the model. The most important of these assumptions is that transportation costs for goods increase with distance. This assumption is plausible in real space, where expenditures of fuel and other resources are required to move tangible goods over geographic distances. However, the type of goods best suited to Internet commerce are information goods carried in digitized form; such arrangements of bits lack the physical form that generates conventional transportation costs. The same is true for the "raw materials" that go into creating finished information goods: computer code, digitized music or text, and numerical data require no costly physical transportation. Transfer of information goods over the Internet is by no means costless, given that it requires telecommunications infrastructure that has limited bandwidth. But incremental transfer costs on the net are certainly relatively low, and are not necessarily tied to geographic proximity.

This stems from the lack of homology between cyberspace and real space. As discussed above, Internet transfers do not necessarily map well onto physical distance: rather than choosing the most direct route, a packet-switching network will route information transfer via the least congested route. This makes highly efficient use of bandwidth, but is not necessarily the shortest physical route—contrary to conventional models of spatial ordering, choosing the shortest distances between sender and receiver might actually increase costs. This, together with the overall "transparency" of the Net vis-à-vis physical distance, suggests that a regular spatial distribution of Internet production centers is unlikely: the economic constraints that dictate location of such centers in real space are absent or radically altered in cyberspace.

If the Internet largely frees centers for production of information goods from the location constraints inherent in physical transportation costs, they instead will locate according to the dictates of other economic constraints. But, as in the case of transportation limits, such constraints are unlikely to be traditional physical limitations. Neoclassical economics predicts that industries will locate on the basis of the "comparative advantage" of particular locations; such advantages might include proximity to transportation, availability of raw materials, or access to skilled labor. I have already suggested that the Internet makes physical proximity less important for production of information goods; in addition, the inputs for such production may differ in mobility from those of traditional industries.

For example, unlike industries in which heavy equipment must be located to create manufacturing facilities, the equipment involved in information production is relatively mobile. A few thousand dollars' worth of computer equipment will quickly put an Internet information supplier on-line, and such equipment tends to be highly portable. The raw material essential to information products—human creativity—is also fairly mobile or, as suggested above, can be supplied via Internet link. Skilled technical personnel, if not available locally, should also be relatively portable. Local availability of telecommunications infrastructure may pose a real constraint, but increasingly sophisticated Internet linkages are becoming available in most portions of the globe.

This does not mean that information creators and providers will not choose to locate on the basis of comparative advantage—quite the contrary. However, the availability of Internet linkage may drastically change the type of advantage that assumes prominence in the choice. In particular, public goods and services may assume a dominant role in dictating the location of information producers. It is already increasingly apparent that producers of physical goods and real-space services may choose their location on the basis of such factors—direct subsidies, local tax structure, environmental regulation, municipal services, and quality of life play important roles in the decision to locate traditional industries. Such considerations will similarly affect the decision to locate information industries that are otherwise relatively unconstrained as to location. In addition, given the nature of the industries under consideration, the class of regulations most directly affecting the creation and distribution of information products—intellectual property laws—may be expected to assume considerable importance in determining the physical location of information producers.

Public Goods and Information

Current positive and normative theories of intellectual property owe much to analysis of public goods as formulated nearly half a century ago by Paul Samuelson.[5] Samuelson observed that there are certain classes of "goods" that are public in nature, that is to say, which are non-rival and non-exclusive. A good such as "national defense" provides a now-classic example: it is non-rival because, unlike tangible goods, a unit of national defense may simultaneously benefit more than one person. It is non-exclusive because, again unlike most tangible goods, once a unit of national defense is produced for the benefit of one individual, it is nearly impossible to prevent others from simultaneously benefiting from its production.

Because public goods are non-exclusive, there may be little incentive for anyone to be willing to pay for their production. The optimal strategy for a given consumer would be to let someone else pay for production, and then because he cannot be excluded from consuming the good, "free ride" off of what is produced. Naturally, if everyone adopts this strategy, no one will pay at all and no goods will be produced. At the same time, because public goods are non-rival, the marginal cost of providing the benefit to additional consumers is zero or nearly zero. This means, first, that it would actually be inefficient to exclude additional consumers from enjoying the good, even if a method could be devised to do so. But it also means that there is little if any incentive to produce more than one unit of the good because everyone can simultaneously hold the first unit. This combination of attributes is anticipated to lead to chronic underproduction of public goods in a competitive market.

Information products tend to resemble Samuelsonian public goods in many respects. In their pure form, information products are at least non-rival—ideas, facts, songs, and poems can be "held" or known by many people simultaneously.[6] The cost of distribution for such pure information products, or "ideal goods," is also close to zero; telling an idea to another individual is generally a fairly low-cost proposition. However, this is not true non-exclusivity, as in the case of a true public good like national defense—unlike additional consumption of national defense, additional consumption of an ideal good can be curtailed by concealment or secrecy. Nonetheless, ideal goods are sometimes said to be "non-exclusive" because they are very cheap to reproduce. Each consumer of an ideal good becomes a potential source of secondary distribution, and proliferation of such secondary sources at some point causes the availability of ideal goods to approach true non-exclusivity.

Intellectual property law almost never protects ideal goods in their ideal form. Fundamental tenets of patent and copyright law forbid the protection of ideas or principles; rather, the specific embodiment of the idea in, respectively, an invention or a tangible medium of expression is protectable. In this embodied form, intellectual property more closely resembles what might be called a local public good rather than a "pure" or general public good.[7] For example, in copyright law, even though different copies of a copyrighted work can be held simultaneously by more than one individual, a particular copy is limited to a discrete physical location. This quality of intellectual property differs substantially from that of a classic Samuelsonian public good such as national defense, which is embodied at no discrete site. The non-rival nature of the protected work therefore lies in the ability to generate multiple copies, rather than in its diffuse or inchoate nature.

Most information products are not in fact ideal goods, but are rather ideal goods embodied in some tangible form, such as compact disks, books, magnetic tape, and so on. Such embodied goods cannot be reproduced as effortlessly as ideal goods. Thus intellectual property law tends to protect information goods only in a particular embodiment. Because the non-rival aspect of embodied ideal goods is in fact an artifact of reproducibility, control of reproduction and distribution represents a choke point in the availability of the good, and hence in the price. Restriction of reproduction and distribution allows the controller to extract a higher price for access to the goods. Such restriction can be used to counteract the tendency to undersupply such goods. Copyright law, for example, uses this "bottleneck" as a point of control to allow authors to recoup their investment in creative works. Copyright extends only to works embodied in a tangible medium of expression, but it grants to authors the exclusive rights to reproduce, distribute, and similarly exploit such embodied works. Unauthorized reproduction is discouraged via legal penalties; thus the copyright holder is able to sell copies or licenses to copy at an artificially—but necessarily—inflated price. By restricting reproduction and distribution of information goods, creation is fostered.

However, technology has tended to greatly enhance the "nonexclusivity" of information products by lowering the cost of reproduction and distribution: from hand-copied manuscript to printing press to photocopy to floppy disk, the distributional bottleneck exploited by copyright is widening. The Internet continues this trend, both by making information resources available to distant users and by facilitating distribution of information products in a digital form that approaches that of an ideal good. By pushing the marginal cost of distribution close to zero, the Internet enables dissemination of information products that is highly efficient— some might argue too efficient. As described above, such efficient distribution enhances the "pure public goods" nature of information products, allowing free riders to reap the external benefits of information producers, and potentially undermining incentives to produce the goods in the first instance.

The Market for Information Products

This restrictive effect creates something of a paradox for intellectual property: jurisdictions that encourage "piracy" are in fact encouraging a type of efficiency, whereas jurisdictions with stringent copyright laws are encouraging a type of inefficiency. This paradox may be in part resolved by considering that these strategies are in fact directed to different phases in the life cycle of an information product.[8] The creation of information products, like the creation of other products, may be conceived of as comprising several phases. An initial phase may involve generation of the information or creative work. A subsequent phase may involve "adding value" to the work through processing, tagging, verifying, indexing, standardizing, packaging, or similarly "institutionalizing." Yet a third phase involves distribution or dissemination, which will generally include reproduction of the work. Each of these phases may entail considerable cost, and each may be thought of as generating a separate "good": raw information sources, "value-added" information resources, and information products or services.

Each of these separate information goods exists to some extent in its own market, although the markets are interconnected: the good from each successive phase is an input to the next phase, leading eventually to distribution of information products. As noted above, copyright law has tended to use the bottleneck in the distribution phase to allow authors to recoup the costs of their creative investment in either the generation or institutionalization phases. Thus stringent control of a work tends to promote production, but at the cost of inefficient distribution. Jurisdictions adopting restrictive copyright regimes thus foster efficient production, whereas jurisdictions adopting permissive copyright regimes foster efficient distribution. Both approaches tend toward efficiency, but only at one particular stage in the product's life cycle.

This dichotomy between approaches has long been apparent in the approaches to copyright taken by different nations. Some nations, such as the United States, have tended to focus on restrictive copyright that promotes production of creative works. Other nations, typically underdeveloped nations, have tended to focus on permissive regimes that promote distribution to their populace at the cheapest cost. These two approaches to some extent focus on different markets—either generation or distribution—but the race to the top in one market entails a race to the bottom in the other. From these competing races charges of "piracy" are born. Efficient distributors must still have something to distribute—most frequently, what the permissive regimes have distributed has been unauthorized copies of works fostered under restrictive regimes.

Physical barriers have tended to keep the effect of pirating localized—unauthorized copies of works have tended to circulate within a given nation or region, but generally not globally in sizable quantities. This tendency toward localization arises from the non-ideal nature of the works at issue; recall that copies of works are embodied in tangible media tend to resemble local public goods rather than general public goods. The physical copies have bulk, weight, and other characteristics that make them costly to transport. In a Löschian system, these characteristics impose limits on efficient distribution. Transportation costs across geographic distances will naturally curtail the circulation of physical copies. Other barriers to circulation may also be interposed to frustrate low-cost transborder distribution: sizable shipments of infringing works entering a "producer" nation can be interdicted at a point of entry.

However, as discussed previously, the Internet violates the assumptions of a Löschian system, particularly in that digitized information products can be distributed unconstrained by the limitations commonly associated with transporting physical goods over distance. This aspect of the network threatens to breach the regional compartmentalization previously associated with information piracy. Distance and transportation costs may no longer pose a significant barrier to distribution of unauthorized copies of a work. The network potentially extends the reach of information pirates, transforming regional permissive distribution into global permissive distribution.

Additionally, interdiction of infringing products may become nearly impossible. As a practical matter, the sheer volume of Internet traffic would make it prohibitively time-consuming to examine each packet coming into the territory of a copyright-restrictive nation, and to sort among them for potentially infringing copies. Infringing packets might enter a territory at almost any point on the border, via microwave broadcast, fiber-optic or copper wire transmission, or satellite downlink. Even if all the packets in all these media were monitored, works traversing the net are likely to be broken into multiple packets that may be simultaneously routed through a variety of entry points. The Internet's feature of piece-meal transmission could thus further obscure a determination of whether the final reassembled transmission would be an infringing work.

The result is that the national borders of restrictive copyright jurisdiction will be rendered highly porous to delivery of cheap information products from permissive copyright jurisdictions. Infringing information products that formerly had the character of local, or at least regional, goods may be freed from their physical embodiments and suddenly begin to resemble true general public goods. The Internet will therefore act not merely as a product delivery system that will free information producers to relocate where they will because they no longer require close proximity to information consumers; it will simultaneously act as a conduit for externalizing the costs of local information regulation choices.

Local Public Goods

It is at this point that Samuelson's insight into the nature of public goods again plays a critical, albeit corollary, role in analyzing the informational market effects of the Internet. Samuelson's observations regarding underproduction of public goods did not go long without an answer. In 1956, Charles Tiebout published his now classic paper modeling local provision of public services on a theory of interjurisdictional competition that closely resembles market competition for provision of private goods.[9] Tiebout theorized that if citizens are free to migrate between jurisdictions, competition for desirable citizen immigrants will arise. Local communities will offer potential immigrants the most attractive packages of goods and services at the lowest tax rate possible. Similarly, migrants will relocate to jurisdictions offering the maximum package of public goods at the tax rate that the migrant is willing to pay. Local communities may even tailor their offerings to appeal to particular types of immigrants, and immigrants would be expected to sort themselves out into groups of similar means and tastes by jurisdiction.

The production of local public goods and services might thus resemble the production of private goods in a competitive market: competitive pressure from other jurisdictions will prevent any given jurisdiction from offering too much or too little in the way of public services. Jurisdictions that offer too much will experience an influx of immigrants from less generous jurisdictions; jurisdictions that offer too little will experience an exodus to more generous jurisdictions. Migration in or out of the jurisdiction will continue until parity with competing jurisdictions is reached. These forces therefore act as a check on over- or underproduction of local public goods. By "voting with their feet," or exiting, citizens force efficiency in allocation of resources to such goods.[10]

The Tiebout model, like most pure economic theories, rests upon a number of simplifying assumptions. The model assumes that voters have full knowledge of the package of local services offered in various jurisdictions; that there are a large number of jurisdictions from which to choose; that individual mobility is relatively unconstrained; and that communities have an optimal size which will be dictated by the balance between resource constraints and economies of scale. Most important for this discussion, the Tiebout model assumes that jurisdictions are tightly compartmentalized so that no external costs or benefits accrue from the local provision of public services. If jurisdictions are "leaky," then individuals could perhaps enjoy the positive benefits of a neighboring jurisdiction's policy without actually incurring the cost of migrating there.[11] More significantly, in a world of "leaky" borders, jurisdictions could lower the costs to local firms by imposing all or part of those costs on neighboring jurisdictions; this would serve to attract firms, but not necessarily by generating a net gain in efficiency.

Ironically, this final assumption implies that even on its own terms, the Tiebout model is an inadequate answer to the problem of inefficient productions of Samuelsonian public goods.[12] If all the necessary assumptions are in place for operation of the Tiebout model, then the problem of Samuelsonian goods is not addressed. The Tiebout model applies only to allocative efficiency of local public goods, that is, production of public goods that are local in nature, having no external effects. However, Samuelsonian public goods are almost always general public goods, that is, true public goods whose effects are not locally circumscribed. For such goods, allocative efficiency will not arise through inter-jurisdictional competition, because the positive or negative external effects will be felt outside the jurisdiction. Tiebout competition will arise only where public goods can be securely compartmentalized.

Law as a Product

Although business firms were not part of Tiebout's original model, his insight was quickly expanded to encompass strategic preferences of local governments regarding such firms. Just as in the consumer/citizen model, businesses too may "vote with their feet," locating their operations in jurisdictions that offer the most attractive set of local public goods. This in turn implies that jurisdictions may tailor their offerings to attract businesses, or to attract certain kinds of desirable businesses, or even to repel undesirable businesses.

However, the "location" of a business is a problematic question, because unlike an individual consumer, a business may have no discrete situs of existence—offices may be in one physical location, manufacturing in another, distribution in another, and sales in yet others. To the extent that a business as a juridical person is "located" anywhere, it may be located in the state of incorporation; the law governing the state of incorporation has a profound effect on the rights and structure of the organization. As a consequence, one might expect that local laws governing incorporation might attract or discourage incorporation under those laws, and that jurisdictions might compete for the benefits—taxes and fees—to be garnered from incorporation franchises.

This type of competition in fact appears to occur, giving rise to the so-called "Delaware phenomenon." It is fairly widely recognized that in the United States, a surprisingly large number of corporations choose to incorporate or re-incorporate under the laws of the state of Delaware. The proper explanation for this phenomenon is less well settled than is the observation itself. Analyses of the phenomenon tend to fall into two broad schools of thought. The first of these schools, originally set out by law professor William Carey, suggests that competition for incorporations represents a "race to the bottom," that is, a race to liberalize incorporation law for the benefit of officers and directors.[13] By enacting laws to appeal to the interests of officers and directors, states may attract incorporations, but at the expense of shareholders' rights. As states vie with one another for incorporation franchises, they successively liberalize their laws until the rights of shareholders are entirely subordinated. Carey recommended federal intervention to halt what he perceived as a downward spiral of ruinous interstate competition.

The second school, which coalesced in response to Carey's claims, questioned whether shareholders would in fact be stupid enough, or oblivious enough to their own interests, to leave their investment dollars with firms incorporated under laws detrimental to the shareholders' interests.[14] If in fact jurisdictions such as Delaware were subordinating shareholder rights, one might expect to see shareholders "vote with their feet" by abandoning Delaware corporations for firms incorporating under laws more favorable to investors. Such a loss of investment dollars to Delaware corporations might in turn provide an incentive for firms not to incorporate there. The fact that there appeared to be no such migration of investors from Delaware firms, or of firms from Delaware itself, led commentators of the second school to interpret Delaware's success in attracting franchisees as indicating that such incorporations are attractive to investors, probably due to the superior returns on investment received from such firms.

This latter analysis suggested that Delaware, far from winning a "race to the bottom" for inefficient incorporation laws, had won a "race to the top" for efficient incorporation laws that permitted maximum returns to investors. A subset of the "race to the top" school, typified in the writings of Roberta Romano, particularly emphasized the Delaware phenomenon as a competition between jurisdictions for "law as a product."[15] Delaware may not necessarily have attracted the lion's share of incorporations because of the absolute superiority of its governing rules, but because of Delaware legal system has specialized in corporate law, offering additional certainty to firms seeking incorporation. Thus, Delaware offers not merely a highly developed statutory system, but also a court system with a high degree of expertise in resolving corporate conflicts, as well as a considerable body of case precedent governing such conflicts. Thus, these scholars argue, the total package of Delaware's law succeeds in the incorporation marketplace as a superior product.

Subsequent studies have suggested that inter-jurisdictional competition for "law as a product" operates in areas besides incorporation, such as bankruptcy law.[16] However, the intangible nature of businesses as juridical "persons" precludes this effect in many areas of regulation. For purposes other than incorporation, businesses may be present almost anywhere transactions are conducted. This raises an important issue with regard to the provision of local public goods. Because a firm is physically diffuse rather than physically discrete, certain types of legal regulation will not constitute local public goods with regard to a firm in a given jurisdiction. For example, a firm that manufactures a given product may be subject to tort liability in a large variety of jurisdictions—the place where a tort occurs will weigh heavily in a legal conflict of law analysis to decide which jurisdiction's law should apply to the question of liability. No matter where a firm's central offices are located, or where its manufacturing facility is located, it is the place where its goods are sold and used that will determine its liability for injuries caused by its goods.

Consequently, we would not expect local tort regulation to appreciably affect where businesses locate their headquarters or manufacturing facilities. Tort law may instead affect where the business decides to sell or not sell its products. Thus, with respect to the business' decision to locate facilities in a given jurisdiction, tort law is not a local public good, that is, it is not a public good whose effects are circumscribed to a discrete geographic region. Instead, choice of law analysis transforms tort law into a general public good that spills over the borders of any given geographic region to reach businesses incorporated and headquartered in other jurisdictions.

The Market for Intellectual Property Law

In contrast, other types of regulation that have the characteristics of local public goods potentially may affect the location of a business' physical facilities—tax requirements, particularly property taxes, state environmental regulation, worker safety and benefits requirements will all tend to have localized effects, permitting a market in such law "products." The question might be posed as to whether the effects of intellectual property law "products" will tend to be localized, like those of incorporation law, or diffuse, like those of tort law. Most especially, the question must be posed of what effect, if any, the Internet may have on the localization or externalization of intellectual property law products.

The answer appears to be that the externalizing effects of the Internet on the market for intellectual property law products may be as profound as its externalizing effects on the market for intellectual property itself. Much as in the case of corporation or bankruptcy law, jurisdictions may be expected to compete in producing intellectual property law; as suggested above, some may adopt a creation-fostering stance, others a distribution-fostering stance. As also suggested above, distance and border control have previously kept these differing approaches compartmentalized, allowing competition between permissive and restrictive regimes. However, the Internet breaks down that compartmentalization, allowing the effects of permissive regimes to be felt in nations with restrictive regimes. This effectively allows permissive regimes to lower regulatory costs at the expense of restrictive regimes, and spells the end of an efficient Tiebout-type competition in information law.

Although this effect might be characterized as a "race to the bottom" for intellectual property law, the discussion above suggests that it is better thought of as simply "a race to externalize."[17] Jurisdictions may adopt a permissive information distribution regime in order to attract distributors, but the Internet expands the market of such low-cost distributors globally to the territories of restrictive jurisdictions. The availability of low-cost information from off-shore sources may disrupt the restrictive jurisdictions' attempt to foster information generation. In order to compete with the off-shore source, domestic providers may have to lower prices to a level at which the creators of information products cannot recoup their investment costs. This potentially puts information production into a "death spiral" of lowered prices and lower production, ending in the type of underproduction predicted by Samuelson for classic public goods.

It may therefore seem that a permissive intellectual property policy is suicidal for information distributors on the Internet; by undercutting incentives for information generation and institutionalization, they would seem to pronounce their own death sentences. In the past, physical distance and national compartmentalization allowed such activity, but as the Internet ties previously isolated markets together, a permissive strategy may ultimately prove self-defeating. Continuing to engaging in such potentially destructive behavior might appear irrational as a business or political strategy. Yet game theory models such as the classic "Prisoner's Dilemma" predict the existence of situations in which apparently rational choices lead to a sub-optimal outcome.[18] It may well be that the aggregate welfare would be increased if all nations adopted stringent intellectual property regulation, but when linked by the Internet, no nation has an incentive to do so unless every other nation does so—and, in fact, every nation may have strong incentives to "defect" from such cooperation in order to externalize its regulatory costs at the expense of others.[19]

Competition and Cooperation

The classic "Prisoner's Dilemma" assumes that the players are unable to communicate with one another, and that the game is a single-round interaction. Nations are not necessarily constrained by these assumptions; opportunities for negotiation arise with some frequency, and the "players" in the international market know that they will interact again in the future.[20] This latter knowledge may be especially significant, since studies of multi-round games have suggested that cooperative strategies tend to dominate such tournaments, and so cooperative strategies may be the preference of rational actors in international competition.[21] Repeated interaction may lead to "trust," where trust comprises mutual recognition of the strategic advantage of cooperation.[22] If such cooperation can evolve among competitors in the market for intellectual property regulation, the "race for externalization" via the Internet might be avoided.

Certain serious barriers to this kind of cooperation may dim the prospects for such a solution. The first of these objections is the simple recognition that nations are not monolithic. Governments do not have interests; individuals do. Where the state is concerned, the individuals furthering their own interests are politicians, and politicians are engaged not simply in a competitive game with their international counterparts, but with domestic voters as well. This latter game will frequently prove to be the more influential factor in intellectual property policy; despite the importance of the Tiebout insight, voting with one's feet need not always eclipse voting with one's ballot. An explanation of current intellectual property laws does not necessarily require resort to inter-jurisdictional competition; a public choice account of domestic interests would seem adequate. In a post-Internet world, the interest groups that forged the present intellectual property environment can be expected to continue to attempt to influence policy to their advantage.

Thus, voice may be as important as exit in the calculus of intellectual property law production.[23] As discussed above, a jurisdiction that wished to win the "race to the bottom" for international information access and provision might be required to do so at the expense of domestic information product creation. However, the highly permissive intellectual property rules necessary to attract information "pirates" could be unacceptable to domestic information industries. If such protectionist sentiments were manifest at the ballot box, that jurisdiction's ability to attract information capital would be stymied. The loss of information providers to other jurisdictions might eventually overcome domestic reluctance to enact a more permissive regime, but this need not necessarily be the case—the United States, for example, has historically responded to extraterritorial copyright piracy not by loosening domestic law, but by exerting diplomatic and economic pressure on the permissive jurisdiction to tighten its copyright requirements.

The second barrier to cooperation is to some extent a corollary to the first: governments are comprised of people, and people do not remain in the same position forever. At minimum, exercise of "voice" through internal elections will periodically change the identity of those representing the nation.[24] Cooperation between nations may be a multi-round game, but, at least so far as nations with democratic process are concerned, it is a game in which the players change every few rounds. Cooperative relationships may be exceedingly difficult to maintain under such conditions because the time horizon for exit of a particular player is finite. If an agreement is concluded with a player who may shortly leave the game, then the value of the agreement becomes uncertain, whereas the value of cheating on the agreement is known. This difficulty is to some extent blunted by organizational mechanisms within governments that promote continuity. However, reversals of international information policy may be as frequent as the elections of a chief executive or majority of the legislature.

Public Choice and the Internet

Public choice theory suggests that politicians will engage in an international race to attract information providers only to the extent activity furthers their personal or political goals.[25] Where the requirements for Tiebout competition are met, this may tend to work in favor of efficient provision of local public goods due to internal forces, as well as external competition. The availability of more attractive regulatory regimes abroad may attract industry out of a jurisdiction, putting politicians in that jurisdiction under considerable voter pressure to streamline domestic regulation.[26] First, politicians faced with a net emigration of firms or citizens may be inclined to enact more efficient local regulation to stem the tide of departure, or to avoid it completely. The threat of exit thus forces regulators to set the "price" of regulation closer to the competitive "price."[27] Additionally, if domestic voters are aware of policies in other jurisdictions, they use this information to gauge the performance of their leaders, and demand comparable policies.[28] Failure to implement such policies may result in the removal of local politicians from office by disgruntled constituents who have not yet exited.

This reasoning indicates that there is implicit in the Tiebout model an answer to the problem of "capture" that is predicted by public choice theory.[29] Because the marginal value of a vote is almost nil, voters in democracies may tend to be rationally ignorant or even rationally indifferent to the electoral process: their ability to affect the outcome of an election may not be worth the time investment to become an informed voter, or even to cast a vote. In the face of such indifference, representative governments may be captured by "rent-seekers"; that is, special interest groups who find that it is worth their time to attempt to influence government. Generally such rent-seeking groups will seek special interest legislation that benefits them, but may not be efficient for society generally.

However, a nation that faces stiff extraterritorial Tiebout competition cannot afford the "drag" of such inefficient legislation. As in the case of firms in private markets, nations may be forced to become more efficient in order to compete. In some instances, law products may do well in the legal market because they embody true regulatory innovation, but more often, rules may be made competitive by paring away inefficient special interest regulation. What this means for information policy is that stiff inter-jurisdictional competition to attract information providers and distributors may help to keep local politicians honest. Nations competing with other jurisdictions in the market for intellectual property law will have to avoid special interest boondoggles, or watch new industries migrate offshore to compete in the information product market.

Current proposals for amending the U.S. copyright laws arguably provide a concrete example of this effect: the proposals, drawn from a Department of Commerce white paper, have been criticized as heavily favoring information producers at the expense of information distributors and consumers.[30] If these criticisms are correct, then the proposals may be the result of "rent-seeking" by powerful entertainment and publishing lobbies. But, even assuming this is the case, it is difficult to see how the proposals will assist the rent-seekers in the face of international competition. The proposals, if enacted, may allow special interests to seek higher prices for the information goods they produce. But lower-cost distributors will simply migrate off-shore to more permissive jurisdictions, and via the Internet undercut the inflated content prices. This in turn will force the beneficiaries of the legislation to lower their prices, negating the effect of the proposals.

This explanation of the white paper proposal would predict that, because of foreign competition for both law products and information products, the rent-seekers' only hope to protect their proposed prerogatives would be to seek homogenous international enforcement of the proposals. This prediction in fact fits the currently available data; the same U.S. bureaucrats who championed the proposals in the United States are now vigorously advocating the same proposals before the World Intellectual Property Organization (WIPO), seeking their widespread adoption. International adoption of uniform intellectual property standards might serve to avoid the "race to the bottom." But in preventing the "race to the bottom," an agreement may also cripple the "race to the top." Such a cure may be no better than the disease; an international intellectual property agreement may resemble cooperative equilibrium less than it resembles anti-competitive collusion in a private sector cartel.

Cooperation and Collusion

Much like a classic economic cartel, governments that participate in an international intellectual property agreement may be able to avoid "ruinous competition" in the market for law as a good. This may be highly advantageous to politicians at the national level. First, through collusion with foreign politicians, domestic politicians can protect themselves against superior foreign law products.[31] Exodus of firms to more attractive regulatory regimes may place domestic politicians and bureaucrats under pressure to streamline local regulation, perhaps at the expense of favored but inefficient rent-seeking constituents. Such streamlining may, however, be avoided by agreement with foreign counterparts to cooperate in suppressing formulation of more efficient regulation in their respective jurisdictions.

At the same time, local politicians may use an international agreement to deflect domestic voter dissatisfaction over special interest legislation by characterizing the protectionist measures as a necessary part of international cooperation.[32] This in essence facilitates intra-jurisdictional externalization of regulatory costs: rather than shifting costs to other jurisdictions, costs are shifted to a different constituency within the jurisdiction.[33] Thus, international collusion may prevent both "voice" and "exit" from correcting political improvidence.[34] Sad to say, elements of both these political ploys seem apparent in the recent domestic U.S. legislation aimed at on-line copyright protection. Several commentators have suggested that the proposed amendments to the Copyright

Act appear strongly partisan, favoring information producers over information distributors and consumers. Not only have U.S. politicians sponsoring the amendments gone before WIPO to seek international implementation of the same or similar copyright provisions, but in Congressional hearings on the domestic legislation, WIPO officials have been paraded before the legislature to certify the importance and necessity of the amendments as part of international cooperation.

However, cartels of any sort are notoriously unstable.[35] In the case of economic cartels, a collusive organization is believed to be most feasible and stable where the quality of the product is homogeneous, the price elasticity of demand for the product is low, barriers to entry are high, all suppliers of the product have similar cost functions, and there is a dominant supplier who can act as price-leader. In the case of international collusion for intellectual property law "products," several of these requirements may be met, in part because the universe of law producers on an international scale is closed. The number of sovereign states is relatively large, but certain nations, particularly the United States, are able to exert considerable diplomatic and economic pressure toward conformity. In this regard, it is particularly worth noting that in pressing its white paper recommendations to WIPO, the United States appears suspiciously like a supplier attempting to act as "price-leader" in the market for intellectual property law. By promulgating its new white paper copyright law products as a proposed standard, the United States is attempting to coordinate the international market for such law products.

The international inefficiencies resulting from uniform intellectual property standards may be no less serious than national inefficiencies. The drawbacks to international cooperation follow naturally from the principles outlined previously in this discussion. First, by homogenizing national intellectual property systems, an international agreement forces international businesses to operate in a world where "one size fits all." Opportunities for jurisdictional experimentation and innovation are curtailed. New information industries that might arise under innovative schemes may be stifled. Established information industries will be confined to an international norm rather than offered the opportunity to select from a diversity of systems that which is best suited to their operation. As a corollary effect, information firms will be exposed to greater business risk because they will be less able to diversify across jurisdictions.[36]

Centralization and Competition

Theories of international cooperation predict that, much as in the "Prisoner's Dilemma," a nation will remain party to a cooperative agreement to the extent that the agreement is "self-enforcing," that is, only so long as the nation has more to gain from cooperation than from defection.[37] If in fact cooperative strategies prove impossible or unworkable, rational competitors may have yet another option. If "horizontal" cooperation between jurisdictions proves unstable, the creation of a "third party" standing in a vertical relationship to the competitors may be necessary.[38] Tiebout recognized this in his original model by noting that where externalities exist, centralized decision-making, rather than inter-jurisdictional competition, may be required to achieve an efficient outcome. Stated in game theory terms: because states know that their own rational short-term competitive preferences will inevitably lead to their own detriment in the long term, states may choose to voluntarily surrender all or part of their decision-making power to a third party.

This is in essence the strategy adopted by the individual states of the United States in acquiescing to the constitutional compact that creates a centralized federal government; similar benefits may be found in the federal compacts of Canada, Australia, and to some extent the European Community. Interestingly, it is also much the same strategy adopted by the GATT signatory nations in creating the World Trade Organization (WTO). However, in the United States and elsewhere, even when some types of interstate regulation have been centralized, the benefits of interstate competition have also been preserved to the extent deemed practical. Because competitive benefits will be lost in whichever markets are centralized, centralization must be considered a drastic measure to be taken only where no such efficiencies are to be had; that is, where externalities prevent the development of competition in the first instance.

International centralization for Internet-related information rights should likewise be approached with a minimalist attitude, if at all. Although the Internet promises to lower distance barriers, other economic barriers may help maintain sufficient compartmentalization such that precipitous international action need not be taken—at least not yet. The first of these barriers is the reputational capital accumulated by nations offering established law products. For example, in Romano's study of the "race to the top" for incorporation, firms that incorporated in Delaware repeatedly referred to the large body of settled case law on corporations as a reason for incorporating there. Similarly, nations with a long history of well-developed copyright law may be especially attractive to information distributors seeking to locate their operations, especially if the jurisdiction sports "specialty courts" with a high degree of expertise in copyright. The certainty offered by a well-developed body of copyright law may in many instances offer greater business value than would relaxed regulation of information distribution. New entrants into the information law market may have their work cut out for them in order to displace the law products of well-established jurisdictions.

These effects would likely tend to favor developed information-producing nations such as the United States over developing nations with immature information law precedents. Of course, the unsettled nature of law on the Internet may blunt this comparative advantage; to the extent that production of "cyber law" represents entry into a new market, no nation yet enjoys an unassailable market share. However, the existence in some nations of courts with a developed expertise in copyright and related law could offer a significant advantage even in the absence of precedential decisions directly addressed to the Internet. This may mean that a stampede of firms to permissive but untried jurisdictions will not develop.

Second, law is in many senses a "bundled" product—the decision to "exit" for an alternative venue will be made on the totality of the public goods package offered off-shore.[39] Even if a permissive intellectual property law product is offered, other regulation in that jurisdiction will be taken into account, and may outweigh the competitiveness of the intellectual property offering. Indeed, nonlegal "factor endowments" such as climate or quality of life may be in essence bundled with the intellectual property law product of the jurisdiction. Restrictive intellectual property jurisdictions may be able to remain competitive if their total package of taxes, climate, labor regulation, import duties, and other local public goods remains attractive.

Similarly, with regard to the market for intellectual property itself, there may be no stampede of consumers to off-shore providers because of barriers of presentation.[40] A common complaint regarding on-line reading material is the inconvenience of moving between screens; it is difficult to "skim" or quickly "thumb through" the displayed material as compared to a hard-copy version. Even the most compact notebook computer is fairly awkward and bulky compared to a paperback book; until the advent of some major and ubiquitous advance in flat-panel technology, this will likely remain the case. And, even with rising printing costs, the present price of a paperback is difficult to beat. Thus it seems unlikely that novels downloaded off the Internet will displace books for pleasure reading in the near future: readers curling up on the sofa with a palm-top computer and a large mug of cocoa is not a scenario that the publishing industry need fear.

Similarly, downloaded graphics seem unlikely to cause imminent displacement of glossy magazines or wall posters. Certainly graphics of all kinds are available in digitized formats on the Internet, and a lively exchange of infringing graphic works is carried on via Usenet and the World Wide Web. But consumers are unlikely to turn to the Net for high resolution photographs of their favorite supermodel or of stunning mountain landscapes—even on high-quality monitors, such scenery lacks the resolution and permanence to be had in the pages of *National Geographic* or *Sports Illustrated*. Additionally, few consumers have the capability to print high-quality copies, nor are many likely to make the investment in such capability when high quality prints may be had for a few dollars in the pages of a magazine.

Comparable barriers exist with regard to other copyrighted works. Digitized music can easily be uploaded to the Internet, and downloaded to a home computer, but generally not in a format that would allow it to be played on home stereos. Playback on standard

computer multimedia speakers is unlikely to be satisfying, especially for fans of Wagner, Pink Floyd, or other artists whose work
cries out for high-fidelity treatment. Similar problems apply to
playback of movies on personal computers, at least for a populace
that is becoming accustomed to home video on big-screen TVs with
surround sound.

Additionally, transmission of movies on the network presently
consumes prohibitive amounts of bandwidth, but may become
feasible as digital compression improves. Alternatively, movie files
may be compressed to be downloaded and played back locally.
However, if anything is known about consumer preferences, it is
that movies on demand will not be the "killer app" of the network—
consumer interest appears lukewarm, and it will be difficult for
Internet content providers to undersell the minimal charge of the
ubiquitous local video rental store.

Of course, many of these presentation barriers may be overcome
as the separate home appliances of computer, stereo, and television begin to merge, allowing seamless transfer of digital works
between video, audio, and information-processing systems. But
that convergence has not happened yet, and—as the history of Bell
Laboratories' abortive "Picture Phone" or Knight-Ridder's failed
videotext "Viewtron" project warn—may never happen.[41] Assuming that such a convergence does occur, the form it may take is
unlikely to be foreseeable in current forecasts. At least for the
present, though, it appears that the Internet has not magically
transformed aesthetic and entertainment works into general public goods—quite the contrary, the particular embodiment of such
works remains an important aspect of consumer enjoyment, and
the preferred embodiments continue to show characteristics of
local public goods. So long as this remains true, "spillover" into
other jurisdictions may be containable.

For other classes of copyrighted works, however, current computer presentation formats will remain perfectly acceptable. Such
works might include databases, factual or instructional documents,
and, of course, computer software. Because such works are not
intended to be enjoyed aesthetically, their presentation format is
less important than their content. It is interesting to note that such
"utilitarian" works tend to be those not traditionally protected by

copyright, and hence those works for which copyright protection is most problematic or "thin." Nonetheless they appear to be the type of works that will most closely resemble general public goods in Internet commerce; consequently, some special provision for such works may be in order.

Conclusion

The Internet promises to facilitate both trans-border delivery of information products and trans-border migration of information producers. Thus the competitive effects of the Internet may prove a mixed blessing, depending on one's perspective. The challenge will be to preserve the competitive benefits enabled by the network while minimizing its externalizing effects. To meet that challenge, a carefully crafted international agreement on copyright and information policy may be necessary, but the necessity of an agreement is by no means clear, and present calls to conclude such an agreement appear premature, even if well-intentioned.

Given the potential for international collusion via such an agreement, action on such an agreement should be postponed until it is quite clear that a "race for the bottom" is more than speculation. This means that periodic "reality checks" regarding the actual extent of Internet externalization will be necessary. If an agreement appears necessary, it should extend only to media that display the characteristics of pure public goods rather than those of local public goods—in the near term, such media might include little more than software, text, and databases.

Additionally, any agreement should leave maximum opportunity for jurisdictional experimentation and variation. This likely means doing no more than specifying minimum standards for copyright protection by the signatories. Interestingly enough, this is already the approach taken by both the Berne Convention and, by incorporation of the Berne standards, the WTO. Thus the sensible approach at present may simply be to seek increased enrollment in existing agreements rather than new or drastically modified agreements.

Notes

1. See Bruce Sterling, *Islands in the Net* (New York: Arbor House, 1988), p. 37.

2. See Vinton G. Cerf, "Networks," *Scientific American* (September 1991), p. 72.

3. See August Lïsch, *The Economics of Locations*, trans. W.H. Woglom & W.F. Stolper (New Haven: Yale University Press, 1954).

4. See R. Sohns, "Lïsch and the Theory of Trade" in *The Analysis of Regional Structure: Essays in Honour of August Lïsch* (New York: Metheun, 1978), pp. 119, 122–124.

5. See Paul A. Samuelson, "The Pure Theory of Public Expenditures," *Review of Economics and Statistics* 36 (1954), p. 387.

6. See Richard P. Adelstein and Steven I. Peretz, "The Competition of Technologies in Markets for Ideas: Copyright and Fair Use in Evolutionary Perspective," *International Review of Law and Economics* 5 (1985), p. 209.

7. See Joseph Stiglitz, "The Theory of Local Public Goods" in *Local Provision of Public Services: The Tiebout Model after Twenty-Five Years*, ed. George R. Zodrow (New York: Academic Press, 1983), pp. 17, 19.

8. See Karen B. Levitan, "Information Resources as 'Goods' in the Life Cycle of Information Production," *Journal of the American Society for Information Science* 44 (1982).

9. See Charles Tiebout, "A Pure Theory of Local Expenditures," *Journal of Political Economy* 64 (1954), p. 416.

10. See Albert Hirschman, *Exit, Voice, and Loyalty: Responses to Decline in Firms, Organizations, and States* (Cambridge, Massachusetts: Harvard University Press, 1970).

11. See Stiglitz, "The Theory of Local Public Goods," p. 48.

12. See Ibid., p. 47.

13. See William L. Carey, "Federalism and Corporate Law: Reflections upon Delaware," *Yale Law Journal* 83 (1974), p. 663.

14. See Daniel Fischel, "The 'Race to the Bottom' Revisited: Reflections on Recent Developments in Delaware's Corporation Law," *Northwestern Law Review* 76 (1982), p. 913; Peter Dodd and Richard Leftwich, "Federal Regulation," *Journal of Business* 53 (1980), p. 259.

15. See Roberta Romano, "Law as a Product: Some Pieces of the Incorporation Puzzle," *Journal of Law, Economics and Organization* 1 (1985), p. 225.

16. See, for example, Margaret F. Brinig and Francis H. Buckley, "The Market for Deadbeats," *Journal of Legal Studies* 25 (1996), p. 201 (empirical study indicating that jurisdictions compete for desirable immigrants by offering absolution from former debts).

17. See Joel P. Trachtman, "International Regulatory Competition, Externalization, and Jurisdiction," *Harvard International Law Journal* 34, (1993), pp. 47, 73.

18. See R. Duncan Luce and Howard Raiffa, *Games and Decisions* (New York: Wiley, 1957) (explaining the "Prisoner's Dilemma" game theory scenario).

19. See Trachtman, "International Regulatory Competition, Externalization, and Jurisdiction," p. 76.

20. See John E. Chubb, "How Relevant is Competition to Government Policymaking?" in *Competition Among States and Local Governments: Efficiency and Equity in American Federalism*, ed. Daphne A. Kenyon and John Kincaid (Washington, D.C.: Urban Institute Press, 1991), pp. 57, 58.

21. See Robert Axelrod, *The Evolution of Cooperation* (New York: Basic Books, 1984).

22. See J.S. Coleman, "Recontracting, Trustworthiness, and the Stability of Vote Exchanges," *Public Choice* 40 (1983), p. 89.

23. See Chubb, "How Relevant is Competition to Government Policymaking?"

24. See Albert Breton, "The Existence and Stability of Interjurisdictional Competition," pp. 38, 49.

25. See Roland Vaubel, "A Public Choice View of International Organization," in *The Political Economy of International Organizations*, ed. Roland Vaubel and Thomas D. Wilbert (Boulder: Westview Press, 1991), pp. 27, 31.

26. Ibid., p. 30.

27. See Breton, p. 40.

28. Ibid.

29. See Mancur Olson, *The Logic of Collective Action: Public Goods and the Theory of Groups* (Cambridge, Massachusetts: Harvard University Press, 1965); James M. Buchanan and Gordon Tullock, *The Calculus of Consent: Logical Foundations of Constitutional Democracy* (Ann Arbor, Michigan: University of Michigan Press, 1962).

30. See Pamela Samuelson, "Intellectual Property Rights and the Global Information Economy," *Communications of the ACM* (January 1996), p. 23.

31. See Vaubel, "A Public Choice View of International Organization," p. 32.

32. Ibid.

33. See Trachtman, p. 57.

34. See Vaubel, p. 34.

35. See George Stigler, "A Theory of Oligopoly," *Journal of Political Economy* 72 (1977), p. 44.

36. See Vaubel, p. 29.

37. See Lester Telser, "A Theory of Self-Enforcing Agreements," *Journal of Business* 53 (1980), p. 27.

38. See Breton, pp. 48–49.

39. See Trachtman, p. 79.

40. See I. Trotter Hardy, "Contracts, Copyright, and Preemption in a Digital World," *University of Richmond Journal of Law and Technology* 1 (1995) (http://www.urich.edu/~jolt/v1.1/hardy.html).

41. See John Markoff, "Building the Information Superhighway," *New York Times,* January 24, 1993 (discussing Picture Phone); Karen Wright, "The Road to the Global Village," *Scientific American* (March 1990), pp. 83, 85 (discussing Viewtron).

A Regulatory Web: Free Speech and the Global Information Infrastructure

Viktor Mayer-Schönberger and Teree E. Foster

National restrictions on freedom of speech on the nascent global information infrastructure are commonplace not only in the United States but around the globe.[1] Individual nations, each intent upon preserving what they perceive to be within the parameters of national interests, seek to regulate certain forms of speech the content of which is classified as reprehensible or offensive to national well-being or civic virtue.[2] The fact that this offending speech is technologically dispersed instantaneously to millions of potential recipients enhances rather than diminishes the impetus to regulate.

At the same time, outspoken advocates of free speech vigorously advance their absolutist position of noninfringement into what appears to be an unrelenting struggle for every inch and aspect of unregulated information infrastructure territory.[3] The information infrastructure is a communicative device of such broad scope and accessibility that it raises serious issues for free speech absolutists, who characterize it as a tool for democratizing speech on a global basis and insist that it remain insulated from any regulatory mandates.[4]

Activists at both ends of this spectrum disregard an integral aspect of the global composition of the information infrastructure. Those who advocate unfettered Net communication and those who espouse some form of national Net regulation are similarly constrained in the pursuit of their objectives by the very structure of the thing they fight about. It is this global aspect of the information infrastructure that shapes the debate on freedom of speech and limits absolutists and regulators at the same time.

The nature of this conflict and its potential resolution will be outlined in the following pages.[5] Thereafter, assuming that national policy makers will not want to cede their authority to regulate the information infrastructure, we will suggest a mechanism by which policy makers who do elect to regulate speech can begin to deliberate about this objective in a structured, principled, and internationally acceptable manner.

International Constraints on National Information Infrastructures

The international nature of the information infrastructure places substantial constraints upon both the free speech absolutists and those who would regulate speech.

Restraint by Nations on Domestic Speech

Advocates of an unobstructed flow of speech conceive of the Net as an anarchic communicative medium that is an inappropriate forum for governmental regulatory intrusion, and as a medium capable of advancing freedom on a global scale by razing barriers to accessing information, even in closed societies.[6] In the United States, these speech advocates rely on the words of the First Amendment, which is framed in absolute terms, and on the Supreme Court, which on occasion has endorsed an absolutist interpretation of the Amendment's dictates.[7]

But speech is not—and never has been—inviolate, either in the United States or in any other country of the world. Communicative acts on the Internet fall within such national speech restrictions because the Net is not extraterritorial and its users are not otherwise exempted from existing national speech regulations. And in fact, many nations have begun the process of constricting the content of speech on the Internet. A sampling of regulatory rules in force in various countries throughout the community of nations follows.

Libel. Most nations deal severely with speech that denigrates the reputation of another. These national libel laws directly apply to Net communication.[8]

Pornography. In England, the Obscene Publications Act defines as "obscene" material that "tends to deprave and corrupt persons" and subjects such material to regulation. *Penthouse* magazine's World Wide Web site lists 25 countries that outlaw its so-called adult material, including Egypt, India, Japan, Korea, Mexico, Saudi Arabia, Spain and the United Kingdom. The government of Singapore has implemented a licensing scheme for local Internet operators and content providers that is designed to constrain all forms of sexual excess in cyberspace.[9] And discussions of sex (as well as religion and politics) are banned in Saudi Arabia and Iran.[10]

In Germany, a group of laws designed to protect children were applied recently in a now-infamous case involving CompuServe. In November 1995, a Bavarian State Attorney ordered a search of the Munich office of CompuServe for evidence of a breach of German child pornography laws, and material was seized by police. The prosecutor pressed CompuServe to prevent all users from accessing through its Internet gateway certain Unsenet newsgroups supposedly disseminating child pornography. In December, CompuServe complied and obstructed its users from accessing 200 groups, including all those prefixed with "alt.sex." CompuServe later lifted this ban in the wake of substantial worldwide protest.[11] By then, CompuServe had developed a software solution to block certain Internet information resources.

Subversive Information. The computer equipment of anarchist groups in Italy, England, and Scotland that advocate anti-government violence through utilization of online sources has been seized by their respective governments. Vietnam, concerned that increasing links with noncommunist nations could undermine the ruling regime, is seeking to control Internet access on the country's two independent computer networks.[12]

Hate Speech. As might be anticipated, the most virulent laws criminalizing hate speech are found in those countries scarred by the Holocaust. In Germany, a number of provisions of the criminal code are directed at expression that is inconsistent with the "dignity of the human personality developing freely within the social community,"[13] a fundamental right preserved in the German Constitution.[14] For example, Section 130 of the Criminal Code condemns attacks on human dignity that incite hatred. Section 131 of the Code proscribes the production or dissemination of hate speech in written form.[15] Section 194 permits prosecution for the denial of the existence of the Holocaust when the disavowal is stated to a person who is a member of a group persecuted by the Nazi regime. Section 86 forbids the distribution of propaganda that promotes the precepts of the Nazi regime, or of unconstitutional parties or prohibited associations. And Section 86a censures the use of insignia—including flags, uniforms, badges, and salutes—of these same proscribed organizations.[16]

The means of enforcing these laws outlawing hate speech and Nazi propaganda are the subject of vigorous debate in Germany. German prosecutors in Mannheim are investigating CompuServe, the T-Online network of Deutsche Telekom, and America Online for aiding the distribution of neo-Nazi material posted on the Internet that questions whether the Holocaust occurred.[17]

The Austrian Prohibition Act similarly prohibits actions on behalf of the Nazi Party as well as advocacy of its objectives or dissemination of its propaganda. Targeting groups of persons for ignominy or justifying their genocide is likewise forbidden.[18] A special investigation of the Austrian Police into terrorist activities has focused in recent months on the Internet and a Nazi computer network information exchange, known as Thule-Net.[19]

In Canada, separate provisions of the Criminal Code outlaw the willful promotion of hatred[20] and the communication of telephone messages likely to expose people to hatred or contempt because of, among other things, their race, national or ethnic origin, color, or religion.[21]

Privacy Protection. Recently, the European Union determined to regulate the flow of information about individuals, ostensibly to prevent corporate intrusion upon individual privacy. The member nations have agreed to obstruct the export of personal data to nations that do not establish "adequate" privacy protection.[22]

These are just a few examples of the many national regulations of Net speech in place throughout the world. Not even among Western, democratic, and liberal countries does there seem to be a consistent approach to restricting the freedom of expression. The Net is not an anarchic, unregulated dominion above and beyond individual state control, but rather a terrain policed by many often outright contradictory national laws. It consists of many regulatory fiefdoms. Yet the internationality of the Net, along with the conglomeration of national regulations and their effects on the flow of information, invariably shape all communicative activity on the Net as a whole. Thus its international nature does not remove discussions on the Net from national regulations but instead subjects them to a panoply of varying and contradictory regulations that breed uncertainty and indeterminacy. The consequence is that speech, subjected to a patchwork of constraints, might be restricted more than intended or necessary. In this respect, the global dimension of the Net could develop into more of a liability than a speech protecting asset, for this state of affairs generates silent silencing rather than clearcut regulations.

Speech is constrained not only in other nations, but also in the United States. The United States Supreme Court has identified varieties of vulnerable expression, or "low value speech,"[23] forms of expression that "are no essential part of any exposition of ideas, and are of such slight social value as a step to truth that any benefit that may be derived from them is clearly outweighed by the social interest in order and morality."[24] These include intentional incitement,[25] obscenity,[26] child pornography,[27] defamation,[28] fighting words,[29] and commercial speech.[30] The Court has constructed a series of quite different standards for each of these varieties of speech to determine, first, whether a particular communication is protected or falls into a vulnerable category and second, for those seen as vulnerable, whether any First Amendment protection is merited.

Obscenity and Related Areas. Obscenity, perhaps the quintessential example of valueless expression, is taken to be bereft of communicative value and thus subject to broad controls. The Court's latest formulation for distinguishing obscenity from speech that is merely distasteful, rough, evocative, or erotic—and therefore protected to some extent—requires a finding that the communication is patently offensive, appeals to prurient interests, and is bereft of serious scientific, artistic, literary, or political value.[31] Integral to these defining principles is the notion that individual communities retain autonomy to set their own statutory standards for the definition of pornography, or communications that are "patently offensive" and appeal to "prurient interests."[32]

However, traditional notions of "community" quickly become confounded in the context of a medium such as the Internet, the characteristics of which obliterate any notions of state or national boundaries. For example, a California couple was convicted in 1994 for dispatching over a computer bulletin board materials found to be obscene when viewed in Memphis.[33] The materials at issue in this case were arguably obscene by any community standard.[34] But this case and others like it raise the question of whether using the Internet to transmit ostensibly obscene materials portends that the applicable community standards will be those espoused by the most priggish among us.

Another recent case demonstrates the power of the Internet to subject individuals to criminal prosecution. A University of Michigan student, Baker, communicating with an unidentified person through e-mail, expressed an escalating sexual interest in violence against women and girls. Baker was charged under federal law with transmitting threats to injure or kidnap another, but the court granted his motion to quash the indictment on the grounds that these private e-mail communications did not constitute statutory threats.[35]

Above and beyond existing judicial decisions and state laws, Congress has decided to criminalize Internet dissemination of not only obscene material but all sexually explicit text or images. The Communications Decency Act of 1996 regulates the carriage and transmission of "indecent" materials on the Internet to persons under the age of 18. In this Act, designated as protecting minors, Congress defines as indecent "any comment, request, suggestion, proposal, image or other communication that describes, in terms patently offensive as measured by contemporary community standards, sexual or excretory activities or organs."[36]

The Communications Decency Act has provoked reaction both swift and strong. America Online threatened to terminate its bulletin boards and chat rooms, opining that only through such severe measures could AOL assure compliance with the Act.[37] The Citizens Empowerment Coalition filed suit challenging the constitutionality of the Act, as did the American Civil Liberties Union. Both groups alleged that the Internet is a unique communications medium that merits unique First Amendment protection at least as broad as that afforded to print media. The challengers argue that parents are the best judges of material that is appropriate for themselves and their children. A federal judge granted a preliminary injunction against enforcement of the Act in February 1996.

In June, a three-judge federal court agreed that the portions of the Act that attempt to regulate non-obscene communications do not pass constitutional muster and upheld the injunction.[38]

Subversive Advocacy. Intentional incitement, or subversive advocacy, is a special case of the Court's approach to appraising the validity of content-based regulations. The Court permits regulation of expression that qualifies as incitement only if as a consequence of the utterance there exists a genuine likelihood of imminent unlawful conduct and if the speaker intends this result.[39] *Brandenburg v. Ohio*[40] declares as a general First Amendment tenet that advocacy of even the most alarming notions is absolutely protected against direct criminal prohibition regardless of dangerousness and intent. Interdiction of ideas or perspectives deemed intrinsically dangerous—and perhaps justifiably so—by the government is forbidden.

National Enforcement and International Structures

As we have established, the Internet, even if global in scope, is not an absolutist free speech domain, but is subject to innumerable national restrictions. At the same time, the very structure of the Net substantially diminishes the chances for enforcement of national regulations.[41]

National speech restrictions can be enforced directly only within the territory to which they apply.[42] But the Net is global, and so is the flow of information. People who disseminate information through the Net that is illegal in one country can easily transfer their activities to a country with no similar prohibitions and effectively redeploy their operations within a matter of hours.

For the recipients of such information, redeployment is hardly noticeable in an environment dominated by the World Wide Web and allowing for information access and retrieval by simply clicking on information links. Because distance from or location of information sources within the World Wide Web is irrelevant to the recipient, relocation of information sources is easy and access to such redeployed information straightforward.

Already there exist numerous examples of exiled political groups taking advantage of information infrastructure networks located in countries with regulatory environments more sympathetic to their causes to widely disseminate political information to countries with more restrictive speech and information regulations. Chinese human rights activists use the World Wide Web to advocate for their cause,[43] and Tibetan women in exile castigate the Chinese government for its tretment of their sisters still in Tibet.[44] CAPA, an organization that supports Cubans fleeing their country, broadcasts accounts of their rescue and survival on the Web,[45] while German Nazis use American and Canadian Web sites to discuss fascism and to issue denials of the Holocaust, a crime under the German Penal Code.[46]

Information sources need not necessarily be redeployed for information to be disseminated across porous national borders. Other tools are available on the global Net to channel information in a way that obscures its source and place of origin. Anonymous remailers allow electronic information to be stripped off all identifying bits and sent without attribution to any recipient.[47] Together with widely available tools of public key encryption,[48] remailers allow worldwide electronic communication on a totally anonymous level, thus circumventing any national attempts at speech regulation.

Continued information redeployment will eventually shape and reshape the global information infrastructure. Nations with little speech regulation or inefficient enforcement structures will attract vast quantities of data and information illegal in other countries. The global infrastructure will experience sustained economic pressures similar to those experienced on the high seas by the "flags of convenience" phenomenon. By redeploying their fleets under "flags of convenience," shipping companies can economically coerce countries to deregulate.[49] A similar phenomenon could materialize on the Net. Some countries might evolve into booming "data havens," while others might face a choice between economic hardship and relinquishing their speech constraints and thus compromising their national or civic values.

Consequences

In the world of a global information infrastructure, an escalating national de jure regulation of speech meets a similarly pervasive de facto futility of enforcement. Herein, indeed, lies a strange paradox: the international dimension of the information infrastructure strengthens *and* weakens both speech regulation and free speech protection simultaneously.

Given this paradox, national legislatures might continue to enact regulations, but their regulatory endeavors are unlikely to be as effectively enforceable as they desire. To circumvent the limitations of national regulatory attempts, one might advocate for an international regulatory measure to restrict the content of Internet communications. In principle, as global a phenomenon as the Internet propels nations to strive for international regulatory cooperation and partnership.

National legislatures differ dramatically in the kinds of content they prefer to regulate. Any attempt to regulate the global information infrastructure must be acceptable to the vast majority of nations in order to become enforceable. Hence, any method or tool to devise a framework for an internationally acceptable and enforceable content-based speech restriction must conform to a rigorous set of requirements. Cognizant of the specific structural qualities of global information infrastructures, we posit several such essential requirements.[50]

The Net is a global phenomenon. In order to be feasible, any regulatory attempt must be based on an internationally acceptable, or already accepted, principle. While speech has never enjoyed—and will never enjoy—absolute protection, the principle of freedom of speech has become part of a minimum standard of freedoms for the great majority of nations. So a method must be devised for defining certain categories of regulable speech while at the same time staunchly protecting all other speech. Regulatory lines must be drawn circumspectly. Only speech that is encompassed within certain specified, albeit narrow, confines can be regulated on the basis of its content. All speech outside these narrow boundaries should be assiduously sheltered from content-based regulation.

Even more important, the method for selecting categories of regulable speech should ensure results that will be accepted by the community of nations. The method must include a mechanism for reaching a broad international consensus. This consensus should be multinational in its reach in order to avoid vulnerability to chauvinistic national interests or sentiments. Shifting attitudes in one nation should not alter the overall definitional landscape of what is globally offensive or outrageous.

The mechanism must also be multicultural in scope in order to circumvent any charges of cultural imperialism and to stimulate cross-cultural exchanges of ideas. Moreover, this consensus broad and inclusive in concept, should be behavioral in character: nations must deem themselves bound by the dictates of this consensus, and must adhere their conduct to it. Only if such a consensus is already experienced throughout the world by the vast majority of nations, can we expect the world to accept it in the telecommunications domain as well.

Creating anew a general principle and agreeing on it internationally will prove to be difficult, if not outright impossible. Thus, we suggest use of an already-existing international legal principle as a basis on which to structure a regulatory mechanism.

The international law concept of *jus cogens* might provide such a basis for regulating speech content on the Net. *Jus cogens* is linked to the foundational work on international law by the seventeenth-century Dutch jurist Hugo Grotius.[51] Grotius theorized that nations do not conduct their affairs in chaos, devoid of underlying universal principles. He was convinced that without binding rules of international conduct—a common law among nations that binds them—interactions between nations would be impossible. He traced these norms to natural law precepts and envisioned these precepts functioning as a "set of mutual links"[52] tying nations together.

Since Grotius, many jurists and writers have accepted and reaffirmed the principle of such binding international law norms.[53] Almost 60 years ago, Verdross was the first to advance a coherent view of the relationship between *jus cogens* and other sources of international law.[54] Verdross suggested that the concept of *jus cogens* would be consistent with other interntional law norms only if international treaties violating *jus cogens* norms would be void. Thus, Verdross's conception of *jus cogens* creates in essence yet another layer of international law above and beyond treaty law and customary international law. International law violating such peremptory norms is void, similar to national laws that violate the national constitution.[55]

In 1969, the precept of *jus cogens* was incorporated into the Vienna Convention on the Law of Treaties.[56] According to leading experts of vastly disparate legal, political, and cultural backgrounds, the issue of whether *jus cogens* is accepted is now settled.[57] The Vienna Convention defines *jus cogens* as follows:

> [A] norm accepted and recognized by the international community of States as a whole as a norm from which no derogation is permitted and which can be modified only by a subsequent norm of general international law having the same character.[58]

Thus, *jus cogens*, gleaned from verifiable behavior across the community of nations, structurally fulfills the methodological requisites we posit and offers the potential for achieving the necessary substantive consensus in the global telecommunications arena. As a "peremptory norm of international law,"[59] *jus cogens* represents a corpus of international law rules that are binding upon every nation and every people. It comprises by definition the multicultural and multinational consensus that we assert is essential. *Jus cogens* norms mandate that certain forms of behavior are unequivocally intolerable.

This global consensus commends *jus cogens* norms as the touchstone for identifying types of speech that are amenable to an internationally acceptable content-based regulation. However, we suggest here that—especially given the scope and power of the Net—a paradigm shift is appropriate. Not only can speech that incites behavior condemned by *jus cogens* principles be regulated, but speech that advocates conduct that *jus cogens* terms depraved can be also banned if a nation so deems a broader ban appropriate. To be sure, the varieties of speech regulable under a *jus cogens* based system would be few and narrowly defined; only speech that advocates the following irrevocably reprehensible behavior could be constrained: piracy, slavery, genocide, apartheid, aggressive warfare, terrorism, and torture.[60]

Because a *jus cogens* based approach narrows the parameters for restrictions to the common denominator among the community of nations, this approach avoids the constant danger of cultural imperialism. It also averts the impulsive, ultimately devastating reflexes that characterize national majoritarianism. As such, *jus cogens* is uniquely qualified to serve as a methodology for regulating globally connected information infrastructures.

Defining the substantive categories of speech to be regulated is the first step. But no regulation will be effective without a working enforcement strategy. Because the information infrastructure is global, so must be the enforcement. The international instrument that implements the *jus cogens* approach to regulation of speech on the information infrastructure must address the enforcement issue. Reciprocal extension of the principle of territoriality among the state parties and the broadening and strengthening of international criminal law and its procedural aspects can be a first level for addressing the area of enforcement.[61]

But the objectives of an international agreement are even broader in scope. State parties must recognize the importance of speedy national implementation and rigorous enforcement of the internationally agreed regulations. Moreover, state parties need to execute and implement an enforcement mechanism among themselves to guarantee continued national support for such an agreement.[62]

International consultative organizations with existing substantial factual knowledge of the matters at issue, such as the Organization for Economic Cooperation and Development (OECD), could facilitate discussions and negotiations leading up to such an international agreement.

Conclusion

Regulating the content of speech on the Net is still thought of as a national issue. Free speech absolutists and national legislators discuss these matters without considering the international dimension of the information infrastructure, which diminishes the significance of these national debates.

The international aspect of the information infrastructure places unique, albeit unexpected and largely unrecognized, constraints upon both free speech advocates and regulators. The former must come to terms with the fact that the global Net is not an anarchic medium, above and beyond legal restrictions, but on the contrary, is cluttered with numerous—even contradictory—national speech regulations. On the other hand, national regulators must recognize that domestic controls and enforcement are futile regulatory mechanisms for an international structure in which information can be redeployed and disseminated in a matter of seconds.

Only an international perspective can overcome the current shortsightedness of free speech absolutists and regulators alike. Speech restrictions on the Net must be elevated to the international level to be both subjectively acceptable to the world's nations and globally enforceable. An international legal instrument, *jus cogens*, which by definition embodies this global consensus and positively binds all nations, could provide a useful tool in drafting a possible solution. *Jus cogens*, limiting regulation to specific, defined areas such as advocacy of genocide, slavery, torture, or apartheid, together with creative international enforcement structures might facilitate the creation of speech regulations for the nascent global information and communication networks that are both sensible and feasible.

Notes

1. C.T. Mien. "Steps Taken in Other Countries to Regulate the Internet," *The Straits Times (Singapore)*, March 9, 1996, p. 35. In Austria, a broad study on the subject of regulating the information infrastructure was commissioned by the federal government; see Ursula Maier-Rabler, Viktor Mayer-Schönberger, Gabriele Schmölzer, and Georg Nening-Schöfbänker, *Net Without Qualities* (1995), http://www.komdat.sbg.ac.at/nikt. For the restricting effect on speech through a European Union Directive on Data Protection, see Stewart Baker, "The Net Escape? Ha!," *Wired*, Sept., 1995, p. 125. In the United States, the Communication Decency Act of 1996, outlaws distribution over the Internet of material from child pornography to profanity. 47 U.S.C. §609 *et seq.*

2. Thomas Pangle, *The Spirit of Modern Republicanism* (Chicago, IL: University of Chicago Press, 1988); J.G.A. Pocock, *The Machiavellian Moment: Florentine Political Thought and the Atlantic Republican Tradition* (Princeton, NJ: Princeton University Press, 1975); Michael J. Sandel, *Liberalism and the Limits of Justice* (Cambridge, UK: Cambridge University Press, 1982), pp. 59–65, 147–174; Symposium, "The Republican Civic Tradition," *Yale Law Journal* 97:1493 (1988).

3. Howard Rheingold, "Why Censoring Cyberspace Is Futile," *Computer Underground Digest* 6.40 (1995); David Johnson, "Taking Cyberspace Seriously: Dealing with Obnoxious Messages on the Net," http://www.eff.org/pub/Censorship/content_regulation_johnson.article.

4. Jeff Selingo and Charles Kelly, "Sleaze Imperils Freedom on Wide-open Online Chat; Down a Dark Alley Along the Information Superhighway," *The Arizona Republic*, June 15, 1995, p. A1.

5. The debate concerning the prudence and legitimacy of content-based speech regulation is beyond the scope of this paper. For analysis of the contention that some forms of speech are so horrifying and potentially destructive that they can be regulated and a proposal for the nature and structure of that regulation, see Viktor Mayer-Schönberger and Teree E. Foster, "More Speech, Less Noise: Amplifying Content-Based Speech Regulations Through Binding International Law," *Boston College International and Comparative Law Review* 18:59, pp. 134–135 (1995).

6. Donald E. Lively, "The Information Superhighway: A First Amendment Roadmap," *Boston College Law Review* 35:1067 (1994); "The Message Is the Medium: The First Amendment on the Information Superhighway" (Note), *Harvard Law Review* 107:1062 (1994). Baker, "The Net Escape? Ha!," p. 125. "Silencing the Net: The Threat to Freedom of Expression On-Line," *Human Rights Watch* 8 (May 1996); http://www.epic.org/free_speech/hrw_report_5_96.html.

7. *Yates v. United States*, 354 U.S. 298 (1957), *New York Times v. Sullivan*, 376 U.S. 254 (1964), *Brandenburg v. Ohio*, 395 U.S. 444 (1969), *Cohen v. California*, 403 U.S. 15 (1971); *Texas v. Johnson*, 491 U.S. 397 (1989); *R.A.V. v. City of St. Paul*, 505 U.S. 377 (1992).

8. *The Sunday Times v. The United Kingdom*, 2 E.H.R.R. 245 (1979); Ulrich Sieber, "Strafrechtliche Verantwortlichkeit für den Datenverkehr in Internationalen Computernetzen," *Juristenzeitung* 1996:429–442. Recently in England a physics lecturer and a nuclear physicist brought separate actions against former colleagues, each alleging that defamatory remarks about his professional competence had been disseminated on Usenet: "Electronic War of Words in Cyberspace Is Heading for Very Real Confrontation in a UK Courtroom," *The Financial Times*, August 13, 1994, at 24.

9. "Lee Kuan Says Yes to Internet, No to Sex and Violence on TV," *Agence France Presse*, Oct. 6, 1995; C.T. Mien, "Steps Taken in Other Countries to Regulate the Internet," p. 35.

10. "On-Line Boundaries Unclear: Internet Tramples Legal Jurisdictions," *Computerworld*, June 5, 1995, p. 1; Faiza S. Ambah, "An Intruder in the Kingdom," *Business Week*, August 21, 1995, p. 40; "Chat Rooms and Chadors," *Newsweek*, August 21, 1995, p. 36.

11. "Censorship Issues on the Internet Continue to Confuse Governments," *New Media Age*, January 12, 1996, p. 5; "Sex on the Internet," *The Economist*, January 6, 1996, p. 18, where the author inquires, "[w]hen Bavaria wrinkles its nose, must the whole world catch a cold?"

12. "Scotland and Italy Crack Down on Anarchy Files," http://www.eff.org/pub/Legal/Cases/ BITS-A-t-E_Spunk/eff-raids.article. Adrian Levy and Ian Burrell, "Anarchists Use Computer Highway for Subversion," *British Sunday Times*, March 5, 1995; http://www.eff.org/pub/LegalCases/BITS-A-t-E_Spunk/bits_seizure.article (Italy); "Cyber Notes," *The Christian Science Monitor*, Sept. 21, 1995, p. 11. Similarly, Germany tried to ban access and availability of the web version of the anarchist publication *radikal*: "Germany Censors Dutch Website," http://www.xs4all.nl/~felipe/press /persverklaring.html.

13. The Lüth Case, Judgment of Jan. 15, 1958, Federal Constitutional Court, 7 BVerfGE 198, translated in Donald P. Kommers, *The Constitutional Jurisprudence of the Federal Republic of Germany*. (Durham, NC: Duke University Press, 1989), p. 370.

14. Grundgesetz [German Basic Law], Article 1.

15. Strafgesetzbuch [German Penal Code] (StGB) §§130, 131. Outlawed are writings that "incite to race hatred or which describe cruel or other inhuman acts of violence against human beings in a manner expressing glorification or intentional minimization of such acts of violence or demonstrating the cruel or inhuman acts in a manner injuring human dignity.

16. StGB §§194, 86, 86a. "Recent Developments," *Harvard International Law Journal* 34:563 (1993). In December 1992, the German government banned the sale and distribution to youths under the age of 18 of neo-Nazi rock music advocating violence and death to foreigners. By this measure the German government sought to staunch the precipitous rise of right-wing violence.

17. "America Online Faces Probe over Alleged Nazi Material on Internet," *The Jerusalem Post*, Feb. 4, 1996, p. 2; "CompuServe Still Blocks Access to Internet," *The Reuter European Community Report*, Feb. 16, 1996; W. Boston, "Germans' Internet Crackdown A Sign of the Future," *Reuters*, Feb. 4, 1996; Sieber, "Strafrechtliche Verantwortlichkeit." German Research and Technology Minister Juergen Ruettgers affirmed that Bonn respected free speech but declared that the German government must do more to regulate the Internet. He stated that "[w]e cannot tolerate a situation in which anything goes" and suggested that the Group of Seven leading industrial countries take up the issue.

18. Verbotsgesetz [Austrian Prohibition Act] §3.

19. Nina Weissensteiner, "'Rechte' Irrwege im Internet," *Kurier*, March 7, 1996, p. 3; see generally Burkhard Schröder, *Neonazis und Computernetze* (Reinbek: Rowohlt, 1995), p. 41.

20. Criminal Code, R.S.C. 1985, ch. C46 §319(2). See *R. v. Keegstra* [1990] 3 S.C.R. 697 (Can.), wherein the statute was upheld in a case involving a teacher charged with wilful promotion of hatred against an identifiable group for promoting anti-Semitism to his students and penalizing the grades of those who did not respond favorably to his rantings. See also *R. v. Andrews* [1990] 3 S.C.R. 870 (Can.).

21. S.C. 1976–77, ch. 33, § 13(1). This statute was upheld in Canada (*Human Rights Commission v. Taylor* [1990] 3 S.C.R. 892 Can.). It is not yet clear whether these provisions apply to electronic communications. A government council concluded that obscenity and hate speech on the Internet should be regulated: Alana Kainz, "Information Highway: Advisory Report Leaves Uncharted Roads," *Ottawa Citizen*, Sept. 18, 1995.

22. Baker, "The Net Escape? Ha!," pp. 125–126. An issue concomitant to privacy is the right to anonymous communication on the Net. Whether a right to anonymous speech does or should exist is beyond the scope of this paper. For contrasting views, compare Tom W. Bell, "Anonymous Speech," *Wired*, Oct. 1995, p. 80, with Richard P. Klaus and Erik J. Heels, "Online," *Student Lawyer*, Sept. 1995, pp. 33–36.

23. Geoffrey R. Stone, "Content Regulation and the First Amendment," *William and Mary Law Review* 25:189, p. 195 (1983).

24. *Chaplinsky v. New Hampshire*, 315 U.S. 568, 571–572 (1942).

25. *Dennis v. United States*, 341 U.S. 494, 544–546 (1951) (Frankfurter, J., concurring); *Brandenburg v. Ohio*, 395 U.S. 444 (1969).

26. *Miller v. California*, 413 U.S. 15 (1973).

27. *New York v. Ferber*, 458 U.S. 747 (1982).

28. *Gertz v. Robert Welch, Inc.*, 418 U.S. 323, 340 (1974); *New York Times v. Sullivan*, 376 U.S. 254 (1963); *Henry v. Collins*, 380 U.S. 356 (1965); *Time, Inc. v. Firestone*, 424 U.S. 448 (1976). See generally, Harry Kalven, "The *New York Times* Case: A Note on the Central Meaning of the First Amendment," *Supreme Court Review* 1964:191 (1964); Nimmer, "The Right to Speak From Times to Time: First Amendment Theory Applied to Libel and Misapplied to Privacy," *California Law Review* 56:935 (1968); Eaton. "The American Law of Defamation Through *Gertz v. Robert Welch, Inc.* and Beyond: An Analytical Primer," *Virginia Law Review* 61:1349 (1975).

29. Fighting words are not inherently menacing in a constitutional sense, but become so only when such words "by their very utterance inflict injury or tend to incite a breach of the peace." *Chaplinsky v. New Hampshire*, 315 U.S. 568 (1942); *R.A.V. v. City of St. Paul*, 505 U.S. 377 (1992). *Chaplinsky* and its fighting words doctrine, similar to obscenity and defamation, seems to raise many more questions than it answers. For example, Chaplinsky addressed his epithets— "God damned racketeer" and "Fascist"—to a city marshall who had interrupted Chaplinsky's soapbox speech: idem at 569. Why should this outburst not be construed as a cry of frustration at the overweening power of government and therefore as protected political or civic speech? See Martin H. Redish, "The Value of Free Speech," *University of Pennsylvania Law Review* 130:591, p. 626 (1982). What of the emotive content of protected First Amendment speech? *Cohen v. California*, 403 U.S. 15 (1971). Could Chaplinsky be convicted for uttering fighting words had he written the same phrases on a poster that he carried while walking the public streets? It has been suggested that the fighting words doctrine's distinction between suppressible rough language and protected provocative words—both of which might that stir a listener to anger—operates more to repress "low value" speakers than "low value" speech. Stanley Ingber, "The Marketplace of Ideas: A Legitimizing Myth," *Duke Law Journal* 1984:1, pp. 33–34.

It is interesting that since *Chaplinsky*, no conviction for uttering fighting words has been sustained by the Court. See, e.g., *Gooding v. Wilson*, 405 U.S. 518 (1972); *Lewis v. New Orleans*, 408 U.S. 913 (1972); *Brown v. Oklahoma*, 408 U.S. 914 (1972); *Plummer v. City of Columbus*, 414 U.S. 2 (1973). Yet, the fighting words doctrine retains technical validity. *R.A.V. v. City of St. Paul*, 505 U.S. 377 (1992). A number of commentators have criticized the continuing constitutional validity of *Chaplinsky* and called for its modification or elimination. Kent Greenawalt. "Insults and Epithets: Are They Protected Speech?," *Rutgers Law Review* 42:287 (1990); Toni

M. Massaro. "Equality and Freedom of Expression: The Hate Speech Dilemma," *William and Mary Law Review* 32:211 (1991); "The Demise of the Chaplinsky Fighting Words Doctrine: An Argument for Its Interment" (Note), *Harvard Law Review* 106:1129 (1993).

30. *Virginia St. Board of Pharmacy v. Virginia Citizens Consumer Council,* 425 U.S. 728 (1976). Commercial speech was once utterly vulnerable to regulation. See *Valentine v. Chrestensen,* 316 U.S. 52 (1942). However, both the Burger Court and the Rehnquist Court have enhanced the respectability afforded to speech that proposes a commercial transaction. Unlike that of the aforelisted categories of vulnerable speech, the validity of commercial speech is assessed by means of a balancing test similar to the one used by the Court to evaluate incidental regulations of otherwise protected communication. *Central Hudson Gas & Electric Corp. v. Public Service Comm'n,* 447 U.S. 557 (1980); *Posadas De Puerto Rico Associates v. Tourism Company of Puerto Rico,* 478 U.S. 328 (1986).

31. *Paris Adult Theatre I v. Slaton,* 413 U.S. 49 (1973); *Miller v. California,* 413 U.S. 15 (1973). In *Roth v. United States,* 354 U.S. 476, 484 (1957), Justice Brennan opined:

> The protection given speech and press was fashioned to assure unfettered interchange of ideas for the bringing about of political and social changes desired by the people . . . . But implicit in the history of the First Amendment is the rejection of obscenity as utterly without redeeming social importance.

Another justification for categorizing obscene speech as taboo is offered by Professor Schauer—that obscenity is specifically designed to evoke a entirely physical effect, and thus is a physical, and not a mental, stimulus. "[A] pornographic item is in a real sense a sexual surrogate." Fred C. Schauer, "Speech and 'Speech'—Obscenity and 'Obscenity': An Exercise in the Interpretation of Constitutional Language," *Georgia Law Journal* 67:899, pp. 922–923, 926 (1979).

32. Child pornography is a special case. Materials depicting children in sexual poses or activities can be criminalized even if the same materials depicting adults would pass First Amendment muster. *New York v. Ferber,* 458 U.S. 747, 756, 773 (1982). Moreover, mere possession of child pornography, even in the privacy of one's own home, can be criminalizedy despite the contrary holding of *Stanley v. Georgia,* 394 U.S. 557 (1969), concerning possession of adult pornography. *Osborne v. Ohio,* 495 U.S. 913 (1990). But see *Jacobson v. United States,* 503 U.S. 540 (1992) (conviction for receiving child pornography in the mail overturned where defendant, the target of a government "sting" operation, was entrapped into the purchase).

33. *United States v. Thomas,* 74 F.3d 701 (6th Cir. 1996), cert. denied. Mark L. Gordon and Diana J. P. McKenzie, "A Lawyer's Roadmap of the Information Superhighway," *John Marshall Journal of Computer & Information Law* 2:177, p. 203 (1995).

34. The materials "depicted images of bestiality, oral sex, incest, sado-masochistic abuse, and sex scenes involving urination." 74 F.3d at 705.

35. Baker also posted to an Internet newsgroup, alt.sex.stories, a story that graphically described the torture, rape and murder of a woman who was designated by the name of one of Baker's classmates at Michigan. This story was the basis for a superseded indictment, but was not mentioned by the government in the later indictment that was the subject of this case. *United States v. Baker*, 890 F. Supp. 1375 (E.D.Mich. 1995). The court declared: "While new technology such as the Internet may complicate analysis and may sometimes require new or modified laws, it does not in this instance qualitatively change the analysis under the First Amendment. Whatever Baker's faults, and he is to be faulted, he did not violate 18 U.S.C. §875(c)." 890 F. Supp. at 1390–1391.

36. 47 U.S.C. 609 *et seq.*

37. Leslie Miller, "New Law May Silence On-Line Chat, AOL Says," *USA Today*, Apr. 2, 1996, p. 6D.

38. "Shakespeare, Bible Restricted?," *Communications Daily*, Vol. 16, No. 58, p. 4; "America Online Says Censors in Some Cases," *Reuters*, Apr. 1, 1996; Matt Godbey, "Internet 'Smut' Law Challenged." *Pennsylvania Law Weekly*, Apr. 1, 1996, p. 12; "Best of the Net," *The Village Voice*, Apr. 2, 1996, p. 21.

39. *Brandenburg v. Ohio*, 395 U.S. 444 (1969).

40. 395 U.S. 444 (1969).

41. "The on-line world's lack of respect for state and national borders is making a mockery of outdated laws." Attempts to erect national barriers against subversive or culturally polluting information are readily circumvented. "On-Line Boundaries Unclear: Internet Tramples Legal Jurisdictions," *Computerworld*, June 5, 1995, p. 1.

42. However, the United States has occasionally, and with some degree of success, extended its territorial reach. For example, in *United States v. Alvarez-Machain*, 504 U.S. 655 (1992), the Supreme Court upheld the United States' assertion of jurisdiction over a Mexican national who was forcibly kidnapped and brought to the United States for trial for murder of a Drug Enforcement Agent that occurred in Mexico.

43. "Support Democracy in China," http://christuarex.org/wwwl/sdc/sdchome.html.

44. "Report on Tibetan Women," http://www.igc.org.

45. "Flotilla to rescue refugees," http//www,capatudio.com/capa/rnainmenue.html.

46. The Institute for Historical Review, an organization denying the Holocaust, is present on the WWW through a server in the United States. Its Internet offerings include "Auschwitz Myths and Facts" and "What is a Holocaust Denial?" and include outrageous quotes presented in a quasi-scientific context. The *Stormfront* magazine is a fascist publication operating servers in the United States and Canada. It maintains the White Nationalist Resource Page and contains explicit references to notorious Nazi Gary Lauck. Lauck has used electronic and conventional mail to massively disseminate Nazi propaganda in Germany. He

was arrested in Denmark while on a lecture tour and later extradited to Germany, where he is currently awaiting trial for violation of the German Penal Code prohibiting national socialist propaganda. Other web sites include The White Nationalist Page and the Counter-Revolutionary Resource Page. Electronic mailing lists are available a well. For extensive information, see Schröder, *Neonazis und Computernetze*, p. 41; Maier-Rabler et al., *Net Without Qualities*, p. 72.

47. The best known anonymous remailer was operated without charge by Johan Helsingius in Finland. Unfortunately, the Church of Scientology brought charges against Helsingius and, faced with the choice between releasing user information and closing the remailer, he chose to close. See "The Closing of anon.penet.fi," http://epic.org/privacy/internet/anon_closure.html. Some remailers might even be run by intelligence agencies: see John Dillon, "Are the Feds Sniffing Your Re-Mail?," *CovertAction Quarterly*, July 3, 1996. See generally Andre Bacard, *Anonymous Remailer FAQ*, http://www.well.com/user/abacard/remail.html.

48. David Chaum, "Achieving Electronic Privacy," *Scientific American*, Aug. 1992, pp. 96–101.

49. R. Tali Epstein, "Should the Fair Labor Standards Act Enjoy Extraterritorial Application? A Look At the Unique Case of Flags of Convenience," *University of Pennsylvania Journal of International Business Law* 13:653, p. 655 (1993). The "Flags of convenience" phenomenon refers to a situation in which registration of foreign-owned and foreign-controlled vessels is permitted by certain countries under conditions that are convenient and opportune for the registrant. Flags of convenience have been variously referred to as "flags of necessity," "cheap flags," and "free flags."

50. Consuelo Lauda Kertz and Lisa Boardman Burnette, "Telemarketing Tug-of-War: Balancing Telephone Information Technology and the First Amendment with Consumer Protection and Privacy," *Syracuse Law Review* 43:1029, pp. 1053–1055 (1992). To be effective, any regulation of speech—on the Net, as well as In conventional forums—must focus on the party who disseminates the communicative act. Attempts to focus on the party who delivers or receives the message have proven to be ineffective, cumbersome, or plain wrong in the past, and no necessity dictates a resurrection of such plans. For example, a telephone carrier is not culpable for a fraudulent 900 service, and media are not responsible for the accuracy or good faith of advertisements unless the publisher undertakes to guarantee the soundness of the advertisement or the product it describes. *Pittman v. Dow Jones & Co.*, 662 F. Supp. 921, 922 (E.D. La. 1987).

51. Murphy, "The Grotian Vision of World Order," *American Journal of International Law* 76:477 (1982).

52. Ibid., p. 480.

53. See Mayer-Schönberger and Foster, "More Speech, Less Noise," pp. 90–96, for extensive discussion of the *jus cogens* doctrine.

54. Alfred von Verdross, "Forbidden Treaties in International Law," *American Journal of International Law* 31:571 (1937).

55. In 1945, the concept of *jus cogens* was applied and extended in the Nuremberg trial of major war criminals. "The Nuremberg Legacy: An Unfilled Promise" (Note), *Southern California Law Review* 63:833 (1990). The Allied court not only concluded that Germany had violated peremptory norms of International Law, but also extended the concept of *jus cogens* from the realm of states to the level of the individual. Louis Sohn, "The New International Law: Protection of the Rights of Individuals Rather than States," *American University Law Review* 32:1 (1982). See Charter of the International Military Tribunal, in *Trial of the Major War Criminals Before the International Military Tribunal* (New York: Andronicus Pub. Co., 1946), p. 11.

Since Nuremberg, *jus cogens* not only prohibits states from engaging in certain conduct, but also holds individuals accountable for conduct that violates *jus cogens*. "The Nuremburg Legacy," pp. 868–870. See also Charter of the International Military Tribunal, articles 7 and 8. This acceptance of peremptory norms of International Law is the significant legacy of the Nuremberg trials, and since Nuremburg, *jus cogens* has become a widely accepted mainstream principle: "The Nuremburg Legacy," p. 883.

56. "Vienna Convention on the Law of Treaties," *American Journal of International Law* 63:875 (1969), signed and ratified to date by 48 nations. During the drafting process, 43 out of 44 nations commented positively on the proposed *jus cogens* regulation. Comments by Governments, ILC Reports on 2nd part of its 17th Session and on its 18th Session, General Assembly, 21st Session, Official Records, Supp. No. 9 (A/6309/Rev.1), Annex.

57. For a socialist view, see Geoffrey Hazard, "Book Review of Aleksidze, Some Theoretical Problems of International Law: Peremptory Norms: *Jus Cogens*," *American Journal of International Law* 78:248 (1984); for a western view, see W. Paul Gormley. "The Right to Life and the Rule of Non-Derogability: Peremptory Norms of *Jus Cogens*," in B. G. Ramcharan, ed., *The Right to Life in International Law* (Dordrecht: Nijhoff, 1985). For a general treatise of *jus cogens* see Lauri Hannikainen, *Peremptory Norms in International Law* (Helsinki: Finnjish Lawyers Pub. Co., 1988).

58. Article 53, Vienna Convention on the Law of Treaties, May 23, 1969, 1155 U.N.T.S. 331, reprinted in 8 *I.L.M.* 679 (1969).

59. Mayer-Schönberger and Foster, "More Speech, Less Noise," pp. 90–96.

60. Ibid., pp. 97–102.

61. For example, the Genocide Convention of 1948, 78 U.N.T.S. 227, has been ratified by more than 100 nations. Persons charged with genocide, an offense against the community of nations, can be tried by any nation.

62. A possible, albeit dramatic, consequence of continuous, open and systematic non-enforcement of the international agreement by one nation could be the restriction of access for information flows from that country, or by that particular government. For example, these domains could be temporarily disabled in the network domain name files.

Conflict and Overlap in Privacy Regulation: National, International, and Private

Robert Gellman

Introduction

Governmental activities designed to protect privacy[1] interests have expanded greatly in the last 20 years. The collection, maintenance, use, and disclosure of personal data are now significant public policy concerns in much of the industrialized world. There are new laws, oversight agencies, and codes of conduct. With the notable exception of the United States,[2] the institutionalization of privacy continues to expand and to deepen its roots.

It may be no coincidence that interest in privacy revived in the 1960s when computers began to take a prominent place in public awareness. In many ways, the growth of privacy as a public policy concern in the last 30 years parallels the growth of computer usage and the emergence of the so-called Information Age. When the executive branch proposed a computerized federal data center in the United States in the mid-1960s, it sparked wide-ranging congressional hearings that continued for years exploring different aspects of privacy.[3] The United States was a leader in the development of privacy policy in the 1960s and 1970s. The Europeans have taken over policy leadership in the past two decades.

Most privacy regulatory activities are found at the national level, although there are some local[4] and international[5] rules as well. There are also many voluntary private attempts to develop and implement privacy rules. As national, international, and privately promulgated privacy rules expand, there is a real prospect of overlapping rules and direct conflict. This possibility creates uncertainty for both record keepers and record subjects.

The emergence of the global information infrastructure and a set of new jurisdictional questions only compounds the uncertainty. Computer networks make distance and national borders irrelevant to communications, information disclosures, and economic transactions. Traditional distinctions between types of records and classes of record keepers are fading as technology evolves and businesses merge and restructure. It becomes increasingly difficult to determine what rules apply to what institutions at any given time or for any set of transactions.

The purpose of this chapter is to identify and discuss jurisdictional issues about privacy regulation. Modern information technology and multinational business activities call into question the ability of individual countries to regulate the use of personal information about their citizens. Existing privacy regulatory mechanisms, both public and private, face the prospect of becoming obsolete or irrelevant. Whether the world has the will or the ability to write privacy rules that can keep pace with the results of changing technology is an open question. A first step in addressing that question is understanding the scope of the problem.

Jurisdictional Conflicts

Jurisdictional battles are familiar in the United States as state and federal governments have long fought over power and over which offers the most appropriate forum for legislation. Current debates over American privacy legislation illustrate different aspects of multilevel regulation. Two major issues are the level at which legislation should be passed and whether the laws should be exclusive or overlapping. The purpose of this discussion is to illustrate tensions that result when there is the prospect or the reality of conflicting rules and multiple jurisdictions. The same tensions can arise with private, self-regulatory activities and with overlapping national and international privacy rules.

Health Records

There is no federal statute that regulates the privacy of health records in the United States. It is largely a matter of state law, and each of the 50 states has a different law. Health records maintained by federal agencies are covered by the Privacy Act of 1974 in the same manner as other federal records about individuals,[6] but most medical practitioners are not covered. Treatment records for alcohol and drug abuse are covered by other federal laws if the records are maintained by a person who receives federal funds.[7]

The result is a legal, policy, and practical mess. Protections for health records are inadequate, inconsistent, and incomplete.[8] Patient privacy interests are largely unprotected. Many studies and congressional reviews have sharply criticized the current legal structure.[9]

Until the second half of the 20th century, the patchwork quilt of health record confidentiality rules was not perceived to be a significant problem. Two principal reasons for heightened concern about the lack of health record confidentiality are the expansion of third-party payers for health care and the increasing computerization of health treatment and payment records. Insurance and computers have turned health care into an interstate business, beyond the control of state health record privacy laws. Those laws that do exist actually create impediments to the interstate flow of health information.

With only limited exceptions, there is a now broad consensus that favors replacing state privacy laws with a uniform federal law. That was not so as recently as 1980. When Congress considered the Federal Privacy of Medical Records Act[10] during the 96th Congress, there was strong opposition to federal preemption from major elements of the health care establishment. For example, in 1979, the American Hospital Association was opposed to federal legislation, preferring to leave the issue to state regulation.[11] By 1994, the AHA had completely changed its position and supported federal preemption, finding the argument for federal preemption to be "compelling."[12]

During consideration of health privacy legislation in the 103rd Congress, groups representing different interests were able to agree on the need for federal legislation because no one benefited from the existing diversity and inconsistency. Civil liberties groups supported federal legislation because it represented improved privacy protection.[13] Privacy protections under state laws or under common law are generally weak, and it is easier to effect change through a single federal statute than through 50 state laws. Hospitals, doctors, and insurers supported federal legislation because the modern system of medical treatment and payment requires greater efficiency, computerization, uniformity, and privacy protection.

The emergence of broad-based support for uniform national health privacy regulation was the result of different factors. Most now agree that the United States has outgrown diverse state health record privacy laws. Whether that agreement will result in the passage of a federal medical privacy bill remains to be seen. However, the interests of privacy advocates and industry with respect to uniform national privacy regulation do not always coincide in this fashion.

Fair Credit Reporting Act

The first modern American privacy law, the Fair Credit Reporting Act[14] (FCRA), was a response to the growth and importance of third-party record keeping about consumers. Problems with confidentiality, accuracy, relevance, and fair use grew along with the size and importance of the industry. Following media attention, consumer frustration, and congressional hearings, Congress passed the FCRA in 1970 to regulate the collection, use, and disclosure of consumer credit information.

In the last 25 years, the credit-reporting industry has changed significantly. While credit reporting was once characterized by small, local credit bureaus, there are now three main national consumer reporting agencies.[15] Without any doubt, credit reporting is an interstate business, and a nationwide market exists for the services.

The FCRA has been little changed since originally enacted. In the late 1980s, Congress began consideration of amendments to the law.[16] There was widespread recognition that the law was out of date and that change was required. Legislative proposals were actively considered during the 101st, 102nd, and 103rd Congresses. Disagreements over some aspects of the legislation were so sharp, however, that they prevented final passage in the 103rd Congress although both House and Senate passed largely similar bills.

A principal area of dispute was the degree to which the federal government should preempt the states from enacting legislation regulating consumer reporting. Industry strongly supported a total federal preemption of state laws. Compliance with different, over-lapping, and inconsistent laws presents an obvious problem for national credit-reporting companies, their information providers, and their customers, all of whom operate in an interstate environment. Consumer groups and state officials opposed preemption of state laws. Consumer advocates supported a federal legislative floor, but they found that they had been able to obtain stronger standards through some state legislatures. The disagreement over this issue proved to be irreconcilable, at least over the course of three different Congresses.

On both sides of the credit preemption issue, there were strategic and tactical concerns. The credit industry initially opposed any change in the FCRA, preferring to continue existing law rather than risk stronger federal requirements. The attention focused on credit reporting by congressional debates pressured industry to make voluntary changes. Eventually, industry came to favor legislative change as a way of institutionalizing the new practices and preventing additional legal requirements. The price for this support was a demand for federal preemption. Preemption was not a high priority for industry at the beginning. Because existing law was on their side, preemption was not an original concern of consumer groups either. When industry demanded preemption, consumer groups naturally took the opposite, pro-consumer position. In this fight, the battle line was drawn on a secondary front. That did not make the confrontation any less intense. The contrast with consensus for uniform federal health records legislation is striking.

Self-Regulation

There is growing interest, especially outside the United States, in the use of industry privacy codes to implement or extend statutory privacy rules.[17] Self-regulatory privacy codes offer the prospect of a different type of jurisdictional conflict than may result from privacy rules. It is only a matter of time before conflicts arise over the scope and applicability of these activities.

One reason is the sheer diversity of available self-regulatory[18] activities. Self-regulatory efforts may focus on individual companies, sectors (e.g., banking), functions (e.g., marketing), technologies (e.g., computer networks), or professionals (e.g., doctors). For example, TRW Information Systems & Services, one of three leading credit bureaus in the United States, has established and published a set of "Fair Information Values" that are intended to "form the foundation of [TRW] practices in information handling and privacy."[19] At the same time, TRW is a member of the Direct Marketing Association (DMA), which has adopted a code of fair information practices. The DMA code is not binding on its members.[20] TRW is also a member of the Information Industry Association (IIA), a trade association representing the interests of creators and packagers of information content. IIA also has adopted fair information practices guidelines. The guidelines are not binding on IIA members.[21] TRW is also a member of Associated Credit Bureaus (ACB) which has promulgated its own policies on privacy and other consumer issues.[22] The ACB code is binding on ACB members. In addition, individual members of the TRW staff may be subject to professional ethics codes, such as the Hippocratic Oath or the rules of bar associations. TRW also has extensive foreign operations, and there may be additional self-regulatory efforts for these operations as well.

The result is that there is a reasonable likelihood that a company like TRW will find potential or real conflicts or overlaps even at the voluntary level. A hypothetical example makes the point more clearly. For purposes of discussion, assume that there are privacy codes for the banking, direct marketing, and insurance industries. Assume further that a bank is a member of all three industry associations that promulgated the codes. Which code applies when the bank sells insurance through direct mail? Which code applies to corporate activities of the bank holding company that operates banking, insurance, and marketing subsidiaries, each of which has promised to comply with the applicable industry codes? If all codes are general or identical, then there may be no problem. But if the codes have different standards or procedures, then jurisdictional conflicts will occur.[23]

A different level of conflict is foreseeable as well for a company that operates internationally. If, for example, national privacy codes for the banking industry have different substantive or procedural rules in different countries, international bankers will face conflicts. As national industry codes for privacy spread around the world, this type of conflict is likely to arise. The European Union data protection directive refers to the possibility of community codes of conduct, but the process for approval and the effect of these codes are not clearly described.[24] This is an area where more development can be anticipated in the future.

Legal and Technological Overlaps

Conflicts, overlaps, and gaps in regulation also can arise within the same level of government because of changes in technology[25] and the way in which laws are drafted. This is not the same type of conflict as discussed earlier in this section, but it illustrates another way that data controllers and consumers can be significantly affected by inconsistent privacy policies.

An example comes from two laws that attempt to protect the privacy of consumers of movies and television programming. The Video Privacy Protection Act[26] limits businesses that sell or rent videotapes to consumers from disclosing some information about the interests of customers. Similarly, the Cable Communications Policy Act of 1984[27] places limits on the collection and use of information about cable subscriber viewing habits. The details of these laws are not important here. What is notable is that both laws attempt to protect consumers from commercial exploitation of transaction information resulting from the consumption of video services.

A recent report from the National Telecommunications and Information Administration in the Department of Commerce points out that the Video Privacy Protection Act may not extend to video programming transmitted through telecommunications networks. Only the rental of movies from video stores may be covered. Similarly, the Act's privacy provisions do not expressly apply to video carriage by direct broadcast satellite or wireless cable service operators.[28] A broader look at rules governing use of consumer information about consumption of information products and services reveals that there are no federal privacy laws that protect customers of libraries or purchasers of books or magazines.

Only video rentals are protected. The result is that essentially identical consumer activities are subject to different privacy rules. Both consumers and merchants suffer from these differences, and there may eventually be a demand for equal treatment. The Electronic Communications Privacy Act (ECPA)[29] was passed in part because changes in technology created new forms of communications that were not protected by existing privacy laws.[30] For ECPA, a level playing field was established with a reasonably high degree of privacy protection. Demands for equality can also be met with a low level of privacy protection.

As long as the United States approaches privacy with separate, uncoordinated, and occasional legislation applying to separate record systems and separate industries, these problems are certain to arise. The omnibus approach adopted by most European countries establishes general privacy standards that are more independent of technological and market considerations. By establishing broader policies, the Europeans ensure that privacy is considered in the planning stages of new technology or activities rather than at a less efficient and less effective point in the process. The United States is rarely, if ever, able to anticipate technology with privacy laws or policies. This increases the prospect of inconsistent rules.

Analysis

There are several lessons to be drawn here. First, for both health and credit records, pressures of technology and interstate commerce are important drivers of industry support for federal preemption. The computerization and concentration that made it easier for credit-reporting companies to operate without regard to state boundaries also made it more difficult to comply with differing state laws. Consider a credit application from a customer who has a business in Maryland and resides in Pennsylvania. The application is received by a California bank that orders a credit report from credit bureaus headquartered in Georgia, Illinois, and Ohio. The application is ultimately rejected by a bank subsidiary in South Dakota. It may not be immediately apparent which state credit-reporting law applies to the processing of this application. The same degree of interstate activity and computerization is common in the health treatment and payment process. This appears to provide the principal motivation for industry support for federal preemptive health privacy legislation.

Second, support for federal preemption is not always determined by core federalism principles. Interest groups are result-oriented, supporting preemption when federal action is more likely to produce a better result for their goals and opposing preemption when the states are more likely to pass more favorable legislation.[31] The ACLU supported federal preemption for health records but opposed it for credit records. This shows a strong conviction for privacy and an indifference to federalism. The business community does not uniformly favor federal preemptive legislation either. While there is no currently active federal legislative issue that illustrates this point directly, the life insurance industry has opposed federal privacy legislation in the past.[32]

A third factor in federalism battles is the extent to which state regulators may lose power if existing state laws are preempted. Some states actively oversee credit-reporting laws, and this prompted opposition to federal preemption from state attorneys general who might have lost their authority over credit reporting in their states. In the health arena, there was no visible opposition to federal preemption from the states. One reason may have been that there was no active regulation or oversight of health privacy by state agencies so no existing power center felt threatened by federal preemption.

Conflict between private regulators also seems possible. Sponsors of overlapping self-regulatory codes, such as trade associations, may compete for membership, influence, or revenues by establishing differing codes. This could raise a different level of forum shopping for record keepers and add to the overall confusion about privacy rules.

Extrapolating from national to international jurisdictions, one may speculate that industry demand for international uniformity of regulation is likely to depend in part on the extent to which business activities routinely involve the transfer of personal information across national borders. Information and communications technologies play an increasingly important role in shaping international business activities, and the pressures of technology and commerce are likely to increase support for uniformity.[33] While many in the business community may prefer no regulation at all, differential, incomplete, or inconsistent regulation may be less welcome than comprehensive, rational, and equal regulation.

Another factor will be the extent to which different interest groups can advance their privacy agendas with more favorable (stronger or weaker) rules at the international level. If more favorable rules are likely at the national level, then there will likely be strong opposition to international rules. Finally, conflicts between national regulators also will play an important role in shaping international regulation.

Tentative Steps toward International Coordination

Some common international data protection rules and policies have already been established, and European institutions have been at the forefront of these efforts. In the past 20 years, a remarkable international consensus has been achieved about the broad objectives of privacy policy. Many controversies and differences still remain, of course. Also, technological developments are creating new threats to privacy as well as new options for the protection of privacy interests. Finally, there are still sharp disagreements about implementation details and enforcement.

The OECD and the Council of Europe

The Organization for Economic Cooperation and Development (OECD) is an international organization that promotes economic and social welfare and stimulates and harmonizes efforts on behalf of developing nations. Along with nearly all industrialized free-market countries, the United States is a member of the OECD. In the late 1970s, the OECD began work on guidelines for protecting privacy in transborder flows of personal data. Final guidelines were adopted in 1980.[34]

The Council of Europe promotes a greater degree of collaboration among the democratic states of Europe, especially in the area of law and human rights. Questions about the effects of technology and privacy came under review at the Council beginning in the late

1960s. Eventually the Council adopted a Convention for the Protection of Individuals with Regard to Automatic Processing of Personal Data in February 1980.[35]

As they were developed in concert, a good deal of similarity exists between the OECD Guidelines and the Council of Europe Convention. Both documents are based on the general principles of fair information practices. Colin Bennett has described how privacy policies around the world have converged around the notion of fair information practices, and the work of the OECD and the Council of Europe institutionalized the harmonization that was already well under way.[36]

Despite the broad policy similarities, there are some significant differences in scope and application. The Council of Europe Convention applies only to automated processing of personal data while the OECD Guidelines are not limited to automated data. Also, the Convention is legally binding[37] for countries that have ratified it while the Guidelines are not. Neither document offers specific details on practical application of the established standards. Both contain very general provisions on enforcement. The OECD Guidelines provide that data controllers should be accountable for compliance.[38] The Convention requires signatories to establish appropriate sanctions and remedies for violations of data protection laws.[39] Countries can meet these general requirements by adopting enforcement methods suitable for their culture and legal system.

Adoption of common privacy principles is an important step toward uniformity. However, there can be less to professed adherence with voluntary guidelines, like those of the OECD, than meets the eye. In the early 1980s, the Reagan administration encouraged private American companies to voluntarily adopt the OECD Guidelines. The National Telecommunications and Information Administration (NTIA) of the Department of Commerce sponsored the effort. By 1983, 182 major U.S. multinational corporations and trade associations had endorsed the guidelines.[40] The United States officially trumpeted these activities as evidence of a commitment to privacy.

Considerable doubt exists about the sincerity and effect of the NTIA effort, however. There is substantial evidence that NTIA's purpose was to avoid embarrassment and possible limitations on the transfer of personal data to the United States that were being widely discussed under the banner of transborder data flows.[41] Further, there is little evidence that the endorsements of the OECD Guidelines by American companies resulted in changes in actual privacy practices.[42]

The Clinton administration has continued to pay lip service to the OECD Guidelines in developing privacy principles for the national information infrastructure (NII).[43] These NII privacy principles were intended to be consistent with the spirit of the OECD Guidelines. Following the pattern set during the Reagan administration, however, no steps have been taken to change federal or corporate privacy policies. The Clinton privacy principles were not binding on anyone, even the federal government. A recent report from NTIA on privacy and telecommunications continues the now familiar pattern of threatening government intervention if industry does not take steps on its own to address privacy needs.[44] These threats seem hollow when there have already been years of inaction by both government and industry.[45]

European Union Data Protection Directive

In July 1995, the Council of Ministers of the European Union adopted a directive on "the processing of personal data and on the free movement of such data." A major purpose of this EU data protection Directive is to establish a common, high level of protection for personal data in all member-states to remove obstacles to flows of personal data within the European Union.[46] The Directive seeks harmonization rather than uniformity of laws.

The first version of this data protection Directive was proposed in 1990,[47] and it took five years and several drafts before final approval. The length of time that this Directive was in process is a measure of the amount of controversy that the Directive attracted. There are some rough parallels between the debate on the EU Directive and the debate in the United States over reform of credit-reporting laws. Privacy advocates, industry, data users, and regulators were all actively engaged in trying to shape the Directive to suit their own agendas.

A major area of interest and controversy involved the EU rules on the transfer of personal data to third countries.[48] The original draft provided that personal data could be transferred only if the third country "ensures an adequate level of protection."[49] The final version contains new language that added interpretative guidance and offered a considerable amount of flexibility on third-country transfers.[50] Several specific conditions have been included in the Directive that justify some transfers to third countries even when there is no adequate level of protection.[51] Importantly, the Directive expressly provides a procedure for preventing the transfer of personal data to countries with inadequate protections.[52] An elaborate notice procedure applies when a member-state or the Commission of the European Communities determines that a third country does not ensure an adequate level of protection.[53] There is considerable uncertainty about how these provisions will be interpreted and applied. It is unclear, for example, whether the EU Directive permits a sector-by-sector or company-by-company assessment of the adequacy of laws or whether a country must be assessed in toto.

The third-country provisions illustrate the difficulty of maintaining personal data protections when other jurisdictions do not have similar laws or practices. A term sometimes applied to a third country that deliberately avoids having privacy regulations is a "data haven." If personal data from a country with privacy regulations can be freely transferred to a data haven where there are no privacy rules, then the legal protections available in the source country may be lost. The controller in the data haven may have no legal obligations or restrictions on use, and the data subject may have no enforceable rights.

The third-country problem is not trivial, and the United States is a major reason. The United States does not have any general private sector privacy laws that are equivalent to most European data protection laws. For example, if a company transfers a personnel file for its employee from an EU member-state to the United States, that file will have no federal statutory privacy protections in the United States, and only limited protection in a few states. Another difference is the absence of an oversight or enforcement mechanism, such as a data protection agency, in the United States. It is an open question whether the EU will find that United States privacy policies and practices meet the standard of adequacy either in whole or in part.

Because of the central importance of the United States in the world economy, this is a high-stakes issue. If the United States is found to meet the adequacy test in the EU Directive despite American resistance to modern, comprehensive privacy laws, then the credibility of the Directive may be undermined. A broad ban on data flows to the United States, however, would be disruptive, expensive, and, seemingly, unlikely. The exceptions that permit transfers to third countries notwithstanding inadequate privacy laws may be invoked to lessen the disruptions. Other intermediate steps might be taken to minimize the economic impact, including the possibility of allowing the United States more time to bring its privacy house in order.

The attempt by the EU Directive to address the third-country issue will highlight, and perhaps exacerbate, differences in national privacy rules. Much will depend on how the Directive is interpreted and enforced when it becomes effective in 1998. The Directive may provide a useful vehicle for international harmonization or it may accent existing differences.

Practical Problems of National Privacy Regulation

The European Union has come the closest to confronting the problems of coordinating national privacy rules in an international environment. The data protection Directive, however, is a complex and obscure document. It is far from clear how the Directive's vague rules on international data transfers will be applied in practice. However, it is still possible to describe the types of problems that may result from the lack of international rules for data protection and that are not squarely addressed in the EU Directive.

Technology and Conflicting Privacy Rules

International data transfers, transactions, and activities are already routine and are certain to increase. Computer networks, like the Internet, currently support routine communications without regard to geographical location or national boundaries. It is just as easy to send an electronic-mail message around the world as it is to send one around the corner.

There is a defined set of rules regulating the international transfer of regular mail, and the risks and consequences are well understood. For electronic mail, however, the situation is more complex. There are no fixed routes for electronic mail.[54] An electronic message from New York to Australia might pass through and be stored temporarily in several intermediary countries before it reaches its destination. It is impossible to predict in advance what path the electronic message will take, and the path may be different each time a message is sent. The degree of privacy that an electronic message will receive may be determined by the countries through which the message passes or in which the message temporarily resides.[55] The United States, for example, affords substantive and procedural legal protection to electronic messages.[56] Equivalent protections are not necessarily available in other countries connected to the Internet. As a result, there is a significant degree of uncertainty regarding the privacy rules governing electronic mail.

International economic transactions are commonplace today. According to one privacy scholar, "[i]nformation sharing now takes place on an international scale and involves a tremendous amount of data referring to individuals."[57] Credit cards have been used internationally for many years, and information about credit transactions flows routinely from the country where charges are incurred to the country where the bill is ultimately sent. An example illustrates the potential complexity of overlapping or conflicting regulation. Suppose that Country E prohibits the use of information from credit transactions for marketing purposes without the affirmative consent of the customer. Suppose further that Country U has no restrictions on the use of credit data for marketing. What rule applies when a citizen of Country E incurs a charge in Country U? There can be many players in the transaction, including the merchant, the merchant's bank or processing agent, a transaction clearinghouse, and the credit card issuer. Some players are located in Country E, some in Country U, and some could be located elsewhere. Can a company that has the transaction information in Country U use the data for marketing although such use in prohibited in Country E? Can two companies that have the same information from the same transaction be subject to different rules depending on the location where the information resides at any given moment? Can one company that operates in two different countries be subject to different rules at different times depending on the country in which the information is maintained? There are no clear answers to these questions, and it is easy to develop even more complex examples with single transactions having a nexus with three, four, or more countries.

Even if each country is determined to have "adequate" levels of protection relative to a specific standard, there may still be substantive or procedural differences between the rules that apply to specific record categories. For example, two countries may both require consumer consent before allowing unrelated uses of transaction data. One country may require affirmative consent (opt-in) while the other permits negative consent (opt-out). Lacking affirmative consent, are marketing uses permissible in one country but prohibited in the other?

International marketing activities are certain to increase as computer networks expand. There is already a considerable amount of marketing activity on the Internet. Eventually, international marketing may be just as commonplace as, and indistinguishable from, domestic marketing. This will increase the routine transborder flow of consumer information and the pressures on privacy regulators. Even a casual connection through a World Wide Web page on the Internet can produce a remote record of an inquirer's electronic-mail address and the subject of the inquiry. Those who engage in targeted marketing may find it profitable to identify Internet users who have shown an interest in a particular subject, service, or product.

An example shows how potential regulatory conflicts may arise from network activities. Presume that the collection and use of consumer transaction information with the consent of the consumer is lawful everywhere. In a country with a data registration or licensing requirement, a local merchant on the Internet will have filed the requisite forms with the country's data protection authority. A foreign Internet merchant, offering identical goods from an identical Web page may not be legally subject to the same requirement. The consumer may not even be aware of the country in which the merchant resides or in which the data will be maintained.

The situation could be equally uncertain for the merchant. Must an Internet vendor comply with data protection laws in each country that is connected to the network? Does the vendor have to comply with the laws of a country only when there is a transaction that originated or is completed in that country? Depending on how data protection laws are structured, more interesting and more complex options and choices are possible. Suppose one country provides that registered data controllers are subject only to actual damages for privacy invasions. Suppose further that those who do business through the Internet from other countries who have not registered their data activities are subject to actual damages, punitive damages, and liquidated damages. The merchant engaging in a normal transaction who uses transaction data in a manner that is lawful in the merchant's country but unlawful in the consumer's country may discover a potentially large legal liability as a result.

Computer networks support transactions in which neither party is aware of the physical location or nationality of the other party. Neither party may be aware of the locations through which transaction data flow or are stored. Even the data controller may not be aware of where a computer service firm stores data. National laws that depend on traditional jurisdictional hooks may be more difficult to apply in an environment characterized by international data transfers over computer networks. Applying privacy laws in this environment without broadly accepted, uniform international rules and procedures may be expensive, difficult, or completely impossible.

Enforcement

Deciding what privacy rules, laws, or standards may apply to any given set of data, consumers, or merchants in an international environment is difficult enough. Another important concern is enforcement. What can aggrieved consumers do when their rights have been violated? How can a nation enforce its own privacy laws? Enforcement is a central concern for privacy statutes, and it presents some especially difficult problems in a transborder context.

The basic privacy law for U.S. government records is the Privacy Act of 1974.[58] There is no centralized enforcement mechanism under the Act. Individuals can bring lawsuits to enforce their own rights, but the former general counsel to the Privacy Protection Study Commission testified that the Act was "to a large extent, unenforceable by individuals."[59] The main reasons are that it is difficult to recover damages and that no injunctive relief is available.

Enforcement of the Privacy Act is impossible for most foreigners as a matter of law. The Act only applies to citizens of the United States and to aliens admitted for permanent residence.[60] However, even if foreigners were given rights under the Privacy Act, they would have the same enforcement problems as Americans. In addition, they would face the difficulty of managing a lawsuit in another country. This is a problem as well when enforcing privacy rights against private sector companies.

For those seeking to enforce privacy rules in countries with formal data protection authorities, alternatives to litigation may exist. Data protection authorities may accept and investigate complaints from individuals. This is not a practical remedy, however, for most consumers. The ability to file a complaint with the French data protection authority is a remedy that few, if any, Americans would welcome or use. It is difficult enough for an average individual to pursue an administrative or legal remedy within his or her own country. Expecting consumers to pursue remedies with additional barriers of distance and language is not realistic.

Data protection authorities also can initiate their own oversight and enforcement activities. It is not a simple task, however, to audit or review activities of data controllers in other countries. It may be possible to establish effective incentives for self-enforcement of privacy rules. Meanwhile, the issue of transborder enforcement of privacy laws remains a largely unexplored subject. The EU data protection Directive offers little guidance.

Conclusion

Conflicting and overlapping international privacy laws and rules present unavoidable political, legal, and policy problems. Agreement on general principles, such as those reflected in the OECD

Guidelines and the Council of Europe Convention, will not establish the common processes and procedures that are needed to implement common international privacy rules. General policies do not inform data controllers of their specific responsibilities or record subjects of their rights. Implementation requires additional rules. Whether those rules come from national laws, self-regulatory codes, or company activities, differences across nations and industries seem inevitable.

Differences are not, by themselves, necessarily bad policy. Applying common policies in varying ways to diverse categories of personal information is a potential strength of privacy regulation. Nevertheless, procedural and substantive rules determine whether an average individual will, as a practical matter, be able to pursue substantive rights. As differences proliferate, meaningful remedies for aggrieved individuals will be difficult at best and practically or legally unavailable at worst. Data controllers face the same problems.

For example, a standard that record subjects should have access to their files will be implemented differently for different records. Health records require more detailed and elaborate access rules and due process rights than pizza delivery records. When an access policy is prescribed by national regulators or through industry codes, rules may vary to reflect local priorities, cultures, industries, and needs. These differences are certain to produce conflicts when records and people cross borders. Neither national legislation nor voluntary action by record keepers will avoid the complexities of adapting general standards to specific classes of personal information.

Second, a government that has an investment in an existing data protection law may be more reluctant to coordinate with other countries. Even though the EU has a substantial commitment to common positions on difficult policy and legal matters, it took years to achieve general and vague agreement on data protection. Add more countries to the mix, and substantive international agreements at a level more detailed than general policies will be even more difficult.

The EU Directive goes beyond the Council of Europe Convention and the OECD Guidelines in providing more specifics about the obligations of member-states. Nevertheless, the problems of consistency are hardly avoided by its adoption. Spiros Simitis, the first data protection commissioner in the German state of Hesse, sees existing national laws as a serious handicap to common regulation. Simitis also sees the political pressures for accommodating existing laws as a threat to a high level of protection and to the scope of common regulations. Extensions beyond existing national laws were too difficult to achieve in the EU drafting process.[61] In effect, existing national laws may create a straitjacket that can stifle creativity, responses to new technology, and willingness to conform to new international rules.

Third, information technology is eroding traditional jurisdictional theories used to apply laws to individuals, corporations, and data. None of the international privacy activities directly recognizes current computer network technology. The OECD Guidelines and the Council of Europe Convention were adopted long before computer networks were commonplace. The EU data protection Directive is more recent, but it too fails to address network issues. Technology has simply overwhelmed some traditional approaches to privacy protection and some legal assumptions upon which the approaches rely.

Fourth, the United States will likely be the major impediment to any attempts to standardize privacy regulation, whether for traditional or networked records, whether through governmental or other mechanisms. There is no substantial political support in the U.S. business community for even the appearance of privacy regulations, let alone substantive protections. American industry is likely to continue this resistance, perhaps until it finds itself closed out of foreign markets for lack of domestic privacy rules. There are some American companies, especially those that operate internationally and comply with foreign data protection laws, that may be more amenable to privacy rules. They are, however, a distinct minority.

Finally, if governments are unwilling or unable to address the details of international privacy regulation in an effective or timely manner, other options are available. The private sector may find it appropriate and necessary to develop and adopt voluntary international privacy codes without the direct participation of governments.[62] The international standards movement may offer one alternative. While many traditional standards activities are aimed at technical issues, there are standards for quality management and quality assurance developed by the International Organization for Standards.[63] Fair information practice standards present similar management and procedural problems, so the standards process may be compatible with privacy regulation. The Canadian Standards Association has already developed a model code for the protection of personal information.[64]

Standards alone, however, without common procedures and effective enforcement, including realistic remedies, are only partly responsive to the problem. The U.S. experience with the OECD Guidelines shows some practical shortcomings of general standards. Many companies agreed to the OECD standards, but few changed their practices or policies. There was no external pressure or enforcement. The government was uninterested, and individual consumers were unable or unwilling to push for compliance. By contrast, a manufacturer might effectively be pressured by customers to comply with quality control principles.

A step beyond standards is a detailed voluntary international privacy code adopted jointly by merchants and consumers. A cooperative privacy code may offer some alternatives that would be difficult to achieve through governmental organizations or through the traditional standards process. For example, merchants and consumers might agree upon a set of cooperatively developed privacy standards and procedures for network transactions. The rules would set out basic fair information practices for the collection, maintenance, and use of personal information created by network activities and transactions. This could include uniform rules for notice, individual participation, use and disclosure, security, and accountability.

To be effective, a cooperative privacy code would have to include two elements. First, there should be substantive and procedural details that go beyond general principles. Specific responsibilities of merchants and network service providers must be adequately described, along with the rights of consumers. Second, there should be an enforcement mechanism that offers some oversight of the activities of record keepers as well as a practical remedy for individuals. This might include independent[65] auditing and electronic dispute resolution.[66] Adjudication could be accomplished through a private service based on mediation or arbitration rather than litigation. Companies engaged in international privacy-affecting transactions could support both the development of rules and the operations of an oversight/disputes resolution entity. The dispute resolution entity could be completely independent of its supporters, collecting a subscription fee from vendors and a filing fee from complaining consumers.

Much, if not all, of the dispute resolution process could be accomplished electronically, reducing the cost to all participants. Consumers would benefit from the availability of a practical, inexpensive process. To offer equivalent benefits to merchants, the remedies available to consumers could be limited. For example, damage awards might be limited to actual damages, and punitive damages would not be available.

Internet merchants and network service providers might welcome the certainty and uniformity of the process. They have an interest in establishing workable rules that they and their customers would find acceptable, practical, and responsive to existing and future problems. Consumers would welcome uniform, realistic, and accessible remedies that are available without regard to borders. Those offering goods and services through international networks who agree to comply with a privacy code could include notices on their network postings. This would inform and reassure consumers about their privacy rights. Because current Internet users appear to have stronger concerns about privacy than the public at large, vendors who subscribe to a cooperative privacy code might attract more business than those who do not.

A cooperative scheme might well result in more than one privacy code. Just like industry codes apply common principles differently to different record environments, multiple codes might develop in the networked environment. Rules that might be suitable for a system that provides electronic-mail services might not be appropriate for electronic commercial transactions. There could even be competition among codes, with some merchants adopting stricter privacy codes as a way of attracting privacy-sensitive customers. Conflicts would not be totally eliminated, but because each network transaction would come with a set of privacy rules and remedies, the consumer and the merchant would know their respective rights and responsibilities.

If large global companies took the lead in developing and implementing cooperative privacy codes along with appropriate consumer representatives, national governments and international organizations might be encouraged or pressured to conform disparate laws to those codes.[67] For example, the European Union might find it convenient to determine that a suitable cooperative privacy code for the Internet meets the adequacy test for network data transfers to third countries. It would certainly offer a way to avoid third-party enforcement problems that would be difficult to address otherwise. The EU Directive and some national laws clearly support industry codes so this is not an unreasonable expectation. Cooperative privacy codes could even be adopted domestically in the United States as a way of avoiding conflicting state rules or unwelcome federal rules. If privacy problems are solved or significantly diminished through private means, pressure for formal legislation may diminish.

Cooperative privacy codes are not a panacea. Computer networks may make it relatively easier to develop and apply cooperative codes, but the barriers will be higher for other, more traditional types of activities. Also, even when consumers and merchants can agree on solutions among themselves, the presence and needs of government cannot be completely ignored. Cooperative privacy codes would have to consider the possibility of law enforcement or national security demands for information and surveillance. Still, that possibility does not prevent consumers and merchants from addressing their own activities and resolving their own disputes.

Privacy was a public policy issue long before the invention of the computer and the computer network. Modern technology has moved privacy issues from the local to the national and now to the international realm. Those countries that are willing to address privacy concerns may nevertheless be unable to offer their own citizens assurances that personal information in an international networked environment will be fairly used in accordance with fair information practice standards. Additional efforts at internationalization or privatization of privacy policy and regulation may be necessary if privacy protections are to be maintained anywhere.

Notes

A version of this chapter was presented at a Villanova Law Review Symposium on International Regulation of Emerging Computer Technology in October 1995.

1. In the United States, the term "privacy" is used to include everything from control over personal information to personal reproductive rights to limits on government intrusion into the home. In Europe, the term of choice is "data protection." This offers a more precise way of referring to privacy values that arise concerning the collection, use, and dissemination of personal information. In this chapter, "privacy" and "data protection" are synonymous.

2. See Gellman, "Fragmented, Incomplete, and Discontinuous: The Failure of Federal Privacy Regulatory Proposals and Institutions," *Software Law Journal*, 6 (1993), p. 199 [hereinafter cited as Gellman].

3. For a history of the early congressional hearings, see Priscilla M. Regan, *Legislating Privacy* (Chapel Hill, NC: University of North Carolina Press, 1995) pp. 71–86 [hereinafter cited as Regan].

4. The first data protection law was passed in 1970 in the German state of Hesse. See David H. Flaherty, *Protecting Privacy in Surveillance Societies* (Chapel Hill, NC: University of North Carolina Press, 1989), p. 22. In North America, the Canadian province of Quebec is the only jurisdiction with a comprehensive privacy law regulating the private sector. Act Respecting the Protection of Personal Information in the Private Sector, S.Q., ch. 17 (Supp. 1993) (Canada).

5. The leading international privacy policy is the European Union's recently adopted Directive on the Protection of Individuals With Regard to the Processing of Personal Data and on the Free Movement of Such Data, 95/46/EC, 1995 O.J. (L 281) 31.

6. 5 U.S.C. §552a (1988).

7. 38 U.S.C. §7332 (1988); 42 U.S.C. §290dd-2 (Supp. 1993).

8. There are ethical rules that define confidentiality responsibilities for physicians and other health care professionals. These rules are also incomplete and out of date. See Gellman, "Prescribing Privacy: The Uncertain Role of the Physician in the Protection of Patient Privacy," *North Carolina Law Review* 62 (1984), p. 255.

9. See, e.g., Office of Technology Assessment, *Protecting Privacy in Computerized Medical Information* (1993), pp. 12–13; Institute of Medicine, *Health Data in the Information Age: Use, Disclosure, and Privacy* (1994), p. 15; Committee on Government Operations, H.R. Rep. No 103-601 Part 5, 103d Congress, 2d Session (1994), p. 83 (report to accompany H.R. 3600).

10. H.R. 2979 & H.R. 3444, 96th Congress, 1st Session (1979), and H.R. 5935, 96th Congress, 2d Session (1980).

11. *Privacy of Medical Records*, Hearings on H.R. 2979 and H.R. 3444 before a Subcommittee of the House Committee on Government Operations, 96th

Congress, 1st Session (1979), p. 1089 (Statement of the American Hospital Association).

12. *The Fair Health Information Practices Act of 1994*, Hearings on H.R. 4077 before the Information, Justice, Transportation, and Agriculture Subcommittee of the House Committee on Government Operations, 103rd Congress, 2d Session (1994), p. 222 (Testimony of Frederic Entin, Senior Vice President and General Counsel, American Hospital Association).

13. See, e.g., ibid. at pp. 451–463 (statement of Janlori Goldman, Director, Privacy and Technology Project, American Civil Liberties Union).

14. 15 U.S.C. §§1681–1688t (1988).

15. Senate Committee on Banking, Housing, and Urban Affairs, *The Consumer Reporting Reform Act of 1994*, S. Rpt. No 103-209, 103rd Congress, 1st Session 2 (1993).

16. *Fair Credit Reporting Act*, Hearing before the Subcommittee on Consumer Affairs and Coinage of the House Committee on Banking, Finance, and Urban Affairs, 101st Congress, 1st Session (1989).

17. For example, the Netherlands data protection law permits private organizations to voluntarily establish codes of conduct to further self-regulation. Wet Persoonsregistraties 19 095 at Part 4.6 (1987). The European Union Data Protection Directive encourages the use of industry privacy codes. Article 27.

The Privacy Commissioner of Canada recently came to the conclusion that voluntary privacy codes are inadequate and recommended that the Canadian Privacy Act be extended to cover the private sector. See Privacy Commissioner of Canada, *Annual Report* (1994–95).

18. The term "self-regulation" is often used loosely. When regulatory authority is delegated by government to a private entity, then the term is used appropriately. When a private entity establishes its own rules without any government delegation, there is no real regulation. In the absence of governmental enforcement, the term "voluntary standards" may be more appropriate. See Michael, "Federal Agency Use of Audited Self-Regulation as a Regulatory Technique," *Administrative Law Review* 47 (1995), p. 171. This distinction, important in other contexts, is not crucial here, and the term "self-regulation" is used here to cover self-regulatory activities, delegated or otherwise.

19. TRW, *Fair Information Values* (brochure) (July 1994).

20. Direct Marketing Association, *Fair Information Practices Manual* (1994). In contrast, the Canadian Direct Marketing Association has privacy rules that are binding on its members. See Canadian Direct Marketing Association, *Code of Ethics and Standards of Practice* (undated), Parts I & J.

21. Information Industry Association, *Fair Information Practices Guidelines* (February 26, 1994).

22. Associated Credit Bureaus, *Setting the Standard: Implementation Guide for Consumer Initiatives in the Credit Reporting Industry* (1994).

23. See Reidenberg, "Setting Standards for Fair Information Practice in the U.S. Private Sector," *Iowa Law Review* 80 (1995), pp. 497, 528.

24. Article 27.3.

25. The alternatives provided by technology are important because, in many ways, technology can direct policy choices. The architecture of computer networks may create problems that policy-makers must confront (e.g., global interconnections) and may foreclose options by not making them available (e.g., use of high-level encryption). See Reidenberg, "Rules of the Road for Global Electronic Highways: Merging the Trade and Technical Paradigms," *Harvard Journal of Law and Technology* 6 (1993), p. 288.

26. 18 U.S.C. §2710 (1988).

27. 47 U.S.C. §551(a) (1988 & Supp. 1993).

28. National Telecommunications and Information Administration, *Privacy and the NII* 16 (1995).

29. Public Law 99-508, 100 Stat. 1848 (1986).

30. See Regan, pp. 129–137.

31. See "Privacy Laws—State or Federal," *Privacy & American Business* 4–5 (May/June 1995).

32. See *Confidentiality of Insurance Records*, Hearings on H.R. 5646, H.R. 6518, and H.R. 7052 before a Subcommittee of the House Committee on Government Operations, 96th Congress, 1st & 2d Session (1979–80) (Testimony of Robert R. Googins, American Council of Life Insurance).

33. See Schwartz, "Privacy and Participation: Personal Information and Public Sector Regulation in the United States," *Iowa Law Review* 80 (1995), pp. 553, 554.

34. *Recommendations of Council Guidelines on the Protection of Privacy and Transborder Flows of Personal Data*, 1981 I.L.M. 422, O.E.C.D. Doc. No. C(80)58 final.

35. 1981 I.L.M. 377, Euro. T.S. No. 108 (Jan. 28, 1981).

36. Colin J. Bennett, *Regulating Privacy* (Ithaca, NY: Cornell University Press, 1992).

37. The Convention does not directly impose binding norms on signatories, but it requires nations to establish domestic data protection legislation. Article 4.1.

38. Part 2, para. 14. The OECD Guidelines, Council of Europe Convention, and the EU data protection Directive use the term "controller" or "data controller" meaning the person who determines the purpose and means of processing personal data. A more familiar, but less precise, American equivalent would be "record keeper."

39. Article 10.

40. Gellman, p. 230.

41. Gellman, p. 231. See also House Committee on Government Operations, *International Information Flow: Forging a New Framework*, H.R. Rep. No 96-1535, 96th Congress, 2d Session (1980).

42. Gellman, p. 232.

43. Information Infrastructure Task Force, *Privacy Principles for Providing and Using Personal Information* (June 6, 1995) (Privacy Working Group, Information Policy Committee).

44. National Telecommunications and Information Administration, *Privacy and the NII* 27 (1995).

45. Compare the Clinton administration's stance with the statement of Bruce Phillips, the Privacy Commissioner of Canada: "The protection of privacy cannot be left to the whims of the marketplace." Quoted in Ann Cavoukian and Don Tapscott, *Who Knows* (Toronto: Random House, 1995), p. 69.

46. Clause 1.

47. Commission of the European Communities, *Commission Proposal for a Council Directive Concerning the Protection of Individuals in Relation to the Processing of Personal Data*, Com(90) 314 Final Syn 287 and 188 (Sep. 13, 1990).

48. By contrast, neither the OECD Guidelines nor the Council of Europe Convention requires restrictions on transfer to third countries with nonconforming laws. See Greenleaf, "The 1995 EU Directive on Data Protection—An Overview," *International Privacy Bulletin* 1 (1995).

49. Commission of the European Communities, *Commission Proposal for a Council Directive Concerning the Protection of Individuals in Relation to the Processing of Personal Data*, Art. 24, Com(90) 314 Final Syn 287 and 188 (September 13, 1990).

50. Article 26.

51. Article 26. The conditions are: (1) consent; (2) necessary for performance of a contract in response to a data subject's request; (3) necessary for performance of a contract in the interest of the data subject; (4) important public interest or in connection with legal claims; (5) necessary to protect the vital interest of the data subject; and (6) from a public register.

52. Article 25.4.

53. Articles 25, 26.

54. Perritt, "Dispute Resolution in Electronic Network Communities," *Villanova Law Review* 38 (1993), p. 349, 352.

55. Messages could theoretically be stored for lengthy periods in intermediate countries. A routine backup of the contents of a forwarding computer could capture a message and store it indefinitely.

56. Electronic Communications Privacy Act, Public Law 99-508, 100 Stat. 1848-73 (1986).

57. Schwartz, "European Data Protection Law and Restrictions on International Data Flows," *Iowa Law Review* 80 (1995), p. 477.

58. 5 U.S.C. §552a (9188).

59. *Oversight of the Privacy Act of 1974*, Hearings before a Subcommittee of the House Committee on Government Operations, 98th Congress, 1st Session 226 (1983) (Testimony of Ronald Plesser).

60. 5 U.S.C. §552a(a)(1) (1988).

61. Simitis, "From the Market to the Polis: The EU Directive on the Protection of Personal Data," *Iowa Law Review* 80 (1995), pp. 445, 449–452.

62. Another approach is to build into network operating systems protocols and procedures that define and perhaps even enforce the rights of participants. For example, some degree of privacy might be assured if the network automatically provided encryption of all communications and transactions. Network protocols can establish rules of practice that are the same as or perhaps even stronger than formal legal restrictions because it can be impossible for network users to avoid or evade the rules.

63. The International Organization for Standardization (ISO) is a private international agency headquartered in Switzerland and dedicated to voluntary standardization. See National Research Council, Standards, Conformity Assessment, and Trade (1995), pp. 46–48. The ISO Committee on Consumer Policy has established a working group to assess whether there should be an international standard for the protection of personal data and privacy.

64. Canadian Standards Association, *Model Code for the Protection of Personal Information* (1995) (Final Draft). See generally Bennett, "Implementing Privacy Codes of Practice" (1995) (Canadian Standards Association).

65. Independence is a critical attribute of a data protection authority. The EU Directive (Article 28) requires "complete independence" for the supervisory authority.

66. For a discussion of modes of dispute resolution in an electronic environment, see Perritt, "Dispute Resolution in Electronic Network Communities," 38 *Villanova Law Review* 38 (1993), pp. 349, 388–395.

67. There is precedent for the development of private law. See, e.g., Note, "The New Law Merchant: Legal Rhetoric and Commercial Reality," *Law & Policy In International Business* 24 (1993), p. 589.

International Regulation of Encryption: Technology Will Drive Policy

Richard C. Barth and Clint N. Smith

Government Encryption Policies

Encryption, the process of protecting the confidentiality of information by the application of mathematical formulae, was until recently the exclusive domain of governments. Only when the international financial services industry became more automated in the 1970s did it begin to incorporate strong encryption to secure payment and clearing systems. Other components of the private sector began to follow the financial services industry's lead as their needs for secure information became apparent. Today encryption is considered an essential element of the infrastructure for electronic commerce and information exchange.

Since its advent government encryption regulation has been driven by two distinct interests: (1) a foreign intelligence interest in collecting all information implicated in national security; and (2) a law enforcement interest in collecting evidence of criminal activity. The military concerns itself with the first interest, the police with the second. The prospect of widely available strong encryption threatens both.

Governments have taken different policy approaches in their efforts to contain the threat they see posed by encryption. Mechanisms for controlling encryption can be placed into three general categories: import controls, export controls, and use controls. The summaries that follow of encryption policy in the United States, France, Israel, Russia, and China explore these forms of control.

A small minority of governments, most notably in Scandinavia, do not control encryption at all because they view encryption as an important tool for protecting personal privacy. Other governments, especially in the developing world, do not regulate encryption at all, perhaps because domestic use of encryption has not become widespread and the government has not had cause to focus on the need for controls. These encryption "safe havens" free from government regulation threaten to undermine the efforts of governments seeking to contain the spread of strong encryption, principally because some of these countries have highly educated cadres of scientists who understand and can use the tools of encryption.

Only recently, encryption has emerged as the object of industrial policy. In a departure from Western governments' efforts to stifle private sector encryption developments, Japan has embarked on an initiative to finance encryption research and development. This nascent policy, which also has the potential to undermine the efforts of governments seeking to contain the spread of strong encryption, is described below, after a review of other nations' efforts.

United States: Export Controls

Like most Western countries, the United States does not control domestic use of strong encryption. While the Arms Export Control Act provides the President authority to control the import of encryption for national security reasons, to date encryption imports have not been regulated. Instead, United States encryption policy is focused on controlling and monitoring the export of strong encryption.

The United States in theory controls the same encryption products as controlled by its former COCOM allies—the scope of what is controlled is contained in the International Munitions List. As a matter of law, the State Department has final say in decisions about strong encryption exports. As a matter of practice, the State Department defers to the judgment of the National Security Agency, part of the Department of Defense.

U.S. export control regulations authorize unrestricted encryption exports to Canada and most encryption exports to foreign subsidiaries of U.S. corporations to secure their corporate communications. The State Department also has a liberal policy regarding the export of strong encryption products which are limited to functions such as digital signatures, access control, and authentication. Additionally, the State Department has shown a willingness to authorize the export of strong encryption to financial institutions so long as its use is limited to protecting the security of financial transactions. In sum, U.S. export policy reveals a bias in favor of: (a) certain destinations, such as Canada; (b) certain reliable end-users, such as the financial services industry and the foreign subsidiaries of U.S.-based corporations; and (c) certain end-uses (e.g., digital signatures and PIN codes) necessary to establish an electronic commerce infrastructure but which do not include a capability to encrypt communications.

The U.S. government's liberalization of encryption export controls has been incremental and always in response to private sector demands. For instance, in 1992, under pressure from the software industry, the government agreed to reduce controls on exports of encryption software with a key length of 40 bits or less. More recently, the State and Commerce Departments have reduced the time necessary for processing export licenses for those encryption products which are still controlled; they have also exempted from license requirements certain exports made only for a U.S. national's personal use (the "laptop rule"). But the government has successfully stonewalled broader decontrol campaigns waged by encryption producers.

Recent U.S. policy reflects a concerted government effort to use export controls to encourage the development and use of key escrow encryption systems both within and outside the United States. The first step was the controversial 1993 Clipper Chip proposal which required the escrow of private keys with the government. The less controversial 1995 commercial key escrow initiative would require surveillance the escrow of private keys with trusted third parties. Commercial key escrow is potentially attractive because it would provide both the private sector and the government the capacity for data security and data recovery. But to date, industry response to the initiative has been lukewarm because of the numerous conditions, in the form of exportability requirements, imposed by the government.

There are signs that the United States believes international coordination is necessary to prevent widespread international deployment of strong encryption. The U.S. government spearheaded the December 1995 OECD information exchange on national encryption policies, perhaps in part because of the unprecedented degree of government coordination required to operate an international commercial key escrow system.[1] The United States can be expected to continue its efforts to forge consensus in support of encryption controls.

France: Reasonable Use Controls

France imposes controls on the use of encryption products within France, in addition to export controls similar to those in the United States. French encryption use controls are based on a December 1990 decree and are administered by the Service Central de la Sécurité des Systèmes d'Information (SCSSI), an office reporting to the Prime Minister through the Secrétariat Général de la Défense Nationale (SGDN). SCSSI embodies the French view that technology and industrial policy are critical elements of national defense.

French use controls differentiate between two categories of products that incorporate information security functions. A company wishing to distribute or use a product containing authentication, digital signature, or access control security features must submit a "declaration" to the SCSSI. Because the use of such products is routinely approved, the declaration requirement as a practical matter functions as a registration requirement. A prior "authorization" from the government is required only if a product contains data, file, or text encryption features. If a product incorporates both types of features, both types of approval must be obtained. For certain products employing strong encryption (apparently including PGP), this authorization may be denied or restricted to specifically identified individuals or groups.

SCSSI has come into serious conflict with a number of large foreign software companies. In the process, both the foreign software giants and SCSSI have had their hubris dented a bit. One U.S. software company faces very substantial potential liability for its distribution of unapproved encryption. SCSSI has received far less support at the top of the new French government than it expected. As a result, SCSSI seems to have accepted that it cannot control cryptography policy by fiat but must be perceived as reasonable and willing to work with industry.

The French government appears willing to participate in international discussions of encryption controls, as evidenced by their participation in the December 1995 OECD conference. Additionally, based on the French representatives' comments at that conference, it is clear that France supports the U.S. goal of encouraging the development of key escrow, or trusted third party, encryption. However, highly publicized allegations concerning France's conduct of industrial espionage against foreign multinationals will cause industry to be wary of any international policy under which the French government could gain access to private keys of foreign companies.

Israel: Use Controls

Israel, like France, controls not only the export but also the import and domestic use of encryption. The legal authority for Israel's controls is a 1974 court order, issued pursuant to the Supervision of Products and Utilities Law of 1957. The order requires a license from the Minister of Defense for the import, export, production or use of any encryption product.

Russia: Import and Use Laws

Russia has import and use laws on the books, but to date there has apparently been no enforcement of these measures. President Yeltsin's April 3, 1995 Edict on Measures to Observe the Law on Development, Production, Sale and Use of Encryption Devices and on Provision of Services in Encrypting Information restricts the use of encryption technologies by state-owned, private, and foreign entities, as well as by Russian government agencies. The Edict complements a rapidly growing body of law publicly regulating activities which previously were the exclusive domain of the KGB, other national security agencies, and the military.

The Edict bans the development, import, sale, and use of uncertified encryption devices, including "protected technological means of storage, processing and transmission information." Any person engaged in the development or sale of such products must obtain a license, and all encryption products must be approved by the government. The Edict directs the Federal Counterintelligence Service and other enforcement agencies to ensure compliance and prosecute violators. The Edict also directs the Central Bank to require that all communications between commercial banks and the Central Bank employ only certified cryptography and encryption devices.

Review of applications and issuance of licenses and use approvals is conducted by the Federal Agency of Government Communications and Information (FAGCI). FAGCI reports directly to the President and is responsible for the security of government communications and intelligence operations in connection with encrypted and coded information.

So far, the Russian bureaucratic apparatus for issuing licenses and certifications has not been established and the procedures are not yet in force. According to one commentator involved in the Russian cryptography industry there is no evidence that the edict has been enforced because there are still no FAGCI certified products.[2]

The prospects for Russian participation in international encryption policymaking are uncertain. Russia is not an OECD member and did not participate in the December 1995 OECD meetings. However, Russia will participate in any discussion of multilateral encryption control rules conducted in the "New Forum," COCOM's successor.

China: Strict Controls

In the People's Republic of China, a company wishing to import or export encryption products must first obtain a license. License applications can be reviewed either by the Ministry of Foreign Trade or the province's foreign trade bureau. The Ministry of Foreign Trade maintains the List of Prohibited and Restricted Imports and Exports. This list, enacted in 1987, indicates that

China restricts the import and export of voice-encoding devices. Anecdotal evidence from U.S. multinationals indicates that approval to use encryption products inside China is not necessarily easy to obtain.

Among the major powers, China is perhaps one of the least likely to join in an international consensus on encryption policy. China is not part of the New Forum, is not an OECD member, and has not sent representatives to major international meetings on encryption such as the December 1995 OECD meeting. Moreover, given that China is the frequent target of sanctions as a result of its arms proliferation and human rights practices, it is questionable whether China would participate in, or be welcome at, an international initiative that would require broad cooperation with the other advanced nations of the world on the sensitive issue of encryption.

Japan: Potential Industrial Policy

Japan's encryption policymaking is in its early stages and not transparent to outsiders. But there are strong signs that encryption is increasingly seen as a national economic priority because encryption is a key technology for improving Japan's penetration of the Global Information Infrastructure.

In the United States and Europe, encryption policy is formed by a mix of governmental interests. Advocates of business, national security agencies, and more recently the police all play a large role in the policy debate. This policy triumvirate is difficult to see in Japan. For a variety of reasons, commercial interests are predominant in Japanese government thinking about encryption. As an island nation, Japan has not had to defend itself for fifty years and so has not had to confront the national security concerns associated with encryption. Additionally, Japanese police face severe political and constitutional constraints on wiretapping, so the prospect of losing this criminal investigative tool seems less troubling to the Japanese government than to the United States and many European nations.

Unlike the United States and Europe, encryption policy in Japan apparently is not dominated by the military intelligence and law enforcement agencies. Rather the powerful Ministry of Posts and

Telecommunications (MPT) is hoping to take the lead in driving this area of policy. Likely competitors for control of cryptography policy include the Ministry for International Trade and Investment and the Bank of Japan—also agencies with a predominantly commercial focus. The MPT has sponsored three study group reports relevant to Japanese cryptographic policy. Each report treats cryptography as a central enabling technology for digital commerce.

The Ministry of International Trade and Industry (MITI) has its own computer technology initiative. It funds the Information-Technology Promotion Agency (IPA). The IPA and MITI, like MPT, have concluded that cryptographic technology is important for Japan's competitiveness as the Internet grows in importance and as electronic commerce increases. The IPA intends to spend more than $300 million on research and development to evaluate cryptography for electric commerce. MITI is spurring as much Japanese industry and academic work as possible on cryptography.

Because of the commercial focus to Japanese encryption policy, and the traditional U.S. dominance of the commercial market for information security, Japan could resist U.S. efforts to promote the adoption of key escrow encryption and to stop the spread of strong unescrowed encryption. If unescrowed strong encryption from Japan is widely available on the world market it will be difficult for governments of other countries to justify continued controls.

The Problems with Restrictive Governmental Approaches: Technology Will Drive Policy

Two relatively recent technical developments have caused a boom in demand for encryption: (1) the explosive growth of electronic communications for both social and economic transactions; and (2) the global deployment of networked computer systems.

Private sector interests in encryption policy are represented by two distinct groups. The first group is encryption users, who require encryption to secure the information they value. Five years ago this group represented the computer activist fringe and a few major multinational corporations, particularly financial institutions. Today it has grown dramatically in size and political power, increasing in proportion to the growth in the aggregate value of the information stored and transmitted in electronic form. The second group is the information security industry. Five years ago this group represented a small core of companies dependent on either government contracts or sector-specific security applications. Today it includes a wide array of the world's most sophisticated technology companies who have targeted the lucrative global market for products that secure electronic information. Neither group favors any form of government regulation which limits the availability of strong encryption.

Demand for Strong Encryption Is Legitimate

Governmental controls on encryption technology often interfere with legitimate private sector needs for strong encryption. Government controls to date have made weak security for private sector information more readily available than strong security. As indicated above, technological advancements in the broader information technology industry have generated a growing class of users who require strong encryption to protect their information.[3]

For those companies and individuals transmitting valued information across borders, reports of widespread government-sponsored industrial espionage add urgency to the demand for strong encryption. For companies such as Motorola and many others whose global growth is outstripping U.S. growth, the imperative for strong protection of company proprietary information and communications is advancing as fast as the technology is evolving to meet its needs. Sensitive Motorola data on software development for the next generation of products need to flow freely through many countries to tie together key software centers in India and the United States. Motorola sales data for Europe and Asia need to flow to Motorola headquarters in Illinois without unauthorized access or unanticipated delays. This information must be safe against both commercial and state-sponsored surveillance. Yet much of the encryption that governments make available without restrictions would pose little trouble to cryptographers who have access to the government-strength decryption resources.[4]

For example, the strongest encryption readily exported under United States export control laws has a key length of 40 bits.[5]

Because of U.S. export controls, 40-bit encryption is widely used in the U.S. origin commercial software that dominates the global market. Recent developments have called into question whether 40-bit encryption offers sufficient security. In July 1995, a group of Internet users broke the 40-bit algorithm used by Netscape, known as RC-4. Using mostly desktop computers, this group was able to exhaust every possible 40-bit key in about a week.[6] One month later a French graduate student broke 40-bit RC-4 encryption in eight days by networking 120 workstations and two supercomputers at an estimated cost of less than $10,000.[7] Even the security of 56-bit DES is in doubt: a private sector report claims that for an investment of $10 million a company could build a computer capable of decrypting any DES-encrypted communication in six minutes, at a cost of $38 per key.[8] As the cost of computing power goes down, the demand for stronger encryption is certain to rise.

These recent events demonstrate that the encryption that governments readily make available can be broken relatively quickly and at a reasonable expense. The communication of valuable commercial information demands stronger security than is available under current governmental controls.

Users' urgent need for information security will inevitably lead them to search out the strongest available encryption. The higher the stakes, and the higher the value of information which a user seeks to protect, the more likely the user will at least bypass, or at worst flaunt, applicable government regulations. Witness the ongoing debacle over the U.S. government's long-standing prohibition against carrying overseas even modest levels of encryption on one's laptop computer or in a cellular phone without obtaining a munitions license—the same type of license required for billion-dollar tank or fighter aircraft exports. While the government made commitments to industry over two years ago to alleviate this requirement, no action was taken until February 16, 1996.[9] How many CEO's or marketing managers traveling around the world realize that they are committing a felony every time they leave U.S. airspace?

What is driving the emergent need for strong security on these data flows, including the sales and marketing data in one's laptop computer, is certainly not user desire for a new game or toy in their suitcase. The driver is technological advancement in information technology and data handling in a global economy. Success in this environment means being part of your company's information flow anywhere at any time. That imposes a requirement for using security, both encryption and other forms of security that protect one's identity, as the legitimate duty of responsible employees who want to protect their company's proprietary information. No longer a toy or optional feature, such easy-to-use, even transparent data security has become a necessity to workers who now assume that it is built into any computer their employers makes available to them. At the same time that governments are warning of commercial espionage and the need to keep America's economy strong in the face of growing competition, government is fearful that encryption and other security techniques will limit their access to individual and institutional data. This conflict must be resolved if the users of the information superhighway are ever to move above the speed of a one-horse buggy.

Information Security: Know-How Is Spreading Worldwide

Controls on encryption technology, especially export controls, can harm national industries that stand to benefit from the booming demand for information security products containing strong encryption. This harm occurs because of the diffusion of encryption technology and is exacerbated by differences in control levels among governments. National companies burdened by controls which are not imposed by the governments of their commercial competitors are at a distinct competitive disadvantage.

Encryption controls impose costs on producers, though the costs are difficult to quantify.[10] In some cases it has been necessary to develop and produce two or more versions of the same software or hardware—one for domestic use and one for export. The need to deal with complex governmental licensing or authorization requirements also imposes legal and administrative costs that are not incurred by competitors in countries with fewer regulations. Finally, companies operating in countries with strict controls may be forced to license their products to companies in other countries, foregoing the profits that would accrue if they could manufacture and distribute the products themselves.

These costs will deter companies in highly regulated countries from developing products to meet the global demand for secure communications. This will create an opportunity for companies in countries where the controls on cryptography are less burdensome. It also creates an opportunity for companies with a global presence to develop encryption in unregulated countries to meet global market demand. Whether controlled or not, technology will migrate to those locations offering a "safe haven" from encryption controls. As the potential profits from sales of encryption products increase, the incentive to bypass or violate government encryption controls will also rise—and increased amounts of encryption know-how will filter out to companies in a position to profit unimpeded by government controls.

We may already see evidence of this. Encryption products are produced in 35 countries.[11] The United States is no longer the sole source of information security—of 1035 encryption products worldwide, 455 are produced outside the United States.[12] RSA Data Security, a leading U.S. encryption company, has entered into product development agreements with partners in China and Japan.[13] While it is impossible to attribute the increasing availability of foreign products to U.S. encryption controls, it is easy to acknowledge that absent U.S. controls, U.S. companies would exploit their dominant position in the software and hardware markets and their massive installed base of users, and as a result foreign production would be lower.

What is indisputable is that this proliferation of security products is a response to the boom in global demand for encryption. Just as there is no indication that demand will drop, there is no reason to believe that migration of encryption technology will decline and there is no indication that the government controls discussed above will prevent the widespread deployment of strong encryption as the market demand for it grows.

Interoperability Is Inevitable and Imminent

Government encryption policies will not hinder the development of interoperable software and hardware. That standards have not yet emerged is due not to government policy, but rather the lack of infrastructure and, until recently, the lack of demand. Strong encryption, previously an insignificant commercial niche, is increasingly in demand.[14]

With the well-documented proliferation of personal computers, modems, and quality telecommunications service, the technical capability to use encryption is a reality for an enormous class of users. In response to market demand for products that allow the large class of users to communicate with one another, a handful of standard encryption algorithms, such as DES, IDEA, and RSA, have emerged. The recently announced Visa/Mastercard agreement on a standard for electronic transactions using these two globally dominant credit vehicles is an important indicator of the trend toward private sector standard-setting.[15]

Key exchange and interoperability standards are also under discussion, also driven by user demand. As more of the private sector becomes technology-enabled, and more information is exchanged and stored in electronic form, encryption will become ubiquitous, no longer an obscure technique clouded in secrecy and understood only by the government.

Controls Are Ineffective

In the face of these technology and global market changes, governmental controls are ineffective today and in danger of becoming irrelevant tomorrow. The proliferation of DES and other strong algorithms in foreign-supplied software and the absence of enforcement of the munitions controls on laptop exports provide ample evidence of this.

Export controls cannot stop the global spread of encryption technology; they can only slow its development and export from the United States. As a technical matter, encryption can, and has been, made widely available over the Internet. Internet FTP sites allow easy, and often anonymous, access to encryption software. The Software Publishers Association has identified more than 450 foreign encryption products.[16] Although the strength of some foreign products was questioned by a January 1996 government study (parts of which remain classified),[17] there is still ample evidence that government controls are stifling sales opportunities outside the United States.

Import and use controls cannot stop the use of the technology within the country's borders since encryption software is so readily available on publicly available distributed networks. The uses least likely to be deterred by such controls are the criminal and hostile government uses of encryption at which these controls are presumably aimed. Moreover, as more consumers and companies pass information over unsecured networks, the public will demand the right to use strong encryption. Government use restrictions, once attacked by only a cadre of libertarian computer activists, could become the target of a new, large and powerful lobby of encryption users.

Controls will become even less effective as the profit potential of evading controls rises. Companies developing encryption products and wishing to profit from the international market take advantage of loopholes in export control laws. For instance, under U.S. law the owner of a U.S. encryption invention can license a foreign company to manufacture and distribute products which have reduced the invention to tangible form. A U.S. company with a marketable encryption invention could license the right to have it built in Taiwan, then import the product back to the United States for domestic use, even though the U.S. company could not build that product in the United States and export it. Aggressive use of such loopholes and intentional violations of encryption controls will become more common as the commercial market for strong encryption grows.

Unilateral national government efforts to limit the availability of encryption are especially prone to ultimate failure. Only through a combination of strict use controls and limitations on access to the Internet can a government effectively limit the availability of strong encryption within its own borders. Such strategies run the risk of attack from both local users and producers of encryption. Such strategies, if maintained over time, will only isolate that country from the benefits resulting from secure access to the developing Global Information Infrastructure and prevent national participation in the ever-increasing amount of commerce that is conducted electronically.

The only prospect for effective government controls is tightly coordinated international policymaking coupled with strict national enforcement, yet there is little indication that this will occur in the near term. Japan, for example, is suspicious of the U.S. commercial key escrow initiative. Scandinavian and certain EU governments value privacy rights and oppose the concept of mandating the escrow of keys with trusted third parties. Only a glimmer of cooperation was reflected at the December 1995 OECD meeting; it remains to be seen if this can mature into effective policy coordination.

Conclusion

Market realities based on continued rapid advances in technology make it likely that strong encryption will be an essential component of the international infrastructure for electronic commerce. Internationally accepted encryption standards will inevitably emerge, and sophisticated companies, especially new, small entrants to this global business, will become better able to sidestep government controls on the export, import, and use of encryption. Together these developments will doom the unilateral efforts of individual governments to prevent the emergence of secure international communications.

If Japan puts the weight of its government and industry behind strong encryption, competitive pressure could further undermine isolated government attempts to limit the deployment of encryption through export controls and other measures. The recent agreement between Chinese government entities and RSA Data Security, a leading U.S. encryption company, provides further indication that the dike is leaking through more than a few small breaks.

The immediate emergence of international consensus on encryption policy poses the only potential obstacle to the otherwise inevitable global deployment of strong encryption. Governments could choose between overt domestic regulation in the Russian and French manner or the export-focused policies that now prevail in the domestic markets of countries like the United States. But any international effort will run a high risk of failure unless enforcement is closely coordinated. This currently is not the case with encryption export controls. And given the rapid pace of technical developments discussed in this paper, any effort undertaken to coordinate encryption policymaking at an international level may be too late.

Notes

1. An international system would need to provide a means for a foreign government to receive a surveillance target's keys from a foreign escrow agent.

2. Anatoly N. Lebedev, "New National Encryption Policies and Regulations in Russia" (unpublished paper, 1995).

3. A study funded by the Computer Systems Policy Project found that global demand for secure computing will increase to 60% of system sales by 2000. William F. Hagerty, *The Growing Need for Cryptography* (1995).

4. A recent report estimated that a government intelligence agency making a $300 million investment in hardware could break 40-bit encryption in .0002 seconds at a cost of $.001 per key. *Minimal Key Lengths for Symmetric Ciphers to Provide Adequate Commercial Security*, Report of an Ad Hoc Group of Cryptographers and Computer Scientists (Jan. 1996).

5. The example of 40-bit encryption also demonstrates that government ability to regulate encryption cannot keep up with the pace of technological development. In the United States, the 40-bit limit on readily exportable encryption has not been adjusted since 1992. In that same time, the cost of computing power necessary to break such a code has declined dramatically. In response to U.S. key-length limits which are deemed to offer inadequate security, the Business Software Alliance has advocated adoption of a "Cost of Cracking Adjustment" (COCA) that would automatically adjust the key-length limit upward every two years.

6. Stephen Somogyi, "Cyberpunks Go Home: U.S. Business Can't Compete in Global Net-based Market Under Current Law," *Digital Media*, September 11, 1995, p. 29.

7. "French Hacker Cracks Netscape Code," *Wall Street Journal*, Aug. 17, 1995, p. B3.

8. *Symmetric Ciphers to Provide Adequate Commercial Security*, Report of an Ad Hoc Group of Cryptographers and Computer Scientists (Jan. 1996).

9. Amendment to the International Traffic in Arms Regulations, 61 Fed. Reg. 6111 (Feb. 16, 1996).

10. A study funded by the Computer Systems Policy Project predicts that revenues of U.S. systems suppliers will reach $200 billion by 2000 and that $50 billion of these revenues could be lost to foreign suppliers as a result of export controls. William F. Hagerty, *The Growing Need for Cryptography* (1995).

11. Software Publishers Association, Worldwide Survey of Cryptographic Products (June 1995).

12. Ibid.

13. RSA Data Security, Inc. and People's Republic of China Sign MOU on Encryption Technology and Joint Research, RSA Press Release, Feb. 2, 1996.

14. For instance, the financial services industry, which has long relied on DES security, is actively looking for a stronger algorithm which would provide greater security.

15. "Visa and Mastercard Adopt Joint Internet Standard," Reuters News Service, Feb. 1, 1996.

16. Software Publishers Association, Worldwide Survey of Cryptographic Products (June 1995).

17. *A Study of the International Market for Computer Software with Encryption*, Report Prepared by U.S. Department of Commerce and National Security Agency (Jan. 1996).

International Information Policy in Conflict: Open and Unrestricted Access versus Government Commercialization

Peter N. Weiss and Peter Backlund

Introduction

U.S. domestic federal information policy is based on the premise that government information is a valuable national resource and that the economic benefits to society are maximized when government information is available in a timely and equitable manner to all. Maximizing these benefits depends, in turn, on fostering diversity among the entities involved in disseminating government information. These include for-profit and not-for-profit entities such as information vendors and libraries as well as state and local governments. Policies such as charging no more than the cost of dissemination and prohibitions against restrictions on the reuse or redissemination of government information are aimed at achieving this goal.

Other nations do not necessarily share these values. Although an increasing number are embracing the concept of open and unrestricted access to public information—particularly scientific, environmental, and geographic information of great public benefit—other nations are treating their information as a commodity to be commercialized. Whereas the U.S. Copyright Act[1] has long provided that "[c]opyright protection under this title is not available for any work of the United States Government," some other nations take advantage of their domestic copyright laws that do permit government copyright to assert monopoly control over certain categories of information in order to generate revenues. Such arrangements tend to preclude other entities from developing markets for the information or otherwise disseminating the information in the public interest.

Agencies of the U.S. government involved in international data exchanges sometime face problems stemming from differing national treatment of government copyright. For example, a country may assert copyright and attempt to condition the sharing of data with a U.S. federal agency on an agreement that the agency will withhold release of the information or otherwise restrict its availability to the public in order to facilitate revenue generation. But U.S. policy holds that public information is a national resource, the value of which is maximized to society through the "diversity principle," discussed below. Therefore, there is a tension between the recognition that public information is a national resource that needs to be openly shared on the one hand and the perceived need of public managers to find new revenue sources on the other. This tension, and its manifestation in the differing information policies of various countries, will need to be resolved in the context of the emerging global information infrastructure (GII).

This chapter examines the sources of the "open and unrestricted" information policy embraced by the U.S. government and compares them to the growing trend toward "government commercialization"[2] of information, particularly among a number of European countries. The authors argue that fundamental democratic values, many of which are reflected in U.S. law, make government commercialization of public information an unwise policy. The authors further argue that even in countries in which these values are not shared, some fundamental characteristics of the economics of information preclude any realistic ability to use government information as a significant revenue raiser. A case study of international negotiations over the sharing and use of meteorological data is presented to illuminate these points. This chapter concludes with some observations regarding a possible resolution of the emerging frictions in international relations caused by divergent national treatment of government information resources.

U.S. Domestic Information Policy

To address these issues, we first need to place them in the broader context of the role played by government entities and government information in the emerging GII. The GII is a combination of facilities, services, and people that allows anyone to send and receive information when and where they want at an affordable cost. The GII includes the physical facilities used to transmit, store, process, and display voice, data, and images. It includes software and services that will integrate and interconnect these physical components through the efforts of a wide variety of private sector providers. Most relevant for the purposes of this chapter, the GII also includes vast quantities of government-generated information as well as the valuable information produced by the private sector.[3]

While much of the infrastructure already exists, information will be so strategic a resource in the 21st century that conscious and deliberate government action—in concert with industry and the public—is needed. Of course, governments are in no position financially, technically, or managerially to design or build the information highway or even to repave it. So the GII will be designed, built, owned, and operated primarily by the private sector, with some significant government involvement.

Governments should strive to be in step with the change from paper to electronic information. The U.S. government, for example, is a major creator, collector, user, and disseminator of information. Sound scientific research, the public health and safety, and the equitable collection and distribution of tax receipts are a few of the national priorities that depend on federal information systems. In addition, the unique nature of information in a free society—Thomas Jefferson called it "the currency of democracy"—gives government policies special importance.

Over the past decade, a broad consensus has developed in the United States that government information is a public asset and a valuable national resource to be managed in accordance with the following principles.[4] The government should make information available to the public on timely and equitable terms. It is also necessary to foster the existing diversity of information sources, in which the private sector, along with state and local governments, libraries, and other entities, are significant partners. On the one hand, this means that the government should not try to duplicate value-added information products produced by the private sector. On the other hand, it means that the government should actively disseminate its information—particularly the raw content from which value-added products are created—at cost and not attempt to exert copyright-like controls or other restrictions.

These consensus principles are set forth in OMB Circular A-130, parts of which were reissued in June 1993 and most recently republished in the *Federal Register* on February 20, 1996.[5] The core information dissemination principles of Circular A-130 are codified in the Paperwork Reduction Act of 1995,[6] which was signed by President Clinton on May 22, 1995, following unanimous passage in both houses of Congress.

Section 3504(d) of the Paperwork Reduction Act of 1995 provides that the Director of OMB will develop and oversee implementation of policies that relate to federal agency dissemination of information, regardless of form or format, and that will promote public access to public information including through the use of information technology. Section 3506(d) provides that agencies shall ensure the public timely and equal access to public information. It also charges agencies with "encouraging a diversity of public and private sources for information based on public information" (3506(d)(1)(a)). This "diversity principle" is key to understanding the issues raised by this chapter.

Diversity as the Key to Maximizing the Benefits of Government Information

Diversity is critical to a robust economy. The "currency of commerce"—which Adam Smith once called "the wealth of nations"— is created, shared, and used by diverse entities. These include large and small businesses in many sectors from farming to manufacturing; financial institutions; governments; and individuals. Each must play varied but complementary roles for the economy to thrive. Diversity is also critical to a robust democracy. Just as Smith's "currency of commerce" helps to demonstrate the diversity principle, so too does Jefferson's "currency of democracy." Information, Jefferson's "currency of democracy," is created, shared, and used by diverse entities. These include federal agencies, for-profit information businesses, libraries and nonprofit organizations, state and local governments, and individuals. Each of these entities must also play varied but complementary roles for democracy to thrive.

In the United States, state, local, and tribal governments cooperate as major partners with the federal government in the collection, processing, and dissemination of information. For example, state governments are the principal producers of information in the areas of health, welfare, education, labor markets, transportation, the environment, and criminal justice. The states supply the federal government with data on Aid to Families with Dependent Children; Medicare; school enrollments, staffing, and financing; births, deaths, and infectious diseases; population trends that form the basis for national estimates; employment and labor market developments; and statistics used for census geography. National information resources are greatly enhanced through these major cooperating efforts.

Another major element of this diversity is the nonprofit sector, particularly libraries, which serve as critical links in the chain of information distribution. Located in nearly every community, libraries not only serve educational needs but also form part of the nation's economic "safety net" by distributing information on various important government health, welfare, and other services to those who need it.

This diversity has also resulted in the growth of a number of vibrant new industries utilizing government information. These industries contribute to the economic health of the nation through job creation and to the government itself through their, and their employees', tax receipts. Here are a few examples:

• A number of firms take government-produced weather data and package them into various products, including commercial weather broadcasts. Indeed, there is now a nationwide cable weather television station broadcasting weather information 24 hours a day. There is even a specific trade association in Washington made up of commercial weather services firms.

• Industrial productivity is enhanced by the growing number of specialized companies that take patent information from the

Patent Office and package it in a variety of ways for various industries and that provide custom-tailored information products to manufacturers who want to keep abreast of developments in particular technologies. This is a service that the government cannot provide to industry given its limited resources.

• We take for granted the maps we buy and use, whether for travel or for work. U.S. maps are largely derived from government-produced geographic data bases. Indeed, one can now buy a privately manufactured CD-ROM product showing all the roads in the country, including the dirt roads in our national parks and forests. Just hook it up to your portable computer and to an inexpensive Global Positioning System receiver in your recreational vehicle, and you're ready to explore.

• The now almost ubiquitous CD-ROM itself is perhaps the best example of the diversity principle at work. Today CD-ROMs offer a wide range of services, from computer games to interactive encyclopedias, and the United States CD-ROM manufacturing industry is by far the largest in the world. This industry got its start, however, largely because of the vast amount of copyright-free government information that was available in the United States.

The information activities of governments, the for-profit sectors of the economy, and the volunteer community can and must coexist. Those information activities should be complementary, not competitive. There is more than enough room and need in the economy for all to play their respective roles.

The policy advocating a diversity of sources and channels of information is based on the reality that no one supplier can design modern information products to suit the needs of all users. Instead, market forces and entrepreneurial energy are crucial for determining user needs and for experimenting in the marketplace with different distribution and marketing techniques and different value-added features in order to satisfy those needs.

In addition, maintaining a diversity of channels and sources protects against censorship and manipulation of public information for political purposes. In this respect the diversity principle is central to the free speech policy embodied in the First Amendment to the U.S. Constitution, with which any state-maintained or state-granted monopoly over public information would be in conflict.

Of course, many public managers perceive a competing policy interest: the need to find new sources of financing for public activities. For them, the best way to raise money for new electronic information systems and public access features is to ensure a sufficient revenue stream from the information access. One obvious way to do so, in effect, is to sell franchises. Strategies for public financing that depend on selling franchises to perform public functions are not new. One of the main ways that King Charles I of Britain financed his government without seeking parliamentary approval for new taxes was through franchises. Some of the revolutionary fervor for both the English revolution and, more than a century later, the American revolution came from a reaction to perceived corruption in the granting of franchises. Franchises are currently disfavored because they deprive the public of the benefits of competition, although the temptation to set up monopolies continues in the background of public finance discourse.[7] In any event, this tendency is antithetical to maintaining the diversity necessary for the health of an economy or a democracy.

The case of *Legi-Tech v. Keiper*[8] illustrates this point. The plaintiff challenged a New York law that created a state-sponsored monopoly on legislative materials expressly to deny the possibility of private sector firms electronically disseminating such information. The court first rejected the assertion that the government's arguable "natural monopoly" over the creation of certain types of information somehow justified assigning rights in that natural monopoly to a preferred franchisee:

The evils inherent in allowing government to create a monopoly over the dissemination of public information in any form seem too obvious to require extended discussion. Government may add its own voice to the debate over public issues . . . but it may not attempt to control or reduce competition from other speakers . . . . When the state creates an organ of the press, as here, it may not grant the state press special access to governmental proceedings or information and then deny to the private press the right to republish such information. Such actions are an act of censorship that allows the government to control the form and content of the information reaching the public.[9]

The court then rejected the argument that the government was behaving as a rational economic actor and was not acting from political motivation, noting that "the profit motive which is the incentive for creation is also a disincentive for suppression of the work created, a premise of doubtful strength in the case of government."[10] A rational copyright holder would be expected to license others to publish a work as long as the price was sufficient to offset the loss from free riders.[11] Rather, the court noted:

The profit motive's weakness where government is concerned is starkly evident in [the State's] own provisions, which prohibit potential retransmitters from subscribing to them at prices that eliminate the potential for free riding. To revert to the copyright analogy, [the State agency] is refusing to license reproduction at any price even though reproduction would increase purchases of the product without reducing [the State agency's] incentive to produce more information.[12]

In sum, U.S. information policy has significant First Amendment components. On the federal level, these can clearly be seen in the Copyright Act's preclusion of government copyright and the Freedom of Information Act's insistence that government information not specifically exempt be released at no more than the cost of search and duplication. These values stand in the way of efforts by government agencies to commercialize their information. However, even in countries that do not share these values, and in unusual situations in the United States when they are sought to be superseded by short-term expedients,[13] other barriers exist to the commercialization of government information. These will be examined in the following sections of this chapter.

The Emerging Trend toward "Government Commercialization" of Information

U.S. domestic federal information policy is relatively straightforward: a strong freedom of information law, no government copyright, fees limited to recouping the cost of dissemination, and no restrictions on reuse. In contrast, European countries vary greatly in their information policies. The Scandinavian countries have strong public access laws, while Germany and the United Kingdom have none. France's public access law is weak and subject to significant exceptions.

The availability of copyright is of particular importance in instances in which governments seek to commercialize their information holdings. Government copyright permits the exclusion of the private sector or the maintenance of exclusive arrangements with preferred franchisees. Although the Berne Convention results in great uniformity in most copyright matters worldwide, Article 2, Section 4, permits signatory states to determine for themselves whether to assert copyright in government information. This discretion reflects a great diversity of approaches. The United Kingdom is at the opposite end of the spectrum from the United States. There, the doctrine of Crown Copyright extends to virtually anything that is not copyrighted by a private entity.[14] Most European states are in the middle of the spectrum, with government copyright being permissible where it is expressly reserved.[15]

The Royal Ordnance Survey of the United Kingdom is an example of an attempt to take certain governmental functions "off budget" by requiring the agencies to recover the costs of operations through commercializing government information. As its name implies, the Ordnance Survey was established in 1791 to create maps for the national defense. Chartered as a semi-independent Executive Agency in 1990, the Ordnance Survey is required to maximize its reliance on revenue generated from information sales. Making aggressive use of Crown Copyright, the Ordnance Survey recovered approximately 70 percent of its operating costs of approximately US$116 million in the fiscal year 1993–1994, with the remainder made up by a parliamentary appropriation. However, the Ordnance Survey is not attempting to recoup the capital for plant equipment and technology spent prior to 1990. Instead, these underlying costs of collecting the data, converting it to computer form, etc., are treated as "sunk costs" and are not recoverable.[16] Thus, the Ordnance Survey has not yet demonstrated the ability to recover its entire operating costs through fees or to raise investment capital without seeking additional appropriations.

In contrast, The Royal Ordinance Survey's sister agency in the United States, the Interior Department's Geological Survey, operates very differently. The basic costs of generating and processing information are covered by appropriated funds, and the Geological Survey sets its prices for information products to cover the costs of reproduction, handling, packaging, and distribution. Its copyright-free and low-cost data policy allows the Geological Survey to focus on strategic planning without being distracted by attempting to assert protective copyright and worrying about possible data misuse, although it is certainly not free from the exigencies of budget limitations.[17]

Although nations are free to adopt either approach, conflicts can and do arise when governments with such disparate information policies attempt to collaborate on data-sharing initiatives. The following sections explore this problem in the specific context of the sharing of meteorological information.

Government Meteorological Information as a Battleground of Conflicting Information Policies: A Case Study

The production, use, and exchange of meteorological data illustrates the complexity and difficulty of resolving information policy issues on an international scale. Two models for financing government production of information are coming into direct conflict. This conflict is occurring within the context of a long-accepted international framework for the production and distribution of information. The conflict between the public good/private enterprise partnership arrangements followed in the United States, exemplified by the diversity principle discussed above, and the efforts of some government entities to restrict the flow of information for quasi-commercial purposes is threatening the traditional framework of open and unrestricted exchange of weather-related data. It is possible that this open framework, which has played a significant role in creating a world in which people take forecasting of the weather for granted, will not survive in its present form.

The International Tradition of Sharing Meteorological Data

The physical characteristics of weather and attempts to understand and mitigate its effects gave the existing framework its present character. The value of meteorological information is well understood by all nations, indeed by all people. The weather affects everyone every day and has an overwhelming influence on agricultural productivity and water resources and thus on the economy of all human communities. Weather prediction is a practical science with tangible benefits that has been supported by governments at all levels for hundreds of years.

Out of this experience has come a recognition that weather is dynamic, with considerable daily variability within broad seasonal patterns. Furthermore, weather is local, regional, *and* global: the world's weather is all one interconnected system, which moves from place to place with no respect for national boundaries.

Measurements taken in one place help predict the weather in other places. The combination of many different observations from many different places makes it possible to construct models of the weather system and to understand how the many different processes within it fit together and affect each other. Sharing information and measurements has resulted in a constantly improving predictive capability. Common recognition of the value of such sharing resulted over time in the creation of a formal international regime for weather prediction in the form of a United Nations agency, the World Meteorological Organization (WMO), which was created in 1951 as the successor to the International Meteorological Organization, which was established in 1853.

Almost every nation is a WMO member. It has numerous technical and scientific functions,[18] but for the purposes of this discussion, the relevant aspect is its dual role in organizing both a global system of weather measurements and the distribution of data and forecasts through programs such as the World Weather Watch. It is important to note that the WMO does not actually take measurements or make predictions; it is rather a cooperative organization that depends on national member agencies to perform tasks according to agreed upon procedures and policies.

One of the WMO's most fundamental, albeit unstated, traditions has always been the open and unrestricted sharing of data collected by members. This is understandable considering the basic physical characteristics of weather described above, and the techniques for predicting it. This ethic of open and unrestricted sharing is also rooted in the scientific method itself, which is premised on every stage of the inferential process being open to scrutiny and replication by peers. Weather prediction has been greatly facilitated by information sharing, and the modeling and observational sciences upon which it depends have been greatly advanced by the open sharing, replication, and testing of techniques, ideas, and theories.[19]

In fact, the sharing of data and information products produced from data, such as forecasts, has been so fundamental that until recently it has not been the subject of any official WMO policy. Some members provide more data and some less, depending on size and capability, but all rely on information from others. Even the United States, with the most elaborate and advanced weather prediction system in the world, needs measurements provided by other nations for input to its models. Data have been exchanged fully among WMO members, and data provided by WMO members to the World Weather Watch are provided to users free of charge. This system has been very effective, with remarkably broad participation.

The Emerging Conflict

In recent years, the widespread willingness to share data and information within the WMO framework has begun to change, primarily because of the combination of budget restrictions affecting members and the increased costs of data collection. These conditions are common to all nations and participants, but responses vary widely, and this variation is producing significant strains in the WMO system as it tries to accommodate traditional government-only activities, public-private partnerships, and now, government commercialization.

The government commercialization approach has been adopted by a number of European nations, including France, Germany and United Kingdom. Essentially, the paradigm is to finance the operations of national meteorological services by charging users for services—as in the example of the Royal Ordnance Survey discussed above—instead of financing their operations through direct appropriations. Since this has in some cases significantly reduced the direct cost to the government of running the agencies, an apparent savings can be claimed by advocates of such policies.

Ironically, the users who are charged include, often to a significant extent, other government agencies within the country. For example, the United Kingdom's Meteorological Office gets about 70 percent of its funding by charging the nation's military for its services. In other words, most of the agency's revenue still comes from tax monies. Furthermore, despite the economic justification for moving the service "off-budget," the provision of this service is still seen as a critical national need, and the United Kingdom has not been willing to simply shift to actual competitive private sector supply of weather information, nor have the other European nations which have adopted the government commercialization approach. Rather, they have tended to grant their national meteorological services what is effectively a monopoly status as the sole supplier of weather information. Such "information monopolies" do not tend to view the unrestricted flow of information as being in their best interest.

The response to budget pressure in the United States has been quite different. Given significant streamlining of the federal meteorological workforce, a different type of public-private division of responsibilities has evolved: the government continues to maintain large-scale measurement systems and modeling and analysis activities and makes its results available to anyone who wants them at the cost of dissemination. In addition, commercial services can pay for "special" (direct and faster, but not exclusive) access to government-provided information and then use this information in creating value-added services and products, such as specialized regional forecasts, that they price according to the market. In this way, a whole class of value-added local and regional forecasting activities and the delivery of high-level information to users has been left to the private sector, creating a significant industry with gross revenues in the range of $200 to $250 million per year and growing. This is a concrete example of the beneficial economic effects of the diversity principle in the context of government information policy.[20]

The result is that data and information products produced by the government are available to all at the cost of dissemination. This minimizes the financial burden of using information for research and education, and assures that there are no barriers to the entry of additional competitive actors in the value-added arena. The competitive value-added industry results in a high level of services available to specialized users, and the public gets quality information as part of popular, low-cost information products such as newspapers and cable television channels, as well as through commercial broadcasting. This value-added information product industry has also become capable of providing service on an international scale, creating a perceived competitive threat that has led some European nations to seek to restrict this competitive force in a number of ways.

The Negotiations over the WMO Accord

These strains came into full view at the last WMO Congress in June 1995. For several years preceding the Congress, various WMO members had begun to withhold, or threaten to withhold, data from the World Weather Watch system, where it would be openly available free of charge. They also began to increase the prices for data supplied to individual scientists, research institutes, and government agencies for research use and to make data available for such use only under bilateral agreements that restricted the ability of the recipient to redistribute the data, including sharing it with research colleagues. The increasing prevalence of charging for data that had previously been made available without charge was recognized by the WMO as a significant problem, and a working group was set up to develop, for the first time, a formal WMO policy on data availability for consideration by the full Congress. The working group had members from the United States and a number of European nations. It is important to note that they were serving on the working group as experts rather than national representatives, and they were attempting to develop a proposal that could be supported by a consensus of the WMO members.

The proposal that was developed called for making certain meteorological data fully and openly available, but divided the data into two "tiers." Tier 1 data would have no restrictions on use at all. Tier 2 data would have no restrictions on research and educational use but would have restrictions on the reexport of the data for commercial purposes from nations that receive it.

Some WMO members asserted that unrestricted redistribution of their data would cause them economic harm, i.e., it would threaten their control over, and ability to sell, information. Specifically, they wished to restrict the ability of private sector entities, both domestic and foreign, to compete with their national meteorological services. Under the proposal that was developed, private sector firms in the United States could not use foreign data obtained at low cost through the United States National Weather Service to compete in foreign services markets. They would have to obtain such data directly from the national weather service in the country of origin, at the price set by that weather service.

This initial proposal was modified significantly during the course of negotiations, primarily because of United States opposition. In light of the policies contained in OMB Circular No. A-130 and the then Paperwork Reduction Act of 1995, the United States argued strongly for adoption of an explicit policy of broadening the open and unrestricted international exchange of meteorological data and products, such as forecasts, with explicit recognition of the desirability of unrestricted exchange and low-cost access for research and education. The United States also argued against adoption of a two-tier system that placed a burden on national governments to restrict the reexport of data.

However, while United States policy is inconsistent with government commercialization, the United States recognizes that other nations have the legal right to impose restrictions within their borders if they choose to do so and to assert copyright on their government-produced works. What the United States argued against was explicit adoption of an internationally agreed policy to limit the flow of information. In essence, the United States position recognized that particular nations might chose to impose restrictions such as copyright or perhaps even tariffs to define and regulate markets within their national territory, subject to international trade agreements. But it opposed adopting an international policy of specific across-the-board restrictions on the use of environmental data. The original two-tier proposal would have required recipients to actively monitor and control the reexport of data. This was unacceptable to the United States and to a number of other countries.

The United States delegation to the WMO Congress stressed the importance of the principle of unrestricted access to and use of environmental data. In doing so, they were representing very serious concerns voiced by the scientific community and the United States value-added industry about the perceived trend of increasing restrictions on the availability of data. The United States position was explicitly endorsed in a contemporaneous report issued by the National Research Council (the operational arm of the National Academies of Sciences and Engineering in advising the federal government), which proved helpful in the deliberations.[21]

The initial reaction to the United States position from the European meteorological services was quite negative. They questioned whether national legal solutions such as copyright were practical, and whether they provide a workable solution to their goal of preventing private sector competition with government commercial activities.

In the end, the WMO adopted a three-part practice that can be summarized as follows: (1) A minimum set of essential data and products "required to accurately describe and forecast the weather and climate" shall be provided on a free and unrestricted basis; (2) additional data and products required to sustain WMO programs at the global level shall be freely exchanged, although members may be justified in placing conditions upon their reexport outside the receiving country for commercial purposes; and (3) open and unrestricted access shall be provided to all data and products exchanged under WMO auspices for the research and education communities for noncommercial use.

This formula seemed to address the primary United States concerns. Open and unrestricted exchange was endorsed with explicit emphasis on research and educational use. On the more difficult issue of restrictions on commercial use, the United States interpreted the language as allowing the originators of data to place conditions on the reexport of data by recipients but not requiring recipients to enforce such restrictions. The United States interpretation was that data could be labeled as not for commercial reexport, and if the ultimate recipient ignored the label, the originator could take national-level actions, e.g., an action for infringement of the originating government's copyright.

Unfortunately, and perhaps predictably, differing intentions and perspectives are resulting in different interpretations of the accord. A group of European weather services has proposed a draft set of conditions on use of data that is at odds with the United States interpretation. These conditions would make national weather services responsible for enforcing conditions on use of data they received including ensuring that data are not reexported by third parties to whom they are furnished. It is also proposed that data can be made available only for research and educational activities that have no commercial application, which is more restrictive than prohibiting the commercial use of data. Finally, any release of data "which may be followed by a transmission by a nonencrypted radio, satellite broadcast or publicly accessible information system and which are thus available for commercial use, directly or indirectly, is considered to be in breach of these conditions" and would be prohibited. If the conditions are violated, access to data for all purposes could be denied to the recipient.

In other words, if British Meteorological Office data designated as not for reexport were obtained from the United States National Weather Service by an American value-added company and the company then reexported the data, or a product made using the data, the British could simply withhold data from the National Weather Service for all purposes. If United States researchers were to use the data for an experiment and post the results on a Web page or transmit them to a colleague on the Internet, where some commercial vendor might conceivably intercept them, they would be violating the conditions. If the United States National Weather Service did not cut them off, the British could stop supplying data to the Weather Service. These are as yet only proposed conditions, but that they are proposed at all is evidence that substantial differences remain. Indeed, agreement on a common interpretation of the WMO accord may not be possible in the foreseeable future.

The most productive course for the United States is probably to continue discussions and to remain very firm in support of open and unrestricted data access. Reaching an agreement on data policy in the WMO is important both for maintaining high-quality weather prediction for all nations and for the continued advance of meteorological science and climate change research. But reaching such agreement is a long-term rather than immediate need, and we have more to lose by excessive compromise than by delay. After all, the WMO has operated effectively since its inception without a formal agreement, and the restrictions on data availability have so far occurred at the margins. They represent a disturbing trend, but they have not yet had a dramatic effect on the quality of forecasts or the ability to conduct research. The process of dialogue is constructive and reduces the risk of further deterioration in the exchange of information.

Outlook: Is "Government Commercialization" the Wave of the Future?

Over the long term, it is not clear that the cost recovery goal of some European governments' commercialization approach can succeed. The private user base that can be charged is probably not large enough to support a comprehensive weather service, especially one that includes observation systems. Charging government users the bulk of these costs merely shifts the expenses from one agency to another rather than actually saving the national treasury any money. Furthermore, it is very difficult for a government agency trying to provide a comprehensive service to compete effectively with commercial entities pursuing specific market opportunities.

More generally, we question whether any governmental entity, even one enjoying copyright and not subject to open access laws, can successfully raise revenue adequate to pay not only for the dissemination of its information but also for the costs associated with creating the information for governmental purposes. This is due to some of the fundamental economic characteristics of information as a commodity. First, the demand for information is highly elastic, unlike food, clothing or shelter. When the price of information is subjectively perceived by users as being too high, they tend to do without. The United States Geological Survey learned this lesson in 1981 when it tried to increase its prices for digital data products in order to recover more of the costs of producing the data. As a result, demand dropped so precipitously that the Survey was forced to quickly reduce its prices. Sales took three years to return to their previous level.[22] The Geological Survey now has a more formalized pricing analysis that covers dissemination costs such as reproduction, handling, packaging, and distribution in accordance with the policies set forth in OMB Circular No. A-130.

In addition to price elasticity, information is notoriously "leaky." Since possession of information is nonexclusive—i.e., giving information to another does not deprive the original holder of possession—information tends to be widely shared, often in contravention of copyright. This would make any regime attempting to control and capitalize on the secondary use of information extremely cumbersome and difficult, if not impossible, to effectively administer. Finally, when information is priced at a level that meets the costs of the barriers to entry in the particular market, other information providers will enter and "skim the cream" of the most lucrative information products.

These characteristics of the economics of information were highlighted by a recent experience in which Congress legislatively mandated a fee for use of information in the Automated Tariff Filing and Information System (ATFI) operated by the Federal Maritime Commission.[23] ATFI was designed to improve efficiency and reduce paperwork by requiring the electronic filing of maritime tariffs. The Commission was required to charge 46 cents per minute of remote computer access, and the same fee was to be imposed on any entity that obtained the data directly or indirectly from the Commission and that operated a tariff system. The purpose of the law was to generate sufficient revenue to permit the repeal of a politically unpopular user fee on recreational boats. A recent audit by the General Accounting Office disclosed that "while the original congressional budget estimate for [fiscal years 1993 through 1995] totaled $810 million, it is currently estimated that the actual user fee will be only $438,800, or 0.05 percent of the original budget estimate."[24] The impossibility of policing downstream uses of the data and the emergence of competing private sector maritime tariff information providers contributed to this dismal performance.

In the area of meteorological information, the issue seems clear. The United States is by far the largest supplier of meteorological data in the world. In fact, the United States National Weather Service is presently the only consistent source of global satellite observations from polar-orbiting satellites. This means that United States policy enjoys considerable leverage and that denying data to the United States potentially carries a much greater cost than benefit. All weather services rely on data provided by others to some extent, but the United States relies the least on other nations and provides the most to other nations. The benefits of international cooperation outweigh the costs of potential confrontation. The combination of satellite and information technologies is vastly increasing the capacity for information transfer and likewise vastly increasing the difficulty of controlling information.

Conclusion

Beyond the specifics of the WMO case is a larger issue: Forging an international consensus that supports the widest possible access to and use of government information without precluding commercial opportunities is a critical need for environmental research in general and an important aspect of the evolving information economy. The unrestricted flow of information is necessary for science and commerce and may prove critical in the context of a global information infrastructure. The conflict between differing national information policies will continue to boil as the commercial value of environmental data products is more fully recognized and government budget pressures remain severe. Although the outcome of the conflict is not clear, we believe that any consensus international information policy will ultimately more closely resemble the United States model of open and unrestricted access than it will the government commercialization model.

Notes

1. 17 U.S.C. 105.

2. The idea of "government commercialization" is to be distinguished from the idea of "privitization". The former presumes governmental or quasi-governmental entities utilizing copyright or copyright-like controls to preclude possible private sector competition and thereby maximize revenues and minimize taxpayer support. "Privitization" is the quite different idea that government information should be turned over to the private sector for exploitation. The economic arguments at the end of this paper apply to both concepts.

3. See "The National Information Infrastructure: Agenda for Action," Information Infrastructure Task Force (September 15, 1993), available at http:// iitf.doc.gov.

4. The development of this consensus is traced in Perritt, "Commercialization of Government Information: Comparisons Between the European Union and the United States," 4:2 *Internet Research* 7, 19 (Summer, 1994).

5 61 *Fed. Reg.* 6428. Available at http://www.whitehouse.gov/WH/EOP/omb.

6. Pub. L. 104-13, 44 U.S.C. Chapter 35

7. Perritt, "Sources of Rights to Access Public Information," 4:1 *William & Mary Bill of Rights Journal* 179 (1995).

8. 766 F.2d 728 (2d Cir. 1985).

9. Id. at 733.

10. Id. at 735.

11. For further discussion see Gellman, "Twin Evils: Government Copyright and Copyright-Like Controls on Government Information," 45:3 Syracuse Law Review 999 (1995).

12. 766 F.2d at 735.

13. See discussion accompanying note 23, infra.

14. For a primer on Crown Copyright and a summary of a similar debate presently raging in Canada, see Marshall, "Crown Copyright: Navigating the Waters," 1993 *Canadian Law Libraries* Vol. 18, No. 4.

15. In contrast with the "government commercialization" trend discussed here is a European Commission initiative to foster greater openness in government information. The so-called PUBLAW initiative contains principles remarkably similar to those expressed in the PRA of 1995 and OMB Circular A-130. The European Commission's draft guidelines encourage making public information available for use by the private sector and for exploitation through electronic media. They encourage procedures for access to public information, and discourage exclusivity and restrictions on redissemination, and would exempt public information from copyright. See Perritt, supra, note 4. It is unclear whether this initiative will have any real effect on "government commercialization" initiatives.

16. See Rhind "Spatial Databases and Information Policy: A British Perspective," Proceedings of the Conference on Law and Information Policy for Spatial Databases, National Center for Geographic Information and Analysis (October 1994).

17. Blakemore & Singh, "Cost-Recovery Charging for Government Information. A False Economy?," Gurmukh Singh and Associates Ltd. (November 1992).

18. See generally, U.S. Congress, Office of Technology Assessment, "International Cooperation and Competition in Civilian Space Activities," and "The Future of Remote Sensing from Space: Civilian Satellite Systems and Applications." (Government Printing Office, Washington, D.C.)

19. National Research Council, "On the Full and Open Exchange of Scientific Data" (1995).

20. There are, of course, still issues within this U.S. model as well, mostly having to do with the question of where to draw the line between government and commercial activity, with some parties, particularly the industry, seeking to further reduce the government role. The activities of the value-added industry also overlap with research activities, leading to the existence of a gray area between publicly funded research whose results are freely available and the development of techniques that are later used for profit-making. We would assert that the existing policy framework seems largely able to deal with such concerns, provided that the parties approach these issues in a spirit of cooperation implied by the diversity principle.

21. See National Research Council report, supra note 19.

22. See Blakemore & Singh, supra note 17 at p. 32.

23. See Gellman, supra note 11, at p. 1065 for a full discussion of this case.

24. B-260055 (March 10, 1995).

Netting the Cybershark: Consumer Protection, Cyberspace, the Nation-State, and Democracy

John Goldring

Introduction

This chapter is divided into three sections. The first takes a broad look at the social context of consumer protection laws. The second examines some limitations of law in protecting consumers under modern conditions, including the changes wrought by the establishment of a new Global Information Infrastructure. The last draws some conclusions, that, if one extrapolates from observations about a particular form of lawmaking to the wider legislative process, have profound implications for democracy.

Historically, consumer protection laws have been the device used to catch the sharks of the marketplace. These laws are a typical outcome of the democratic process. They flow directly from an exercise of people's political sovereignty that expresses popular interests effectively, in ways that other mechanisms—particularly those of the market—rarely can. Such laws represent a means by which the people control or proscribe antisocial behavior.

Some new technologies pose a challenge to laws of this type and ultimately to the democratic process. They may make life far easier for many people, and far more profitable for businesses, but potentially open the way to forms of antisocial behavior as yet unimagined.

By presenting opportunities for new forms of antisocial behavior, these new technologies, and the development of a global economy, may together destroy benefits which national laws provide for consumers and other social groups that lack economic power, such as workers, women, and members of minority cultural and ethnic groups. People concerned with the environment, which cannot protect itself, are in a similar position. These groups have struggled to achieve protection against antisocial behavior that affects them by securing enactment of national laws.

The laws of most countries recognize degrees of antisocial behavior. Some attract severe criminal sanctions; some merely attract disapproval. In the middle is a range of behavior that attracts no more than a liability to compensate people injured by it.

In European-style democracies, informal pressures have not been enough to stop people from behaving in antisocial ways. Historically, if enough people objected and were able to influence the exercise of power within society, those who engaged in such behavior were punished with retaliatory physical violence or restraint. Since we have supposedly become more civilized, laws have been enacted that impose sanctions on people who behave antisocially.

Most of us prefer law to force. The problem is that some new technologies may not come within the power of law. As a result, the Internet and other new technologies may provide means for people to act antisocially with impunity. This raises some important questions about the law, the state and democracy.

Consumer Protection Law, Technology, and Antisocial Behavior

Consumer Protection Laws

Consumers of goods and services, although generally not well organized as an interest group, have achieved some political gains leading to the enactment of laws such as truth in advertising, truth in lending and product safety laws.

How might consumers of goods and services be protected against antisocial behavior that uses the Internet and cyberspace technology? Existing laws in most developed countries provide a measure of protection against a range of antisocial behavior that damages consumers, including deliberate fraud, unintentional but misleading or deceptive conduct, and anti-competitive behavior.

A combination of technological change, recent economic developments, and the limited practical effectiveness of both international agreements and national laws may mean that existing national laws will no longer effectively protect consumers from these perceived evils. There will be a gap not covered by the laws of any nation (Trubek, 1987; Aman, 1995). Similar "gaps" have also been identified in relation to environmental law (Stewart, 1992).

The forms of antisocial behavior most likely to affect consumers adversely are deceptive practices in advertising and marketing and in the delivery of financial services; and the supply of dangerous goods or goods that do not fulfill legitimate expectations.[1] Those who engage in such antisocial behavior are one species of cybershark, but the genus is wider. Because markets themselves do not encourage or preserve competition (if anything, the converse is true), most economic communities have found it necessary to enact laws ensuring competition. These laws, such as the U.S. antitrust laws, have similar ends to those of most regulatory consumer protection laws, and their enforcement in modern times gives rise to similar legal problems. Market predators who seek to take advantage of new technology or economic conditions to undermine or destroy competition are also a species of cybershark, but they are not central to this particular fishing expedition.

Consumers have sought protection through legislation because neither general laws nor market forces have provided it. Consumer protection laws take several forms: either they may proscribe specific types of conduct or they may establish standards of behavior, either general or specific, that manufacturers, marketers, distributors, or suppliers of products must meet if they want to avoid either a criminal or civil sanction. They may standardize the terms and conditions of contracts that consumers make for the supply of goods and services, or conduct intended to encourage the making of such contracts (marketing, packaging, advertising and provision of information).

Previous generations assumed that ordinary law, especially the law of contracts, would protect consumers; they assumed, without foundation in practice, that the parties to contracts were equal in terms of power and information as well as legally. In real markets, almost invariably consumers have markedly less power and information than suppliers. The law deems the action of a consumer in buying a commodity to be the making of a contract—in theory a free, consensual act. In practice, legal consequences are attributed to the action by the law without any consideration of what the consumer actually knows or wants. The common law of contracts simply cannot afford consumers the protection they would seek if they were rational, fully informed, and equal in economic power to the supplier. Because contract law is an inadequate basis for the legal protection of consumers, it must often be modified or supplemented by legislation (Goldring, 1990).

Consumer Protection Law as Public and Private Law

The distinction between "public" and "private" law within a national legal system (Goldring, 1978), though not as important in Anglo-American legal systems as in the civil law systems of continental Europe (or their derivatives in Asia, Africa and South America), remains important. Legal rules, procedures and orders that involve physical or financial penalties, in general, can be imposed under public law, on the initiative of the state. The procedures and structures through which the state operates to make, implement and enforce laws are the subject of public law. In contrast, relations between persons are the subject of private law.

Consumer protection laws include elements of both public and private law. When the law relates to the formation, content and performance of contracts between persons, or when it imposes obligations to compensate loss or damage suffered by another person as a result of an unlawful act, it is private law. When it involves the creation or workings of a governmental structure; the making of laws; the prosecution of crimes or offenses; or the imposition of penalties, such as imprisonment, fines or confiscation of property, it is public law. The definition and prosecution of crimes, the criminal law, is a special part of public law.

Public law differs from private law principally in its far greater emphasis on procedure. Bureaucrats and government institutions are controlled and made accountable through procedural requirements enforced by courts and tribunals. The rules of criminal procedure ensure that no penalty is imposed unless strict procedural safeguards have been observed. Private law, though still imposing procedural requirements, places more emphasis on substantive transactions and outcomes.

Consumer protection laws, then, either create criminal offenses enforced by government agencies through use of public, criminal laws, provide compensatory remedies under private law, or both. Good examples of both types of consumer protection laws may be found in the Australian Trade Practices Act, 1974 (Commonwealth). Part V, Division 1 of this Act makes various kinds of deceptive marketing practices criminal offenses, and provides that the Australian Competition and Consumer Commission or the Minister for Consumer Affairs may commence proceedings against those accused of these practices. If convicted, violators are subject to fines. In those proceedings, the standard and burden of proof are those of criminal law; for example, the prosecution must prove every element of the offense beyond reasonable doubt. Part V, Division 2 of the same Act provides mandatory terms and conditions which are implied into specified types of contracts made by consumers. The consumer is entitled to recover compensation for breach of those implied conditions in a civil court of competent jurisdiction in exactly the same way as a claim for damages for breach of an express term of the contract would be made. In those proceedings, the plaintiff need only establish a case on the balance of probabilities. Division 1 may be described as public law, Division 2 as private law.

To avoid problems of bureaucratic capture,[2] the Act also provides (s. 82) that any person who suffers loss or damage as a result of a contravention of any relevant provision of the Act may recover compensation for that loss or damage in civil proceedings; it also provides (s. 80) that the Commission, the Minister, or any other person who has suffered or fears that he or she might suffer damage as a result of a contravention of provisions including Part V, Division 1, may seek an injunction in the federal court to restrain further conduct that contravenes the Act. These remedies are private law remedies and require the civil burden and standard of proof.

Impact of New Technologies on Consumer Protection Law

Travel, trade and communications, health care and agriculture—indeed, virtually every aspect of material life in the developed world—have changed almost beyond recognition within the century because of new technologies. Until recently, technologies could not overcome many of the barriers created by distance. Now converging communications/entertainment technologies mean that people all over the world can engage in simultaneous talk and interchange of vast bodies of different types of data. People all over the world, in their own houses and villages, can watch events that the media owners consider newsworthy as they are taking place, on satellite TV. New technologies (especially communications technologies) affect our daily lives if we are rich enough to buy access and live in developed countries. Electronic technology is almost entirely limited to the rich communities of the world. People in poor communities—to which business is rapidly moving its repetitive and dirty operations—may not know what a computer, or even a telephone, is.

New manufacturing and resource-extraction technologies affect us all, rich and poor, wherever we may be. There are imperatives for people to think in ways that accommodate new technologies (see, for example, Katsh, 1993; Johnston et al, 1995; Negroponte, 1995). By and large, the new technologies have brought benefits, but without any serious thought about their impact on the natural environment and the health and well-being of all forms of life.

The introduction of certain new technologies without regard to their impact on the world and its peoples has led to a reaction, even a new Luddism. Such extreme reactions are probably necessary to bring about a political climate in which the countervailing forces of the state can be invoked to prevent excesses resulting from the introduction of new technology. If there is no state intervention, degradation of the natural environment and people's health will continue.

Technological changes can bring benefits, but they also provide new opportunities to the economic predators of the world, who, in the past, have been somewhat constrained by laws, and even by market pressures in small markets.

The Geographical Challenge—Locating the Cybersharks

The natural history of the shark is very interesting. Biologists believe that this predator is one of the oldest forms of marine life. It has changed very little over time, as it has not needed to change. It survives through generations, feeding on whatever passes by. Its sole motive is to stay alive, and it cares little how it does so. The shark has counterparts in the economic game; cyberspace is a very receptive and supportive environment for predators. The odd cybershark may stray serendipitously into the net of national laws, or rise to a random bait. Nevertheless, they are a potential danger, and very difficult to catch.

Most international trade now involves communications technology to a high degree. Transport and financial documentation is exchanged electronically. Reservations for cargo space and seats for passengers on aircraft are made by computer link. Institutions store records from all of their global operations in a central data base located in the territory of a single national state, but data can be accessed electronically from anywhere in the world. Anyone can access bank accounts and credit across national and continental borders, provided the magnetic stripe on his or her credit card is compatible with the local hardware.

Cybersharks are already learning to use the new technologies. Within the last three years, a number of Australian and New Zealand investors lost millions of dollars through a long-distance fraud, which consisted of a series of letters and faxes sent from Belgium soliciting investment in what appeared to be a mutual fund. Money was sent by credit card transfer or telegraphic bank transfer to a bank in Liechtenstein. It proved impossible to find the perpetrators of the fraud, but even if they had been found, exacting a legal remedy or punishment would have been difficult. The scheme was not new: at the time, the medium was new, but transborder scams are now a regular event, especially between Canada and the United States (see, for example, *Libman v R* [1985] 2 Supreme Court Reports 178; 21 Dominion Law Reports (4th) 174 (Supreme Court of Canada)).

When—and the word is "when," rather than "if"—large-scale fraud and other crimes are committed using the Internet as a vehicle, the criminals are likely to be even more difficult to trace than they have been previously; if they are smart, as speakers at the Federal Trade Commission Hearings pointed out, they will use aliases and will access the Net from a public and anonymous source.

Not all cybersharks are malicious, but they all hunt and kill in order to survive. Some otherwise reputable businesses, in the course of competitive market behavior, do things that have the effect of misleading or deceiving consumers, regardless of intention. Sometimes these actions result directly from the pressure to compete. Some consumer protection laws are directed at businesses in that position.

The U.S. Federal Trade Commission now has a World Wide Web page of "on-line scams," but some appear to be inadvertent. In November 1995, Virgin Atlantic Airways Limited was fined heavily after pleading guilty to a charge of misleading advertising on its World Wide Web page. The advertisement contained details of a promotional offer which had expired, but no dates were stated. The fact that Virgin pleaded guilty and paid the fine suggests that law enforcement may be relatively easy, even though the medium carrying the false advertisement was a new technology not envisaged when the law was made. Available reports did not say which country's law had been infringed, who started the proceedings, where the Web site was located physically or the place at which the Web was accessed. Such variables are often highly relevant in legal proceedings, and it may have been a fortunate coincidence that Virgin pleaded guilty. The reported facts are not clear, but such cases could raise many complex legal issues.

Manufacturers of hazardous products are certainly cybersharks. Some laws prohibit the promotion and sale of products that harm people. Tobacco advertising is banned in many countries on health grounds, but lawyers argue that it is constitutionally protected in Canada and the United States. Is it possible to catch the cybersharks who produce tobacco advertisements in the United States, and beam them by satellite to, say, Australia, where such advertising is prohibited?

Technology, Law, and Politics

Laws apply to everyone. They are the end product of politics: the means by which political gains become part of the institutional and social framework of the political community, the body of norms to which people in that community conform.

Lawyers are often like the workers who clean the streets after the triumphant procession when the elephants and horses have left (Rosett, 1992: 683, 684–687). Their job is to ensure that the legal system, which underpins a great deal of social activity, does not unduly frustrate community or commercial activity. Legal change is slow and usually piecemeal. Courts change the law if they are required to decide cases which require them to apply established rules to new facts. Their decisions may be reversed by legislation. Legislatures change laws only when there is sufficient pressure from the bureaucracy or political interests. Ultimately the decision of whether to change the law is political.

The Australian National Information Services Council, reporting in 1995 on commercial laws governing cyberspace activities, advised that there was no need for lawyers to panic: for most purposes existing laws were adequate, though a few changes were necessary. In most aspects of life, we tend to think that the existing system can cope, until it breaks down under the pressure of trying to deal with a load beyond its capacity. In fact, new technologies and the new horizons created by cyberspace may demonstrate that some national laws cannot cope with the changing demands on them.

Technologies produce pressure for legal change. For example, until approximately 1980 most international trade transactions were supported by traditional paper documentation: bills of lading, bills of exchange, bankers' documentary credits, etc. This documentation had acquired a legal patina after years of operation in practice (and consideration by courts in disputed cases). New technologies introduced in the early 1980s made business more efficient. These included: container transport, just-in-time manufacturing and inventory procedures, facsimile transmissions, affordable air cargo transport, and electronic data interchange. The substance of the old transactions changed radically, leaving only the patina. The traders had no further use for the documentation, and kept these records only because of legal requirements. In some cases—financing of international sales, for example—the insistence by banks and insurers on retaining outmoded documentation of international transactions because it is legally tested may be making business inefficient.

Commercial laws originated in mercantile custom, and have always served mercantile interests. When those interests require change, change will occur. Because commercial transactions affect commercial profits, if profits are likely to be impeded by outmoded laws, business has the political will to take action and exercise its considerable power in the legal, commercial, bureaucratic, and political worlds to support change. Then the law will change. The major problem is that changing the law of one nation is not enough, and the major obstacle is securing international agreement to the form of change (a point considered later).

However, where laws enacted to protect consumer or environmental interests are frustrated by the introduction of new technologies, achieving change is far more difficult. For example, changing Australian consumer credit laws originally passed in the 1930s to protect consumers against oppression by lenders proved far more difficult than changing banking laws to enable banks to undertake new types of business because the interests of commerce were ranged against the interests of consumers. It was not just a matter of government responding to powerful interests. Whether or not these laws changed became politically controversial. Today, consumer groups find that the framework of politics has changed. Relatively disempowered groups which previously had relied on gaining the support of the legislature to establish their basic demands now find it more difficult to do so. The dominant political rhetoric asserts that only the purity of market forces will protect the true interests of society and inveighs against any intervention by the state. Relatively weak groups, such as consumers, have no political power to balance against that of organized business.

Democracy and Globalization

Democracy in the Western form is a recent development. Universal male suffrage is scarcely a century old in the United States and Europe; women have been permitted to exercise their democratic rights over a much shorter period. The founders of many modern states, including the United States, Canada, and Australia, distrusted democracy. They foresaw the possibility that democratic power might be used to redistribute wealth and sought safeguards against extreme redistribution, but probably did not foresee that it would be used to the extent that it has been for the protection of special interests (Hobsbawm, 1995: 103–104, 409–410).

Democratic politics has offered the only avenue to relatively disadvantaged groups, including consumers, to influence the exercise of public power in a systematic, continuous way. These groups have used that power not to influence directly the setting of the nation's economic priorities, but rather to correct blatant market failures that have produced the greatest physical and moral damage.

Globalization of the market, to the extent that it nullifies the laws resulting from the democratic process, is antidemocratic—it allows international commerce to reproduce domestic market failures on a global basis, without any prospect of legislative remedy.

The "global economy" may frustrate the interests of consumers, workers, and other disadvantaged groups by ensuring that if workers in one place demand a share of profits that is too large, businesses will move operations to a place where there is a pool of unorganized labor. If governments try to redistribute wealth through taxation businesses will move their operations to tax havens or low-tax, low-welfare venues. Similarly, if governments attempt to protect the environment or consumer interests, business may move elsewhere. There are indications that, with increasing enactment of product safety laws, businesses will move their manufacturing operations to "liability havens" or adopt other liability avoidance devices. Each example of legislation listed in this paragraph reflects legitimate expressions of popular interests and popular sovereignty.

The extension of the General Agreement on Tariffs and Trade to nontariff barriers[3] and trade in intellectual property has the potential to prevent nation-states from acting effectively to protect a wide range of interests of their populations. Free trade may have benefits in lower prices for commodities, but consumers may want more than low prices; consumers are not always rational and have values other than the bottom line. The General Agreement on Tariffs and Trade, the World Trade Organization, and various common markets may be seen as devices for using international law to prevent nation-states from exercising political sovereignty.

The Internet and cyberspace are convenient for both the cybershark and the economic libertarian. State power is irrelevant to many cyberspace activities. Cyberspace has no physical location, and, by design, is dispersed and exceedingly difficult to control. This presents some significant potential dangers for democracy.

It is difficult enough for nation-states in times of economic prosperity to protect the interests and welfare of their citizens. What they can do depends very much on exercising power—countervailing that of powerful transnational forces whose motivation takes no account of the welfare of disadvantaged groups.

Will Nation-States Survive?

For the foreseeable future nation-states will continue to play a significant role in government and politics. Those who want to dismantle impediments to international trade also often assert a need for strong domestic policies such as more public and private police services and heavier penalties for crime. For this reason alone, nation-states will continue to exist. No matter how libertarian a government may be, citizens still expect basic state services, including those ensuring physical safety and integrity, as well as, though they may be loath to admit it, basic welfare services. Businesses expect nation-states to support commerce by providing "last resort" mechanisms for enforcing contracts (Hirst and Thompson, 1995). National states will be tolerated as long as they do not attempt to interfere with global economic policy. It is important for consumers and economically disadvantaged groups to ensure that nation-states have more than a community policing role; if this is all that is left to them, their consumer protection laws will lose even the limited power to catch cybersharks they now have.

Nation-states are also required to satisfy the demands of ethnic and cultural groups who assert that they form a distinct political community. Some of these communities are based on language and customs, some on religion, some on geographic ties and links with land. The former USSR and Yugoslavia have broken into a series of relatively powerless states based mostly on ethnicity and language. Other ethnic groups—such as Francophone Quebecois, Tibetans, Kurds, Basques, Zulus, and Catalans—wish to establish their own nation-states. Within the United States, Canada, Australia, and elsewhere, aboriginal people deny the legitimacy of the European conquest and seizure of their lands and assert rights to sovereignty (Williams, 1986; Otto, 1995). These nationalist demands may not make sense economically, but they are a fact of modern political life.

Legal Rights and Remedies

Constitutional Power

The constitutional laws of most states allow legislation only when there is a territorial or personal link[4] between the state and the subject matter of the legislation. States may legislate with respect to all matters within their territorial boundaries, and with respect to the activities of their nationals and citizens. The law treats ships, aircraft, and embassies as extensions of territory. (Some constitutions, especially federal constitutions, further restrict those powers.) In theory, the Parliament of the United Kingdom could prohibit smoking in the state of New York, but this would be senseless, as the laws would affect only citizens of the United Kingdom and would not be recognized by any other person or state.

International Law

What a nation-state can achieve legally outside its geographical boundaries is determined by two bodies of rules: public international law (formerly called the law of nations and now often called transnational law), and private international law (in the United States and other federal systems more accurately called "conflict of laws" because the rules determine which of two different legal systems applies within or outside a particular political institution, where more than one legal system claims to determine at least some of the issues). I have used the terms "public" and "private," however, because they contain the kernel of an important practical distinction, which is quite different from the distinction discussed above between public and private law within national legal systems.

Both public and private international law limit the powers of nation-states to provide legal sanctions and remedies to those who have suffered a legal wrong. These limits are the fundamental boundaries within which any legal controls of cyberspace activities can occur. For the foreseeable future, if there are to be controls on these activities, they must come from nation-states, because the nature of cyberspace is essentially anarchic and players cannot afford to trust other players or voluntarily accept limitations on what they may do.

Public international law governs the relations between entities recognized as having legal status or personality—usually nation-states. There is no supreme, authoritative ruler with legal or formal authority to discipline states that do not toe the line. The content of the rules of public international law comes from practice of states toward each other (usually referred to as "custom," itself a problematic concept) and from international agreements. For this reason, much public international law is "soft" (Chinkin, 1988) in the sense that breach does not necessarily attract the imposition of a sanction. For legal positivists[5] the possibility of imposing a sanction is the defining characteristic of law, and they deny international law the status of law, though they concede that the rules of public international law have significant moral and political force. States that continually offend attract odium which can translate into economic and political consequences. To have an effective impact on people and corporations, public international law must receive legislative backing within nation-states—either, as in the United States, through ratification by the Senate, or, in most other countries, by enactment through routine legislative processes.

Private international law, by contrast, is law in the fullest possible sense: it forms part of the system of rules administered and enforced by the municipal law of the nation-state. This body of rules determines, most importantly for this discussion, whether any state has the legal power to entertain disputes between citizens or between citizens and governments ("judicial jurisdiction"); whether any state may enforce a judicial determination of such a controversy ("recognition and enforcement"); and which body of rules will be applied to resolve any issues that arise ("choice of law").

Public international law itself has no direct effect on the behavior of individuals or collectivities. It operates indirectly, through the national or "municipal" law systems. Infringement of any rights afforded to individuals by international law provides them a legal remedy only if their national government decides to take up their cause, as the Turkish and French governments did in the seminal case of the *Lotus* (PCIJ Series A, No. 10, 1972).

In contrast, while in the past the rules of private international law may have seemed remote from the lives of ordinary people, today's easier communications mean that these rules affect many individuals every day. Every individual who travels from one country to another (or, in a federation, from one state or province to another) is immediately subjected to the operation of private international law; so too are businesses that operate outside their own country or state. Everyone who logs onto the Internet immediately becomes exposed to some operations of the rules of private international law.

Enforcing the Rules

Once a person has been identified as the perpetrator of antisocial behavior that a nation-state has proscribed, it still remains for someone to enforce a legal sanction. Legal sanctions are generally of two types: civil and criminal.

Civil remedies are, in a technical sense, generally easier to enforce across international boundaries than criminal sanctions, though the process of imposing civil remedies is cumbersome and expensive. Western legal systems generally accept the principle that judgments or orders of courts in other countries should be recognized and enforced if to do so would not offend the public policies of the place where enforcement is sought (referred to as "the forum") and provided it is clear that the court making the order had jurisdiction, or power, to entertain the suit that led to the order.

The rules relating to jurisdiction are quite complex. In general, a court has jurisdiction over a person who is physically present in its territory, even if only for a fleeting instant. Corporations are legal persons recognized by national laws. Usually they are regarded as being within jurisdiction if they have a regular place of business or an agent in the territory or if they transact business there.

Jurisdiction rules are much simpler and easier to apply to contracts and other commercial transactions than to civil wrongs. International trade has been a fact of life for a long time. International tourism and large-scale international environmental pollution—the major potential areas of litigation that do not arise out of contracts—are more recent, and have not yet generated similar bodies of practice or rules of private international law. Road accidents involving tourists frequently lead to extremely complex problems in private international law.

In commercial transactions, the courts normally respect the autonomy of parties—the right of parties to choose where their disputes will be litigated, which nation's laws will govern the relationship, or even that disputes will be settled according to privately established rules and procedures outside the legal system of any country. Where legal obligations arise by operation of the law—that is, where obligations result from particular combinations of facts rather than from the agreement of the parties—there may be disputes about which nation's law applies and whether other nations with an interest in the outcome will recognize and enforce the application of that law.

One example of obligations arising as a result of a national law is product liability. These laws are most stringent in the United States, but other nations, including the European Union nations, Australia, Israel, Japan, Korea, and Taiwan, have recently introduced legislation imposing a liability on manufacturers and importers of unsafe goods to pay compensation to those injured by defective goods, without proof of any "fault." Some major manufacturing countries—Thailand and Singapore, for example—do not have such rules. If a manufacturer in Singapore produces goods that cause injury to a consumer in, say, Ontario, the current private international law rules of the Canadian provinces would probably deny the injured person a remedy. Like similar rules in most common law countries, they impose liability only when the defendant would have been liable if the facts had occurred in Ontario and the events would also be illegal under the laws of Singapore.

Another example comes from hire-purchase legislation in Australia. The consumer credit laws introduced by state governments in the 1930s required disclosure of effective interest rates and restricted remedies for lenders if borrowers failed to repay. Some financial institutions instructed their lawyers to evade the scope of these restrictive laws. The lawyers achieved this and retained the commercial substance of the credit transaction, but took it beyond the scope of the restrictive laws. They prepared a standard form contract that stated expressly that the transaction was to be governed by the law of another state that imposed less stringent restrictions, even though neither the borrower nor the lender normally had any other connection with that state.[6] In the United States, courts may have disregarded this choice of law in the circumstances, but the Australian courts did not. Borrowers from such companies were obliged to enter into a transaction without any of the protections that the law was designed to provide.

The general rule in international law and practice is that no state will attempt to exercise its power or public authority within the territory of another state, without the express agreement of the other state. The power to tax is regarded, like the power to punish, as an exercise of sovereign power. In the absence of bilateral agreement or treaty arrangements, neither the civil nor criminal courts of any country will recognize or enforce the penal or revenue judgments or orders made by courts (or other aspects of the implementation of public policy) of those countries. Countries have been known to arrest and abduct persons accused of crime under their own law in the territory of other states.[7] These countries offend international law and the feelings of other states, and even they rarely attempt to carry out sentences of their courts in other countries. This is the one major exception to the principle that foreign laws are recognized and enforced. The operation of penal laws or revenue laws of another country is restricted to the geographical territory of that other state.

International law regards the operation of national laws as confined to national territory or citizens. U.S. antitrust laws are essentially criminal laws. The United States on occasion attempts to enforce its antitrust laws against foreign persons as a result of activities in their own countries, on the basis that those activities affect competition in the United States. The prevailing world legal opinion is that the United States is acting contrary to international law and that even if it is not, it is being a bad member of the international community. Nations that are normally sycophantic in their relationship to the United States, specifically the United Kingdom, Canada, and Australia, have had major and serious diplomatic differences with the United States over this issue and have gone to the extremes of public criticism and enacting legislation blocking the impact of U.S. antitrust laws.

The solution seems to lie in extradition, by which one state requests another to apprehend and surrender to it a person accused of committing a crime against its laws (Shearer, 1971). Although ad hoc extraditions are possible, extradition generally takes place under a treaty between the two states that generally sets out conditions. In addition, each state also usually has legislation setting out general procedures for, and conditions of, extradition orders.

After initial contact between governments, leading to police action (including issuing and executing an arrest warrant), the accused person must be brought before a court in the country of arrest. That court must be satisfied of the matters specified in the legislation of that country. The accused may argue that extradition is improper—for example, that the crime is not an "extradition crime" within the relevant treaties or legislation. Most extradition crimes consist of activity prohibited by the criminal law of both countries and are not political or ideological. If the prosecution succeeds, the court orders that the accused be taken into custody and surrendered to the authorities of the prosecuting state. That state then disposes of the matter, generally by a criminal trial in its own courts. The procedure may be complex and time-consuming, and the authorities of the prosecuting state may decide that the time and expense are not justified relative to the result.

If any activities in cyberspace are to be made criminal, the only acceptable, though cumbersome, means of enforcing the laws may be through international agreements under which governments agree that each will make criminal, under its domestic laws, the conduct that all desire to prohibit.

Harmonizing National Legal Rules

National laws, then, are the only effective legal means of regulation. The sort of cyberspace activities that people might want to regulate, however, know no national boundaries. If the response to an antisocial activity requires national laws, nations may discover a common interest in harmonizing their laws. Different regulatory regimes in different countries mean that the unscrupulous may play off one nation against another. They will locate in countries with no regulations, or with less stringent ones. The policies of other countries will be frustrated by such maneuvering.

Here the best analogy may be with intellectual property laws, whose application to cyberspace activities is already controversial. Intellectual property rights include rights like patents, trade marks, and copyright. Problems arise when entrepreneurs who own intellectual property carry on business in countries whose laws do not recognize or protect the intellectual property rights they have acquired in their home countries. For this reason, governments have tried to protect the interests of national businesses. They have sought agreement with other governments on basic standards of recognition and protection of intellectual property rights. The current framework of intellectual property laws reflects a degree of international agreement on the protection of some forms of property, and a significant bureaucratic body—the World Intellectual Property Organisation—exists to ensure the smooth operation of those agreements. Under international conventions it may be possible to register title to an item of intellectual property in one country which is a party to the conventions, with a reasonable assurance that those rights will be recognized and enforced by all the other states that are party to the convention. All member-states have legislation to this effect. The conventions are among the oldest international commercial conventions and their lack of success is largely due to the fact that the United States has never been a wholehearted supporter of the international protection of certain types of intellectual property rights that it sees as restricting trade (patents and trade marks)—in contrast to its strong support for the application of free-trade principles to intellectual property transactions, as represented by the Trade in Intellectual Property (TRIPS) agreement.

International agreements are usually the result of a long period of diplomatic negotiation and maneuvering, during which each state attempts to protect what it sees as its national interests. Agreement on one issue may be the trade-off for concession on some totally unrelated matters. Powerful states usually get their way in this type of negotiation. If no powerful state has a particular objective, international agreements tend toward the lowest common denominator of the interests of the states involved. The Montreal Convention on greenhouse gas emissions and the international agreements on the slaughter of whales, seals, and other wild and endangered species are good examples of the compromise process, which satisfies nobody. A compromise is probably the symbol of success in both domestic politics and international diplomacy.

"Harmonization" of law requires harmonization of policy as well. If a state undertakes that its laws are to be harmonized with those of another state, it circumscribes its own freedom to legislate as it thinks best; it abrogates its own sovereignty.[8] This is a major criticism of both the European Union and also of the expanded General Agreement on Tariffs and Trade and World Trade Organization agreements that followed the Uruguay Round of discussions in the 1980s. These agreements require harmonization of national laws on trade (Schaefer and Singer, 1992; Dunleavy, 1993; Howse, 1994; Schneiderman, 1994).

There are fundamentally two different methods of harmonizing laws internationally. The first is the legislation model, in which the provisions of an international treaty bind the parties to do, or to refrain from doing, certain things, including making new laws or amending or repealing existing laws.

The legislation model ensures that the law of each country is identical, allowing for problems of translation. A state that has accepted the terms of an international agreement, however, is bound to preserve it as part of municipal law, or risk offending international law. Unless the reasons for acceding to the treaty are compelling, states are often reluctant to take the first step.

The other means is the model law, used with conspicuous success in Canada and the United States. Experts prepare a summary of the existing rules together with any desired changes; these are reviewed by a body representing governments and, if approved, submitted to the individual governments for enactment. In this way the laws of each country, if not identical, are sufficiently similar to provide uniform standards of conduct. The best known example is the Uniform Commercial Code, but there are successful examples in many other areas of law. The model law approach is more attractive to states that are reluctant to commit themselves to maintain uniformity of legislation. Internationally, this method has been used successfully in the area of settlement of international commercial disputes, with many countries adopting by legislation the Model Rules developed by the United Nations Commission on International Trade Law (UNCITRAL).

A model law is simply a model. There is no compulsion to adopt the whole of the text. Local drafters are tempted to add their own embellishments to provide for local circumstances; local politicians often need little pressure to be persuaded that variations that cater to the needs of particular local interest groups are desirable.[9]

Democracy and National Laws

Because commerce takes place in increasingly global markets over which no single national state has control, these markets are very congenial environments for cybersharks. Some large cybersharks are inhibited from predatory behavior because they are accustomed to obeying national laws, and there may be some benefit in seeking to ensure that the laws of the several nation-states are similar if not identical.

Harmonization of law can be antidemocratic, even if the text of a uniform law is adopted by a democratically elected legislature. At times, politicians—and even voters, if, as happens only too rarely, they are fully informed—may place a higher value on something that requires internationally uniform rules than on the right of the people to make and change their own laws. It is a valid exercise of political sovereignty for a state to surrender some of its power temporarily. Once the surrender becomes more permanent, or if the scope of the surrendered power widens, questions must be asked about whether the state can truly be said to have remained sovereign. For example, many Canadians wish to preserve a distinct national culture by, for example, requiring Canadian radio and television stations to broadcast a minimum proportion of "Canadian content" material though there is currently litigation as to whether laws containing such requirements are consistent with the legislation establishing the North American Free Trade Agreement. The value of Canadian content rules is, for most Canadians, cultural rather than economic. Similar questions arise for people in European nations that have joined the European Union.

The nation-state is, realistically, the only forum in which democratic politics can take place. Smaller political divisions with limited powers within nation-states are sometimes required in very populous political communities (such as the United States of America or the European Union). In other situations, for example as a response to aggressive behavior by large trading blocs, smaller states must stand together because none is individually sufficiently strong to provide the countervailing power to corporate strength that is a major justification for the state in modern politics.

Cyberspace and the Law

Sharks sometimes eat each other, or destroy each other by exhausting all the available feed stock of smaller fish. The price is the lives of the smaller fish! It has been suggested that cyberspace should remain unregulated, and that those using it as a medium for their transactions should be left to organize their relationships by contractual agreements (Johnson and Marks, 1993; Hardy, 1994; Burk, 1993, 1994) just as medieval merchants were content to have their transactions governed by the *lex mercatoria* or "law merchant" which was, according to the theory, not part of the law of any state or nation, but recognized by all (Trakman, 1983).

These suggestions assume a model of the law merchant that may not be historically accurate because it ignores the role of nation-states. The law merchant depended, in the last resort, on the existence of some national law. People are usually happy to act on informal agreements, but a time comes when one of them tries to get away with behavior that is not permitted, and may be prohibited, by the agreements. Though informal, those agreements have the legal status of contracts, and national laws are revealed as the ultimate foundation for the legal effects of all the informal transactions, because the injured party falls back on rights under national laws, in the last resort, to enforce commercial obligations. Self-imposed restraints are effective only while the parties accept them. Predators, almost by definition, do not observe such self-imposed restraints.

Major economic forces, as well as special interest groups, require a foundation of order rather than the anarchy of a Hobbesian state of nature, a war of each against all where life is nasty, brutish, and short. To some extent this need for order is demonstrated by the form of commercial arrangements for various international electronic trading transactions. The parties agree in writing at the beginning of their commercial relationship what the terms of that relationship will be. The agreement is generally a "standard form" agreement, and may be transmitted electronically; however, it takes effect as if it were a formal written contract. Invariably these agreements are prepared by lawyers and contain a "choice of law" clause stipulating that the law of a particular place (usually the law of one of the United States) will govern the contract; a "choice of forum" clause stipulating that claims may only be brought in the courts of a particular nation or state (usually the place where the supplier carries on business); and often an alternative dispute resolution clause that precludes the parties from enforcing legal rights in a court, at least until they have attempted to use other, often more costly, forms of dispute resolution. Each clause is predicated on the existence of a national legal system.

Part of the agreement is usually a protocol or set of protocols, in standard form, which assign meanings and consequences to the transmission of specific electronic signals. Such protocols are normally the foundation of any transaction that uses or requires interchange of electronic data and are commonly used also when subscribers apply for one of the many commercially available electronic services.

It may also be appropriate for cyberspace to be regulated by the private (or quasi-private, such as universities) interests that provide electronic services (Johnson and Marks, 1993). These service providers require subscribers to behave in certain ways, at the risk of losing access. Whether or not individuals have a right of access to these services is a different and highly problematic question.[10]

The very existence of consumer protection laws indicates that enough people to influence politicians accept that market forces do not always work or, if they do, that they do not work in the interests of consumers. Those laws represent a triumph of democracy and human values over the values of the market which are not neutral or impersonal, but coincide with the interests of the large businesses that are the most powerful players. To say that market forces—or their legal counterpart, contractual arrangements—should be left to govern cyberspace would represent an immediate surrender of consumer interests. Sharks can only be caught with strong, effective equipment.

Is Regulation Possible?

Convergent Media and National Laws

The Internet was designed so that the physical equipment would survive multiple nuclear attacks (Katsh, 1993; Johnston et al., 1995; Negroponte, 1995). The hardware through which it operates is physically dispersed. Satellite and wireless technology mean that the Internet is not restricted to a single, fixed physical means of transmitting electronic impulses. No national government can, in the last resort, regulate the Internet, though clearly many would like to do so. Other current technologies may be more dependent on physical plants but the various communication technologies are converging rapidly and becoming ever less subject to governmental supervision.

The fax machine brought the real news of Tiananmen Square to the people of China when their local news media published distorted accounts. Satellite TV can reach most audiences with the resources to install the necessary equipment. People are prepared to do this despite the efforts of repressive governments to prevent access. The government of Singapore, for example, forbids construction without a permit of the dishes needed to receive signals.

If regulation is to operate at all, it must operate on people or physical objects that have a geographical location. But databases and other information sources are totally mobile, and can be moved instantaneously to storage sites in more congenial legal climates. Regulating cyberspace may be impossible.

Information is a commodity, and it has its consumers. The supply of other commodities is usually in the hands of national markets that, to some extent at least, are subject not only to national consumer protection laws but also to laws designed to preserve and enhance competition (such as antitrust laws), and to ensure that consumers receive the benefits of competition.

The danger posed by the Internet is that control of the content of major databases and access to them through the Internet will be restricted to those who receive permission from the owners or controllers, normally on payment of a fee. As many databases are unique, this price is likely to be a monopoly price. There are already complaints that media magnates such as Rupert Murdoch, Ted Turner, Conrad Black, Kerry Packer, and the late Robert Maxwell acquired controlling interests not only in conventional print and electronic news media but also in film archives and other databases. The information in those databases—or such of it as the controllers see fit to release—will be made available on the information superhighway at a price. Access may increase but consumers will not know whether or not what is released is accurate or complete because the information is in private hands.

The fact that control of the databases rests with private corporations rather than government is itself a major cause for concern. Governments are at least subject to constitutional and administrative law requirements of procedural fairness or due process of law. Public sector organizations are prohibited from discrimination on improper grounds, including grounds of gender, race, and religious or political beliefs. The controls on private organizations, especially those with no accessible physical location, are much more limited, so that their power, including the power to discriminate, is potentially absolute and despotic. Media convergence must lead to speculation about the power of the major media proprietors in the future. Because of their monopolistic or oligopolistic positions, they may turn into cybersharks of a different species, but still threaten consumers. History shows that those who have power and privilege will do what they can to prevent competition and to preserve what they have.

We have learned not to trust governments to promote the dissemination of information, especially about their own activities, and we have learned that corporations are even more secretive about their activities than governments. In the advanced societies of the West, the United Kingdom excepted, extensive freedom of information legislation allows most citizens access to the vast majority of information held in the public sphere. Because of the push toward privatization, this sphere is shrinking. In any event, the greatest danger in misuse of personal information has always resided in the private sector, rather than government. Financial institutions, especially major banks and insurers, accumulate data about individuals that may prove invaluable to marketing institutions and other commercial interests. In most countries, the only limits on disclosure of this information are contractual, and any individual or business making contractual arrangements with the financial institutions is obliged, as part of a standard form contract, to agree to waive the right of privacy as a condition of gaining the financial or insurance service provided.

Freedom of Expression and Access

The right to express ideas is not the same as the right of access to the means of disseminating them. In democratic societies, there is no equivalent of the publications that flourished in the former Soviet Union and ensured that the work of some writers was better known than if it had been published commercially in the West. Perhaps there should be. People who wish to disseminate ideas have relatively easy access to print media. Electronic broadcast media reaches a wider audience, but most individuals cannot express their ideas though them because they have no access. Prime-time major network television simply does not encourage the dissemination of radical ideas or those critical of powerful interests if to do so would threaten its advertising revenue. Despite this, both environmental and consumer movements have succeeded in creating newsworthy incidents or spectacular and unusual demonstrations in order to publicize ideas, some of which are now widely accepted. While advocates of unpopular causes may not have been punished for expressing their ideas, their ability to convey those ideas to a wide audience was limited—until the Internet made that possible. Now anyone with a small amount of technical knowledge—and access to the Internet—can secure relatively wide publicity for ideas.

There are obvious dangers in curbing freedom of expression through the Internet, but some regulation may be necessary to prevent social harm. The danger of regulation may be less if other media which do not reach as wide an audience as the Internet are available. There is great controversy about whether or not to restrict access to the Internet, but that question may be entirely academic because restriction may be physically or legally impossible. National laws can only operate on people—natural persons—and things physically or otherwise within their control.

An Analogy: Intellectual Property Law

Any international move to impose legal controls on cyberspace is likely to start in the area of intellectual property. Many patents and copyrights are owned by powerful interests. The right conferred by a copyright or a patent is a right to make money from the invention or creation. When these rights depend on national laws for enforcement, there is concern that use of new technologies, especially the Internet and associated technologies, will enable "pirates" to copy text, sounds, and images and reproduce them in breach of the property owner's rights, provided they do so outside the boundaries of a state whose laws protect that right.[11]

In the past, it was to reach a high degree of international agreement about the content and scope of national laws governing intellectual property rights. While powerful interests have these rights, national laws that protect them are assured and the extension of such protection as widely as possible is almost inevitable. Other interest groups may therefore have a precedent that may assist them to ensure that governments will continue to support the existence of national laws.

Conclusions: Democracy and Market Forces

Interest group politics are probably the only way in which consumers can gain any protection against large and powerful forces in society, such as businesses and groups of businesses. Competition has virtues, but we should be foolish to accept it as a panacea for all consumer ills.

Despite the theory that consumers benefit from market competition, in practice, markets are not perfect: barriers to entry and externalities inevitably produce, in both global and national markets, a tendency toward concentration of market power, rather than competition with its attendant benefits (Lindblom, 1977; Ogus, 1994). The combination of growing concentration of market power and the introduction of new technologies makes the need for consumers and other disadvantaged groups to enlist some countervailing power stronger than ever. The growing concentration of economic power and monopoly or oligopoly is readily recognizable in states that have introduced extensive economic deregulation. When U.S. airlines were deregulated, market power became concentrated, and there was less competition, not more. The same may happen with the deregulation of global communications. Businesses tend not to compete but wherever possible form oligopolies and cartels to shield themselves from competition. Mergers are often an enemy of competition, especially in large economies; in small economies, the market may not bear more than one supplier and competition is not feasible. In practice, it is impossible to generalize or fit concrete situations into abstract economic theories.

People and governments in states such as Canada, the United Kingdom, Australia, and most of Europe are not always convinced by the value of "rugged individualism" which, in the popular image, characterizes the United States. Even though they may have a common language or religion, these states have markedly different social and cultural heritages, which are reflected in social attitudes. Many individuals in such states would rather suffer the minor inconveniences of regulation and a public welfare and health system than reap the "benefits"—never yet fully demonstrated—of a totally market-driven economy. They are not convinced of the virtues of totally untrammeled free markets and are skeptical of the existence of even relatively competitive markets because of the obvious distortions, inequalities of power, and simple market failures they have experienced. If markets are to work, popular experience suggests that assistance from the state is required.

Consumer organizations agree that consumer interests require a degree of intervention by the state, if only to maximize competition. When the state does intervene for these purposes, this is a clear example of democracy at work.

It is a characteristic of political sovereignty that the people of a nation can choose whether to submit to the interests of free trade and transnational business. Their choice need not be rational, any more than the definition of a "political community" is rational. It need not even be a choice that is objectively beneficial to the choosers. There are many examples of communities rejecting inclusion of smaller political units in larger ones, though this choice is often irrational in the sense that people who choose the option of the small nation are worse off economically.

Political sovereignty may only be possible within a nation-state. That sovereignty requires that people are allowed to exercise political rights, including the right to influence legislation that regulates aspects of the economy, redistributes wealth and income, and provides social security. Cyberspace technology, either alone or in combination with the globalization of the economy, may make the exercise of those political rights impossible.

Who Benefits?

There is no doubt that new technologies bring some short-term benefits for everyone, but they may come at a cost. Those who stand to gain heavily from the introduction of new technologies—those who control access to the Internet, those who own the physical means of encoding and carrying signals, and the producers of hardware—are not vocal about those costs. Neither are other business groups. They stand to benefit from the decline of any institutional machinery through which the democratic will can redirect, channel or curtail the unlimited quest for profit, at whatever long-term cost. People whose leisure and even working hours are made easier by the new technologies may not realize that the very limited opportunity they have to influence the course of events, gained over centuries through political struggle, may be destroyed by the inability of nation-states to control many of those technologies.

The nation-state is the best instrument, possibly the only instrument, for effective democracy. It is the only means ordinary people have for redressing the inequalities of the market. Anything that erodes the power of the nation-state to control antisocial behavior destroys democracy, which is valuable only because of the power it provides to the people as a whole, and to interest groups that they form. Some may benefit from the new technologies, but consumers and other disadvantaged groups need to be aware of what those new technologies are destroying as well as what they bring. Few would want the Hobbesian state of nature that would result from the destruction of the nation-state.

If cybersharks cannot be netted by national laws, they will swim free, wreaking random destruction in the knowledge that they will remain free. Is it acceptable to allow such predators free range? National laws are the only alternative. By embracing the short-term benefits of new technologies and globalization, we may expose everyone to the risk of attack.

Notes

1. In 1995, the U.S. Federal Trade Commission held hearings on the Global Information Infrastructure's impact on consumers. The proceedings are available on the FTC's Web page. The testimony was far from unanimous, but raised a number of very interesting issues.

2. Bureaucratic capture occurs when an agency entrusted with the task of regulating a particular section of business becomes so close to those over whom it exercises power that it absorbs the values and attitudes of the regulated group (Gunningham, 1974; Cranston; 1979; Grabowsky and Braithwaite,1986).

3. A nontariff barrier is a control on importation of a commodity other than in the form of a fiscal impost. Regulations that prescribe standards for classes of commodities risk characterization as nontariff barriers if their effect is to discriminate in favor of domestic products and against foreign-produced products, even though the purpose of the regulation may be to further interests of health, quality or safety. For example, the *New York Times* of January 18, 1996, reported that the World Trade Organization had found that U.S. laws governing emission controls on gases emitted by oil refineries constituted a non-tariff barrier that discriminated against foreign oil refiners.

4. In law, a "personal" link is established by factors such as residence, citizenship or domicile.

5. Legal positivists assert that law is comprised exclusively of written rules made by legislatures or courts. They deny that moral values or international custom

can ever have the status of law.

6. In the United States, the obvious analogy is the use by business of the so-called Delaware corporation.

7. As the United States did in the *Escamilla* case (referred to in LaForest, 1970). In that case and subsequently in the cases of General Manuel Noriega and others, United States law enforcement officers have arrested foreign nationals in foreign countries with the purpose of removing them physically, regardless of the wishes of the state where the persons were found, for trial in the United States (Nadelmann, 1993). The legality of acts of this type was upheld by the United States Supreme Court (*Ker v Illinois* 119 US436, 1886). In the cases of Adolf Eichmann and some others, Israel has also abducted persons accused of crimes under its laws committed in the territory of other states.

8. Municipal constitutional law may make this invalid: see the judgment of the Privy Council in *In re Initiative and Referendum Act* (1919) AC 935, which, although relating specifically to a Canadian province, is taken to represent the position in all Commonwealth countries.

9. Patchel (1993) points out that the Uniform Commercial Code in the United States was drafted by lawyers who were close to commercial interests and totally ignored the interests of consumers, who were equally affected by the provisions of the UCC. See also Rosett (1992): 683, 694–696.

10. A Committee of the Australian Senate considering delivery of pornographic material through on-line services has recently recommended legislation requiring access providers to regulate access to such material, subject to criminal sanctions (Senate Committee on Computer On-Line Services, Australia, 1995).

11. The United States and China recently disagreed strongly over respect for intellectual property rights; the only item that overshadowed nontariff barriers in recent GATT negotiations was the negotiation of the TRIPS agreement which is supposed to ensure free trade in intellectual property, and about which the United States was extremely cautious. Intellectual property laws have, one must remember, been used to restrict the flow of information; in Australia, the High Court has allowed the government to restrict publication of information not under administrative law rules but by upholding the government's copyright in documents published in the media (*The Commonwealth v John Fairfax & Sons Ltd*, 147 Commonwealth Law Reports 39, 1980).

References

Aman, Alfred C. Jr. "A Global Perspective on Current Regulatory Reforms: Rejection, Relocation or Reinvention?" *Global Legal Studies Journal* 2 (1995).

Burk, Dan L. "Patents in Cyberspace," *Tulane Law Review* 68 (1993): 1.

Burk, Dan L. "Trademarks Along the Infobahn," *University of Richmond Journal of Law and Technology* 1 (1995): 1.

Chinkin, Christine M. "The Challenge of Soft Law: Development and Change in International Law," *International and Comparative Law Quarterly* 38 (1988): 850.

Cranston, Ross. *Regulating Business* (Manchester: Manchester University Press, 1979).

Dunleavy, Michael W. "The Limits of Fair Trade: Sovereignty, Environmental Protection, and NAFTA," *University of Toronto Faculty of Law Review* 51 (1993): 204.

Goldring, John. "Public Law, Private Law and Consumers' Remedies," *Australian Quarterly* 50, 4 (1978): 58.

Goldring, John. "Consumer Law and Legal Theory: Reflections of A Common Lawyer," *Journal of Consumer Policy* 13 (1990): 1.

Grabowsky, Peter, and John Braithwaite. *Of Manners Gentle: Enforcement Strategies of Australian Business-Regulating Agencies* (Melbourne: Oxford University Press, 1986).

Gunningham, Neil. *Pollution, Social Interest and the Law* (London: Martin Robertson, 1974).

Hardy, I. Trotter. "The Proper Legal Regime for Cyberspace," *University of Pittsburgh Law Review* 55 (1994): 993.

Hirst, Paul and G. Thompson. "Globalisation and the Future of the Nation-state," *Economy and Society* 24 (1995).

Hobsbawm, Eric. *Age of Extremes: The Short 20th Century 1914–1991* (London: Abacus, 1995).

Howse, Robert. "NAFTA and the Constitution: Does *Labour Conventions* Really Matter any More?" *Constitutional Forum* 5 (1994): 54.

Johnson, David R. and Kevin A. Marks. "Mapping Electronic Data Communications onto Existing Legal Techniques," *Villanova Law Review* 38 (1993): 403, 415.

Johnston, David, Deborah Johnston and Sonny Handa. *Getting Canada Online: Understanding the Information Highway* (Toronto: Stoddart, 1995).

Katsh, Ethan. "Law in a Digital World," *Villanova Law Review* 38 (1993): 403.

LaForest, G. V. *The Ambit of Criminal Law,* Working Paper, Law Reform Commission of Canada (Ottawa: 1970).

Lindblom, Charles E. *Politics and Markets* (New York: Basic Books, 1977).

Nadelmann, Ethan A. *Cops Across Borders: The Internationalization of United States Criminal Law Enforcement* (University Park, PA: Pennsylvania State University Press, 1993).

National Information Services Council, *Legal Issues on the Information Superhighway* (Canberra, Australia: 1995).

Negroponte, Nicholas. *Being Digital* (New York: Knopf, 1995).

Ogus, Anthony. *Regulation: Legal Form and Economic Theory* (Oxford: Clarendon Press, 1994).

Otto, Dianne. "A Question of Law or Politics? Indigenous Claims to Sovereignty in Australia," *Syracuse Journal of International Law and Commerce* 21 (1995): 65.

Patchel, Kathleen. "Interest Group Politics, Federalism and the Uniform Law Process: Some Lessons from the Uniform Commercial Code," *Minnesota Law Review* 78 (1993): 83.

Rosett, Arthur. "Unification, Harmonization, Restatement, Codification and Reform in International Commercial Law," *American Journal of Comparative Law* 40 (1992): 683.

Schaefer, Matt, and Thomas Singer. "Multilateral Trade Agreements and US States: An Analysis of Potential GATT Uruguay Round Agreements," *Journal of World Trade* (1992): 631.

Schneiderman, David. "Canadian Constitutionalism and Sovereignty after NAFTA," *Constitutional Forum* 5 (1994): 93.

Senate Committee on Computer On-Line Services, *Second Report* (Canberra, Australia: 1995).

Shearer, Ivan A. *Extradition in International Law* (Manchester: Manchester University Press, 1971).

Stewart, Richard B. "Environmental Regulation and International Competitiveness," *Yale Law Journal* 102 (1993): 2039.

Trakman, Leon E. *The Law Merchant: The Evolution of Commercial Law* (Littleton, CO: Fred B. Rothman & Co, 1983).

Trubek, David M. "Consumer Law, Common Markets and Federalism: Introduction and General Concepts," in *Consumer Law, Common Markets and Federalism in Europe and the United States,* edited by Thierry Bourgoignie and David Trubek, Vol. 3 of *Integration Through Law: Europe and the American Federal Experience,* edited by Mauro Cappelletti, Monica Seccombe and Joseph Weiler (Berlin and New York, Walter de Gruyter, 1987).

Williams, Robert A. Jr. "The Algebra of Federal Indian Law: The Hard Trail of Decolonizing and Americanizing the White Man's Indian Jurisprudence," *Wisconsin Law Review* 7 (1986): 219.

Contributors

Peter Backlund (pbacklund@ostp.eop.gov) is a NASA representative to the National Science and Technology Council (NSTC), where he works on environmental science and technology policy issues and serves as the liaison to the NSTC Committee on Environment and Natural Resources (http://www.nnic.noaa.gov/CENR//cenr.html).

Richard C. Barth (Rich_Barth-ARB005@email.mot.com) directs telecommunications strategy and regulation at Motorola's Corporate Government Relations Office in Washington, D.C. His team works closely with U.S. government agencies, especially the Federal Communications Commission, that deal with spectrum and telecommunications regulatory issues. He also is developing a broader strategic program to deal with other telecommunications issues, such as encryption policy and export controls.

Dan L. Burk (burdanl@lanmail.shu.edu) is Assistant Professor of Law at Seton Hall University, where he teaches torts, patents, and intellectual property.

Teree E. Foster (tfoster@wvu.edu) is Dean and Professor of Law at West Virginia University College of Law. Her research has focused on the areas of evidence, the First Amendment, capital punishment, and law and literature.

A. Michael Froomkin (froomkin@law.miami.edu; http://www.law.miami.edu/~froomkin) is Associate Professor at the University of Miami School of Law. Before entering teaching, he practiced international arbitration law in the London office of Wilmer, Cutler & Pickering.

Robert Gellman (rgellman@cais.com) is a Privacy and Information Policy Consultant in Washington, D.C., and Executive Director of the Virtual Magistrate Project, an Internet arbitration service. He served for many years as chief counsel to the Subcommittee on Government Information in the House of Representatives.

John Goldring (j.goldring@uow.edu.au) was Foundation Dean of Law at the University of Wollongong in Australia (http://www.uow.edu.au/law/law_web_main/lawhome.html) from June 1990 until July 1995. He remains Professor of Law at that university. He has practiced law in Australia, Papua New Guinea, and the United States and has taught law in those countries and also in the United Kingdom and Canada. He has been a member of the Australian Law Reform Commission and the Australian Consumers' Council.

David R. Johnson (david.johnson@counsel.com) is Chairman of Counsel Connect, an online meeting place for the legal profession, and Co-Director of the Cyberspace Law Institute. He previously practiced computer law as a partner of Wilmer, Cutler and Pickering.

Christopher R. Kedzie (c.kedzie@fordfound.org) is a Moscow-based Ford Foundation Program Officer supporting democratic reform in Russia. As a Doctoral Fellow at RAND, he analyzed the relationship between communication technologies and global democratization. He has also founded organizations in Ukraine and Uzbekistan that exploit new communication technologies to assist reform efforts.

Viktor Mayer-Schönberger (vms@gii.priv.at) has directed the postgraduate program in Legal Informatics at the University of Salzburg and taught at a number of universities in Europe and the United States. He works at the University of Vienna School of Law and is former Head of the Information Law Project at the Austrian Institute for Legal Policy.

Henry H. Perritt, Jr. (perritt@law.vill.edu), is Professor of Law at Villanova University School of Law (http://www.law.vill.edu) and author of *Law and the Information Superhighway* (John Wiley). He served on President Clinton's transition team, working on telecommunications issues.

David G. Post (david.post@counsel.com) is Co-Director of the Cyberspace Law Institute and Visiting Associate Professor at the Georgetown University Law Center, where he teaches courses on constitutional and copyright law as well as the law of cyberspace.

Joel R. Reidenberg (jreidenb@counsel.com) is Associate Professor of Law at Fordham University School of Law. He serves as chair of the Section on Computers and Law of the Association of American Law Schools and is a Fellow of the Cyberspace Law Institute. He has served as an expert advisor to the U.S. Congress's Office of Technology Assessment and to the Commission of the European Communities. He has coauthored with Paul Schwartz the book *Data Privacy Law.*

Clint N. Smith (Clint.Smith@mci.com) is an assistant technology counsel in the Law and Public Policy Department at MCI Communications Corporation. He is responsible for legal issues relating to MCI's Internet and electronic commerce services. Prior to joining MCI, he was an associate in the technology and international practice groups at the law firm of Steptoe & Johnson LLP in Washington D.C.

Ingrid Volkmer (Ingrid.Volkmer@post.uni-bielefeld.de) is Associate Professor of Media/Communication Studies at the University of Bielefeld. Her primary field of research is global/international communication. She is Director of Global Media Consultants Ltd. in London and a member of the Advisory Board of Nickelodeon in Germany.

Peter N. Weiss (WEISS_P@A1.EOP.GOV) is a Senior Policy Analyst/Attorney in the Office of Information and Regulatory Affairs of the Office of Management and Budget. He is the primary author of the information policy provisions of OMB Circular No. A-130, "Management of Federal Information Resources," and staffs the Information Policy Committee of the Information Infrastructure Task Force.

Index